AF768392

Qualitative Methods for Health Economics

Qualitative Methods for Health Economics

Edited by Joanna Coast

ROWMAN &
LITTLEFIELD
INTERNATIONAL
London • New York

Published by Rowman & Littlefield International Ltd
Unit A, Whitacre Mews, 26-34 Stannary Street, London SE11 4AB
www.rowmaninternational.com

Rowman & Littlefield International Ltd. is an affiliate of Rowman & Littlefield

4501 Forbes Boulevard, Suite 200, Lanham, Maryland 20706, USA
With additional offices in Boulder, New York, Toronto (Canada), and Plymouth (UK)
www.rowman.com

Selection and editorial matter © Joanna Coast 2017

Copyright in individual chapters is held by the respective chapter authors.

All rights reserved. No part of this book may be reproduced in any form or by any electronic or mechanical means, including information storage and retrieval systems, without written permission from the publisher, except by a reviewer who may quote passages in a review.

British Library Cataloguing in Publication Data
A catalogue record for this book is available from the British Library

ISBN: HB 978-1-7834-8561-1
PB 978-1-7834-8562-8

Library of Congress Cataloging-in-Publication Data
Names: Coast, Joanna, editor.
Title: Qualitative methods for health economics / edited by Joanna Coast.
Description: London ; New York : Rowman & Littlefield International Ltd., [2017] | Includes bibliographical references and index.
Identifiers: LCCN 2017010823 (print) | LCCN 2017011960 (ebook) | ISBN 9781783485635 (ebook) | ISBN 9781783485611 (cloth) | ISBN 9781783485628 (paper)
Subjects: | MESH: Qualitative Research | Economics, Medical | Research Design | Evaluation Studies as Topic
Classification: LCC RA410.55.E83 (ebook) | LCC RA410.55.E83 (print) | NLM W 20.5 | DDC 362.1068/1072—dc23
LC record available at https://lccn.loc.gov/2017010823

∞™ The paper used in this publication meets the minimum requirements of American National Standard for Information Sciences—Permanence of Paper for Printed Library Materials, ANSI/NISO Z39.48-1992.

Printed in the United States of America

This book is for Steve, Iain, Ned and Alfie, with all my love, and thanks for much patience and many cups of tea while I was putting it together!

Contents

List of Figures xi

List of Tables xiii

List of Boxes xv

Acknowledgements xvii

PART I: CHOICES ABOUT METHODS **1**

1 Theoretical and methodological positions and the choice to use qualitative methods 3
Joanna Coast and Louise Jackson

2 Designing qualitative research studies in health economics 19
Joanna Coast, Philip Kinghorn and Amanda Owen-Smith

3 Understanding sampling and recruitment 42
Amanda Owen-Smith and Joanna Coast

4 Understanding data collection: Interviews, focus groups and observation 59
Amanda Owen-Smith and Joanna Coast

5 Understanding primary data analysis 92
Joanna Coast and Louise Jackson

6 Understanding secondary data analysis 119
Hareth Al-Janabi and Amanda Owen-Smith

7 Presenting and publishing qualitative research in health economics 139
Joanna Coast

PART II: CASE STUDIES **153**

8 Introduction to the case studies 155
Joanna Coast

PART II A: USING QUALITATIVE METHODS TO DEVELOP AND ENHANCE QUANTITATIVE RESEARCH **161**

9 Constructing statement sets for use in Q methodology studies 163
Rachel Baker, Neil McHugh and Helen Mason

10 Qualitative methods in discrete choice experiments: Two case studies 175
Jane Vosper, Joanna Coast and Terry Flynn

11 Using qualitative methods to develop a preference-based health-related quality of life measure for use in economic evaluation: The development of the Child Health Utility 9D 193
Katherine Stevens

12 Incorporating novel qualitative methods within health economics: The use of pictorial tools 205
Alastair Canaway, Hareth Al-Janabi, Philip Kinghorn, Cara Bailey and Joanna Coast

13 Using non-participant observation and think-aloud to understand and improve modelling processes 217
Samantha Husbands, Sue Jowett, Pelham Barton and Joanna Coast

PART II B: USING QUALITATIVE METHODS TO INTERPRET QUANTITATIVE FINDINGS **229**

14 Using 'think-aloud' and interview data to explore patient and proxy completion of health and capability measures at the end of life 231
Cara Bailey, Philip Kinghorn, Rosanna Orlando and Joanna Coast

15 Getting beyond the numbers: Using qualitative methods to explore the validity of health state valuation techniques 245
Suzanne Robinson

16 Use of deliberative methods to facilitate and enhance understanding of the weighting of survey attributes 257
Philip Kinghorn, Alastair Canaway, Cara Bailey and Joanna Coast

PART II C: USING QUALITATIVE METHODS TO ENHANCE AND GENERATE ECONOMIC UNDERSTANDING **275**

17 Using qualitative methods in impact evaluation: The case of the results-based financing for maternal and neonatal care impact evaluation in Malawi 277
Manuela De Allegri

18 An assessment of an international declaration on aid effectiveness through qualitative methods at the country level 293
Melisa Martínez-Álvarez

19 Using cost-effectiveness evidence in making priority gradings: The case of the Swedish National Guidelines for heart diseases 307
Nathalie Eckard and Ann-Charlotte Nedlund

20 Contributions of qualitative methods to the study of priority setting and resource allocation in health care 319
Neale Smith

PART III: AFTERWORD **333**

21 Afterword: Walking the disciplinary tightrope 335
Joanna Coast, Hareth Al-Janabi, Louise Jackson, Philip Kinghorn and Amanda Owen-Smith

References 339

Index 377

Contributors 385

List of Figures

9.1.	Q grid and sorting instruction	165
9.2.	An illustration of Q factor analysis	166
12.1.	Example of completed hierarchical map	212
16.1.	Recruitment process for public	263
16.2.	Task one example question	265
16.3.	Patients versus close persons (task three)	266
16.4.	Number of participants recording a change on one or more tasks	269
18.1.	Example of analysis of the theme ‘mutual accountability’	302
19.1.	Schematic description of the work process for the National Guidelines (Socialstyrelsen 2008)	310

List of Tables

3.1.	Extract from AOS doctoral thesis: qualitative sampling in practice	44
5.1.	Example definitions associated with first- and second-level analytic categories for citizen–agent example (Coast 2000b)	111
6.1.	Reciprocal translation of selected themes across two qualitative studies	123
6.2.	Qualitative data repositories currently available	126
6.3.	Translation of the 'concept' of control into individual studies in a meta-ethnography of six studies of the experience of informal care (Al-Janabi 2009)	132
9.1.	Sources of statements for study of values and life extension and terminal illness	169
9.2.	Example of Q set design matrix	172
10.1.	Attributes and levels included in the TREAD discrete choice experiment	183
10.2.	Attributes and levels included in the drug treatment discrete choice experiment	189
16.1.	Coding and the emergence of themes	268
18.1.	Key informant and in-depth interview participants	298
19.1.	Identified themes for the use of cost-effectiveness evidence in priority gradings	316

List of Boxes

4.1.	Example topic guide for patient interview	64
4.2.	Example topic guide for citizen interview	65
4.3.	Example of a distress protocol	89
5.1.	Excerpt from first analytic account for citizen informant, based on first four interviews transcribed	113
5.2.	Excerpt from final analytic account for citizen informant, based on all interviews	115
14.1.	Stages of the think-aloud interview	236
15.1.	Details of the main valuation study	246
15.2.	Outline of the interview schedule	251

Acknowledgements

The inspiration for this book on the use of qualitative methods in health economics came about through discussions with Alison Howson, and I would like to thank her for that and for her backing for the book. I would also like to thank two other publishing staff for their assistance later in the project: Martina O'Sullivan and Michael Watson.

There are a number of people, institutions and funding bodies that I would like to thank. I would particularly like to thank Jenny Donovan, who introduced me to qualitative research and provided invaluable mentoring during my early work in this area. Over the years I have enjoyed working with, and learning from, a number of researchers using qualitative methods in health economics. I would like to thank them all for their enthusiasm and persistence in working in an area that falls between disciplines, but particularly Hareth Al-Janabi, Cara Bailey, Alastair Canaway, Oya Eddama, Sue Horrocks, Sam Husbands, Tom Keeley, Phil Kinghorn, Amanda Owen-Smith, Rosanna Orlando, Eileen Sutton and Jane Vosper.

This book was written while I was based in two universities, University of Bristol and University of Birmingham, and I would like to thank both institutions for their support and encouragement.

Acknowledgements for funding bodies for the individual case studies are given at the end of each chapter, where applicable. A number of organizations also require thanks for funding the different qualitative research projects that are discussed in the first part of the book, including the Economic and Social Research Council, European Research Council, Medical Research Council, National Institute for Health Research and the South and West Research and Development Directorate.

I would like to thank the International Society for the Scientific Study of Subjectivity for permission to reproduce Figure 9.2.

Finally, I would like to offer my greatest thanks to all of the chapter contributors for their hard work and the informants who participated in the various research studies without whom there would be no qualitative research to report!

Part I

CHOICES ABOUT METHODS

Chapter 1

Theoretical and methodological positions and the choice to use qualitative methods

Joanna Coast and Louise Jackson

It is assumed that the main audience for this book comprises (health) economists with an interest in using qualitative methods in their own research; this chapter therefore begins the book with a relatively accessible discussion of issues around ontology, epistemology and methodology. The nature of training in economics (Lawson 1997; Lee, Pham, et al. 2013) means that many economists reading this book may be unaware of these terms and will not have thought about these issues previously (Coast 1999). Indeed, when publishing her first article exploring these issues in a health economics journal in the late 1990s, Coast was asked to include a glossary detailing these terms, as they were deemed to be terms that health economists would generally be unfamiliar with (Coast 1999). It has been noted that economists' training does not tend to provide an understanding of data collection processes or the role of qualitative methods in complementing quantitative research, with Berik stating that 'such training would be an eye-opening and humbling experience – an essential antidote for arrogance – for economists who do not question their data' (Berik 1997, p. 124). Those with an existing sophisticated understanding (e.g., qualitative researchers reading the book because they are working with economists) may want to read this chapter not so much for its content but to become aware of the different understandings of ontology and epistemology that the economists they are working with may have.

This chapter begins by considering theories of knowledge and their application in economics, drawing on Coast's earlier paper (Coast 1999). There is much work of an explanatory nature examining issues relating to the nature of health care systems as well as health more generally. The vast majority of this work is conducted within the neoclassical framework (indeed Murphy and colleagues have noted the 'narrowness of the range of economic thought that is currently being deployed on the problems of health technology and health services' [Murphy, Dingwall, et al. 1998, p. viii]) although explanatory work can also be conducted within alternative frameworks. Normative (welfare or extra-welfare), institutional, behavioural and feminist economics are all briefly considered, as is the potential for approaches based on critical realism. The chapter then details the nature of qualitative research methods as well as the constructivist philosophy with which they are most frequently associated. From this discussion it is apparent that such a philosophy is very different from that usually associated with the discipline of economics. The nature of enquiry associated with qualitative research is briefly examined, covering details of specific data collection methods, sampling, analysis of data and ensuring rigour. Despite differences in philosophy from mainstream economics, it is apparent that qualitative methods are useful to economists, and the use of qualitative methods in health economics is then examined. It is argued that robust qualitative research can provide scientifically valuable contributions to health economic knowledge both through improving quantitative data collection, such as when generating attributes for discrete choice attributes, and through contributing directly to economic theory, particularly in complex areas such as priority setting or developing financial incentives.

UNDERSTANDING RELEVANT TERMINOLOGY

Health economists embarking on qualitative research first need some understanding about the ways in which different types of researchers understand the world. Many are likely to have a view similar to that of Coast when she started work as a junior health economist in 1990. She had completed a first degree in economics and a master's degree in health economics, and throughout these degrees, theories had been largely presented either as self-evident, and thus without the need for any supporting evidence, or in terms of economists developing hypotheses based on deductive thinking and then testing these hypotheses using quantitative data.

An example of the former was the basic underlying principles of demand and supply, and the elaborations on these such as Giffen goods. These were presented as clear, logical and internally consistent interpretations of how the world works. But there was little in the way of evidence for many of these theories, perhaps underlining the views of some that economics is largely a branch of applied mathematics, with little relationship to the world outside (Rosenberg 1992).

An example of the latter might be the theories of supplier-induced demand, where economists have developed theories about how medical physicians might act in ways that shift the demand curve for health interventions from its 'true' level (the level that fully informed consumers might choose), perhaps to achieve higher income for themselves (Evans 1984). Hypotheses are then generated based on these theories, and various quantitative econometric techniques might then be utilized to test these theories. For example, the hypothesis might be around physicians not being able to achieve their target income if more doctors arrive in an area and thus choose then to increase their provision of services to achieve this income. This might then be tested using quantitative information about the levels of consumption of medical services alongside data about numbers of physicians working in a location (Evans 1980). The hypothesis can then be accepted or rejected.

In applying economics to health, health economists constantly come up against the problem that theories developed to explain 'the economy' (with varying degrees of success and with varying degrees of acknowledgement of that varying success) will very often not apply readily and simply to the 'health economy'. For Coast, her first job, as a lone health economist in a university department of epidemiology and public health in the United Kingdom, made this abundantly clear, as her relatively 'neat' views of the world did not reflect those of her new non-economist colleagues, nor as she could quickly see for herself the complexities of health care provision in the UK health economy. There was clearly a need for something more, and qualitative methods seemed to have potential in achieving a better understanding of the health economy and how it works. Even a small foray into this different research paradigm, however, suggested a very different perception of the world.

UNDERSTANDING ONTOLOGY, EPISTEMOLOGY AND METHODOLOGY IN (HEALTH) ECONOMICS

Ontology means the view of the nature and form of reality (Lincoln 1992). Epistemology is concerned with the theory and nature of knowledge, in particular the relationship between what is to be known and the researcher (Lincoln 1992). There are very different views of the nature and form of reality, although many health economists are unlikely to have given these issues much thought. Indeed, they may well assume that their own view of reality is universally shared because of the way in which the nature of the discipline is conveyed.

As suggested in an earlier paper (Coast 1999), most health economics explanatory research is achieved within an orthodox neoclassical framework. The standard view of reality within this 'positive' or 'explanatory' economics has had a number of influences including positivism, the notion that there is a single reality that can be researched (Hollis 1994), and the falsificationism of Popper (Blaug 1992; Hausmann 1994). Essentially, within this world view, there is a belief that there is a single, knowable reality and that research can help to find out about this reality. This reality comprises a set of rules that it is possible to determine (Lawson 1997; Graça Moura and Martins 2008).

Methodology is concerned with the means by which the person inquiring tries to find out what is to be known, the practice of research (Lincoln 1992; Creswell 2013). Methods of investigation within explanatory neoclassical economics are long standing (Mill 1994) and start from the individual; that is, assumptions about 'individual' preferences, both from consumers and from firms, are used to generate the behavioural assumptions from which the economic theory is built. This is known as methodological individualism (Hodgson 1986; Dugger 1994; Toboso 2001). In an explanatory research conducted within a neoclassical paradigm, the economist starts with a set of these assumptions, referred to as axioms, which are high-level principles that are regarded as being established and accepted (although the accuracy of these starting assumptions is often seen as less important than the resultant predictions [Friedman 1994]). From these axioms, often concerned with rationality or optimization (Lawson 2006), the economist can infer logically, through a deductive process, what might be predicted, and these predictions can be tested; these predictions then form the basis for explanation.

The testing of these assumptions draws on a particular view of the relationship between the researcher and what he or she is researching, in which it is assumed that the economist tries to be objective. The economist develops and tests hypotheses without allowing himself or herself to influence the findings or be influenced by these findings, so that he or she can confidently accept or reject the hypothesis/hypotheses that have been tested and thus confirm (or not) the accuracy of the theory generated. In general, at least theoretically, it is seen as better to try to test whether hypotheses can be falsified (Blaug 1992). Although the logical sequelae of falsifying a theory is to reject it and move on to generate new theories and test these, it has been noted previously that in economics this may not be the ultimate outcome (Coast 1999), with views expressed that economists may instead try to refine their mathematical expressions (Ormerod 1994), alter assumptions and try to bring more variables into the explanation (Lawson 1997). Indeed, in relation to the example of supplier-induced demand used earlier, it is notable that there has been difficulty in reaching clear conclusions (Labelle, Stoddart, et al. 1994) despite the problem being formulated in a number of different ways.

In testing hypotheses, the aim is to eliminate bias and obtain true knowledge about how reality works. Options for achieving this include the randomized controlled trial with which most health economists will be familiar, given the place of this method within health research as the 'gold standard' basis for determining the effectiveness of health interventions (Bennett 2007). Indeed, many health economists will have particular familiarity with this method through their conduct of economic evaluation alongside such randomized controlled trials (Drummond, Sculpher, et al. 2015). Although there are some famous exceptions, particularly around the use of health insurance (Manning, Newhouse, et al. 1987), randomised trials have not generally been used to explore economic phenomena for practical reasons. Instead, economists employ complex statistical and econometric techniques (e.g., instrumental variables [Angrist, Imbens, et al. 1996] or difference-in-difference approaches [Lechner 2010]) with the aim of reducing bias, applying these techniques to observational data for statistically representative samples of the population. A problem faced by economists, however, is that they generally use existing data sets that may have been collected with quite different purposes and intentions and may therefore not have access to good-quality data for answering their particular research question (Leontief 1982).

It is clear that ontology, epistemology and methodology in neoclassical (health) economics is of a particular kind: belief in a single knowable reality that is accessible through rigorous unbiased testing of hypotheses generated through logical inference from accepted axioms. As this chapter goes on to show, however, this set of beliefs and approaches is very different from that common among the broad set of disciplines where qualitative methods are commonly used.

Although most health economists reading this text are likely to have their academic origins in orthodox neoclassical economics, of course, many will also have other aspects to their interests, backgrounds and concerns. Health economists in particular, and in contrast to other economists, very often work within normative economics, where the concern is how policy should proceed rather than explanation. Health economists may be working from either welfarist or extra-welfarist perspectives (Brouwer, Culyer, et al. 2008; Coast, Smith, et al. 2008) which both ally to some extent with neoclassical economics in the extent to which they focus on the concerns of individuals and their values and preferences (Coast 1999) but draw on differing ethical theories that relate to how well-being is identified. For traditional welfarism, this well-being is identified with the satisfaction of individual utility (Hausman and McPherson 1994; Coast, Smith, et al. 2008), while for extra-welfarism in its usual expression as health maximization it is identified with some form of satisfaction of societal preferences for maximizing health gains (Culyer 1989; Coast, Smith, et al. 2008). Although these branches of normative economics undoubtedly rely on philosophical and ethical thinking about what should be maximized and why, there is also huge effort expended on trying to estimate preferences/values from unbiased samples of the relevant patient or general adult population to inform these normative assessments (see, e.g., Brazier, Roberts, et al. 2002; McCabe, Stevens, et al. 2005; Al-Janabi, Flynn, et al. 2011; Flynn, Huynh, et al. 2015; Ratcliffe, Huynh, et al. 2016). In a similar way to explanatory economics, health economists working in this area, at least until recent years, have tended to start with assumptions about what is valuable and then test these assumptions about what attributes/dimensions of well-being/health/utility are important to people through estimating the values given to them through some quantitative form of preference elicitation (common methods include time trade-off [Buxton and Ashby 1988; Brazier, Ratcliffe, et al. 2007], standard gamble [Baker and Robinson 2004; Brazier, Ratcliffe, et al. 2007], willingness to pay [Donaldson 1993; McIntosh, Clarke, et al. 2010], person trade-off [Pinto-Prades 1997; Dolan and Green 1998] and discrete choice experiments [Louviere 2000; Ryan 2004; Bansback, Brazier, et al. 2012] including best-worst scaling [Flynn, Louviere, et al. 2007; Louviere, Flynn, et al. 2015]) and testing whether they are significant.

Health economists may also use other approaches to explanatory economics than the orthodox neoclassical approach. There have been attacks from both within and outside the discipline, often focusing on the inability of economics to make accurate predictions and the extent to which it engages with the 'real' world (Rosenberg 1992, 1994; Ormerod 1994; Coase 1995, 1998; Lawson 1997, 2003; Lee, Pham, et al. 2013). As Mannion and colleagues note, 'The crude neoclassical model is immensely elegant, but totally unrealistic in that it in no way represents an accurate depiction of actual human behaviour in real world settings' (Mannion, Small, et al. 2005, p. 381). The failure of mainstream economics to successfully predict the 2008 global economic crisis has increased the scrutiny around economic methodology (Colander, Goldberg, et al. 2009; Lawson 2009; Hoover 2010), with Krugman arguing, 'The economics profession went astray because economists, as a group, mistook beauty, clad in impressive-looking mathematics, for truth' (Krugman 2009). It has been suggested that this inclination towards mathematization is perhaps the core unifying characteristic of mainstream economics (Lawson 2006), and, in line with this, some have suggested that economics can be relegated to no more than a branch of applied mathematics (Rosenberg 1992, 1994). If this is the case, the question of using qualitative methods is almost certainly immaterial, but there are others who believe that careful use of data rather than a focus on rationality and abstract theories (Ormerod 1994) is important, and for these groups the use of qualitative methods may be a positive advantage.

Although mainstream neoclassical economics remains the dominant force (Coast, McDonald, et al. 2004), both ontological and epistemological approaches have become more eclectic in recent years, and there is an ever-increasing demand for the economics discipline to accept alternative approaches and methods to better understand the economy (The Cambridge 27 2001). Over the past fifteen years, there has been an increase in the use of qualitative methods in specific fields within economics; indeed, Starr asserts that there has been a 'small explosion' in the use of such methods (Starr 2014,

p. 238). Nevertheless, a narrowing towards the mainstream has also been noted in the U.K. setting (Lee, Pham, et al. 2013).

The potential for using critical realism in economics has been strongly advocated by Tony Lawson. Lawson draws on critical realist thinking (Bhaskar 1989; Lawson 1995a, 1996, 1999, 2003; Graça Moura and Martins 2008) in setting out an alternative approach to mainstream neoclassical economics (Lawson 1997, 2003), identifying the primary problem with current approaches as being its positivist deductive ontology (Coast 1999; Graça Moura and Martins 2008). As Coast stated in 1999:

> [Lawson] describes the form of explanation in economics as requiring universal regularities in the form of 'whenever x then y' (Lawson 1995b, 1997). In neo-classical economics the axioms of orthodox theory, whilst being formulated at a relatively high level of generality, are interpreted as secure event regularities in the real world (Lawson 1995b). The nature of knowledge supported by mainstream economics is that reality is that which is given in experience; thus the task of science is to seek empirical evidence of event regularities (Lawson 1995b). The problem identified by Lawson is that the existence of such event regularities in the social realm of the real world is highly suspect. Hence mainstream economics is destined for failure. (Coast 1999, p. 349)

Lawson's approach derives from the ontological perspective of critical realism (Bhaskar 1989). In critical realism, there is a sense of a single reality, but it is not assumed to be directly accessible as in realism (Maxwell 2012). Instead, there are assumed to be three domains of reality. First, there is the empirical, which comprises impression and experience. Second, there is the actual, which comprises actual events as well as the empirical. And third, there is the real. The real comprises structures, powers, mechanisms and tendencies, as well as the first two domains (Lawson 1997). Here, structures are concerned with how a phenomenon might operate, while mechanisms are related to how the structure works and to the powers (causes) underlying them. These mechanisms may or may not happen in the actual world, depending on whether they are triggered, and so the effects of mechanisms are thought of as tendencies (Lawson 1997). In critical realism, the empirical, the actual and the real, as the three domains of reality, are not in phase with one another, meaning that looking for relationships of the 'when x then y' type will not succeed; causality does not relate to events but to these tendencies and both the extent to which they produce events and the likelihood of these events being detected (Wainwright 1997). This different understanding of reality within critical realism means that the research focus also needs to be different. The aim is to explain (but not predict) by understanding the structures, mechanisms, powers and tendencies which produce the event of interest (Lawson 1995b), constructing theories to explain these mechanisms

(Wainwright 1997). The main method proposed by Lawson is retroduction, or the use of abductive ('as if') reasoning to move towards an explanation of how a phenomenon arises (Lawson 1997). Lawson's aim is to foster a move towards an approach that 'more obviously prioritises the goal of illuminating social reality' (Lawson 2003, p. xix). Although there are a number of critiques of the critical realist approach in economics (Graça Moura and Martins 2008), it provides a useful point of commonality with qualitative research, given that there are also qualitative researchers working from a critical realist perspective who reject notions of multiple realities but who accept readily that there may be different perspectives on a single reality (Maxwell 2012).

Three areas where qualitative methods have been utilized are institutional economics, behavioural economics and feminist economics. In (old) institutional economics, there is a rejection of the methodological individualism of neoclassical economics (Hodgson 1986; Toboso 2001); rather, the institution is conceptualized as the main focus for analysis and can be perceived broadly to include such institutions as money or marriage (Searle 2005). Here, institutions are seen as guiding behaviour, and so individual preferences cannot be the basis for theory development as in mainstream economics. Instead, institutional economists look for patterns to generate theory (Dugger 1994). The evidence used might comprise case studies, historical or anthropological in nature, which can be used to look at these patterns and hence ascertain the plausibility of theories (Dugger 1994). Mixed methods are seen as important in this context. For example, Downward and Mearman argue that such methods allow the combination of different insights on the same phenomena, giving an understanding of individual decision making and the institutional contexts in which this takes place (Downward and Mearman 2007).

Within behavioural economics, in contrast, the emphasis on the individual is retained, but the aim is to incorporate more accurate psychological assumptions (Carmerer and Loewenstein 2004) to improve the explanatory power of economics. Behavioural economists use a wide range of data sources and methods, including field experiments, simulations and modelling, with the emphasis on conducting empirical research (Heukelom 2014). For example, behavioural economists have used a variety of approaches to examine the choices people make and have questioned the idea of rational economic agents seeking to maximize utility (Santos 2011; Berndt 2015). The focus on understanding choices is reflected in health economics, where qualitative research has been extensively employed to ensure that the experimental and preference information obtained through quantitative work is well founded (Coast and Horrocks 2007; Coast, Al-Janabi, et al. 2012; Vass, Rigby, et al. 2017).

Feminist economists have been particularly concerned with the methods employed in economic research, as this is seen as central to addressing the exclusion of women's economic contributions and viewpoints from the traditional concerns of the discipline (Pujol 1997). Qualitative methods or mixed methods have been proposed as a way to overcome some of the limitations associated with orthodox economics and its focus on a narrow range of methods (Nelson 1995). Berik has outlined three core ways in which qualitative methods can enrich economic research from a feminist perspective. First, such methods can help identify the biases that imbue the quantitative large-scale surveys that have traditionally been used within economics, for example, in relation to how 'work' is defined and measured. Second, qualitative methods allow a focus on economic processes rather than just outcomes. For example, the outcome of gender differences in wages can be analysed using econometric methods, but qualitative methods would allow an understanding of the processes. Third, qualitative methods support the consideration of new topics as they enable researchers to gather data on phenomena that have traditionally been excluded from economic studies either because they are not deemed to be 'economic' or because they cannot be measured quantitatively (Berik 1997).

UNDERSTANDING ONTOLOGY, EPISTEMOLOGY AND METHODOLOGY IN QUALITATIVE RESEARCH

The ontologies, epistemologies and methodologies associated with qualitative research are starkly different from those underlying mainstream economics. Indeed, the whole purpose of qualitative research differs, with a focus not on the testing of deduced hypotheses to verify a theory that has already been developed but instead on determining meaning and generating theory inductively (Strauss and Corbin 1990; Swanson and Chapman 1994; Hansen 2006; Creswell 2013; Charmaz 2014; Patton 2015). Qualitative approaches are diverse and varied, originating from multiple disciplines and being described using many different terms (Miller and Crabtree 1997; Creswell 2013). Disciplines with which these approaches are particularly associated are sociology and anthropology, but increasingly also more applied disciplines such as nursing and education. Terms used to describe qualitative research are related to their methodological/analytic approaches and include phenomenology and interpretative phenomenological analysis (Hycner 1985; Cohen and Omery 1994), ethnography (Hammersley and Atkinson 1983; Hammersley 1992), grounded theory (Glaser and Strauss 1968; Strauss and Corbin 1990; Charmaz 2014), thematic analysis (Braun and Clarke 2006), framework (Ritchie and Lewis 2003; Gale, Heath, et al. 2013), narrative analysis (Riessman 2011), conversation analysis (Heritage 2011) and many others. There is not a single paradigm within which qualitative research is undertaken (Atkinson 1995), and even trying to understand how the approaches relate to one another is complex (Miller and Crabtree 1997). Nevertheless, the purpose is to 'grasp phenomena in some holistic way or to understand a phenomenon within its own context or to emphasise the immersion in and comprehension of human meaning ascribed to some set of circumstances or phenomena' (Lincoln 1992, p. 376) often aiming to generate new theory from the data collected (Glaser and Strauss 1968; Strauss and Corbin 1990; Charmaz 2014).

The view of the nature and form of reality taken within qualitative research is very often (but not always) relativist. From a relativist perspective there is no knowable single reality, and the paradigm in which research is conducted is constructivist (alternatively known as 'interpretivist' or 'naturalist') (Hughes 1990; Lincoln 1992; Creswell 2013; Charmaz 2014). Here, the perception is that reality is constructed and that there are multiple such constructed realities (Lincoln 1992). Correspondingly, the interaction between the researcher and what is being researched is seen as producing the findings of the research. Research is undertaken in natural, non-experimental, non-contrived settings (Hammersley and Atkinson 1983), and thus, understanding context and common-sense knowledge is vital in, and central to, qualitative research (Miles and Huberman 1994; Patton 2015).

Interaction between the researcher and the phenomenon under investigation allows the exploration of views and constructions, enabling the researcher to reach an understanding from the perspective of informants. Rather than the linear approach taken to research within the quantitative economic paradigm (of developing a hypothesis, testing it and arriving at a conclusion), qualitative research is much more circular and iterative (Miller and Crabtree 1997; Charmaz 2014). A number of data collection methods can be used, all of which involve intense contact with a particular phenomenon, with the researcher aiming to obtain data from the perspective of informants by becoming deeply aware of their views and by relying on these informants for understanding while suspending the researcher's own preconceptions (Miles and Huberman 1994; Gold 1997; Creswell 2013). The researcher himself or herself is the main research tool used, and so the quality of the research is heavily dependent on the skills of the investigator (Miles and Huberman 1994; Morse 1994; Barbour 1998; Patton 2015). One of the main requirements of the researcher is reflexivity: the idea that the researcher should reflect on his or her role in the research and on what is being found (Glaser and Strauss 1968; Burman 1994; Creswell 2013).

The aim of sampling is not, as in quantitative work, to obtain a sample of sufficient size and representativeness to be able to generalize from the particular sample to the entire population. Instead, sampling is purposeful and is often used to guide data collection as the analysis dictates (Strauss and Corbin 1990; Morse 1994; Charmaz 2014; Patton 2015), with sampling ending only once the analysis is complete (see Chapter 3). Data collection (Chapter 4) and analysis (Chapter 5) proceed concurrently, allowing researchers to pursue new leads as data collection continues. Analysis is conducted by categorizing data (which may include a variety of materials such as interview transcripts, field notes, documents and videos) and by looking for emerging themes in the data obtained (Dey 2003; Grbich 2013). Just as with quantitative work, the goal is to apply rigour to the research, and there are standards that qualitative work is expected to meet (Hammersley 1992; Lincoln 1992; Altheide and Johnson 1994; Lincoln 1995; Dingwall, Murphy, et al. 1998; Popay, Rogers, et al. 1998; Tong, Sainsbury, et al. 2007). These criteria differ from those of quantitative research, however, because the focus is not on objectivity and avoidance of bias but on acceptance of subjectivity and acknowledgement of how the researcher and informants may have influenced the findings, through the process of reflexivity.

USING QUALITATIVE RESEARCH METHODS IN HEALTH ECONOMICS

Qualitative methods allow the detailed exploration of issues, particularly in relation to complex phenomena about which informants may have deeply held beliefs, and are particularly useful where the concern is to understand the attitudes and views expressed (Donovan and Coast 1996; Hansen 2006). This may be advantageous to (health) economists trying to understand complex economic phenomena on the one hand and trying to improve their quantitative methods on the other.

Where health economic phenomena are complex and concerned with issues of meaning, qualitative methods may be particularly appropriate. In these cases the use of simple survey questions with large samples of the population or patient population is unlikely to be informative. A good example of an area that health economists have struggled to explore meaningfully using conventional surveys and quantitative methods is that of the barriers to the use of economic evaluation in decision making (Eddama and Coast 2008); qualitative methods appear to have been much more informative in exploring the complexities and meanings in relation to these barriers than traditional survey techniques (Bryan, Williams, et al. 2007; Williams and Bryan 2007a; Eddama and Coast 2009). The greater success of qualitative methods in this area is likely to be related to the need to explore both individual understandings of meaning and interactions within complex health organizations.

One area where there is undoubted opportunity for improving quantitative methods by using qualitative methods is in eliciting preferences from patients/consumers/citizens for use in economic analysis. This then avoids the sort of prior conceptions that Evans and Wolfson discussed in 1980, when they stated that 'preferences are preferences – economic theory is not supposed to pass moral judgements about what should be in a utility function'; they go on to add in parentheses that 'analysts do so all the time – but are not supposed to admit it' (Evans and Wolfson 1980, p. 11). The use of qualitative methods in preference elicitation is a burgeoning area of research where qualitative methods are increasingly accepted, if not expected, in developing the attributes or scenarios that form the basis for preference elicitation studies (Coast, Al-Janabi, et al. 2012; Vass, Rigby, et al. 2017). Examples of use of qualitative methods in this way are provided in Chapter 10, where Vosper and colleagues report the use of focus groups and in-depth interviews to generate attributes in two studies of depression, and in Chapter 11, where Stevens describes the development of dimensions of a preference-based measure for children.

Qualitative methods might be useful not just in exploring issues in the health economy; they might also be useful for improving processes of both data collection and analysis. Indeed, notable economists both in health and outside have suggested that understanding choices and preferences may require reflection, introspection and discussion, on the part of both informants and researchers (Sen 1973, 1977; Mooney 1998). This is because preferences in some areas may not be fully formed (Boulding 1969; March 1978). Existing research within health economics has used the opportunities for discussion and reflection offered by a qualitative approach to improve data collection (Cookson and Dolan 1999; Dolan, Cookson, et al. 1999; Coast, Donovan, et al. 2002; Litva, Coast, et al. 2002) particularly where informants are operating outside of their usual sphere of experience. Deliberative approaches may be one option for increasing the rigour with which values and preferences are collected (Coote and Lenaghan 1997; Lomas 1997; Harrison and Mort 1998; Burchardt 2014): as Fishkin states 'On many issues, about four out of five citizens do not have stable, nonrandom opinions; they have what the political psychologists call "non-attitudes" or "pseudo-opinions"' (Fishkin 1991, p. 83). The use of deliberative approaches in health economics is explored further by Kinghorn and colleagues in Chapter 16. Analytic practices in health economics are also an area ripe for exploration using qualitative methods (Squires, Chilcott, et al. 2016), and Chapter 13 reports early work in this area from Husbands and colleagues using qualitative methods to explore processes around health economic decision modelling.

The philosophical frameworks most often used in qualitative research (Hansen 2006) clearly provide a contrast to the dominant approach within mainstream economics, with its search for universal relationships within a single reality, but qualitative research is not restricted to such approaches and can be used within alternative approaches more aligned with the traditional economics approach. There are qualitative researchers who see themselves as realists working outside the constructivist paradigm (Hammersley 1992; Miles and Huberman 1994; Maxwell 2012). Miles and Huberman, for example, suggest that analytic frameworks can be theory driven and view qualitative methods as providing a means of testing hypotheses as well as developing them (Miles and Huberman 1994). The dichotomy between realism and relativism may also be too stark. The chapter has already discussed, from the economics perspective, more nuanced approaches to realism such as that associated with critical realism; these are also used by some qualitative researchers (Maxwell 2012), and there are other possibilities as well. Hammersley, for example, suggests an approach of 'subtle realism', which retains 'the idea that research investigates independent, knowable phenomena. But it breaks with [realism] in denying that we have direct access to those phenomena, in accepting that we must always rely on cultural assumptions, and in denying that our aim is to reproduce social phenomena in some way that is uniquely appropriate to them' (Hammersley 1992, p. 52).

There will also be economists who need to use a more pragmatic approach to qualitative data for a particular purpose, rather than focusing on a holistic assessment or theoretical development of the phenomenon of interest; a good example of this is the use of qualitative methods to generate Q sets in Q-methodology, as discussed in Chapter 9 by Baker and colleagues. In such cases, the qualitative elements of the research are explicitly designed to serve the economic purpose of the research. Indeed, increasingly, particularly in health care research, quantitative and qualitative research are used alongside one another, and the view is that the two approaches can be complementary, with different methods being able to inform different aspects of a research question (Hansen 2006). The research as a whole can then benefit from the respective strengths of both the qualitative and quantitative work (Black 1994; Dingwall, Murphy, et al. 1998; Morgan 1998). Within health technology assessments, for example, there might be quantitative elements comprising a randomized controlled trial to look at effectiveness and an economic evaluation to look at efficiency, but also qualitative elements exploring how to achieve the most successful randomization (Paramasivan, Strong, et al. 2015), the fidelity and quality of implementation (Moore, Audrey, et al. 2015) and the nature and acceptability of the particular health technology. The research can benefit from both aspects: the quantitative research provides statistically generalizable data, while the qualitative data aid understanding of issues, particularly where those issues are complex.

The nature of the use of qualitative methods and the theoretical perspective that an economist takes in his or her research are likely to be closely intertwined. Where the qualitative work is a precursor to quantitative work, the methods are likely to be used and applied quite differently compared to where the qualitative work is concerned with exploring phenomena directly;

the depth of analysis required may also be very different. This can be seen both from the existing literature and in the chapters in this book. Using qualitative methods to generate statements for use in Q-methodology (see Baker et al., Chapter 9) requires a different type and level of analysis from that required to generate attributes or dimensions for further valuation (see Vosper et al., Chapter 10, Stevens, Chapter 11, and existing literature [Coast and Horrocks 2007; Coast, Al-Janabi, et al. 2012]), and that again requires a different level and type of analysis from a full explanation of a particular economic phenomenon such as health care rationing (see Smith, Chapter 20, also existing literature [Coast 2001a; Eddama and Coast 2009; Owen-Smith, Coast, et al. 2009; Owen-Smith, Donovan, et al. 2015]) or the effectiveness of international aid provision (see Martínez-Álvarez, Chapter 18).

Although combining qualitative and quantitative methods is increasingly accepted both in health and across the social sciences (Hansen 2006), there remains a danger for health economists in using qualitative methods, which is that they may end up outside the 'disciplinary mode of thinking' (Williams 1997) that is typical of mainstream health economics (Coast, McDonald, et al. 2004). This may be particularly important for those using qualitative methods within an explanatory neoclassical paradigm, where methods designed for building theory grounded in reality may inevitably come up with something other than that derived on the basis of logical assumptions and notions of rationality. Indeed, it has been noted previously that those pursuing the more anthropological research associated with institutional economics have tended to be intellectually located outside the mainstream of economics (Coast, McDonald, et al. 2004). As Coast and colleagues noted in 2004:

> There is thus a tension for health economics between, on one hand, the potential for improving the 'systematic mode of thinking' of economics, particularly, its application and relevance to health care, and, on the other, the potential to threaten the disciplinary basis. Economics tends to be alone among the disciplines in facing this problem because of the extent to which its central paradigm represents a monolithic body of knowledge and beliefs shared by the vast majority of those involved in the discipline, the extent to which this body of knowledge is dependent upon the basic axioms and the extent to which other paradigms are marginalised. (Coast, McDonald, et al. 2004, p. 174)

One response to this would be to conduct qualitative work within a predefined framework, but this may be equally problematic in that it may lead to criticism from qualitative researchers, on the grounds that the work is restricted by the theory to which it subscribes.

Not all use of qualitative methods by health economists may face these problems, or not to such an extent. Where the primary purpose of the work is to enhance quantitative findings, these issues may not arise; they are much more likely where health economists are using qualitative methods for inductive theory development (Coast, McDonald, et al. 2004). Health economists may also be happier than other economists to see themselves outside of the mainstream of economics, with considerable interest in behavioural economic approaches for example.

These issues do mean, however, that economists need to ensure that they embark on qualitative research aware of these issues and having developed for themselves a meaningful theoretical perspective with which they are comfortable (Coast, McDonald, et al. 2004). They need to reflect on their epistemological position (and, of course, all researchers operate with such a position, whether or not they reflect, acknowledge or justify it [Marsh 1999]) and be aware of how it facilitates their use of qualitative methods (Coast, McDonald, et al. 2004). Health economists conducting qualitative work have often accepted methodological individualism but rejected deductivism, focusing instead on developing theory inductively (Coast, McDonald, et al. 2004). They have often been reluctant to accept a relativist or constructivist position (although there are exceptions – see, e.g., Chapters 13 and 20), rather being attracted to nuanced forms of realism such as subtle realism (Hammersley 1992) or 'critical realism' (Bhaskar 1989; Lawson 1997; Maxwell 2012). Lawson's arguments, for example, provide a basis for not attempting to define universal event regularities (Lawson 1995b, 1997), while Hammersley's views about the possibility of avoiding both 'naïve realism' and relativism are potentially particularly useful for economists searching for a theoretical position from which to embark on qualitative work. This is because they allow economists to attend to context while still working within a broad philosophical framework that most economists would find acceptable given that it retains 'the idea that research investigates independent, knowable phenomena' (Hammersley 1992, p. 52).

Health economists could also explore the philosophical approaches used in the 'heterodox economics' approaches explored briefly earlier in the chapter and engage with current debates within the discipline of economics (Lawson 2006). In a number of areas, economists are examining how approaches can be broadened to enable economists to gain new insights and investigate issues that are not readily answered using traditional data sources and techniques (Jefferson, Austen, et al. 2014). Health economists would be well placed to inform such debates given the rich history associated with employing qualitative methods within a health care context.

CONCLUSION

The methodological choice to pursue qualitative research is an important one. It suggests a desire to go beyond theory based on deduction and the numbers associated with econometric analyses, to provide greater understanding and thus improve both the theory and practice of health economics. As one among many examples, research by Geneau et al. in Tanzania highlighted the value of using in-depth interviews to understand the willingness to pay 'researchers working with the concept of "utility" to capture [willingness-to-pay] for health services need to acknowledge that peoples' motivations and behaviours are the results of a complex interplay of individual and socio-cultural factors. This calls for considering broader units of analysis, documenting more thoroughly community values and incorporating these elements when designing a survey or while interpreting survey results' (Geneau, Massae, et al. 2008). This provides just one illustration of the benefits that can be generated through using qualitative methods.

While health economists employing qualitative methods do need to develop a philosophical understanding and perspective to reconcile their use of qualitative methods with their place in the economics discipline, they should not let this put them off using qualitative methods. It is important to 'use the method that fits the research question, which may necessitate crossing the current method boundaries' (Berik 1997, p. 124). Enhanced epistemological understanding and awareness might well enhance economists' quantitative work: returning to the area of supplier-induced demand, it has been noted that much of the controversy in reaching clear conclusions 'can be attributed to ideological dispositions' (Labelle, Stoddart, et al. 1994, p. 350). The potential advantages of using qualitative methods outweigh the potential disadvantages, as they enhance the possibility of obtaining information which will allow the development of economic models and theories that start from a better understanding of the complexities of the health economy and the views and preferences of the actors within that health economy. Ultimately, this might reduce criticisms of the sort made by Hunter, that 'economics may furnish us with endless models and theories to debate but the discipline is weak in making any allowance for, or comprehending, human behaviour in actual real-life situations' (Hunter 1993, p. 8). It is important, though, that qualitative research within health economics takes account of the particular nature of the economic question in its design, and it is to the area of designing qualitative research in health economics that the book now turns.

Chapter 2

Designing qualitative research studies in health economics

Joanna Coast, Philip Kinghorn
and Amanda Owen-Smith

The aim of qualitative research is to collect data to increase understanding of why and how particular social phenomena arise (Ritchie 2004; Pope and Mays 2006b). Key features include a naturalistic and interpretative approach to data collection, which involves investigating the context for social behaviours and the meanings attached to them by individuals (Mays and Pope 2000). Research questions that are particularly suited to qualitative enquiry include those concerned with complex or hitherto poorly understood phenomena, those that relate to process issues (i.e., how something came to be) or those that deal with sensitive or deeply rooted issues, where it is necessary to understand the overall social context for participants' knowledge and understanding (Ritchie 2004). Designing research of this type requires consideration of a number of issues.

This chapter focuses on issues related to the design of qualitative research in health economics, concentrating on three main areas. The first is the theoretical perspective for the research, the second is the particular purpose of the health economics research and the third is the rigour of the research. Qualitative research can be conducted from many different theoretical perspectives, and the choice of theoretical perspective will influence the methodology used and thus the design of the research in terms of sampling, data collection and data analysis. This section of the chapter will briefly outline the main theoretical approaches and will also posit the possibility of an explicitly economic perspective from which to conduct qualitative research, a theme that will be returned to in Chapter 5, when analytic approaches are considered in depth.

The chapter will then turn to focus on the different areas of research where health economists might wish to use qualitative methods, exploring topics where the use of qualitative methods might have quite different purposes. These will include topics where the purpose of qualitative methods is to develop and enhance quantitative methods (e.g., developing attributes for discrete choice questionnaires), topics where the purpose is to better understand findings obtained through quantitative methods (e.g., generating data on completion of questionnaires) and topics where the purpose is to better understand health systems and other economic phenomena (e.g., allocation of scarce resources within different settings). This section of the chapter will distinguish between these topics and explore how these different research purposes might impact on the design of the qualitative research.

Third, the chapter will consider aspects of rigour that need to be built into the research design. It will focus on two specific issues: triangulation and reflexivity. It will also begin to discuss the ethics of conducting qualitative research, an issue that is returned to throughout the chapters. In this chapter, the focus of the ethics discussion will be around the importance of considering ethical issues at the stage of designing the research, and particularly the need to obtain appropriate approvals from the regulatory bodies.

Finally, the chapter will consider two examples of published research in terms of the design choices made in each of these three categories, as an aid to researchers new to this area who may find it difficult to see how this relatively theoretical discussion can be applied in empirical research.

THEORETICAL AND METHODOLOGICAL PERSPECTIVES FOR QUALITATIVE RESEARCH: INFLUENCES ON DESIGN

As already alluded to in Chapter 1, there are a number of underpinning theoretical bases from which qualitative research can be undertaken; indeed Atkinson suggests that the qualitative approach is not so coherent as to constitute a single paradigm (Atkinson 1995). These theoretical bases influence the methodological choices that qualitative researchers make in designing their studies, in terms of both data collection and analysis. They are also important because they influence the issues that researchers choose to study and the questions that they consider to be important; they also help to locate where the answers to these questions might be found and are associated with different ways of presenting findings.

The challenge for economists new to the use of qualitative research is unpicking these various approaches and making choices about how they might be applied in their own research. This task is not aided by the overlapping yet diverse set of approaches, and as Miller and Crabtree indicate, 'The quest for a useful organizational map of qualitative methods is not unlike the quest for the Holy Grail. The methods derive from multiple disciplines and from at least 20 or more diverse traditions, each with its own particular language' (Miller and Crabtree 1997, p. 13). There tends to be relatively complex technical jargon with terminology that has different meanings both from everyday use and across disciplines, ambiguities in explanation and interpretation and extensive debate and conflicting information. For novice (in qualitative terms) economists who are dipping their toes into this literature for the first time, without any training in the different theoretical perspectives or philosophical approaches within the social sciences, this can be daunting (Coast 1999; Coast, McDonald, et al. 2004).

Indeed, Creswell describes the choice of approaches as 'baffling' (Creswell 2013, p. 7) and provides a table outlining how different authors have classified the approaches since the late 1980s, showing the large number of different approaches that have been taken across areas as diverse as sociology, nursing, education, psychology, social science and theatre (Creswell 2013). From these, Cresswell selects five as those that are most frequently used in social, behavioural and health sciences and that contain systematic procedures for data collection and analysis: ethnography, grounded theory, narrative research, phenomenology and case study research (Creswell 2013). Four of Creswell's five approaches are discussed here; case studies are not considered separately in depth as they are very often a feature of ethnographic and other approaches. To these four, however, is added feminist research, which has relevance to this volume both because it illustrates the application of a particular analytic lens, a subject returned to later in this book, and because it is an area where economics, in the form of feminist economics, has already embraced qualitative research methods (Starr 2014).

It is worth noting that these approaches do not apply just to particular aspects of the research process, given that terms are sometimes applied in this way (e.g., an ethnographic approach to data collection, or the use of grounded theory for analysis of data), but rather as overall composite approaches that will ideally inform the methods for sampling, data collection and analysis. It is also important to note that in practice the approaches may overlap significantly and that it is possible to work with more than one approach concurrently. Nevertheless, it is helpful to have some understanding of the key features of these different approaches.

Ethnography

Ethnography is associated with anthropology and sociology (Gobo 2011; Creswell 2013) and involves the study and description of cultures, where the term 'culture' can be interpreted broadly, to include organizations and groups as well as geographical locations (Hansen 2006; Patton 2015). In particular, ethnographers are interested in groups who share a culture and interact over time developing shared beliefs, values and behaviour, and ethnographers look for patterns in these areas (Creswell 2013). As Hansen states: 'Traditionally, ethnographies were conducted in an attempt to understand exotic and unfamiliar places and people. More recently ethnographies have been used to view the familiar with fresh eyes' (Hansen 2006, p. 61). Of particular relevance to health economists who are interested in how organizations within the health economy function might be organizational ethnography, where the focus is to make sense of how the organization works (Eberle and Maeder 2011).

Ethnography tends to involve immersion in a particular situation – the 'field' – and use of multiple and diverse data collection methods including observation, interviews and collection of documentary evidence (Eberle and Maeder 2011; Creswell 2013), with observation being perhaps the defining feature of the approach (Hammersley and Atkinson 1983; Gobo 2011). Cases will often be selected as part of an ethnographic approach (Creswell 2013). Analysis tends to focus on obtaining a detailed 'rich' or 'thick' description of the shared patterns within the culture under study (Hansen 2006; Creswell 2013) and considers both the 'insider' accounts of those being studied and the 'outsider' accounts of the researcher (Hammersley and Atkinson 1983; Creswell 2013).

Chapters within this book that draw on approaches associated with ethnography, using observation alongside other techniques, include the work by Martínez-Álvarez, which involved immersion in the field in Tanzania, exploring aid effectiveness (Chapter 18); the research by Husbands et al., which involved the use of multiple sources of data to understand the processes used by health economic modellers (Chapter 13); and the exploratory research of Eckard and Nedlund, which combined observation and interviews to explore priority-setting processes in Sweden (Chapter 19).

Grounded theory

Grounded theory is an approach derived from sociology and focusing around a process or action (Creswell 2013). The explicit purpose of a grounded theory approach to qualitative research is to generate or build theory by exploring a particular phenomenon in depth (Glaser and Strauss 1968; Strauss and Corbin 1990; Charmaz and Bryant 2011; Charmaz 2014). To achieve this, researchers need to have 'theoretical sensitivity' to the phenomenon, essentially conceptual insight allowing them to comprehend the meaning of the data and to determine what is and is not important. This theoretical sensitivity may in part be a quality of researchers and their experience, in part an understanding derived from previous reading and in part comes from the analytic processes involved in questioning and comparing the data (Strauss and Corbin 1990). The main method of analysis is constant comparison: comparing information from one informant initially with that from another, and then comparing it with emerging categories (Glaser and Strauss 1968).

Analysis is conducted iteratively and can be quite structured, with different types of coding: open, axial and selective. Open coding begins by identifying concepts within the data, most frequently interview transcripts (Creswell 2013), and starting to categorize these into larger units; Strauss and Corbin describe this as 'fracturing' the data (Strauss and Corbin 1990). Axial coding is the next stage and involves bringing these fractured categories 'back together in new ways by making connections between a category and its sub-categories' (Strauss and Corbin 1990, p. 97) with the aim of relating categories within the emerging theory. Finally, there is selective coding, which involves determining the main category within the emerging theory and developing and understanding the relationships between that category and other categories (Strauss and Corbin 1990; Creswell 2013). As the theory is developed, researchers continue to collect data by sampling theoretically until they reach 'saturation', the point at which no more information can be added to the categories (Creswell 2013).

Challenges with the approach are in following all the relevant parts of the theory, which is considerably more prescriptive than other forms of qualitative inquiry (Hansen 2006; Creswell 2013), amid concerns that many claims to the use of grounded theory are questionable (Charmaz and Bryant 2011; Charmaz 2014). A variant of the approach that comes from a more interpretative stance is constructivist grounded theory (Charmaz and Bryant 2011; Charmaz 2014). Constructivist grounded theory is rooted in a relativist ontology and subjectivist epistemology that postulates the existence of multiple social realities which are co-constructed through the interaction between researcher and research participants. The biography and cultural perspective of the researcher, therefore, takes on a more central role in analysis, and a greater degree of power balance between researchers and participants may emerge (Charmaz 2005).

Much of the qualitative work in health economics has drawn on grounded theory procedures, particularly the constant comparative technique and the notion of sampling to saturation in relation to theory development (Coast 2001a, 2001b; Owen-Smith, Coast, et al. 2009; Al-Janabi, Flynn, et al. 2012), and the influence of this approach can also be seen in the chapters in this book from Vosper and colleagues (Chapter 10), Canaway and colleagues (Chapter 12) and Bailey and colleagues (Chapter 14). As will be discussed later in this chapter and more extensively in Chapter 5, this is in part related to the purpose of grounded theory, which is often similar to the purposes of health economics research around model building.

Narrative inquiry

The focus of narrative inquiry is on individual cases with an emphasis on 'how an account was generated, its effects, the positioning of characters and other aspects of narrative construction' (Riessman 2011, p. 312). It is an approach that Creswell describes as arising from the humanities and social sciences (Creswell 2013). Individuals' 'stories' are the basis for data collection (Riessman 2011; Creswell 2013; Patton 2015). These are constructed through the interaction of the individual with the researcher and focus on experiences (Creswell 2013). The primary form of data collection is interviews although other methods can also be used; Patton suggests written texts, and political rhetoric can also be the focus of narrative analysis (Patton 2015). It is suggested that participants often find telling their stories to be 'pleasurable and helpful' (Payne 2007, p. 157). Narratives are evaluated critically, and in analysis, the specificity of these cases is kept intact rather than splitting them into segments to derive overall themes as in other approaches (Riessman 2011) with narratives considered within participants' personal contexts (Creswell 2013). Analysis might focus on the themes, structure and dialogue of narratives and may involve restorying: 'Restorying is the process of organising the stories into some general type of framework' (Creswell 2013, p. 74) with a chronology and story line.

Narrative research has been advocated as a potentially valuable method to study issues around decision making and priority setting in health care (Smith, Mitton, et al. 2009). Smith and colleagues suggest that 'an important goal of narrative research is to put the person at the center of the analysis, rather than to come up with "themes" that emerge from analysis across many cases and which are thus often highly abstract' (Smith, Mitton, et al. 2009, p. 1167). They indicate that understanding different narratives from different actors in the system will indicate the extent to which priority-setting processes are likely to be well received within an organization and thus, ultimately, how successful they are likely to be (Smith, Mitton, et al. 2009) (see also Chapter 20). The approach can be demanding, however, given the need to collect extensive information from those taking part in the research and the importance of reflexivity in the 'restorying' of the narrative (Creswell 2013).

Phenomenology

Phenomenology is associated with psychology and philosophy (Creswell 2013) and is popular in both psychology and nursing research (Hansen 2006). Phenomenological research focuses on 'lived experience', that is, describing individuals' experiences and how they experience them (Hansen 2006; Creswell 2013). It aims to reduce these descriptions of particular experiences down to their very essence (Cohen and Omery 1994; Creswell 2013) understanding 'hidden meanings' (Grbich 2013). The approach derives from philosophy and in particular the works of Husserl and Heidegger (Cohen and Omery 1994). Work tends to focus on a single issue, such as the research by Evans and Hallett on the experience of the work of hospice nurses which explored the meaning of comfort care with fifteen hospice nurses (Evans and Hallett 2007) or the research by Cote-Arsenault and Denney-Koelsch on parents' experiences of pregnancy with a lethal fatal diagnosis which conducted a set of ninety longitudinal interviews with sixteen mothers and fourteen partners (Cote-Arsenault and Denney-Koelsch 2016).

Discussion of the philosophical approach is entwined with description of the study itself, and interviews with those who have experienced the phenomenon under investigation are often used to provide data; sometimes an approach referred to as 'bracketing' is used to keep separate the researcher's personal experiences from those of participants (Hycner 1985; Creswell 2013; Grbich 2013), as in the work by van Wijngaarden and colleagues where bracketing was achieved through ongoing reflection via a reflective research journal and dialogue with others (van Wijngaarden, Leget, et al. 2015). Analysis involves identifying significant statements relevant to the research question and then grouping these into units of meaning; common themes or 'essence' is then used to draw these units of meaning into clusters that can be related together (Hycner 1985; Creswell 2013; van Wijngaarden, Leget, et al. 2015). The aim is to obtain a description of the essence of the phenomenon of interest, based on those experiences that are common to the participants (Creswell 2013). Particular challenges with the approach can be in finding sufficient people who have experienced the issue of interest, difficulties in conducting bracketing and having sufficient understanding of the philosophical underpinnings of the approach (Creswell 2013), as well as in understanding the different streams of phenomenological analysis (Grbich 2013).

Phenomenology is not an approach that appears to have been used in health economics research, though it could potentially be meaningful in identifying the essence of particular experiences about which preference information could then be generated.

Feminist theories

In feminist approaches, the concern is with gender and the focus is more politicized (Hansen 2006). These approaches explicitly examine the experiences of women, focusing on issues such as discrimination and inequity (Berik 1997; Hansen 2006). As Creswell puts it, 'In feminist research approaches, the goals are to establish collaborative and nonexploitative relationships, to place the researcher within the study so as to avoid objectification, and to conduct research that is transformative' (Creswell 2013, p. 29).

Feminist theories provide an approach to data collection and analysis rather than a method in itself: 'In the feminist literature there is considerable agreement that there is no distinctive feminist method, but rather there are feminist applications of methods' (Berik 1997, p. 122). Indeed, this approach can be seen in the work of Austen and colleagues, who suggest the application of grounded theory to understand women's social and economic progress (Austen, Jefferson, et al. 2003), a method applied also by Warren and colleagues in their U.K. study of low and unpaid work among mothers (Warren, Pascall, et al. 2010). Grbich notes that feminist research uses many approaches including grounded theory, phenomenology and ethnography, applying feminist principles within these (Grbich 2013). Rather than providing methodological guidance, the feminist approach provides a particular interpretative lens through which analysis that concentrates specifically on issues around gender is conducted.

Feminist economists have seen the use of qualitative research methods as a means of expanding the range of what is studied by economists. They note, for example, that surveys have often led to findings that are biased towards males, for example, by focusing on the heads of households or paid employment, when many women work in the informal economy (Berik 1997; Austen, Jefferson, et al. 2003; Jefferson, Austen, et al. 2014). They also suggest that the focus on outcomes such as gross domestic product leaves unacknowledged the processes by which these outcomes are achieved (Berik 1997). Qualitative work within feminist economics has particularly focused on issues around the labour market, with researchers explicitly focusing on gender issues giving voice to marginalized groups and often advocating for policies focused on achieving greater equality (Esim 1997; Warren, Pascall, et al. 2010; Jefferson, Austen, et al. 2014).

Approaches to qualitative research in health economics?

One question that economists may have is whether such approaches are required for their own qualitative work. As Creswell indicates, 'Some qualitative studies do not employ any explicit theory. . . . However . . . prior conceptual structure . . . provides the starting point for all observations. . . . Still, one sees qualitative studies that contain no explicit theoretical orientation' (Creswell 2012, p. 66) although it is clear that this is not a choice that Creswell agrees with (Creswell 2012, 2013). It has been noted that much qualitative research conducted in the area of applied health research is 'generic', focusing on 'thematic analysis' and making little reference to theory (Kelly 2010). The aim of such research, it is said, is that it can be applied relatively quickly to practice, but it is noted that 'it may involve a relatively surface analysis of the content of the data or be a preliminary exercise to gain a general overview of an issue' (Kelly 2010, pp. 286–7).

Indeed, this issue is explicitly discussed in relation to the study of priority setting by health economists, in a paper published in *Health Economics* in 2009 (Smith, Mitton, et al. 2009). Smith and colleagues argue strongly that health economists have not gone far enough in working within established theoretical perspectives, suggesting that while there has been an increase in the use of qualitative data, this is not necessarily mirrored by increasing use of qualitative methods or methodologies (Smith, Mitton, et al. 2009); Smith further pursues this argument in Chapter 20. These authors do, however, acknowledge that different uses of qualitative work may require different approaches; that is the area to which this chapter now turns.

PURPOSE OF THE ECONOMIC RESEARCH: INFLUENCE ON DESIGN

Qualitative research within health economics has different purposes, which will undoubtedly impact on the design of the research (Coast 1999). Drawing on earlier work (Coast 1999), this section of the chapter outlines three broad purposes of qualitative research within health economics and considers the methodological choices in designing such work. These three purposes focus on qualitative research to develop and enhance quantitative research, qualitative work to interpret quantitative findings and qualitative work where the primary purpose is economic understanding and theory generation.

In making decisions about study design, economists need to consider not just qualitative theory and methodology but also economic theory, thus increasing the complexity of these choices. Chapter 1 has already discussed in detail the issues around philosophy and economics, but here the implication of these issues for design of a study is highlighted in more detail.

Qualitative research to develop and enhance quantitative research

Within the mainstream neoclassical tradition, as well as beyond it, qualitative methods may be used as a precursor to quantitative analysis. Rather than economists themselves deciding on the questions to include in a survey of one type or another, they could use qualitative research methods to determine what issues to include in the research. Methods such as semi-structured interviews or focus groups can be used to talk to individuals and identify themes relating to what is important to them in a particular context. This might include aspects of preferences that the researcher had not thought about for a preference elicitation study, views from a wide range of perspectives to include in a Q set or issues that had not been considered to be important in a survey of systems or behaviour focusing on economic issues. Using qualitative methods in such a way could prove helpful in ensuring all relevant factors are included in quantitative work while ultimately retaining the advantages of the use of a survey which can be sent to a representative sample of sufficient size to achieve statistical power.

In welfarist and extra-welfarist normative analysis (Brouwer, Culyer, et al. 2008; Coast, Smith, et al. 2008), it has become relatively common, if not expected, in recent years, that preference elicitation studies should begin with a qualitative phase of research that aims to draw out the pertinent issues from those with experience of the area under study (Coast, Al-Janabi, et al. 2012; Vass, Rigby, et al. 2017). In designing such work it is important to be aware of the need within the qualitative research to focus sequentially on two different issues (Coast, Al-Janabi, et al. 2012). The first is the development of conceptual attributes reflecting the areas of importance to those whose preferences are to be elicited, and the second is the development of meaningful language for use in the measure or preference elicitation task (Coast, Al-Janabi, et al. 2012). In some studies these phases are explicitly separated (Al-Janabi, Flynn, et al. 2012; Sutton and Coast 2014), while in others they are merged but still treated as conceptually different tasks (Coast and Horrocks 2007; Canaway, Al-Janabi, et al. 2017).

Although some such studies adopt a generic health services research-type (Kelly 2010) approach to data collection and analysis for 'attribute development' (Miners, Llewellyn, et al. 2016), many studies of this type are more explicitly based on grounded theory approaches, with an iterative approach to sampling and analysis, use of theoretical sampling to saturation (defined as achieving a fully complete set of attributes [Coast, Al-Janabi, et al. 2012; Canaway, Al-Janabi, et al. 2017]) and the use of constant comparison in analysing data. This is in large part because the aim of these attribute development studies is essentially to derive a theory or model of values and preferences in relation to a particular issue, which is then essentially 'tested' using the quantitative valuation techniques, such as discrete choice experiments (DCEs) (Ryan 2004) and best-worst scaling (Flynn, Louviere, et al. 2007; Louviere, Flynn, et al. 2015), or other preference elicitation techniques (Drummond, Sculpher, et al. 2015).

Data for attribute development may be derived from primary research, using interviews (Coast and Horrocks 2007; Ke, Mackichan, et al. 2013; Sutton and Coast 2014; McCaffrey, Gill, et al. 2015), focus groups (Danner, Vennedey, et al. 2016) or a combination of the two (Abiiro, Leppert, et al. 2014; Kinghorn, Robinson, et al. 2014), or they may be generated from secondary analysis (Jackson and Roberts 2015; Ogwulu, Jackson, et al. 2015) or secondary analysis in combination with primary analysis (Al-Janabi, Coast, et al. 2008). Observation is not usually an appropriate technique for data collection of this sort because an individual's values are usually internalized and may not be expressed in everyday life; trying to capture them through observation is likely to be inefficient. More details on designing attribute development studies can be found elsewhere (Coast and Horrocks 2007; Coast, Al-Janabi, et al. 2012); in this book, Vosper and colleagues explore the use of qualitative methods in developing attributes for DCEs (see Chapter 10), and Stevens describes the use of qualitative methods in developing dimensions for an outcome measure for use in economic evaluation of interventions affecting children (see Chapter 11).

Studies using Q methodology in health economics have also often started from the use of qualitative methods to generate a Q set (Baker, Thompson, et al. 2006; Baker, Wildman, et al. 2014). Here the aim is to generate a set of statements that can then be used during the Q sort; qualitative data generated through primary research are often combined with other data to generate this Q set. For example, in a study of economic rationality in people with diabetes, Baker included data from patient interviews but combined this with information from patient resources, medical textbooks and journal articles to generate a set of statements that was then refined to a final set structured within three types of rationality (Baker 2006). Here, the use of theory may be more related to the economic area under investigation than to the qualitative data per se. The use of qualitative data in Q methodology is considered more extensively in the chapter by Baker and colleagues (Chapter 9).

Also falling into this group of studies are those that use qualitative methods to try to enhance health economic methods more generally and thus aim to improve quantitative methods moving forwards. A recent focus of work of this type has been the improvement of the processes used in health economic modelling (Chilcott, Tappenden, et al. 2010; Kaltenthaler, Essat, et al. 2014; Squires, Chilcott, et al. 2016). Much of this work to date has taken the sort of generic approach indicated earlier, with relatively small samples to obtain an overview of the issues, but ethnographic approaches that pay particular attention to observing processes and practices as well as interviewing informants may fruitfully extend this work. Indeed, more recent work by Husbands and colleagues has approached the area with a more interpretivist philosophy and uses observational methods associated with an ethnographic approach (see Chapter 13). There are also other areas to which this approach might be applied; such an example is provided by the work of Canaway and colleagues (Chapter 12), which focuses on issues around who should be included in economic evaluations of end-of-life care.

Qualitative research to interpret quantitative findings

Qualitative methods can be used alongside experimental studies or quantitative observational or survey studies to improve understanding of the quantitative results obtained, essentially as an explanatory adjunct to quantitative work. Objective data are provided by quantitative enquiry, but where results appear confusing or unintuitive, qualitative research can be used to question its meaning. This role for qualitative research has the advantage that the methods used provide a powerful tool for understanding.

A number of health economics studies have used qualitative methods to better understand the use of economic measures (O'Hanlon, Fox-Rushby, et al. 1994; Al-Janabi, Keeley, et al. 2013; Keeley, Al-Janabi, et al. 2013; Bailey, Kinghorn, et al. 2016), their appropriateness in particular contexts (Goebbels, Lakerveld, et al. 2012) and the elicitation of preferences for use in health care decision making (Baker and Robinson 2004; Geneau, Massae, et al. 2008). The former type of study has often concentrated on how people complete standard health economic measures such as EQ-5D (O'Hanlon, Fox-Rushby, et al. 1994), or newer measures such as the various ICECAP (ICEpop CAPability) measures that focus on capability well-being (Al-Janabi, Keeley, et al. 2013; Horwood, Sutton, et al. 2014; Bailey, Kinghorn, et al. 2016). These studies have tended to use relatively structured techniques such as cognitive interviewing or think-aloud approaches as well as less structured techniques that focus on issues such as content validity of measures (Keeley, Al-Janabi, et al. 2013). Cognitive interviewing/think-aloud techniques tend to ask the participant to complete measures while 'thinking aloud' and/or to complete them and then comment on their thoughts as they completed the measures (Tourangeau 1984; Willis 2005). A useful adjunct to completion while thinking aloud is to interview informants subsequently, as with some of the work conducted with the ICECAP measures (Al-Janabi, Keeley, et al. 2013; Bailey, Kinghorn, et al. 2016). The chapter by Bailey and colleagues discusses the use of think-aloud approaches in evaluating economic measures in the context of end-of-life care (Chapter 14).

Similar techniques have also been used by health economists to explore the various valuation techniques used in preference elicitation and generation of Quality-Adjusted Life-Years, including time trade-off (O'Hanlon, Fox-Rushby, et al. 1994; Robinson, Dolan, et al. 1997; Spencer 2003) and standard gamble (Baker and Robinson 2004; van Osch and Stiggelbout 2008), as well as other preference elicitation techniques such as willingness to pay (Smith 2007; Geneau, Massae, et al. 2008) and DCEs (San Miguel, Ryan, et al. 2005; Ryan, Watson, et al. 2009). These studies tend to employ approaches whereby qualitative data are collected alongside, or shortly after, the completion of the relevant quantitative task. In these studies, researchers may be interested in exploring particular assumptions behind the valuation techniques and may therefore ensure that the questioning approach that they use during interviews identifies instances where the assumption is met/violated, enabling the researcher to probe the assumption with the informant (Ryan, Watson, et al. 2009). The chapter by Robinson focuses on using qualitative methods to understand health state valuations (Chapter 15).

A second broad use of qualitative methods included under this heading is their contribution to reflection and deliberation in obtaining quantitative findings. From the early days of the use of qualitative methods within health economics, reflection and discussion has been seen as potentially advantageous both in understanding the results obtained and in obtaining more meaningful findings (Cookson and Dolan 1999; Dolan, Cookson, et al. 1999). Although deliberative processes are not purely qualitative, drawing as they do on political aspects of democracy (Fishkin 1991; Fishkin and Luskin 2005), they provide a means of connecting citizens to the decision-making process (Coote and Lenaghan 1997; Delli Carpini, Lomax Cook, et al. 2004; Burchardt 2014) and are thus potentially valuable to health economists trying to understand values and preferences for resource allocation. Deliberation moves beyond the scope of traditional qualitative methods in two ways: first in terms of blurring the roles of and interaction between the researcher and research participants, and, related to this, by empowering participants not only (consciously or subconsciously) to reveal their beliefs, values and behaviours but also to put forward their own conclusions, recommendations or group verdict based on and informed by those values and beliefs. The blurring of the nature of the interaction between researcher and research participant comes from an explicit objective by the researcher of introducing the research participant to relevant background and contextual information and the alternative sides of related debate. Essentially, both parties are enhancing their understanding of a phenomenon by being exposed to the knowledge, understanding, values and beliefs of the other. Deliberative processes have been used in understanding health state valuations (Robinson and Bryan 2013) as well as in relation to issues around priority setting. In this book, the chapter by Kinghorn and colleagues focuses on the use of deliberative methods to understand values and priorities around the provision of end-of-life care (Chapter 16).

Qualitative research to enhance and generate economic understanding and theory

Although the main focus of qualitative research outside health economics is to generate understanding and theory around particular phenomena rather than to enhance quantitative work, this is probably the least developed use of qualitative methods within (health) economics. As indicated in Chapter 1, this almost certainly reflects the dominance of mainstream economic theory with its approach to theory deduction from standard axioms and assumptions. Nevertheless, qualitative methods have been used, albeit infrequently, in the more inductive development of understanding and theory related to the operation of the market (Mannion and Smith 1997; Holmes, Bate, et al. 2009), aid transactions (Cruz and McPake 2010; Cruz and McPake 2011), health care rationing (Coast 2001a, 2001b; McDonald 2002; Owen-Smith, Coast, et al. 2009; Arvidsson, Andre, et al. 2010; Owen-Smith, Donovan, et al. 2015), pharmaceutical decision making (Ragupathy, Tordoff, et al. 2012; Armataki, Karampli, et al. 2014; Tafuri, Stolk, et al. 2014), health insurance decisions (De Allegri, Sanon, et al. 2006a, 2006b), patient decision making (Durif-Bruckert, Roux, et al. 2015; Walker, Howard, et al. 2016) and the use of economic techniques to induce behaviour change (Junghans, Cheung, et al. 2015). The methods have also been used to consider issues of particular concern to health economists: the appropriateness of health economic outcomes (van Mastrigt, Paulus, et al. 2015) and the use of economic evaluation in health care settings (Bryan, Williams, et al. 2007; Williams and Bryan 2007a; Teerawattananon and Russell 2008; Eddama and Coast 2009; Lafi, Robinson, et al. 2012), with the latter being an area of study where quantitative methods have struggled to provide helpful information (Eddama and Coast 2008).

Qualitative methods have also been used as part of a mixed-methods approach where understanding is generated through the combined use of qualitative and quantitative methods to generate understanding. While it may appear on first glance that this is similar to the two earlier uses of qualitative methods to enhance quantitative research, the difference is in the purpose of the work, with both qualitative and quantitative work contributing to a more rounded understanding of an issue rather than the qualitative work being seen as an adjunct to arrive at stronger quantitative findings or explain those findings. Examples of recent mixed-methods approaches to enhancing theoretical understanding include work to understand payment of health workers in Sierra Leone (Bertone and Lagarde 2016), to understand dual practice among physicians in Africa (Russo, McPake, et al. 2014) and to understand pharmaceutical markets in Mozambique (Russo and McPake 2010).

Some of these studies within this general area of enhancing understanding have focused on providing a description of an issue rather than attempting to move the area forward theoretically, but others have explicitly attempted to improve theory within the mainstream of health economics, to better reflect the operation of health care markets. Principal-agent theory (Ross 1973; Smith, Stepan, et al. 1997), for example, has provided a particular focus for studies in the areas of health care markets (Mannion and Smith 1997), health care rationing (Coast 2001a) and aid effectiveness (Cruz and McPake 2010). Research has also focused explicitly on the nature of utility in relation to health care rationing (Coast 2000b, 2001b). Such theory development has stayed within a mainstream paradigm by using preferences and utility functions as the starting point for the development of theory, but even using this starting point, economists need to be aware that qualitative methods can have the effect of moving the analysis away from the mainstream. For example, Mannion and Smith's analysis of the market for community care, in which semi-structured interviews were conducted with members of social service departments, was explicitly linked with neoclassical principal-agent theory. Interestingly though, their final paragraph indicates the limitations of the neoclassical approach ('the emphasis on relationships intrinsic to any analysis of trust suggests that the relentless individualism of the neoclassical approach may in this respect be of limited usefulness' [Mannion and Smith 1997, p. 159]) and suggests the possibility of ending up outside mainstream theoretical frameworks even when this provides a starting point for the research.

In designing research to aid understanding, therefore, health economics researchers need to think about not just their theoretical perspective from the 'qualitative' side (e.g., theory generation from a grounded perspective, ethnographic study of an aspect of the health economy, understanding of values or narratives) but also their economic theoretical perspective: mainstream or more heterodox approaches, and the particular theoretical area of interest. The economic theoretical perspective may be dictated by the general framework within which the health economist works but also by the particular topic. Whereas economists working within the mainstream neoclassical approach might start from an assumption that individuals' preferences are the main building block for research, this may not be true outside of this mainstream. From these alternative perspectives, the types of questions posed are likely to be very different: theories about the workings of the economy are unlikely to be built (solely) from information, however well embedded in context, about individuals' preferences. Lawson, for example, argues for the reality of social structures that are not irreducible to individuals (Lawson 1997). As an example, work by Culyer within the neoclassical mainstream attempted to explain the existence of the National Health Service (NHS) in the United Kingdom through individual preferences (Culyer 1971; Culyer and Simpson 1980); outside the mainstream, 'alternative' theories would not attempt to explain the NHS's existence and the form which that service takes by consideration of individual preferences. Instead, it would be more likely to consider the historical and institutional conditions which led to the development of such a system. Consideration of individuals' views about the health service would be the wrong starting point for this type of research.

There are a number of chapters in this book focusing on using qualitative methods to better understand economic phenomena and to generate theory around those phenomena. Two chapters draw, at least in part, on principal-agent theory to consider issues in lower- and middle-income countries. The first, from De Allegri, focuses on performance-based financing and is also concerned with theory around financial incentives (Chapter 17), and the second, from Martínez-Álvarez, studies aid effectiveness in health care (Chapter 18). Two further chapters concentrate on the societal decision-making process, with Eckard and Nedlund focusing on theories around the use of efficiency information in health care (Chapter 19), while Smith focuses specifically on design issues in relation to work on priority setting (Chapter 20).

DESIGNING FOR RIGOUR

Research rigour

There are many contrasting approaches to research rigour within qualitative work. Alternative approaches to qualitative research have led to proposals for different sets of criteria by which to evaluate such research, with considerable variation between these (Murphy, Dingwall, et al. 1998; Creswell 2013). These differ according to whether they use criteria drawing on parallels with quantitative research or attempt to define criteria from a more interpretivist perspective (Altheide and Johnson 1994; Lincoln 1995), arguing that unique criteria need to be developed (Hammersley 1992; Denzin and Lincoln 1994), for example, with notions of 'trustworthiness' replacing the quantitative notion of rigour (Lincoln 1995). It is clear, however, that issues of research quality relate to both the fieldwork conducted and the process of interpretation and writing (Glaser and Strauss 1968; Altheide and Johnson 1994; Creswell 2013), and that many of the criteria developed are primarily concerned with the relationship between the researcher and informants (Lincoln 1995). Hammersley perhaps provides an exception here, suggesting validity and relevance as the two main criteria for evaluating all social research. He defines validity in terms of the truth of the claims made, which can be determined by their plausibility and credibility, while relevance relates to the importance of the research and its contribution to knowledge (in terms of the audience for whom it is conducted) (Hammersley 1992).

For economists entering the world of qualitative research, this is a complex literature to grasp. Creswell provides an excellent summary of the current state of thinking in this area (Creswell 2013, pp. 243–68) but also helpfully suggests useful validation and reliability strategies, which can be seen as enhancing the rigour of qualitative research. These are prolonged engagement and persistent observation; triangulation (making use of multiple sources and methods); peer review or debriefing; negative case analysis; clarifying researcher bias (applying notions of reflexivity – the idea that the researcher should reflect on his or her role in the research and on what is being found [Glaser and Strauss 1968; Burman 1994]); member checking – going back to research participants; rich, thick description that enables assessment of the transferability of the research to other settings; external auditing of the research; and multiple coding of data sets (Creswell 2013).

Of further relevance to health economists are those sets of criteria that have been developed for use in health research. Specifically in relation to health, Popay et al. argue that three criteria form the basis of good qualitative research: interpretation of subjective meaning, description of social context and attention to lay knowledge (Popay, Rogers, et al. 1998). The first criterion requires that the meaning, actions and contexts of those being researched should be explained, with research showing how behaviour is viewed from within a particular culture (Popay, Rogers, et al. 1998). The latter criterion relates to the importance of prioritizing lay views rather than using clinical or psychological constructs (Popay, Rogers, et al. 1998). In order to achieve these objectives, Popay et al. suggest that qualitative research should provide evidence that the research has been adapted according to the ongoing analysis; evidence that sampling was adequate to produce the particular type of knowledge with a good description of the sampling process; evidence of detailed description, related to context and meaning; evidence of data quality in which perceptions and experiences are treated as knowledge and different sources of knowledge are compared and contrasted; and evidence of theoretical and conceptual adequacy (interpretative validity), including use of the constant comparative method (Popay, Rogers, et al. 1998). Malterud, writing in *The Lancet*, suggests criteria of relevance, validity and reflexivity (Malterud 2001). An influential paper in health care, used by a number of health journals in terms of required reporting of qualitative research, is the consolidated criteria for reporting qualitative research (COREQ) guidelines, which provides a 32-item checklist for reporting of interviews and focus groups (Tong, Sainsbury, et al. 2007). The COREQ guidelines are discussed more extensively in the chapter on presenting findings (Chapter 7).

Of particular interest for this book, however, is whether (health) economists can or should use these same sets of criteria in the evaluation of qualitative research conducted within (health) economics, whether some sets of criteria are potentially more useful than others and whether there are other, additional criteria that might also be important to consider in conducting and reporting rigorous qualitative research in (health) economics. Inevitably, the answers to these questions will depend on a number of factors: the nature of the qualitative approach taken and its theoretical perspectives, the purpose of the research and the economic theory incorporated into the research.

As an indication, however, that criteria for rigour may differ in qualitative research undertaken in health economics, it is useful to consider the one area for which explicit guidance has been generated specifically for the conduct of qualitative work in health economics. This is for the area of attribute development for DCEs, where Coast and colleagues outline a number of recommendations (Coast, Al-Janabi, et al. 2012). It is important to note that these relate as much to the underlying theory and purpose of DCEs as they do to the conduct of the qualitative research. The first two recommendations concern researcher understanding of the latent construct that the DCE is intended to inform, as a basis for avoiding attributes that are too close to this construct, and the need to focus on attributes that can be manipulated in policy terms (Coast, Al-Janabi, et al. 2012) (see Chapter 10 by Vosper et al. for more discussion of this issue). The third recommendation is focused on the qualitative research itself, but specifically within the context of attribute development; it outlines the importance of the two stages of attribute development (conceptual development and generation of meaningful language) for the design of the research (Coast, Al-Janabi, et al. 2012). The final two recommendations concern awareness of the rationale for the choice of method for attribute development and provide minimum reporting guidelines for attribute development studies, which accept that the space available for reporting may be very small if the entire DCE is reported in a single journal publication, but that still provides a basis for evaluating the qualitative element of the research (Coast, Al-Janabi, et al. 2012).

Ethical rigour

Ethical issues are covered in more depth later, but at the design stage, it is worth emphasizing the absolute importance of seeking appropriate ethical approvals. This is because qualitative research involves conducting research with human subjects. This is an area with which many economists and some health economists will be largely unfamiliar and which other health economists will only have experienced 'second hand' through their involvement in economic evaluations conducted alongside primary research where these ethical and governance issues will have been dealt with by others.

Conducting qualitative research will invariably require ethics approval for at least one of two reasons. The first is that, in many countries, any research with human subjects will require ethics approval. In health care settings and particularly for research with patient groups, this may mean obtaining approval through a national or regional health agency; for members of the public (often a group whom economists, from a societal perspective, are interested in), it is more likely to be some form of institutional review, from the researcher's host institution, that will be required. Individual countries will have slightly different rules on the precise body to be approached.

The second reason for requiring ethics approval is that many journals will not publish research that has not been through an ethical review process. Journals may have good reasons for this stance: it encourages research to be properly checked – important for research that may touch on upsetting or sensitive issues such as access to health care; it ensures that information provided to participants is appropriate and that consent issues are adhered to; and it ensures that the participants' and the researchers' safety and data are protected. Importantly, for journals, it means that the editors of journals do not themselves have to act as mini-ethics committees, deciding what is and is not ethically appropriate for publication.

For readers in the small number of countries where institutional review does not seem to be the norm, it is worth thinking carefully about how to deal with this issue at the design stage, to avoid possible rejection of papers on these grounds; it is extremely disappointing for researchers who have put considerable time and effort into a piece of research to not even have it reviewed when it is sent to a journal. Possible options for researchers in this position may be to ensure that the research is reviewed at another institution (possible, e.g., with international or even national collaborations where institutional policies differ) or to consider setting up a departmental review board that can meet on an ad hoc basis when required. This may also be an option for student research if this is not covered by the institutional review board and if later publication is being considered.

Ultimately, it is the researcher's responsibility to ensure that these ethical and governance issues are adhered to. It is vital that all health economists embarking on qualitative research seek appropriate ethics approvals.

TWO EXAMPLES

This final section of this chapter aims to assist health economists designing their own research study, by being explicit about the design choices made in two pieces of research, with different intentions, from Coast and colleagues. The first of these is the development of the ICECAP-A capability measure for use in economic evaluation of health and social care interventions (Al-Janabi, Flynn, et al. 2012), and the second is the generation of theory around the citizen–agent relationship in health care rationing (Coast 2001a), an example that is returned to in later chapters.

Example 1: designing for attribute development

In developing all of the ICECAP measures, including ICECAP-A, the philosophical approach taken was one of subtle realism: the notion that there is a reality that the researcher is trying to grasp but that it is experienced in different ways by different individuals and that the researcher has to unpick 'cultural assumptions' in attempting to unpick that reality (Hammersley 1992).

Essentially, designing for attribute development is concerned with generating a model of what is valuable to individuals in a particular area, which is then expanded on and tested through the use of quantitative techniques. Given this fundamental research aim of developing a model encompassing all that is important to people, the work was conducted drawing very much on grounded theory approaches (Glaser and Strauss 1968; Strauss and Corbin 1990; Charmaz 2014), with theoretical sampling based on including groups with different perspectives on life, an inductive approach to analysis that started from understanding the influences on well-being (e.g., health, wealth) and moved on to generating a model of the underlying factors that are important in people's lives (more abstract concepts such as stability, autonomy), sampling to saturation (i.e., until these attributes were fully defined) and the use of constant comparison as the analytic approach (Glaser 1965).

The specific economic theory on which the work drew was the capability approach of Amartya Sen (1987, 1993), which conceptualizes well-being in terms of what a person can do and be in his or her life. The capability approach also advocates a deliberative approach to the development of sets of capabilities so as to ensure that the capabilities focused on are those that are important in a particular cultural setting (Robeyns 2005), and that was an explicit focus of the work. The focus of the research was thus to generate a model of the aspects of well-being that adults in the United Kingdom value *in terms of these doings and beings*. It was not expected that a focus on capability well-being would be outside of what was valued by individuals, given that the choice to focus on capability within the research team had itself arisen from earlier qualitative research with older people (Grewal, Lewis, et al. 2006).

In terms of rigour, the research was designed to provide extensive engagement with citizens from a variety of backgrounds through lengthy in-depth interviews. The research design incorporated the development of detailed analytic accounts containing rich information and the exploration of negative cases. It also included checking of findings with informants and with the broader research team, and through peer review of emerging attributes during seminars and conferences and through advisory groups, with the aim of minimizing the influence of a single researcher on the development of attributes. The latent construct for the research was clear from the beginning: capability well-being, making it possible to avoid attributes that were too all-encompassing and close to this construct. All attributes developed were ones that could be expected to change with policies focusing on personal well-being, and the two separate stages of attribute development were designed as distinct elements of the research. Ethics approvals were obtained from the relevant university research committee.

Example 2: designing for theoretical understanding

As with the first example, this research was also located within a subtle realist philosophical perspective (Coast 2000b).

The focus of this research was the preferences that citizens and their agents hold in relation to health care rationing. Although the research was inductive, it was designed to explore this particular area and that focus was explicit from the start of the research (Miles and Huberman 1994). The methods used attempted to develop theory inductively drawing on an approach more usually associated with the constructivist/interpretivist school and, specifically, with the development of grounded theory (Glaser and Strauss 1968; Strauss and Corbin 1990). Sampling was increasingly theoretical as the research progressed: initially participants were chosen mainly because it appeared from the focus group that they would make good informants (i.e., were relatively articulate and willing to be further involved) but, later in the research, informants were also chosen because they had particular views or perspectives that would contribute to the developing theory around the citizen–agent relationship. Analysis incorporated various 'questioning' techniques recommended by Strauss and Corbin to enhance theoretical sensitivity, and used the methods of constant comparison, comparing transcripts initially to each other and then to emerging categories (Strauss and Corbin 1990).

The research aimed to determine values in relation to health care rationing decisions among both citizens and their potential agents. It drew on two aspects of economic theory: principal-agent theory (Ross 1973), as applied to societal health care decision making (Mooney 1994, 1998; Rochaix 1998), and the possibility of process utility as an influence on health care decision making (Mooney and Lange 1993; Coast 1997). In ascribing importance to preferences as a determinant of actions, the resultant organizational system and the maximization of welfare, the thesis began from the sort of individualistic viewpoint associated with a neoclassical mode of thinking. It started from an assumption that citizens would have health care preferences and that someone in health care would be making decisions about the allocation of health care resources from a societal, rather than individual, perspective. Focusing the research in this manner allowed the issues to be explored in a relatively efficient way while retaining an open mind about the issues and allowing other questions to arise during the research. Indeed, as interviews with agent informants continued, the assumption that 'someone' was making societal decisions was replaced with the notion that 'decisions' were the product of interaction between different groups within the health service (Coast 2001a).

The design of this research included, from the beginning, multiple methods (focus groups and interviews) to enable triangulation; these also aided in building rapport with informants and allowed topics to arise, through participant discussion, which may not otherwise have arisen. There was prolonged engagement with the setting in which the research was conducted over a period of more than two years, and the research design included a focus on reflexivity, with explicit consideration by the researcher of her role in the research and likely biases. The analytic design included the writing of rich and detailed analytic accounts (see Chapter 5) as well as the generation of matrices to avoid finding simplified patterns in extended text (Miles and Huberman 1994). Review by peers was achieved through presentation of emerging findings in a number of fora, including presentations to social science researchers, health economists and study participants. Ethics approvals were obtained from the relevant NHS committees, which was the appropriate course of action at the time that the research was conducted (Coast 2001a).

CONCLUSION

This chapter has focused on the design of qualitative research for health economics from a number of perspectives: the theoretical basis for the qualitative research, the economic purpose of the research and the rigour of the research. Two examples have provided information on how these different issues influence the design of two published pieces of research. Chapters later in this book will also consider design issues to a greater or lesser extent. Of particular interest might be the chapter from De Allegri, which specifically focuses on design issues and how the design of her research shifted in response to earlier findings from quantitative data (Chapter 17), and that from Smith, which explicitly considers the possibility of different design choices (Chapter 20).

What may already be clear to readers is that research using qualitative methods has a number of different aspects and that it may not be possible to adhere fully to one type of qualitative research method while also generating information that is useful within the study of health economics. This is clearly a challenge! But health economists should also see it is as liberating in many ways. As Atkinson states, 'The goals of research will not be served by a slavish adherence to the historical accidents and arbitrary boundaries that separate methodological traditions and particular research methods. . . . Qualitative research methods, in all their variety, often in conjunction with quantitative measurement and formal models, serve the development of concepts and theories' (Atkinson 1995, p. 123).

Indeed, as is already starting to become clear, the application of qualitative methods in health economics may require economists to go beyond the theoretical options that exist and start to apply approaches that fit more clearly with economics and with 'what economists do'. Two aspects of such an approach that are already becoming apparent from this chapter are the focus on models, as outputs from qualitative research within (health) economics, and the application of a particular analytic lens that seems to be focused on issues around values, preferences, utility and capability, on the one hand, and society, agency relationships, structures and systems on the other. As Creswell indicates:

> Researchers increasingly use a theoretical lens or perspective in qualitative research, which provides an overall orienting lens for the study of gender, class, and race (or other issues of marginalized groups). This lens becomes a transformative perspective that shapes the types of questions asked, informs how data are analyzed, and provides a call to action or change . . . these theoretical lenses . . . guide the researchers as to what issues are important to examine . . . and the people who need to be studied. (Creswell 2012, pp. 64–65)

In short, perhaps, what health economists need to apply in their qualitative analysis is an 'economic lens'. This issue of an economic approach to analysis will be returned to in Chapter 5; before that though, questions of sampling and data collection arise.

Chapter 3

Understanding sampling and recruitment

Amanda Owen-Smith and Joanna Coast

Most health economists understand sampling in terms of sampling within either intervention studies or surveys where the aim is to obtain representative samples of the general population from which generalizations can be made. Sampling within qualitative research uses very different methods, with the aim of sampling being to generate new theoretical approaches or greater understanding of a phenomenon. Sampling therefore tends to be purposeful, with the 'purpose' of the sampling being related to the research question under consideration. The different nature of sampling in qualitative research is an area that economists typically find difficult to comprehend, with sample sizes 'usually viewed as too small to be informative by economists' (Starr 2014, p. 243) and a tendency to dismiss findings as anecdote (Coast, McDonald, et al. 2004). It is for this reason that an entire chapter of this book is devoted to issues around sampling and recruitment.

Understanding sampling is a critical issue in nearly all forms of research. It is rarely, if ever, possible to include an entire research field in a single study, so understanding the population of interest and how it can be represented within the constraints of the research study, and the resource available to that study, is key. Chapters 1 and 2 have already emphasized that there are fundamental differences between qualitative and quantitative approaches to research, and these are partially reflected in differential approaches to sampling. Qualitative sampling strategies are not generally concerned with issues of statistical representation. Instead, they focus on issues in depth using purposeful strategies to identify information-rich cases (Patton 2015), often achieving theoretical representation through the identification of key characteristics in the population of interest and selecting informants through carefully constructed sampling frames. Sample size per se is not regarded with the same importance as in quantitative economic research (Starr 2014), and instead the focus is on data adequacy and a comprehensive understanding of the phenomena of interest. This does not mean the sampling strategy is of any less importance in qualitative research, however, and indeed it has been argued that where samples are small, their selection is of even greater importance (Ritchie and Lewis 2003).

In this chapter, issues of sampling and recruitment are discussed as an integral part of qualitative research planning. The need to consider sampling techniques alongside cycles of data collection and analysis is emphasized, and the strength of an iterative approach to research design is discussed. The chapter begins with a description of the most commonly used purposeful sampling strategies in qualitative research (particularly among health economists), including maximum variation sampling, theoretical sampling and snowballing strategies. It then goes on to discuss specific sampling techniques common across most of these strategies, including the construction of sample frames, the establishment of sampling criteria, the documentation of inclusion and exclusion criteria and identifying and contacting specific individuals. The chapter then considers sample adequacy, addressing issues such as theoretical saturation and the thorny issue of generalizability, and comments on a number of problems and pitfalls researchers may come across when sampling in qualitative research. References to real-life research studies, including those in the area of health economics, are made throughout, and qualitative sampling is acknowledged to be a complex, iterative process where perseverance is often necessary and research objectives and practical issues are sometimes at odds.

THE AIM OF SAMPLING IN QUALITATIVE RESEARCH

Qualitative research is generally undertaken within an interpretative epistemology (either with a relativist or realist ontology [Maxwell 2012]) where the aim is not to gather quasi-objective social 'facts' or draw broad generalizations about social behaviour but to understand the social world from the perspective of those involved. Appropriate sampling techniques need to fit within this overall paradigm, and therefore, probability sampling (where all participants in the population stand an equal chance of being selected) is rarely used. The point of probability sampling is to make statistical generalizations across a defined population and is therefore out of kilter with the usual aims of qualitative inquiry, which are to investigate social processes or make theoretical insights about a phenomenon of interest; in economic terms these notions may translate as investigating economic phenomena or developing theoretical models relating to the health economy and the actors within that economy.

Without the potential for generalization, statistically representative sampling loses its point, and instead a purposeful strategy is usually adopted to ensure all groups or characteristics of interest are included. Importantly, this does not mean it is impossible to generalize from qualitative research but instead that the concept of generalization needs to be reconsidered in terms of applicability to the broader social context (see later). In addition, the time-consuming nature of qualitative research means that the researcher is unlikely to be able to investigate a sample that is large enough for generalizations to be made to the population as a whole.

SAMPLING STRATEGIES

There are a number of qualitative sampling techniques, but, as with all aspects of qualitative research, flexibility and iteration are key, and it is not unusual for a single study to include two or more of the approaches outlined. For example, in the study described in Table 3.1, which was an investigation of patients' and professionals' attitudes to health care rationing, at least five sampling techniques can be delineated from the reporting of the overall strategy adopted (Owen-Smith 2008).

Table 3.1. Extract from AOS doctoral thesis: qualitative sampling in practice (Owen-Smith 2008)

Thesis text	*Sampling strategies identified*
The researcher decided to undertake a preliminary small-scale study at the meso level of decision making, to gain an understanding of the local context for rationing decisions and to ensure that the selection of case studies reflected the concerns of local health care professionals. Approval from an NHS Local Research Ethics Committee was obtained to interview managers and clinicians working at primary care trusts (PCTs) in a large city in England, which houses three large secondary care institutions and (at the time) four PCTs, providing care for a diverse population of about a million people. The city was chosen for pragmatic reasons and because the researcher already had a managerial contact within a local PCT who was willing to act as an initial informant and to recommend other professionals for interview. Sampling of individuals proceeded on a snowballing basis and was continued until the researcher had adequate information to understand local rationing processes and had gathered enough specialty-specific information to choose the first of the clinical case studies, which was to be morbid obesity care.	Key informants and snowballing

(Continued)

Table 3.1. (Continued)

Thesis text	*Sampling strategies identified*
The first case study was undertaken in the same city where the preliminary study had been carried out, as the researcher had already built up links with the local clinical team through pilot informants. Professional informants were initially identified via informants at the PCT level and were then recruited purposefully to ensure that all staff groups within the small team providing care were represented in the research. Access to patients who had received weight reduction surgery in the public or private sector was negotiated via members of the obesity surgery team, and other appropriate patients who had been unable to access surgery were recruited through a specialist dietician.	Purposeful (quota) sampling Snowballing
The complexity of the data arising from the first case study meant that the researcher had the capacity to carry out only one further clinical case study, if both the breadth of the research within each case study and the depth of data collection and analysis were to be maintained. It was decided that the best way to enhance the explanatory power of the research would be to choose a different clinical area so that the data analysis remained focused on the phenomenon of rationing per se rather than on the phenomenon of the rationing of obesity treatments. It was decided to carry out the second case study in the same geographical area as the first case study so that existing contacts at PCT level could be utilized, and there was a common context within which to interpret findings. The second case study selected was breast cancer treatment, which had been highlighted as an area of controversy in the preliminary study at the community level, and was predicted to yield findings that would constitute a useful contrast with findings from the initial case study.	Maximum variation sampling
The sampling for the second case study proceeded in a similar way to the first, with two early professional informants being nominated by PCT-level contacts and other clinical professionals being sampled purposefully to represent a range of staff groups. One of the specialist nurses involved in breast cancer care facilitated access to patients, whom she contacted on behalf of the researcher. Separate ethical approval for each case study was obtained from an NHS multi-centre research ethics committee prior to any recruitment being carried out.	Snowballing Purposeful (quota) sampling

It should be noted that just because sample sizes are small in qualitative research, this does not mean that the selection of cases is not important. Straightforward convenience sampling involves simply approaching those eligible participants nearest at hand and asking them to participate in research. Convenience sampling differs from purposeful sampling, in that there is no deliberate attempt to select people based on particular characteristics, and is used when the researcher is unable to follow a purposeful strategy for ethical or practical reasons. It is rarely used in health services research, however, due to the obvious pitfalls of skewed recruitment and incomplete population coverage, and Patton describes it as lazy, lacking in strategy and having low credibility because it produces cases that are not information-rich (Patton 2015).

Purposeful sampling is based on deliberately selecting individuals from the population based on their characteristics of interest so that they can contribute meaningfully to understanding the research issue (Bowling 1997; Creswell 2013), and the logic of such sampling is to obtain information-rich cases (Patton 2015). Purposeful sampling is also known as purposive and the terms are largely interchangeable, although Patton justifies the use of the term 'purposeful' because of its ease of understanding and associations of the origins of the terminology of 'purposive' sampling with statistical methods for capturing diversity in populations (Patton 2015). 'Purposeful' is used throughout this chapter and the first part of the book; in the case studies, terminology is used according to individual authors' preferences. Purposeful sampling can be conducted in many different ways (Patton identifies around forty [Patton 2015]); the approaches included here are those commonly used within health economics research and include maximum variation (or contrasting case) sampling, theoretical sampling, straightforward quota sampling, key informant and snowball sampling and purposeful random sampling. In all of these techniques, however, the researcher needs some prior knowledge of the research field before entry so that he or she is able to identify what the characteristics of interest (and therefore the basis for sampling) might be. This does not need to be terribly sophisticated and is normally achievable through a brief review of the literature and discussion with informed colleagues. Where an iterative approach is taken, as in most qualitative studies, these characteristics will be frequently revised as emerging insights are made through ongoing data collection and analysis. Where it is not possible to identify the sampling frame in advance, chain methods such as snowball sampling may be appropriate.

Maximum variation (or contrasting case) sampling

This form of sampling aims to select as wide a diversity of cases as possible based on the dimensions of interest identified during research planning (Patton 2015). In health economics research, it is particularly applicable to the selection of sites, or clinical treatment areas, where the researcher aims to uncover contrasting experiences so that inferences can be drawn through comparison. In the health care rationing study reported in Table 3.1, for example, the two clinical treatment areas selected were morbid obesity and breast cancer, with the aim of picking cases that seemed as different as possible to one another in terms of generosity of NHS funding and general public attitude. In other situations, such as when investigating the successfulness of a health care intervention, maximum variation sampling might be used to select geographical areas where the intervention appears to have been implemented more or less successfully, or in areas of high and low social deprivation.

Maximum variation sampling has also been used as a sampling strategy for obtaining interviewees where the aim is to generate attributes for a discrete choice experiment because such a strategy enables the researcher to capture different experiences that might inform the attribute development as it enables coverage of the range of views that might need to be included in the experiment (Coast and Horrocks 2007; Coast, Al-Janabi, et al. 2012; Abiiro, Leppert, et al. 2014). Depending on its objective, maximum variation sampling could thus be used either as a stand-alone purposeful technique or as part of a detailed theoretical approach to sampling described earlier.

There are other approaches to achieving contrasting cases that focus on explicitly sampling for outliers, deviant cases or sampling using matched pairs with different characteristics (Patton 2015). Such strategies may also to be used to sample within a broader analysis to study specific issues, as in the analysis by Canaway and colleagues (see Chapter 12).

Theoretical sampling

A theoretical approach to purposeful sampling was initially expounded by Glaser and Strauss in their influential volume *The Discovery of Grounded Theory* (Glaser and Strauss 1968). Glaser and Strauss argued strongly that an iterative approach should be taken to sampling and data analysis whereby individuals (or incidents) are sampled on the basis of characteristics relevant to the theoretical hypotheses under construction (Glaser and Strauss 1968). In practice, many studies start out with a more general purposeful approach, and sampling becomes increasingly theoretical as research progresses and confirmatory and negative cases are compared to emerging hypotheses (Strauss and Corbin 1990) and data are obtained that help conceptual development (Charmaz 2014). In the study reported in Table 3.1, for example, the researcher ended up sampling from a particular (small) group of patients who had contested health authority decision making around the availability of certain cancer drugs. This was undertaken with the express aim of developing a theoretical model of patients' reactions to explicit health care rationing (Owen-Smith, Coast, et al. 2009). In theoretical sampling, case selection can only be considered complete once 'theoretical saturation' is reached when no new themes or insights are arising from the research and the relationships between those already identified are well established (Charmaz 2014) (see 'sample adequacy').

Theoretical sampling may also be relevant to other qualitative approaches. In phenomenological approaches, for example, where the focus is on lived experience, the cases sampled will be theoretically sampled based on the phenomenon of interest (Patton 2015). In realist approaches, theory may also be the basis of sampling, with the aim being to test and refine theory based on hypotheses about causal mechanisms, selecting participants who are relevant in terms of the developing theory (Maxwell 2012; Patton 2015).

Quota or stratified sampling

Quota sampling relies on the researcher setting up a sampling frame reflecting the characteristics of interest in the population and sampling until that cell's 'quota' is fulfilled. Similarly, stratified purposeful sampling aims to account for potential variation in the data without necessarily going as far as sampling for maximum variation. An example of the use of stratified purposeful sampling in health economics is the work by De Allegri and colleagues, which sampled informants for a study exploring demand for health insurance on the basis of health insurance, distance to the medical facility and socio-economic status (De Allegri, Sanon, et al. 2006b). These approaches are perhaps less iterative than other forms of purposeful sampling, but they have the advantages of being relatively easy to design and straightforward to execute and report (Wilmot 2005; Patton 2015). In addition, these techniques can provide a useful starting point for sampling early on in a study to ensure all population groups are accessed, before being combined with other sampling strategies (see, e.g., the sampling of professional groups in the study reported in Table 3.1).

Key informant and snowball sampling

Sampling from key informants can be particularly helpful when studying particular institutions or organizations, or in trying to understand a particular pathway or process. In many ways, the collection of information from key clinical collaborators for use in decision modelling in health economics is akin to, albeit a limited use of, a key informant sampling approach in qualitative research. Key informant sampling has been used in a number of areas of health economics research, including in generating attributes for discrete choice experiments (Abiiro, Leppert, et al. 2014), in understanding decision modelling processes (Chilcott, Tappenden, et al. 2010) and in identifying relevant outcomes for economic evaluation (van Mastrigt, Paulus, et al. 2015).

Key informant sampling can be conducted alone or in combination with snowball sampling starting from initial sampling of key informants (Patton 2015). A 'snowballing' technique exists when initial key informant(s) is/are identified to recommend further participants for research, who in turn recommend other participants until the sample size is large enough for the purposes of the research (Patton 2015). Although there are obvious disadvantages to this method, such as over-representing and under-representing certain segments of the population, it is sometimes the only method available, particularly in hard-to-reach groups (see 'problems and pitfalls in the sampling process'). An additional benefit to this approach is the 'sponsorship' researchers engender through their introduction to potential informants by trusted peers. This could be seen clearly in Whyte's seminal sociological study of delinquent subcultures in Chicago, where he gained a level of social acceptance through his association with 'Doc', a trusted member of the subculture and also a key informant in the research (Whyte 1955). However, any key informant, however helpful, will have access only to certain social networks, and securing more than one entry into the field of enquiry might circumvent some of the obvious issues with population coverage. Sampling from within different networks provides a variation on this approach (Patton 2015). Snowball sampling has been used by health economists in understanding pharmaceutical markets in Mozambique (Russo and McPake 2010).

Purposeful random sampling

Purposeful random sampling can avoid accusations of potential selection bias, and even though a sample may be insufficiently small to generalize from, it is, for economists, a potentially useful method of obtaining citizen input in an unbiased manner. Such purposeful random sampling was, for example, used in conjunction with maximum variation sampling (to identify diverse locations in which to conduct the random sampling) for the generation of attributes for the ICECAP-A capability measure (Al-Janabi, Flynn, et al. 2012). An example of the use of purposeful random sampling is given in the chapter by Kinghorn et al. (Chapter 16).

SAMPLING TECHNIQUES

Once the sampling strategy is agreed, the next step is to decide how individual participants for the research should be identified. In many circumstances (e.g., the study reported in Table 3.1), the researcher may find himself or herself immersed in *multi-level sampling* whereby he or she first needs to sample a geographical area or an institutional setting to make the research workable. Although the steps mentioned should be followed at all levels of sampling wherever possible, in practice, higher-order sampling such as the selection of sites is often impacted by practical issues such as geographical proximity and resource availability (Maxwell 2012).

Constructing the sampling frame

Constructing the sampling frame is an important first step and is a way to map the units of the population of interest and explicitly consider the heterogeneity therein (Wilmot 2005). Depending on the needs of the research, this step may not be particularly complex or onerous, and in many cases a pre-existing sampling frame (e.g., a hospital database) may be available. However, it is important to review this information to ensure that the population is complete, that all the necessary sampling units are included (e.g., sex, age, clinical diagnosis) and that included information is up to date (Wilmot 2005). In practice, there will be some compromises here, and the sampling criteria (see later) will to some extent depend on the information available in the sampling frame. The frame should be reviewed for missing groups that might display different attitudes/behaviours in relation to the phenomena under study, and in some cases a second sampling frame may need to be constructed. For example, a study using a hospital database as its primary sampling frame necessarily excludes those patients who have not yet secured a referral to secondary care, and a further sampling frame made up of patients treated in primary care may need to be constructed.

In some research studies, it can be very difficult to initially identify a usable sampling frame, and in these cases a snowballing approach could be used, or even advertising for participants (see 'sampling hard-to-reach groups'). However, these methods of sampling tend to be onerous and may unwittingly exclude some groups within the population who may add valuable information to the research (e.g., illiterate or non-English-speaking populations when recruiting via advertisement). Alternatively, for some studies the sampling frame could effectively be constructed as part of the research process. This is most likely in mixed-methods studies, such as qualitative research nested within a clinical trial, an approach used by Vosper and colleagues (see Chapter 10), although is also possible in wholly qualitative studies, where initial focus groups could be used as a sampling frame for later in-depth interviews as in Coast's work on priority setting where interviewees were selected purposefully from focus groups that had been generated using a mix of methods, including purposeful random sampling, to achieve different types of public representation (Coast 2001a).

Establishing sampling criteria

Having mapped the units within the population as far as possible within the sampling frame, the next step is to decide what the sampling criteria should be, that is, which of the variables identified should form part of the selection process. Depending on the size of the population, the information available in the sampling frame and the resources available for the research, some compromises may need to be made here. For example, although it is normally preferable to include age and gender in sampling criteria, it may not be possible to sample across all diagnostic groups or to include diversity by ethnic group in all age and sex categories. Staying focused on the research question is of paramount importance, and the criteria that are most likely to provide a well-rounded view of the phenomenon of interest should be prioritized. As data collection proceeds, maintaining an open mind and flexible approach to sampling criteria is likely to lead to a more theoretically focused approach.

Documenting inclusion and exclusion criteria

Many studies need to rely on gatekeepers to help identify individuals for participation (Hammersley and Atkinson 1983), particularly where this involves the recruitment of service users, and this may involve some negotiation with these gatekeepers (Patton 2015). It is therefore useful to have some written documentation of the inclusion and exclusion criteria for the research to help keep the sampling strategy on track. This both helps the researcher to maintain control over the research process and is useful to gatekeepers, many of whom, at least in a health care context, are used to dealing with recruitment to clinical trials, where the eligibility (or not) of a patient is usually specified in detail. However, as always in qualitative research, flexibility and iteration are key, and these criteria should be subject to revision depending on emerging findings and the demands of theoretical development.

Identifying and contacting potential participants

Once the sampling frame is complete and sampling criteria are agreed, it is normally fairly straightforward to start to identify individuals eligible for participation. The next step is to send out invitations to participate. Flexibility may be necessary here, and the approach needs to be tailored to the particular participant group. In professional groups, for example, an unsolicited telephone contact is unlikely to be welcome and sending an email invitation may be a more successful (and cheaper) form of initial contact. The subject line should state the intention of the email, but the temptation to 'sell' the research too hard at this point should be resisted – 'invitation to participate in research' is far more likely to prompt opening (and avoid spam filters) than 'unmissable opportunity for research involvement'. The body of the email should give a brief summary of the research and the nature of the participant's potential involvement (e.g., 'an in-depth interview taking an hour of your time'), and a formal invitation letter and information sheet about the research should be attached (see later). It is generally advisable to follow up email invitations by post if no response is received, as this can be a helpful way to reach people who engage better with different modes of communication. In addition, when dealing with senior managers or medical consultants it is worth remembering that a good deal of both mail and email is initially filtered by administrative staff, so if no response is received it may be worth a brief phone call to the administrative team to check if the invitation has been received and passed on. The time frame for response prior to follow-up (if appropriate) should be detailed in the covering letter and will vary according to the needs of the research, but a reasonable rule of thumb is approximately two to three weeks.

When contacting service users, the process is more complicated as there is unlikely to be a publicly accessible sampling frame, and access is usually regulated via data protection legislation and formal ethics agreements. It is important to be aware of the relevant local and national regulations. In the United Kingdom, for example, access to health service user information is regulated by the Data Protection Act (1993) and the National Health Service (NHS) Health Research Authority, who normally require initial recruitment packs to be sent out by a member of NHS staff. This means that most researchers have no access to patient identifiable information (e.g., names and dates of birth) at the time of recruitment, meaning that either an anonymized sampling frame needs to be constructed, or the responsibility for identifying eligible patients needs to be passed to an appropriate gatekeeper. Whatever the particular regulatory requirements, it is important that the researcher maintains sufficient control over the recruitment process; information packs should be made up by the research team and assigned individual control numbers so that a record of distribution according to the sampling criteria can be maintained. This not only makes uncontrolled issuing of recruitment packs (through informal photocopying) less likely but also means that important information about non-responders can be collected and analysed, which might be helpful when analysing low recruitment rates (see later) and has been identified as a key criterion in the robust reporting of qualitative research (Tong, Sainsbury, et al. 2007).

All recruitment packs should contain a clear information sheet detailing the purposes of the research and what involvement will entail along with a covering letter, response slip and prepaid envelope. However, return of the response slip is rarely considered to constitute formal consent to participate in the research, which should generally be undertaken on a face-to-face basis with a trained researcher. In practice, taking consent often happens at the start of in-depth interviews or scheduled observations, so it is useful to ensure the initial information sheet dispatched with the recruitment pack is comprehensive enough to provide a basis for informed consent. Failure to do this may mean a delay to the research process as many ethics agreements require the potential participant to have had a specified minimum time to consider the information prior to signing. Up-to-date guidance on the appropriate composition of information sheets suitable for informed consent should be obtained from within the relevant regulatory setting as this can vary both over time and across jurisdictions. In the case of service users, it may be helpful to include a covering letter from their consulting professional, but caution needs to be taken to avoid causing anxiety to potential participants who may experience this as coercion to participate.

SAMPLE ADEQUACY

In qualitative research, sample adequacy relates to the amount and quality of data collected rather than the number of interviews/observations undertaken (Morse 1994). Adequacy is therefore intimately tied to the objectives of the research and the type of data collection undertaken. As Patton states, 'There are no rules for sample size in qualitative inquiry. Sample size depends on what you want to know, the purpose of the inquiry, what's at stake, what will be useful, what will have credibility, and what can be done with the available time and resources' (Patton 2015, p. 311). Sample size may also depend on the depth of data generated from each informant. For example, a study that aims for rich description of a particular health condition or lived experience to identify attributes for a simple discrete choice experiment around a particular intervention (Coast, Salisbury, et al. 2006; Coast and Horrocks 2007) is likely to require less data than a theoretical study seeking to make explanatory inferences about particular economic issues (Coast 2001a; De Allegri, Sanon, et al. 2006b; Owen-Smith, Donovan, et al. 2015) or complex outcome measurement topics (Grewal, Lewis, et al. 2006; Al-Janabi, Flynn, et al. 2012). Similarly, a study using rich ethnographic techniques encompassing observations and a series of interviews with each informant is likely to require a smaller sample size than a simple cross-sectional interview study, even if the study aims are similar. Sample sizes are rarely specified in advance in qualitative research, and the judgement over whether a data set is complete should be made jointly by the research team with reference to the study's original aims and objectives.

Practical issues (e.g., resource availability and recruitment rates) are also likely to be important factors in final sample size. In particular, attention should be paid to the time available for analysis. Each in-depth interview is likely to yield thirty to forty pages of written text, all of which is usually subjected to line-by-line coding prior to any higher-order analyses being undertaken (see Chapter 5). Bearing in mind that it is unethical to collect data for which there is not sufficient time to analyse, it is not surprising that many qualitative studies are based on what would be considered to be relatively small sample sizes from a traditional, positivist perspective. While data adequacy depends on fulfilling the study aims and answering the research question, as a general rule even large qualitative studies rarely exceed fifty to sixty informants (Britten 2000; Ritchie, Lewis, et al. 2003).

Theoretical saturation

One concept that is frequently invoked (not always faithfully) in the reporting of qualitative studies is that of theoretical saturation. This concept was originally conceived by Glaser and Strauss in the *Discovery of Grounded Theory* and in common with the theoretical approach to sampling described earlier relies on an iterative approach to sampling, data collection and analysis (Glaser and Strauss 1968; Charmaz 2014). For Glaser and Strauss, sampling should be continued until there are no new theoretical insights arising relating to the concepts and categories identified in the data, and relationships between categories are well established. The judgement as to when saturation is reached is necessarily subjective, but it is essentially the point at which no additional data are being found that can add to the theoretical analysis – in practice this is often the point where the erstwhile enthusiastic researcher starts to get 'bored' with data collection and is approaching new interviews and observations with noticeably less enthusiasm. Saturation may be achieved in relation to the overall theory or focus of the work but is unlikely to be achieved across all data, so it is valuable to detail the areas in which saturation has been achieved. Saturation for studies that involve generation of attributes for outcome measures or discrete choice experiments can be seen in terms of fully generating conceptual attributes and appropriate and meaningful wording for those attributes (Canaway, Al-Janabi, et al. 2017).

Generalizability

Generalizability is a thorny issue in qualitative research, and its understanding requires transcendence of traditional quantitative notions around statistical representation. Although there are those who argue that generalizability is not the point of qualitative research, in applied fields such as health economics, research is rarely undertaken without the desire to make broader statements about the applicability of research findings. In qualitative research this applicability can be achieved by careful documentation of contextual factors and making generalizations to theoretically similar situations (Glaser and Strauss 1968; Ritchie, Lewis, et al. 2003); considering the typicality of cases in relation to the general population is also important (Hammersley and Atkinson 1983; Popay, Rogers, et al. 1998). Indeed, since most quantitative research aims only to generalize findings to a particular population, it has been argued that the findings of qualitative research studies may have wider applications than those claiming statistical representations (and usually larger sample sizes) (Hammersley 1992). Clearly the key here is in the documentation and reasonable interpretation of relevant contextual factors. For example, the findings of a recent analysis of rationing techniques applied to the allocation of obesity surgery on the NHS could reasonably be applied to other elective surgical treatments (hip replacement, cataract repair, etc.), but more caution would need to be applied when it came to the rationing of very urgent or immediately life-saving treatments (Owen-Smith, Donovan, et al. 2015).

PROBLEMS AND PITFALLS IN THE SAMPLING PROCESS

As with all types of research, there are a number of problems that may be encountered when using qualitative sampling techniques. Probably the most common problem relates to inadequate samples, but problems may also be encountered through overly large or diverse populations, recruiting hard-to-reach groups, and over-zealous gatekeeping.

Inadequate samples

The biggest fear of many researchers, whether quantitative or qualitative, is that they will end up with an inadequate sample, meaning that research objectives cannot be met and inadequate generalizations can be made. In qualitative research where the concern is more with data adequacy than sample size per se, inadequate sampling often refers to a skewed sample whereby some aspects of the phenomena are unlikely to have been considered and thus the data set is incomplete. Studies involving complex theoretical development may have more problems in establishing adequacy than simpler descriptive studies. The most important tactic to avoid inadequate sampling is to undertake an iterative process of data collection and analysis and carefully document the success of various recruitment strategies, updating sampling criteria and changing tack when needed. Other tactics include adding incentive payments for informants (although the effect of this should be monitored to avoid further skewed sampling) or widening the geographic base for recruitment. In a study of near-fatal suicide attempts, for example, the number of sites had to be increased significantly to obtain the sample of twenty-two patients over a three-year period (Biddle, Donovan, et al. 2010; Biddle, Gunnell, et al. 2012).

Large and diverse populations

A further problem arises where the researcher is seeking to sample from a very large and diverse population. In health economics, for example, citizens may be a group of interest, but citizens inevitably comprise an amorphous group with only one unifying characteristic, which is that they are free members of a country. Health economics studies have used different approaches to tackle this issue. One approach is to use purposeful random sampling as a means of recruitment. Such purposeful random sampling ensures that the initial selection of participants is not biased. However, certain groups may be more likely to respond to such invitations; citizen participation has been noted to be an elite activity in which groups with poorer education, and who are less confident or articulate, may not be included (Klein 1984). It may therefore be advantageous to combine purposeful random sampling with other techniques. An example where such an approach has been used is in the qualitative research used to develop the ICECAP-A capability measure. Here, purposeful random sampling was used initially, but higher numbers of older people responded to the initial invitation and those in less socio-economically deprived areas were also more likely to respond. Two approaches were used to ameliorate this issue. First, higher numbers were invited in the more socio-economically deprived areas. Second, maximum variation sampling was used within the sample to ensure a spread of age (and other characteristics) (Al-Janabi, Flynn, et al. 2012).

Considering the typicality of informants is also important. It should be noted that citizen informants responding to research requests are often small in number and thus can be considered to be atypical in at least one respect: that of applying in the affirmative to the invitation to participate in the research. In Coast's research on priority setting, this choice to participate was discussed with some informants both in interviews and in focus groups. A number of the citizen informants were interested in health care for some particular reason, such as previous or current work within the health service, recent experience as a patient or as the relative of a patient or some familial health service connection. More generally, informants suggested that it was their view that it was a duty of all people to get involved because the health service is for everybody. The group of citizens included in this research may therefore have been more community-minded than others who chose not to participate, and this may have affected their views about willingness to participate in health care decision making, which was an important area of the research (Coast 2000b). It is thus important to interpret findings in the light of such sampling issues.

Over-zealous gatekeeping

A common problem for the researcher seeking to undertake service user research is encountering over-zealous clinical gatekeeping, a problem that may be particularly acute in areas that are perceived to be sensitive such as at the end of life (Campbell, Bailey, et al. 2016). In the study with survivors of near-fatal suicide attempts referred to earlier, for example, informal restrictions on access imposed by psychiatrists or community general practitioners all but paralysed the research, despite sufficient data being amassed by the research team to show that interviews were rarely upsetting for participants (Biddle, Cooper, et al. 2013). Even in less sensitive research, such as that reported in Table 3.1, it was necessary to diversify the sampling technique when it was noted that relying on clinical gatekeepers was resulting in a skewed sample of 'satisfied patients'.

To overcome some of these issues, it is always worth making the time to ensure that gatekeepers are fully familiar with the aims of the research before the research begins and, if there are any concerns, making sure that researchers are physically available during initial rounds of recruitment so that they can observe the process and are on-hand to answer questions as they arise. Involvement of key gatekeepers in the research team can also be beneficial (Bailey, Kinghorn, et al. 2016; Campbell, Bailey, et al. 2016). In one (as yet unpublished) study undertaken by the authors relating to treatment decision making in renal disease, sitting in on a recruitment session revealed that nurses had added a number of informal criteria to documented sampling guidelines, including physical health states, 'known' preferences around travel and research participation and unsubstantiated judgements on cognitive capability. In this situation, the gatekeeping had become so entrenched that the researcher needed to seek written support from the research sponsor and relevant clinical leads to regain control over the recruitment process.

Sampling 'hard-to-reach' groups

Depending on the research question of interest, some fields of enquiry involve the sampling of participant groups that are more difficult to access than others. In these situations a diversification of techniques is likely to be valuable, and the sampling frame is normally constructed as the research progresses. Some researchers have famously relied on the use of 'key informants' who help them to gain entry to particular areas of the research field which might otherwise have been inaccessible (Whyte 1955). Another tactic would be the use of advertisements in recruiting to studies, such as in newspapers or clinic rooms. This approach was used by Canaway and colleagues to sample bereaved friends and relatives with diverse experiences for a study generating attributes for a close person measure for use in the economic evaluation of interventions at the end of life (Canaway, Al-Janabi, et al. 2017).

CONCLUSION

Sampling is a core part of the overall research process, intimately tied up with the plans for data collection and analysis that are considered in the next two chapters. Indeed, there is nothing so fundamental to good research design, in whatever line of inquiry, as the selection and execution of a good sampling strategy. The very point of social science research is to open a window onto a broader social world and make insights and inferences about social behaviours, and it is only through appropriate sampling techniques that such insights are possible. When working within a qualitative paradigm, it is useful to conceptualize sample adequacy in terms of data adequacy rather than simply a number of participants, as it is the richness of the insights that are drawn from the data that will eventually determine whether the analysis is a success, and not achieving some predefined sample size, which only makes sense in very particular forms of research which are based on quantitative objectives and (usually) random sampling techniques.

As noted earlier, sampling strategies do not always work out as planned, and one of the joys of a qualitative approach is the flexibility it provides for the researcher to review and amend strategies while the research is ongoing. Indeed, it is not unusual to see four or five different sampling strategies employed within a complex piece of qualitative research, and provided these are all theoretically justified and comprehensively reported, this is no contradiction to methodological rigour. Sampling choices are also, of course, closely tied to the type of data collection being employed within the research, and it is this topic that the next chapter explores.

Chapter 4

Understanding data collection: Interviews, focus groups and observation

Amanda Owen-Smith and Joanna Coast

The principal methods for qualitative data collection include individual interviews, focus groups and observations, although combining techniques is common and often necessary to gain a well-rounded view of phenomena (Mays and Pope 2000). Document review can also be used as a qualitative research method, but is rarely used on its own, and qualitative data collection generally implies some form of face-to-face contact (Snape and Spencer 2003). Both individual interviews and focus groups can be considered 'generative' techniques whereby individuals are encouraged to reconstruct their experiences and explain their attitudes and beliefs (Ritchie 2004). By contrast, observational techniques involve watching participants in their natural environment and making interpretations and inferences about behaviours in the context of other knowledge.

This chapter provides detailed explanations of all three main forms of qualitative data collection: interviews, focus groups and observation. For each method, a number of issues are explored. These include the overall nature of the method, practical issues around getting started and conducting the fieldwork and the main strengths and limitations associated with each approach. Interviews are considered first, and more space is devoted to this topic, in part because this is the method most likely to be used and in part because many of the issues covered in that section, such as the development of rapport, are also applicable to the methods discussed later. Issues of data recording and transcription are then discussed, and the ethical issues that are commonly encountered when collecting qualitative data are reviewed. Throughout, the issues associated with data collection are considered in relation to their potential uses in answering questions of relevance to health economists. The chapter ends with some concluding comments.

INDIVIDUAL INTERVIEWING

Individual interviews are probably the most common and flexible approach to qualitative data collection. Interviewing is particularly useful for understanding factors underlying particular beliefs or attitudes, motivations behind behaviours and decision-making and the context for particular events and occurrences (Ritchie 2004). It allows the social (or economic) world to be examined from the viewpoint of the participants in that world (Miller and Glassner 2011). Individual interviews are thus commonly used to answer 'why' questions and access reconstructions of past events, which are inaccessible through observation methods. In contrast to quantitative survey techniques, a flexible and exploratory approach is taken, and there is an emphasis on allowing participants to explain their views and experiences in their own words.

There are three main types of research interviews – structured, semi-structured and in-depth (Hancock 1998; Britten 2000; Bryman 2004). Generally, only the latter two are considered qualitative in approach, and structured interviews are normally restricted to the face-to-face delivery of a formal questionnaire, where questions are asked in the same order using the same wording, normally with the aim of addressing an a priori hypothesis (DiCicco-Bloom and Crabtree 2006). By contrast, a qualitative interview allows the informant to dictate the pace and ordering of disclosure, with the researcher adopting a highly skilled position at the 'rudder', gently steering the interview's direction and carefully bringing the conversation back on course where necessary. Moreover, in the qualitative interview, it is the informant who is considered the expert, having access to privileged information about their own beliefs and life experiences, and the researcher who must listen actively and respectfully, probing where necessary to prompt further disclosure and explanation.

Drawing a distinction between semi-structured and in-depth interviewing is a matter of judgement based principally on the amount of detail included in the topic guide and the overall approach taken by the interviewer. In-depth interviews will generally be more informant-led than a semi-structured approach and may be focused on exploring just one or two topics with an emphasis on building rapport and encouraging deeper levels of disclosure (Bryman 2004). A semi-structured interview has similar aims, but the interviewer is generally slightly more directive, prompting informants more regularly with the aim of answering a more specific research question and drawing comparisons between accounts. In practice, a study may include both approaches, with interviews gaining more structure as the study progresses and the researcher aiming for theoretical development (Glaser and Strauss 1968). A semi-structured approach is the most common approach in health services research and is also likely to be more common in health economics, where many questions are quite focused on specific issues.

Getting started

Preparing the interviewer

Qualitative interviewing is a very particular skill, and it is important that the interviewer has undergone appropriate methodological training and is familiar with the aims and practices of qualitative research. The researcher need not be an expert in the topic under question (indeed some degree of genuine naivety is often helpful in prompting full disclosure) but should have sufficient understanding to meaningfully interpret the information provided and probe for further details. The researcher is the key tool in qualitative interviewing and should approach the task with a friendly, inquisitive nature and a genuine desire to learn more of humankind. Judgement needs to be suspended, and individual political agendas need to be put aside. The researcher needs to be aware that he or she may encounter opposing views, but his or her role is simply to investigate the source of these views and never to change them. The role of active listening should not be underestimated, and the researcher should approach each new interview prepared for intellectual and emotional challenge. Clearly an interest in the topic helps demonstrate genuine engagement with the informant, but high stakes in the welfare of particular informants (such as when a clinician interviews his or her own patients to find out about service attributes for inclusion in a discrete choice experiment) are best avoided if a neutral stance is to be maintained.

Contacting informants

Once an informant has made a positive response to an invitation to participate (see Chapter 3), he or she should be contacted as soon as possible to make arrangements for the interview. This is usually the first opportunity to build rapport and should be undertaken by the interviewer wherever possible rather than being left to an administrative member of staff. Where the informant has provided several means of contact (email address, telephone number, etc.), it can be helpful to overcome any initial shyness and telephone to arrange the interview as a means of starting to build rapport with the informant and generate a sense of commitment to the research by the informant. In some situations this may mean calling outside of usual working hours to get a response. Leaving a message on an answerphone or voicemail is not ideal, but if this is the only option it is helpful to leave contact details and a message regarding calling back at a specific time. For example, one agoraphobic informant interviewed multiple times by one of the authors would respond to contacts only if the researcher called, identified herself and said she would call again in five minutes. The additional effort paid dividends in terms of the research, however, as in interviews the informant was able to offer a detailed and heartfelt account of her experiences of her health condition.

For early interviews, it may be useful to have a prompt card by the telephone with a brief sentence of introduction and checklist of things to arrange (time and place of interview, confirmation of address, instructions for parking, etc.). Alongside the practical benefits of being able to clarify all these details in just one contact, speaking on the telephone enables the informant to ask any questions he or she has about the research process and for both parties to feel more comfortable when they meet face to face. The informant may be feeling anxious about the research process, so it is important to explain the study using non-specialist terms and reassure him or her that he or she does not need any specialist knowledge to participate. The use of the term 'research interview' in particular can provoke anxiety for certain groups of informants who may feel they need to provide 'answers', and therefore it is sometimes worth avoiding this term altogether and discussing arrangements for the 'research visit' instead. The researcher may need to be flexible again here and be prepared to offer interview slots outside of normal working hours if necessary.

It is up to the research team to decide which options will be offered for the location of the interview, and this should be clear on the participant information sheet which will normally be circulated with the invitation to participate (see Chapter 3). Experience from both authors suggests that most professionals will opt to be interviewed at their place of work if offered, but they should always be offered an alternative (e.g., a research base or their home) which may sometimes encourage greater disclosure. Similarly in the experience of the authors, if offered, most patients or citizens will opt to be interviewed at home, particularly if they are currently ill or have caring responsibilities. Offering home interviews is usually more resource intensive in terms of travelling time, and it is necessary to put in place safety protocols for the researcher (see 'harm avoidance'). However, it is generally much quicker and easier to establish rapport in someone's home, and the researcher gleans valuable contextual information from informal observations of the neighbourhood and living accommodation. Some people will, nevertheless, prefer to be interviewed in an institutional setting, and an appropriate alternative such as a university or health care setting should always be offered. Wherever the interview takes place, it is important that it is both private and quiet enough for the recorder (if used) to pick up the audio (King and Horrocks 2010). For these reasons, it is rarely appropriate to undertake the interview in a public space such as a café.

In some situations, particularly if the informant is very ill or the interview will address very sensitive issues such as end-of-life preferences or experiences of mental illness, it may be appropriate to ask informants whether they would like a friend or family member present. Sometimes informants will make this request spontaneously (or the acceptability of their presence may simply be assumed), so it is worth deciding how to respond to this issue in advance. Generally, this request should be accommodated wherever possible, although the interviewer may need to tread carefully to ensure that it is the views and experience of the informant (rather than the relative) that are prioritized; any perceived impact on disclosure will also need to be taken into account in analysis.

Compiling an interview topic guide

Most researchers use a topic guide (sometimes known as an interview schedule) when interviewing to ensure some comparability across interviews, although its content and level of detail depend on the extent of structuring of the interview and the experience and confidence of the researcher. The topic guide can be either a list of questions or simply a number of bullet points prompting the researcher to ensure specific points are covered. However, it is a core characteristic of qualitative interviewing that questions are not asked in the same order (or indeed in the same words) to all informants, and ideally, the interviewer will be able to encourage the informants to talk on their own terms, with the flow between topics seeming natural and conversational (Hammersley and Atkinson 1983). In practical terms, it is useful if the topic guide is restricted to one side of an A4 sheet and is split into broad topic areas, so that there is no difficulty with page turning and it is easy to see at a glance if the interview is proceeding according to plan. In addition, it is useful to have a clipboard and a pen to hand so that the topic guide can be annotated while the informant is speaking if there are particular points the researcher wishes to return to later, which is usually preferable to interruption. The researcher should not be overly directive, and it is a hallmark of qualitative research that the most interesting insights sometimes come from 'diversions' or what does not seem immediately relevant (Bowling 1997).

Whether choosing to use written questions or a bullet point approach, it is a good idea to have at least the first question written out in case nervousness strikes, and it is difficult to get the conversation under way. Initial questions are usually broad and 'easy' for the informant to answer, often aimed at eliciting a particular story, which should be allowed to unfold unprompted as far as possible. A good opening question for professionals is to ask them to tell the interviewer about their role, while studies with patients that are focused on obtaining information about preferences often start by asking patients to describe their condition. The topic guide normally becomes increasingly focused as the interviewer guides the conversation to talking about the key phenomena of interest (Glaser and Strauss 1968; Morse 2002). For example, in a study aimed at eliciting rationing experiences in relation to accessing obesity surgery in the UK National Health System, the opening question was concerned with asking about patients' experiences of weight gain before gradually guiding the conversation towards the discussion of the various interventions available and whether they had attempted to access weight loss surgery. It should be noted that it is not wise to leave the core research questions until late in the topic guide, particularly if interviewing professionals who may be pressed for time and may need to curtail the interview if it overruns its allotted time slot, or frail patients who may become fatigued. Two examples of topic guides, laid out in slightly different ways, are given in Boxes 4.1 and 4.2. Robinson, in Chapter 15, Box 15.2, also provides an outline of her interview schedule for research aiming to understand the time trade-off and person trade-off valuation processes.

BOX 4.1. EXAMPLE TOPIC GUIDE FOR PATIENT INTERVIEW

Introduction
Researcher explains research, asks if any queries on PIS, and takes consent.

History of weight gain and help-seeking
- To start off, I was just wondering if you could tell me a bit about when you first started having problems with your weight? [Prompt on different life stages where necessary]

Probe: experiences of stigma; attitudes towards culpability; eating to cope; social support networks
- What sorts of things have you done over the years to try and contain your weight?

Probe: diets / exercise / drugs

Accessing medical and surgical care
- When did you first seek help from your doctor about losing weight? [Prompt – primary / secondary care]

Probe: attitudes encountered; relationship with GP; importance of family / friends
- Did your doctor suggest you taking any medicines to help you lose weight?

Probe: General attitudes to medication; side effects; helpfulness
- When did you first decide weight loss surgery was a realistic option for you?

Probe: where did they hear about it? Did they approach GP or did GP suggest? Do they know about NICE guidance? PCT rules?
- When were you first referred for surgery?

Probe: Waiting times? Do they know of any problems around funding – exceptional funding panels?

Expectations of outpatient appointment
- How are you feeling about your outpatient appointment next week?

Probe: Are they nervous? Do they view it as an assessment? Do they expect doctors to be understanding?
- What sorts of things do you think the doctor might say to you?

Probe: do they expect rationing to be an issue? Do they think they will have to argue their case?

Wind-down and explanation of continuing research process
Researcher checks topic guide for omissions and prompts informant back towards areas of discussion where they seemed most comfortable (e.g. talking about social support networks or relationship with their GP).
Researcher then explains the next stages of the research process (observation of clinics) and assesses whether the informant is prepared to grant their ongoing consent for participation in the research.
[Offer summary of results and stop recorder]

BOX 4.2. EXAMPLE TOPIC GUIDE FOR CITIZEN INTERVIEW

Core		Personal - rationing and the citizen's utility function	
CHECKLIST	* TAPE RECORDING * CONFIDENTIALITY & ANONYMITY * STOPPING * TRANSCRIPTS	• **Rationing**	- Do you think there is rationing in health care? How do you feel about that? - Does it matter how it's done? How do you think it's done now? - Who do you think should be responsible?
• **Willingness to participate**	- Do you want to participate? why? why not? - Would some things make it easier for you to participate? child care etc... - Would it matter how your input was used? (probe issues of responsibility)	• **Denial**	- What about if someone is badly affected by a decision your group makes? how would you feel about that? - What if it affected you or a member of your family? - Could you say "no"? why? why not?
• **Who**	- Who should be involved? why? - Who should decide? why? - Is there anyone who shouldn't be involved? why?	• **Deprivation**	- Telling individuals about the decision - what would you want them to be told? why? - Would you want them to know their care has been rationed? why? - What if it was you? member of your family? a child?
• **Focus group as method**	- What surprised you about the group? - Was the meeting what you expected? - Did you enjoy/dislike taking part? - Did your views change? - Is this a good way of getting people's views? - Are there better ways? - How did you feel when you heard others people's views? why?	• **Health Service**	- Do you think much about the health service? why? - Do you think it's important to have a national health service? why? - Do you want the health service to stay the same as it is now? - Do you think all care should be free? for everybody? for everything? - What's important to you about the health service?
• **Information content**	- What sorts of information would you want if you were going to participate? why?	• **Caring externality**	- Does it matter to you that other people can get health care? why?
• **Information style**	- How should information be provided? When? - What would be the easiest type of information to understand?	• **Health care objectives**	- Is value for money important in the health service? - Are other things as/more important? (probe - fairness/ need/ public input?)

It is important to spend sufficient time developing the topic guide to ensure that the interviews will yield appropriate data. In patient-focused research, consulting with patient and public involvement representatives is helpful in ensuring that key concepts are addressed in a way that will be comprehensible to interviewees. It is rarely necessary to conduct formal pilot interviews, as the appropriate wording for individual questions will vary by participant, and such interviews could even be detrimental if they desensitize the researcher to the 'surprise' of the research field before the researcher enters it properly. The topic guide is also an important documentation of the research process and should be submitted for ethical review and made available as supplementary material to published articles (Bryman 2004). This does not mean that the document is static and unchanging, however, and it is usually necessary to update it as the research is ongoing and additional insights are gained and themes of interest emerge (Kvale 1996; Warren 2001; King and Horrocks 2010). Such changes should be discussed with the research team where possible, and new documents should be version-controlled as part of the documentation of the research process. Some informants may be curious about the topic guide and ask to see it – it is normally reasonable to accept such a request, so it is worth writing the guide with this possibility in mind.

Conducting the interview

Arrival and introductions

The first few minutes following arrival at an interview setting are often critical to its overall success. Before attending the interview it is important to think about self-presentation, including the clothes worn and the vocabulary used, both of which will give the informant cues about the identity of the researcher (King and Horrocks 2010). Particularly when interviewing someone in his or her home, the researcher should behave as a guest, making polite conversation and accepting refreshments until the participant is ready to begin (Legard, Keegan, et al. 2004). The informant will often want to know about the researcher's career and the overall purpose of the research prior to starting the interview, and this should be taken as an opportunity to build trust and rapport. However, it is important to keep in mind the purpose of the appointment and in particular to resist straying into a discussion of the topic of interest before taking consent and switching on the audio recorder. It normally feels somewhat artificial to ask people to repeat their story once the recorder is turned on and will often lead to a curtailed version of events being recorded.

Once the normal social niceties have been observed, it is time to move the interview forward by explaining the research process, completing consent forms and gathering any formal demographic information that is required for the project. This can usually be prompted by simply taking out a file and pen, when most informants will realize it is time for the serious business of the day to begin. When taking consent, it should never be assumed that the informant has read the research information sheet, however, and the researcher should always have a copy and be prepared to talk through it if necessary. Although some informants will try and breeze through this part of the interview, it is important to ensure forms are completed correctly and that informants understand that the interview will (usually) be recorded. Informants are often interested in the recording equipment at the start of the interview, so ensure they are given the chance to ask any questions about it at this point, and they will soon forget about it once the interview is under way.

Questioning techniques

The substantive interview often begins with an open request for the relation of a particular experience, and the role of researchers is to put informants at their ease and demonstrate their interest through actively listening (Kvale 1996). The aim at this point is not to guide informants through the topic guide but rather to avoid interruption and enable them to relate their experience in their own words, raising issues that are important to them. In a very good qualitative interview it is not unusual to hear up to ten minutes uninterrupted talk from the informant at the start of the interview. Where clarifications and explanations are necessary, it is often useful to note these on the topic guide rather than interrupt the natural ordering of events.

As the interview progresses, questioning usually becomes increasingly focused as the researcher works through the topic guide and guides the conversation towards a discussion of the particular phenomena under study. Open questions (e.g., what did you do next?) are generally better than closed ones (e.g., did you go to the doctor next?), and double or leading questions are best avoided (Britten 2000; Legard, Keegan, et al. 2004). Informants should always be given ample time to answer questions, and if time is running short it is preferable to prioritize the most important questions for the research rather than curtail individual responses or ask two questions at once (people invariably answer only one, and it is better that the researcher decide which one this should be!). As far as possible, questions should relate to individual views and experiences (rather than theoretical or conceptual issues), and the researcher should listen out for the terminology used by individual informants so as to be able to frame ongoing questioning in the informants' own terms. Questions eliciting simple 'yes'/'no' responses can be useful for clarifying certain points, but the aim is not interrogation, and such data are rarely useful for in-depth analysis or providing suitable examples for publication.

The researcher should avoid reacting to responses wherever possible and should aim to maintain an interested yet neutral persona (Legard, Keegan, et al. 2004); Hansen recommends making 'neutral sounds and gestures to indicate interest' (Hansen 2006, p. 115). Despite various methodological texts describing the qualitative interview as a 'conversation', this is of a very specific kind that is balanced in favour of the informant, and it should by no means be allowed to become an exchange of views such as one might have with a friend or colleague. A shared background and understanding is not assumed, and researchers may at times exaggerate their own naivety to prompt full disclosure (Johnson and Weller 2001). Silences are permissible where the researcher suspects that further information may be forthcoming but should not be allowed to stretch out to the extent that the interaction becomes strained or the informant uncomfortable. Descriptive questions are generally preferable to too many 'why' questions, although on occasion (but used sparingly) more challenging questions are necessary, such as to clarify contradictory viewpoints or inconsistent versions of events. In addition, it is essential to ensure that informants are prompted to define key terms for themselves, particularly where these are relevant to the conduct of the research – generic economic terms such as 'cost-effectiveness' might have quite diverse interpretations between informants and might vary markedly from the textbook definition of the term (Charmaz 2001; Warren 2001); this approach was used in a study of the use of economic evaluation in decision-making (Eddama and Coast 2009).

Routine summarizing and 'reflecting back' what the informant says should be avoided – it may come across as glib or patronizing and clearly disrupts the flow of the conversation (Bowling 1997). It can be tempting for the just-trained qualitative researcher to use this technique to begin the analysis process in the interview itself, but this is rarely helpful and is a distraction from the core role of the qualitative interviewer, which is to actively listen and probe for more depth where appropriate. In addition, the researcher is neither a counsellor nor an advisor and should resist adopting this stance in the interview – the informant has agreed simply to share his or her experience and not to receive the benefit of the researcher's knowledge and counsel. In some situations, it may be appropriate to share information about external information sources or support groups, although this should be reserved for the end of the interview where possible, usually within the strictures of a predefined 'distress protocol' (see 'harm avoidance'). The role of active listening should not be underestimated – intense concentration is needed to conduct a successful qualitative interview, and emotional resilience is often required, particularly where topics are sensitive. Depending on the travelling distance and sensitivity of the topics addressed, it is rarely advisable to schedule more than two qualitative interviews in a day.

Other elicitation techniques

Although less usual in qualitative research generally, interviews may also incorporate tasks to both facilitate discussion and collect data in their own right. This is particularly common where mixed-methods approaches are being used. For example, priority setting vignettes could be composed where informants are asked which hypothetical patient would have the first call on publicly funded health care resources, or a card-sorting technique could be used to rank treatments in order of importance for funding. Other elicitation techniques include the use of timelines to unearth a chronological sequence of events or the use of hierarchical mapping to collect data on networks. Elicitation tasks are also sometimes used in interviews with children as a means of enabling children to participate and provide their own perspective on particular issues in a way that is suited to their cognitive ability and willingness to communicate with adults who are not familiar with them; such tasks may include strategies to enable anonymous provision of information, using drawing techniques and using photography (Punch 2002; Gabhainn and Sixsmith 2006; Horstman, Aldiss, et al. 2008). More generally, these sorts of elicitation techniques are relatively common in health economics, where the focus of much qualitative research is to enhance quantitative data collection or better interpret quantitative data. These techniques can serve to focus informants on the specific issue under investigation as they complete and reflect upon a task.

It is important that these elicitation tasks are well placed in the interview and do not feel too artificial. For example, in the think-aloud work reported by Bailey et al. (Chapter 14) and other similar work (Al-Janabi, Keeley, et al. 2013; Horwood, Sutton, et al. 2014), it was valuable to ask informants to think-aloud as they completed the relevant questionnaires at the start of the interview and then ask informants about their views of the questionnaires, whereas in qualitative work by Keeley et al., which was focused on the appropriateness of particular questionnaires for use in cost-effectiveness analysis conducted in the randomized controlled trial setting, it was important to obtain information about perceptions of quality of life *prior* to the introduction of the questionnaires (Keeley, Al-Janabi, et al. 2013). Canaway and colleagues (Chapter 12), in particularly sensitive interviews focused around the death of a loved one, found that using the hierarchical mapping early on in the interview was a good way to generate rapport with informants and also aided discussions in that the interviewer knew who the important people were in the decedent's life by the time experiences of care were related.

If such tasks prove to be unhelpful in eliciting the required information, it is important to be aware of this and to make flexible decisions about moving forwards. For example in qualitative research work to generate meaningful wording for the attributes for the first ICECAP capability index (Coast, Flynn, et al. 2008), two approaches were initially used, one of which involved a more structured task in which cards with suggested descriptors were shown to informants and they were asked to place these under the different attribute 'labels'. Informants seemed unsure how to complete the task and found it difficult to engage with, and it therefore seemed to elicit little valuable information. Much more successful was a second, less structured task, which started from potential labels (meaningful wording) and asked informants to say what these labels meant to them. The first task was relatively quickly abandoned in favour of the second.

In many cases, however, the tasks can both provide additional data related to the task (e.g., the physical hierarchical maps generated in the interviews conducted by Canaway et al., detailed in Chapter 12) and generate discussion that would have been unlikely to occur in the absence of the task. It is therefore worth thinking about the potential value of including such tasks in interviews.

The importance of rapport

Already touched on earlier, in interviews it is essential to build rapport with informants (Hammersley and Atkinson 1983; Gold 1997). Having good rapport with informants means that they are more likely to trust the researcher and to be open with their responses, and the data obtained are thus likely to be richer. Even before the start of the interview, it is important to start building the relationship with the informant, which is easier where there has been some prior contact such as participation in an earlier stage of the research study (e.g., through observation or a focus group). Even where there is no prior relationship, however, the interviewer can help build rapport with the informant by doing things such as accepting refreshments offered at the beginning of the interview, as time spent making cups of tea or coffee tends to provide a few minutes of general 'chat', during which time rapport can start to be established and the informant begins to relax. In some settings, more formal initial activities may also help in building rapport. Stevens, for example, included making a name badge with colourful stickers prior to her interviews with seven- to eleven-year-olds, when developing a child measure for use in economic evaluation (Stevens 2010). Some researchers have also found that the inclusion of a task once the interview has started has helped informants to relax into the interview and enabled rapport to develop as the task is conducted; essentially the task forms a shared experience between the informant and the interviewee (Canaway et al., Chapter 12).

During the interview, generating and maintaining rapport involves giving responses that indicate that the researcher is accepting the informant's views and is understanding what the informant is saying (Hammersley and Atkinson 1983). Achieving rapport may be more difficult where the subject under discussion is potentially sensitive. Examples might include sensitive health topics, such as end-of-life care or sexual health, but also topics where the informants might feel vulnerable for other reasons, such as those related to the performance of their role, particularly in cultural settings that have less tolerance for openness and debate. Some have argued that a degree of self-disclosure is necessary to establish rapport (Oakley 1981; Johnson 2001). However, in our experience this is rarely necessary – sympathy and understanding can be demonstrated in other ways, and revealing one's own experience is bound to alter the course of the interview. Where directly asked about one's own views and experiences, the best approach is to acknowledge the relevance of the question but say the purpose of the interview is to focus on informants' experiences and any questions they may have can be addressed at the end of the interview. It is worth remembering that it is only the researcher (and not the interviewee) who is bound by the confidentiality agreement signed, and it is never wise for researchers to disclose information that they would not be happy to be public knowledge.

In developing rapport, it is important to realize that the 'ideal' of the research may not always be achievable. For example, it may be desirable to interview family members separately, but with some informants this may not be achievable without generating distrust or reducing this rapport. For example, in a very early interview conducted by one of the authors, the interview was with a husband and wife, both with different disabilities. Both had participated in an earlier focus group and both were interesting to interview. Their accommodation was such though that it was not possible to ask one informant to wait elsewhere while the other was interviewed, and both were somewhat distrustful of the interview process. Insisting on separate interviews would have resulted in a significant loss of rapport and would possibly have resulted in a refusal for interview or very superficial data. Interviewing the two informants together, however, resulted in rich data.

It has been argued that going beyond a surface level to access true feelings and opinions (a 'private account') is possible only in the context of multiple interviews (Cornwell 1984; Charmaz 2001; Warren 2001). However, this is not necessarily the case – it is perfectly possible to establish rapport within one research interview, and plenty of rich, qualitative work has been published as the result of one-off interviews. For some areas of health economics, such as in studies looking at valuation techniques or generating attributes for preference elicitation studies around particular services, it would be very rare to include more than one interview with each informant. However, multiple interviewing can be helpful if trying to observe a process and examining changes in attitude and opinions over time (Kvale 1996). For example, the authors of this chapter conducted a longitudinal qualitative study to investigate NHS patients' conceptions of health care rationing, which was undertaken in 'real time' so that their views could be sought as the reality of their situation unfolded (Owen-Smith, Donovan, et al. 2015). There are downsides to this approach, however, including complexities in analysis (is the experience of each individual the primary object of analysis, or the comparison between individuals?) and managing complex relationships with participants, which can become intense and start to feel increasingly unequal as participants 'forget' their status as interviewee and start to regard the researcher as a friend and confidante.

Achieving rapport in interviews is a skill that some health economists may have to work hard to achieve. This sort of interpersonal skill is not taught in economics courses and is not a skill that economists are particularly likely to have developed in their past work. It is, however, important in conducting qualitative research that researchers think explicitly about developing these skills, for example, through attending relevant training courses.

Ending the interview

The interview itself should end with topics that informants are comfortable in discussing, and the researcher should check that they have had the opportunity to say all they want to on the topic of interest (King and Horrocks 2010). Informants should always be thanked sincerely for their participation and hospitality regardless of the success of the interview from a research point of view, and researchers should check they have the correct contact details for any ongoing questions about the conduct of the research. In turn, most informants will be happy to be contacted again post interview by researchers if there are any issues they are unsure about. Following the termination of the interview and the recorder being switched off, on occasion the researcher may find himself or herself engaged in further conversation related to the topic of the research. Such 'off-the-record' disclosures are relatively common but can be frustrating if they pertain to key issues that it was not possible to clarify during the interview itself. In some situations it may be possible to ask to switch the recorder back on to capture these comments, although if in any doubt as to whether this is appropriate it is best avoided. In these cases the researcher must simply try and remember as much information as possible and note this down in post-interview field notes (see 'recording and transcription'). It should be noted that King and Horrocks suggest leaving the recording equipment running until the very end of the interview in an attempt to avoid this particular problem (King and Horrocks 2010).

In some situations, it will be important to alert the informant to possible sources of support at the end of the interview. In certain settings, as for example in the hospice research conducted by Bailey and colleagues (Chapter 14), health professionals caring for the patient may need to be alerted that the interview has been completed and, depending on the particular distress protocol, informed if the patient has become upset during the interview.

Strengths and limitations of qualitative interviewing

Qualitative interviewing offers some unique advantages over other forms of data collection. In-depth accounts can be accessed, and views and experiences can be explained in a way that is simply not possible through direct observation or more quantitative questionnaire-based methods. However, despite its popularity there are a number of limitations to qualitative interviewing, which need be taken into account in research planning. In particular, its resource-intensive nature means that samples are usually small, although, as discussed in Chapter 3, this is not necessarily a problem provided they are drawn carefully (Bowling 1997). Nevertheless, the overall success of the data collection exercise is inevitably dependent on what the researcher is able to elicit and what a relatively small number of informants are willing and able to disclose.

For example, when interviewing patients it is possible that some informants are simply too frail or ill to fully articulate their experiences (Morse 2002; Legard, Keegan, et al. 2004). Most people will find it tiring to talk about their own lives for a length of time, but for particularly vulnerable groups, such as dying patients or those with degenerative brain diseases, this may simply not be possible (Warren 2001). Such patients should not be unfairly excluded from research, but all possible accommodations (e.g., using a reduced interview schedule, conducting the interview in two or more sessions or ensuring an experienced carer is present) should be made; the approach of using a reduced schedule and ordering the tasks to prioritize those most important to the research was the approach used by Bailey et al. in their study of hospice patients (Bailey, Kinghorn, et al. 2016). Alternatively, although nearly all informants will tell their story in a disjointed manner, some may ramble excessively and it may be difficult to keep the interview focused on the topic of interest (Legard, Keegan, et al. 2004). There should be scope for some diversions within the context of the interview, but where this is threatening to subvert its course entirely, the researcher may need to be more active in moving the informant through the agenda, which can normally be achieved by simply breaking eye contact and consulting the topic guide (or, as a last resort, one's watch!).

Less commonly, informants who seem to have understood the informed consent agreement but are reluctant to disclose information once the interview starts may be encountered (Adler and Adler 2001). Normally, reticence can be overcome through affirming social behaviours (e.g., nodding and smiling) and emphasizing the confidential nature of the research interview. However, on occasion the researcher may simply come across informants who either seem to have little interest in discussing the topic at hand or are too wary of judgement or retribution to disclose further, which ultimately the researcher has little choice but to accept with good grace. Other informants may display interest and willingness to disclose but try to dominate the research agenda by constantly returning to a particular point or questioning the conduct and purpose of the study (Hammersley and Atkinson 1983; Legard, Keegan, et al. 2004). In such cases it can help to allow them to air their chosen view first and then try and gently steer the interview back on track if possible, although this can be problematic if informants have limited time available. Where key research questions are continually avoided or dismissed as of little relevance, it is worth trying to tackle the question in different ways or even issuing a gentle challenge through introducing the views of other informants to demonstrate the relevance of the issue to their situation.

Although the emphasis in the interview is on eliciting the account of the informant, the influence of the researcher should not be underestimated, and simple characteristics such as sex, age, physical stature and the interviewer's manner of speech can all affect rapport and the information disclosed, alongside more obvious factors such as questioning manner and response to disclosures (Hammersley and Atkinson 1983; Miller and Glassner 2011). It is not possible for the data collected to be completely unaffected by the researcher, but these influences should be minimized wherever possible, such as dressing appropriately for the social situation that is about to be entered and keeping responses and tone of voice neutral. In some cases, these impacts are outside of the researcher's control and should simply be noted as an element of the research process to be taken into account during analysis, but it can also emphasize the value of working in diverse teams where researchers with different backgrounds may capture different facets of an issue (Miller and Glassner 2011). For example, one of the authors of this chapter encountered some difficulties in conducting in-depth interviews with patients who had experienced the rationing of morbid obesity surgery, where her slim stature was frequently an object of comment, and on one occasion resulted in her having a door slammed in her face. If more than one interviewer is collecting data, individual characteristics should be compared and any potential impact on the data collected should be accounted for in analysis.

Telephone interviews – special considerations

Modern technology makes conducting interviews over the telephone relatively easy. These are best accomplished using an in-ear pick-up microphone (available through Internet suppliers very cheaply), plugged into the usual voice recorder. Telephone interviews are being increasingly used in qualitative research, and indeed some whole studies are conducted without meeting informants face to face. However, there is the need for some caution with this approach as communication styles over the telephone may be quite different from those interactions conducted in person (King and Horrocks 2010). It is far more challenging to establish rapport over the telephone, and it is not possible to access non-verbal communication, meaning it is harder to assess emotional reactions or the completeness of accounts. The topic guide tends to become of greater importance, and it is harder to interpret silences remotely. In addition, there is more scope for either researcher or informant to become distracted, and, as good as modern recording equipment is, a widespread reliance on cell phones means it is much more difficult to get a clear recording over the telephone. Nevertheless, telephone interviewing may be extremely useful in the context of multiple interviews, where rapport has already been established. It may also widen the accessibility of research to informants who live very remotely or suffer with social anxiety, or who are busy professionals reluctant to be 'pinned down' to a specific interview time.

FOCUS GROUPS

Qualitative interviews are not always held with individuals, and focus groups (group interviews) are a popular method to gather data on the views and experiences of a group of people (Wilkinson 2011). The core interest is in accessing shared values and understandings, so the research questions are often different from those addressed in individual interviews and the focus of analysis is usually the interaction between participants (Finch and Lewis 2003; Kitzinger 2006); focus groups can also be a useful means of enabling reflection and discussion on topics that are less familiar to informants (Dolan, Cookson, et al. 1999), and it is suggested that being part of a group enables participants to re-evaluate their position (King and Horrocks 2010). It may be for this latter reason that focus groups have been seen as particularly useful for health economists engaging in research on priority setting in health care, with Cookson and Dolan using focus groups to generate debate around particular priority setting vignettes (Cookson and Dolan 1999; Dolan and Cookson 2000) and work by Coast and colleagues using initial focus groups to generate discussion around public involvement in priority setting before conducting individual interviews with purposefully sampled participants (Coast, Donovan, et al. 2002; Litva, Coast, et al. 2002). Examples of the use of focus groups are given in Chapters 10 and 16.

Getting started

Arranging and structuring the group meeting

It is not normally reasonable to ask people to put aside much longer than a maximum of two hours for participation, and this time is often shorter when dealing with professional groups. It is common for groups to take place outside of normal working hours, and a venue may need to be hired in a convenient location. It is important that the setting is comfortable, has adequate facilities for hospitality and meets the access requirements of all participants. Possible venues might include community halls, leisure centres, village halls, conference venues and hotels; choice may be limited in any specific location, so it is important to ensure that sufficient budget is available for the hire of such venues.

The room needs to be set up in a manner that means all participants can see and hear each other. Tables may or may not be used, but if some sort of written task is included, then a table will make this easier to conduct. Name badges (that can be easily seen across a room) for both the research team and the participants are helpful, and water should be available. In a meeting lasting more than an hour, it may be helpful to have a short comfort break with simple refreshments.

All focus groups will need a facilitator to conduct the group interview. It is also advisable, however, to have two further staff, additional to the main facilitator, present during focus groups. The first of these should be a dedicated 'note-taker', whose role is purely to take notes about who is speaking when, to enable accurate transcription; this person may be the person who will ultimately transcribe the data, and indeed, it can be very helpful for the quality of transcription if this is the case. The second should be an additional facilitator, who can operate recording equipment, act as an observer, pick up on any issues that the main facilitator appears to have missed and deal with any issues that arise. These might be simple practical issues, such as dealing with consent for late entrants to the focus group, providing more detailed explanation of tasks for individual participants or ensuring that refreshments are available, but there may also be more difficult sensitive issues where people become upset during the focus group or overwhelmed by the topics under discussion and may need to be accompanied to a comfortable waiting area. Although all facilitators should be introduced, the demarcation of responsibilities should be clear.

More sophisticated recording equipment and/or additional microphones may be required compared to individual interviews, as well as more specialist transcribers (see 'recording and transcription').

Contacting participants

The issues under discussion will often relate to the personal experiences of informants so there is some meaningful basis for shared reflection and discussion, and groups should be composed carefully to minimize social disparities between participants (Finch and Lewis 2003). Consideration needs to be given to the heterogeneity, or otherwise, of group members; where participants are more similar, they may be more willing to share experiences, but this may also narrow the focus of discussion (King and Horrocks 2010). There also needs to be thought about the size of the group. This should not be too large (where it may be too difficult to keep the discussion on track and some participants may be inhibited from speaking) or too small (where it may be difficult to get discussion going) (King and Horrocks 2010). The more people who are included, the less each individual participant will be heard – for example, with a group size of six to ten, there will be an opportunity for each participant to talk only for six to ten minutes on average.

Focus groups are more difficult to organize than individual interviews, since their time and location needs to be convenient for all participants. It is usually necessary to have a reasonable number of responses to initial invitations to participate before the groups can be organized, and some informants may be waiting some weeks (or even months) between returning their initial response and participating in a group. Therefore, it is always worth an interim contact to thank informants for their interest in the research and to provide a time frame within which more details will be provided.

Compiling a focus group topic guide

As with individual interviews, focus groups can be more or less structured, with the facilitator allowing different levels of freedom for the discussion to diverge from the topic guide. Topic guides are composed in a similar way to those for individual interviews but will generally be shorter as there is less time to explore the views of each participant, and it is usually a more difficult task to keep the group on track.

Conducting focus groups

Arrival and introductions

As with individual interviews, it is important to consider the start of the focus groups, and many of the same issues apply. In a focus group setting, however, the research team is always the host, and therefore, it is important to welcome participants, give basic information about housekeeping issues (e.g., location of toilets), provide refreshments if required and generally act in a friendly, welcoming and unthreatening manner. General conversation about neutral issues such as travel to the venue may be required with participants who arrive early, while waiting for all those taking part to reach the venue. This is also a good time to talk individually with participants about any questions they have about the research and to ask them to complete the consent form.

Facilitating the focus group

The role of the main facilitator is critical to the success of the focus group. The facilitator needs to be constantly alert to divergences, and to managing the balance between covering the key points on the topic guide and allowing sufficient flexibility for new themes of interest to emerge. The facilitator may also need to manage interactions to ensure that the views of all participants are reflected in the findings, as some participants may be very vocal and others much less so. As with individual interviews, building rapport with informants is vital.

It is important to stress confidentiality issues at the beginning of the focus group and to request of participants that they do not share information gained through their participation in the focus group. It is also important to emphasize that participants should respect the views of others within the group (King and Horrocks 2010). As with individual interviews, it is helpful to have an easy starting question that engages the focus group participants and encourages them to contribute to the group. It is the task of the main facilitator to guide the discussion and make judgement calls about which topics to prioritize when time is short, as well as to judge the optimal timing of breaks, taking cues from participants.

Using elicitation techniques

Elicitation tasks (e.g., the discussion of vignettes or completion of specific elicitation exercises) can be incorporated into focus groups and can be particularly useful to get the conversation going and provide some common basis for discussion. An example of the use of such tasks during focus groups is given in the chapter by Kinghorn and colleagues (Chapter 16), which uses a more deliberative approach to data collection (Burchardt 2014).

Ending the focus group

As the focus group reaches an end, either through a natural conclusion to discussion or through time constraints, there are a number of issues to cover.

It is good to provide an opportunity for participants to say if there is anything further they would like to say before the meeting ends. Following the end of the meeting, the most important task is to thank the participants for giving up their time to attend the group. There may be requests for further participation in the research to cover, for example, if there are follow-up interviews to conduct; in these cases, participants should be asked if they would be willing to be contacted about further research and if so to provide the best means of contacting them. Travel expenses may need to be paid, and information may need to be provided about possible support, particularly if the topic of the meeting has been in any way sensitive or distressing.

Strengths and limitations

One of the core strengths of focus group research is the ability to access socially contextualized data and ascertain shared knowledge and values. Indeed, in very successful focus groups, participants may start to 'interview' one another or discuss reasons for the differences in their views, to all intents and purposes starting the analysis process in situ. Different perspectives may be highlighted and focus groups can provide a cost-effective form of data collection (Patton 2015); this latter issue may be a consideration for health economics researchers, particularly when conducting qualitative research as part of a larger project where the primary focus is the quantitative data.

A disadvantage of the approach is that it can be difficult to distinguish individual from group views in analysis, and indeed 'groupthink' may be encouraged, with individuals conforming in their views to pressure from dominant member(s) or those perceived to have a higher status (Kitzinger 1995; Gibbs 1997; MacDougall and Baum 1997) or just being reticent within a group setting (King and Horrocks 2010). Some people may find it more difficult to contribute to focus groups than others, and accounting for the composition and characteristics of groups is extremely important in analysing data (Kitzinger 1994, 1995). Further, researchers conducting focus groups need to be aware that the rules and regulations of communication differ across cultures – including gender and racial groups – with some groups communicating to exchange information and others with the aim of building relationships (Dreachslin 1998).

Clearly, the anonymity of informants is to some extent compromised in focus groups, and some researchers view them as less useful than one-to-one interviews for probing individual experiences (DiCicco-Bloom and Crabtree 2006), although others suggest group interaction can be helpful in encouraging informants to give their views as members of the group become aware of others with the same issues or concerns (Kitzinger 2006; King and Horrocks 2010). Nevertheless, dealing with confidentiality concerns is vital.

OBSERVATION METHODS

Observation methods are used to gain direct insights into the social world of participants. They are concerned with capturing naturally occurring data, and researchers should aim for minimum disruption to the normal flow of events (Bryman 2004). Observations can be undertaken as a participant, where the researcher himself or herself becomes a part of the social world under study, or as a non-participant, where the researcher simply observes and interprets the behaviour and events unfolding before himself or herself. In practice, researchers often occupy a position between these two extremes, where they are both within and without the social world under study, accepting both that their shared humanity links them with those under study and that their academic interest in the situation sets them apart (Hammersley and Atkinson 1983). There is also a distinction to be made between overt and covert observation. In the latter, the presence of the researcher is unknown to some or all of the participants in the social world under examination. However, this would rarely be considered appropriate by modern-day ethics committees, and its use has largely been confined to the sociological study of deviant groups (Whyte 1955; Pryce 1979).

The purpose of observation research is to become explicitly aware of what ordinary participants in a social situation take for granted and to interpret ongoing actions and interactions from the perspective of the social actors involved. Eberle and Maeder note the observer 'enters the field with all of his or her senses' (Eberle and Maeder 2011, p. 54), and this can result in findings that would not be obtained in the absence of such observation (Buscatto 2011). Observation alone, however, can be seen as controversial if undertaken entirely by researchers themselves, and therefore, interviews (however informal) are usually undertaken alongside observational research (Hammersley and Atkinson 1983). In health economics to date, observational research has most often been undertaken of the interactions between members of professional groups (e.g., in decision-making committees), or between professionals and patients, in an attempt to better understand decision-making as it happens, rather than relying on accounts of the process where informants may be unwilling to talk fully about all aspects of the process. For example, observational studies have yielded fascinating insights into the use of cost-effectiveness data and evidence-based guidelines in practice, often exposing a gulf between a traditional academic approach to health economics and the political nature of day-to-day health care decision-making (Williams and Bryan 2007a; Eddama and Coast 2009; Russell and Greenhalgh 2012). Although these situations may seem a world away from traditional anthropological studies of indigenous tribes, in essence the process is very similar, with the researcher seeking to understand the relevant social norms and practices and the influence these have on the events observed. In other studies, observations have been made of doctor–patient decision-making in the context of economic scarcity (Owen-Smith, Donovan, et al. 2015), and even the activities of health economists themselves (Mulkay, Ashmore, et al. 1987; Ashmore, Mulkay, et al. 1989). A number of chapters in this book have combined observation with other techniques (see Chapter 13 by Husbands and colleagues, Chapter 18 by Martínez-Álvarez and Chapter 19 by Eckard and Nedlund).

Getting started

There are a number of practical issues to consider in observational research, and inevitably, the researcher has less control in these naturalistic situations than in manufactured research settings such as interviews and focus groups. Most obviously, the researcher has to decide which situations will be observed and may have to negotiate access through a 'gatekeeper' (Pope and Mays 2006a).

A key decision in starting observational fieldwork concerns the extent to which the researcher will be a participant in the field (Patton 2015). This may in part depend on the nature of the setting, and in many situations for health economists there may be little choice on this issue because of the nature of the research question. There are situations, however, where there may be a possibility of participant observation as, for example, in settings focusing on resource allocation decision-making where both participant (McDonald 2002) and non-participant (Eddama and Coast 2009) observation methods have been used. Husbands also had a choice between acting as a participant and non-participant observer in work on observing the process of decision-analytic modelling, ultimately deciding to act in a non-participant role (see Chapter 13).

Researchers also need to devise a process to obtain informed consent from all the social actors involved. Depending on the nature of the research, this may be more problematic than it sounds, as the researcher may not want to disclose information that will disrupt the natural unfolding of events. For example, making it explicit to everyone under observation that the researcher is interested in how health economics evidence is used in practice may well affect how information is dealt with on the day of the observation. Therefore, objectives should be presented broadly in information sheets (for the earlier example 'investigating the important factors in decision-making' would probably suffice), and the importance of observing a naturalistic process where there is no 'right' and 'wrong' practice should be emphasized. In addition, the ethics committee will need to know how the situation will be handled if a potential participant refuses to be observed and/or recorded. Whereas this is relatively straightforward when dealing with one-to-one interactions (i.e., the observation simply does not go ahead), it is more problematic when dealing with a meeting of twenty people, nineteen of whom have agreed to the recording of data! In such situations, audio recording of data is unlikely to be possible, although the researcher may be permitted to stay and take detailed field notes.

Conducting observational fieldwork

The context for the research will dictate how data can be recorded. If the focus for observations is time-limited interactions as is often the case in observations of meetings, clinical encounters or particular processes, then (pending consent) audio recording will probably be the most appropriate technique and will proceed in a similar way to recording focus groups or interviews. However, if the research is broader in scope, particularly if acting as a participant observer, then the researcher will necessarily be more reliant on making field notes, which may have to be written up after the event if constant scribbling is likely to distract participants or be otherwise inappropriate. Whatever the case, it is always useful to carry an audio recorder in case unexpected opportunities to interview participants arise, or researchers simply have so many thoughts in their head that it is useful to 'download' them verbally at the first opportunity. Such contextual field notes, whether written or spoken, should be formally written up at the earliest possible opportunity (Hammersley and Atkinson 1983).

Other forms of observation are also likely to be needed; for example, the researcher will need to take notes on the physical and social environments in which the observation takes place, the nature of interactions and so on (Patton 2015). As Pope and Mays note, observation requires 'not only good observational skills, but good memory and clear, detailed and systematic recording' (Pope and Mays 2006a, p. 37).

A multitude of other issues may need to be thought through depending on the nature of the observation undertaken. As just one example, in some of the work conducted by the authors, the researcher was not physically present for the observation, which involved observations of clinic interactions undertaken solely by audio recording. In this situation, there were issues of who would deal with consent, start/stop the recorder and act as interim custodian of the data. As information sheets had been sent out in advance (as is normally required by ethics committees), there needed to be mechanisms for dealing with last-minute substitutions on the day (e.g., a locum doctor, a deputation at a meeting or last-minute changes to patients on a clinic list). None of these problems were insurmountable, but such issues can be very stressful if not thought through in advance. It can therefore be useful to simply conduct a 'dry run' of the observation process, by going to the proposed site of the research and thinking through all the possible problems and pitfalls that could occur, before 'going live' with the data collection.

Strengths and limitations

The core advantage of an observational approach relates to the full immersion of researchers in the social world of participants, allowing them first-hand access to events and reducing reliance on informants' accounts, which may be incomplete, partial or simply inaccessible (Bryman 2004). In addition, the researcher is less interventionist than in interview research, enabling a more flexible approach, which may lead to the emergence of completely new themes of interest. However, the researcher has far less control in a naturalistic situation, and in some circumstances a large number of observations may need to be made before the phenomenon of interest is captured. For example, in a study undertaken by the authors on the communication of rationing decisions, only one of nine consultants observed ever mentioned the impact of financial factors on care availability, meaning that initial attempts to compare differing disclosure techniques were somewhat limited (Owen-Smith, Donovan, et al. 2015)!

Some aspects of the social world, such as past experiences or participants' interpretations of their own behaviour, are simply not suited to an observational approach to research (Bryman 2004; Lewis 2004; Ritchie 2004). Whereas the observer can carefully document every detail of a social interaction, in the absence of the views of participants, interpretations and conclusions are necessarily those of the researcher, which may be more or less correct (Hammersley and Atkinson 1983). It is also rarely possible for researchers to have no influence at all on the social world under study, and their personal appearance and characteristics can all impact on gaining the trust needed to conduct useful observational research (Hammersley and Atkinson 1983; Pope and Mays 2006a). Maintaining the liminal position between participant and observer can be stressful for even the most experienced researcher and, in some situations, participant observers have been accused of 'going native' where they lose the ability to stand back and analyse unfolding events objectively, even oversympathizing with the views of deviant groups whose actions may be morally abhorrent (Hammersley and Atkinson 1983).

RECORDING AND TRANSCRIPTION

Recording data

Interviews and focus groups are usually audio recorded and then transcribed for analysis. Modern recording equipment is generally discreet and easy to use, and where possible, an encrypted digital recorder will offer the best sound quality and security of data. Always ensure the recorder is fully charged between each interview or focus group and that data are downloaded to a secure server as soon as possible. Although modern recorders are very reliable, it is always useful to carry a backup recorder in case of mishap, and for very important recordings (e.g., focus groups where the data are virtually impossible to reconstruct) using two recorders just in case of technical mishap may be preferable! Even the cheapest digital recorders on the market offer excellent recording quality, but it is important for researchers to check with their IT department that recorders meet the requirements for information security and download in an appropriate file format for transcription. As focus groups normally take place in much larger rooms and there is much more scope for overlapping speech, it may be useful to use one or two external microphones to ensure a high-quality recording. Other useful features include prominent record/pause buttons for unavoidable interruptions and a recording light so that researchers can easily check at a glance that the recorder is active, allowing them to focus all their attention on active listening.

It is possible to document interviews in other ways, including simple note-taking if an informant declines to be recorded (although in our experience this is extremely rare). However, note-taking during interviews is time consuming and distracting, and clearly more subject to researcher bias, so it is best avoided where possible (Bowling 1997; Britten 2000). Contextual field notes, including information such as the time and location of the interview, along with the researcher's initial impressions, should be written up as soon as possible after data collection has ended to aid data interpretation. Other alternatives to audio recording include video recording, which has the benefit of capturing non-verbal communication, but it is generally unnecessary for individual interviews where the researcher is present to make these observations first-hand.

Whereas it is sometimes possible to audio record, or even video record, participants during observational research, in other situations note-taking is the only means of recording data. Field notes should be undertaken chronologically and be a relatively concrete description of the context for observations (the location, who was present, time of day, etc.) and the social processes observed (what was said, the events that transpired, participant reactions, etc.) (Hammersley and Atkinson 1983). This is a central research process and should be conducted with as much care and self-awareness as possible. Note-taking is a skill to be practised and learned, and adequate training should be undertaken if the researcher suspects this will be the dominant means of data recording (Hammersley and Atkinson 1983).

Transcribing data

Where data are transcribed for analysis, a set of transcribing rules are required such that notation is used consistently to record particular elements within the data. A number of transcribing conventions are available (Poland 1995; Atkinson and Heritage 1999). The level of transcription will depend in part on the form of analysis to be conducted, with some types of analyses requiring much more detail in the transcription than others. For example, analytic methods such as conversation or discourse analysis require greater detail to enable features such as lengths of pauses or overlapping speech to be accurately recorded for use in the analysis (Davidson 2009).

Ideally, transcription will be conducted on an ongoing basis from the start of the research to enable analysis to be conducted on an iterative basis. Some researchers prefer to transcribe their own data, which, although time-consuming, has the very real benefit of enabling them to maximize familiarity with the data. Where time constraints mean that transcription is conducted by others, such as secretaries or professional transcribing services, it is important to be clear about the rules that those transcribing the data should follow. It is also important for the researcher to assess transcription quality through listening to all recordings while following the transcript to correct discrepancies and add in any data that the professional transcribers have not been able to identify (Poland 1995). Persons who conducted the interview are much more likely to pick up such errors as they both will be more familiar than the transcription service with the topic of the interview (and thus more aware of any specialist terminology) and may be able to recall the interview to enable meaning to be identified. The types of discrepancies that often occur include problems with word order, the omission of quotation marks and words or phrases that are either missing or incorrectly transcribed.

Alongside this, an increasing minority of researchers send their transcripts out to participants themselves to review. However, this is unlikely to result in increased accuracy in transcription (since participants will not have the recording available to them and are unlikely to remember exactly what was said); it may also provoke further comment or disagreement, and if choosing to do this, it is important to decide in advance how to respond to informants. For example, if persons contradict what they said in interview, how will this be dealt with in analysis? This is a reminder, of course, that the process of transcription is an interpretative process, and transcripts should be regarded as a decontextualized account of the interview, and not the base data themselves (Poland 1995; Kvale 1996). A transcript is inevitably an interpretation from oral to written language and should be regarded as a record of a particular conversation taking place in a particular context and not a stable reflection of the views of informants. In addition, verbatim transcripts of conversations may seem impoverished, when compared to transcripts of written speeches that people are used to seeing in the media, and may unintentionally portray participants as inarticulate, repetitive or even boring, so careful consideration needs to be given to the issue of participant review, with responses being treated as an additional form of data rather than a tool to increase the accuracy of transcription (Hammersley and Atkinson 1983; Poland 1995).

ETHICAL ISSUES

As with all research involving human participants, a number of ethical issues are relevant to the conduct of qualitative research. In particular, full and careful consideration needs to be given to informed consent and voluntary participation, the protection of confidentiality and anonymity and the requirement for non-maleficence or harm avoidance.

Informed consent and voluntary participation

Potential informants should be provided with full and accurate information about the research study wherever possible. They should be provided with a full and clear information sheet outlining the purpose of the study, what their participation will involve and what will happen to their data if they agree to take part; useful guidelines are available (Health Research Authority 2014). Informants should be given the opportunity to consider the information and ask questions about the research before they are asked for their formal consent to participate. Consent should be recorded in writing wherever possible, including separate consent to be audio recorded where relevant. As noted previously, many participants will try to breeze through this part of the interview process ('just show me where to sign'), and there is a balance to be struck between ensuring informants understand the formality of the informed consent agreement and not making it seem overly onerous and threatening emerging rapport.

Other demands of the informed consent process include that participants have not been put under any undue pressure to participate and that they have the right to withdraw from the research (including extracting their data) at any time. Both of these issues can be more complex than they initially appear in qualitative research (Ryen 2011) and deserve careful consideration at the research planning stage. For example, it is common for access to informants to be negotiated via gatekeepers who might hold a more powerful position than others by virtue of their pre-existing relationship (e.g., senior managers and their more junior colleagues, or clinicians and their patients) who may then feel under pressure to agree to participation. If possible, there should be systems in place to ensure the gatekeeper does not have access to information about who has agreed to participate in the research (i.e., all responses are made directly to the research team), and this should be clearly explained in the participant information sheet. In terms of withdrawal, the iterative nature of data collection and analysis in qualitative research means that the contributions of individual informants start to affect the course of the research and influence analysis very shortly following their participation. Indeed, once data have been incorporated into formal analytic techniques such as analytic accounts, it is very difficult to withdraw, and it is important to be clear about this in information provided to informants, perhaps specifying a time point beyond which it may no longer be possible to withdraw data from the research.

The other dilemma often faced when considering consent is, how 'informed' does 'informed consent' need to be? In some cases, such as when trying to uncover a social process generally hidden from view, being entirely explicit about the purpose of the research may discourage participation or even undermine its purpose by highlighting it as an object of interest. In others, explaining the exact purpose of the research may cause needless anxiety to participants, and it may need to be couched in more general terms for their comfort. For example, in a study conducted by the authors into the experience of implicit health care rationing, this could not be disclosed to patient informants, many of whom did not know their care had been subject to financial limitations (Owen-Smith, Coast, et al. 2010).

Confidentiality and anonymity

It is important to protect both the anonymity of research participants and the confidentiality of data arising from their participation (Economic and Social Research Council 2015). In practice this means that no one outside the research team is told who has participated in the study, and the contributions of individual participants are not identifiable in any public presentations of data. Audio recordings should be stored on an encrypted recorder and uploaded to a secure server as soon as possible. A confidential identifier should be assigned to the file immediately, and only the data custodians within the research team should have access to the information to link this to individual informants. All consent forms and information containing personal details (e.g., names and addresses of interviewees) should be kept in a locked filing cabinet for a period not exceeding that laid down by data protection legislation. Similarly, there should be a disposal plan for electronic data after an agreed length of time (usually some years), which has been agreed by the relevant ethics committee and included on participant information sheets.

In writing up results, sufficient contextual information should be changed to ensure that participants are not identifiable publicly or to one another. For example, when interviewing professionals, it is usually best to assign generic job titles, such as 'commissioning staff' or 'senior manager', and names of specific organizations should almost never be given. However, in qualitative research there is some trade-off between protecting anonymity and providing sufficient contextual detail so that theoretical generalizations can be drawn by readers (see purposeful sampling, Chapter 3). In practice, a common-sense view will usually prevail; for example, a description along the lines of 'a large town in north-west England' would normally protect the identity of participants but is specific enough to enable considerations of wider applicability of the data presented. Where there is any doubt, however, the maxim of 'participants first' should prevail and anonymity should be prioritized over providing contextual depth.

Non-maleficence/harm avoidance

Accordingly, despite the scope of qualitative research to investigate individual motivations and ordinarily concealed social processes, there is an absolute duty on the researcher of non-maleficence, that is, to avoid harm to individuals or communities in either the short or long term in the course of the research (Economic and Social Research Council 2015). All risks to informants should therefore be considered at the planning stage of the research and documented in participant information sheets. Although relatively 'safe' compared to some other forms of research, the main risk through participation in qualitative research is usually the potential emotional cost of reflecting on sensitive topics and possibly reliving difficult experiences through the medium of the research interview. The likelihood of this occurrence should not be underestimated, and it is relatively common for informants to display emotional reactions in one-to-one interviews, regardless of the informant group.

Whereas such emotional reactions should never be greeted with alarm, they always require acknowledgement, and if addressing very sensitive topics, it is often useful to have a distress protocol in place that has been agreed with the ethics committee (for an example see Box 4.3). The first step in any distress protocol is usually to offer to pause the recorder and take a break from the interview if required. However, this shouldn't become invalidating for informants (King and Horrocks 2010), many of whom may prefer to continue with their story, in which case simple acknowledgement of emotional content through eye contact and sympathetic body language is usually the best approach. Other elements of the research protocol might include offering information about external help sources at the end of the interview, which should be as up to date and specific as possible, or offering to contact family members for support. In extremely rare cases, it may be appropriate to contact external support without the permission of the informant, although this would normally only be a consideration in research with particularly high-risk groups where there is a realistic concern for the safety of the informant or another person.

In addition, the researcher must ensure that the conduct and reporting of research does not stigmatize particular communities of people, particularly where those communities are already vulnerable or lack a powerful voice in society (Kvale 1996). Researchers should only ever seek to cast light on the social world of participants, highlighting its challenges and difficulties

BOX 4.3. EXAMPLE OF A DISTRESS PROTOCOL

All interviews will be prefaced with a statement about confidentiality and the duty of care. Participants will be told that the interview is strictly confidential, but should they disclose information to suggest that they are at significant risk of harm, the interviewer may have to discuss this with a clinical advisor.

In the event that an interviewee appears to be distressed during the interview (e.g., becomes silent, cries) or discloses information to provoke concern about suicide risk, the following procedures will be followed:

- Respondents will be offered the opportunity to pause for a break from the interview and will then be asked if they would like to resume.
- If necessary, the interview will be terminated and recording equipment stopped.
- At first, the interviewer will listen to the interviewee and offer support in situ. This will allow the researcher to assess whether further action is necessary.
- Should the interviewer remain concerned, he or she will reflect this to the interviewee and depending on the nature of the situation

    1. offer information about local help services,
    2. ask the interviewee if there is anyone he or she should contact and if so attempt to make contact,
    3. offer to make initial contact with clinical services (primary or secondary) on behalf of the individual and with his or her consent.

- In cases of particular concern, the interviewer will

    1. if necessary, remain with the person until the distress has subsided or someone else is present,
    2. contact a local study clinician for advice/assistance,
    3. provide a written report of the incident to (supervisors), including information about the nature of the distress and the actions taken.

Interviewees will be advised to contact their GP should they find subsequently that the interview provokes issues that they need to discuss.

where appropriate, but never to denigrate or cast judgement. The researcher should retain at least some level of self-awareness about the fundamental inequality in the research relationship, where informants give time and energy to the research, usually for no personal reward. It is this inequality that has led some commentators to characterize the qualitative research relationship as exploitative and advocate an 'action research' approach whereby participants are treated as equal partners in a research process which has the explicit objective of improving the conditions of those under study (Oakley 1981).

A further consideration under the theme of non-maleficence is the duty to protect researchers themselves. Rewarding as it is to conduct interviews in informants' homes in diverse locations, this inevitably places researchers at some degree of personal risk, which needs to be properly assessed and managed. Most universities will have in place a lone fieldworker protocol, which should, as a bare minimum, require that a responsible individual in researchers' host institution has information about where researchers have gone, what time they are expected back and a protocol for action if contact is not made by the agreed time (which should range from calling researchers' personal mobile to, as a last resort, contacting the emergency services). To protect informant confidentiality, the address of the informant should be kept in a sealed envelope, which can be returned unopened to the researcher provided there was no need for any further action. The emotional well-being of researchers is also important; if the interviews are addressing difficult or distressing topics, it is important for interviewers to have a scheduled 'de-brief' with a colleague to manage their own emotional reactions to what has been disclosed, a process used with the end-of-life work reported here in the chapters by Canaway et al. and Bailey et al. (Chapters 12 and 14).

CONCLUSION

In this chapter in-depth consideration has been given to the three main methods used in qualitative data collection – individual interviewing, focus groups and systematic observations. The research question is of fundamental importance to the method chosen, and key considerations include the sort of data required (can it be 'observed' or is it only available through recounting?), whose interpretation of the social world is sought (the researchers' or the informants'?) and the nature of any limitations on the availability and completeness of accounts. Depending on the complexity of the research question, one method of data collection might be sufficient, or it may be necessary to combine multiple methods to obtain a well-rounded view of social phenomena. Whatever the case, it is essential that researchers have undergone adequate training in the method(s) used and are prepared for the intellectual and often emotional challenges ahead.

Qualitative research is necessarily a human endeavour. Data are usually constructed through the interaction of two or more individuals, one of whom is often the researcher. Its 'truth', such as it can be determined, is usually dependent on the establishment of rapport with participants, nearly all of whom will give freely of their time and energy and engage enthusiastically with the research objectives. This in turn imposes an absolute duty on the researcher to conduct ethical, scientifically sound research with an overall objective of improving the lot of humankind and, for some commentators, the social situation of communities under study (Oakley 1981).

Although considered sequentially in this book, it is important to regard data collection as part of an iterative cycle with data analysis and ongoing sampling. The sort of data that will be generated and a plan for its analysis need to be considered prior to starting data collection, and the analytic process needs to be started as soon as possible following each episode of data collection (Kvale 1996). New themes and insights should be recorded in field notes or operational memos, and ongoing sampling and data collection should aim to develop theoretical explanations of the social phenomena observed (Glaser and Strauss 1968). Analysis techniques are considered in detail in the next chapter.

Chapter 5

Understanding primary data analysis

Joanna Coast and Louise Jackson

Qualitative data analysis is likely to be the area of qualitative research with which health economists are most unfamiliar, and indeed, it may seem somewhat mystical, with notions of 'themes arising from the data' but little sense of the process by which this might happen. Analysis is also one of the most difficult aspects of qualitative research for the inexperienced researcher to grasp. This chapter therefore takes a very 'hands-on' approach to the notion of data analysis, providing a detailed description of analytic techniques used by the authors in previous work and showing that robust analysis of qualitative data can create rich insights into key economic issues in health.

The chapter begins, however, by considering the nature of analysis that might be required for qualitative data in the economic setting. Given the different methodological strategies outlined for qualitative research in Chapter 2, each of which has its own analytic processes and procedures, it is obvious that this book cannot do justice to them all; it also does not need to do so. As will become clear from early in this chapter, there has been a relatively limited set of analytic strategies used within the existing qualitative research within health economics. There are good reasons for this, which are related to the particular purposes of qualitative research within health economics and the need of qualitative research conducted within the discipline to enhance economic thinking. Other strategies may, of course, sometimes be helpful in studying economic issues, but these are well detailed in more general texts (Creswell 2013; Grbich 2013; Patton 2015).

The first section of this chapter expands this reasoning, focusing on the nature of qualitative data analysis within health economics and important characteristics that such analysis should fulfill. The second section of the chapter then briefly considers general approaches to the analysis of qualitative data. The major section of the chapter then provides a detailed description of an approach to data analysis that draws on the constant comparison approach and that has previously been used within health economics. It has been used in the generation of theoretical models to aid understanding (Coast 2001a, 2001b), in the generation of measures drawing on the economic theory of capability (Al-Janabi, Flynn, et al. 2012; Sutton and Coast 2014; Canaway, Al-Janabi, et al. 2017) and in the generation of attributes for discrete choice experiments (Coast and Horrocks 2007; Coast, Al-Janabi, et al. 2012). The approach to analysis is outlined, and then a detailed example of its use in practice is given, to aid readers in fully understanding how the approach might be applied. The final section of the chapter briefly considers some analytic challenges that economics might face.

QUALITATIVE DATA ANALYSIS FOR (HEALTH) ECONOMICS

While Smith (Chapter 20) makes a passionate plea for greater consideration of methodology and use of established methodological traditions within qualitative health economics research, and in the area of priority setting particularly, it is also important to note that these traditions derive from areas of social science with quite different disciplinary foci from that within economics. The foundations of qualitative research are generally seen to lie within the disciplines of anthropology and sociology, often in the form of ethnographic work (Snape and Spencer 2003). In anthropology, early studies involved the ethnographer reporting on non-Western peoples and cultures and in sociology observations were carried out in local communities and towns (Padgett 2016). Qualitative methods experienced rapid growth from the 1960s, retaining a key concern with inductive analysis, often with priority being given to bringing out the experiences and perspectives of the participants in the research (Starr 2014). Ethnography derives from anthropology, hence its focus on culture; phenomenology from philosophy and psychology, hence its focus on values; and narrative from history and other disciplines, hence the focus on stories.

Within health economics, as indicated in earlier chapters, there is little tradition of qualitative research, and different aspects of research share commonalities with different existing approaches to qualitative research. For example, work focusing on health systems shares much in common with ethnographic approaches, combining data collection techniques within cases studies and very often including both observation and interviews, with researchers working in these areas understanding that generating a rounded view of how a system works may not be achieved without seeing what people within a system actually do, as well as what they say that they do. The case study chapters focusing on aid effectiveness (Chapter 18) and priority setting systems (Chapter 19), and indeed the chapter from Husbands and colleagues which studies systems for conducing decision analytic modelling within health economics (Chapter 13), all show these characteristics of ethnographic approaches. Unlike ethnography, however, the aim is not purely to produce rich description of these systems (cultures) but to generate models and theories around how these systems work. Health economics qualitative research focusing on values and attribute development, however, probably has more in common with phenomenological approaches than ethnography. Generating attributes requires a focus on what is important to people in a particular situation (Coast, Al-Janabi, et al. 2012), to develop understanding about individuals' lived experiences within a particular context. Yet the aim of such health economics research is quite different from the aim usually associated with phenomenological research. It is not to distil that lived experience down to its essence but rather to reduce that lived experience into its constituent parts so that this information can be used to generate quantitative information about preferences for different aspects of a situation. Again, the purpose differs and health economists are more focused on generating a model of what might influence preferences for a particular state, with the intention of testing that model and providing quantitative information about relative strength of preferences. This can be seen clearly in the chapter by Vosper and colleagues (Chapter 10), where the research focuses very much on themes that would be familiar with phenomenological research: experiences of depression and treatments for that depression. But the analytic approach was quite different, drawing on thematic and constant comparative approaches, with the purpose of attribute development for a discrete choice experiment at the forefront. A similar approach can be seen in the work of Stevens (Chapter 11) in relation to the development of measurement instruments for children.

While (health) economists can undoubtedly work within these different methodological approaches, following them fully or unquestioningly may not provide an optimal strategy for understanding economic phenomena or the health economy. In the case study chapters here, as well as in the published literature, health economists have had to make methodological choices around data collection and analysis that might be considered unconventional for other disciplines and which could lead to the accusation that data collection and analytic strategies are uninformed and/or 'generic' in nature because they do not subscribe to a particular approach. This is largely, however, because of the differing aims and objectives for research in health economics and the need to inform research in the economics discipline. Indeed, as in other areas of research, economists' philosophical, methodological and analytic choices when using qualitative methods are often carefully thought through and aim to reconcile the conflicting nature of economic theory and approaches with those more common in qualitative research. Economists, particularly when conducting research to enhance the collection of quantitative data or explain quantitative findings, often start from quite a pragmatic philosophy (Creswell 2013), where they are focused on the end goal of their research. Alternatively, the philosophy may be one that combines a realist ontology with a more interpretative epistemology (Creswell 2013) such as the subtle realism of Hammersley (1992) or the type of critical realist approach discussed by Maxwell (2012).

Indeed, the chapters within this book and the growing, albeit still small, published literature using qualitative methods within health economics give some sense of the prevailing analytic approaches within health economics. They attempt to use, but not be bound by, existing economic theory as, for example, in Baker (2006), alluded to in the chapter by Baker and colleagues (Chapter 9) which used economic theory around rationality to develop the Q sort, or in the work reported by Martínez-Álvarez here (Chapter 18) which started from principal-agent theory within economics but went beyond that in analysing the data inductively as well as deductively. Economic theory, whether normative (as in the case of Canaway et al.'s research on determining social network boundaries for economic evaluation, Chapter 12) or positive (as in the case of De Allegri's research on results-based financing, Chapter 17) provides the context for qualitative research within health economics, and the lens through which these researchers examine data is guided by this understanding of the world.

There appear to be two main things that most frequently characterize the approaches within health economics to the analysis of qualitative data, and that together unite to provide the strongest overall approach to such analysis: the application of an economic lens to the analysis and the generation of outputs in terms of description alongside theory that takes the form of models. These characteristics are vital in generating work that is relevant to (health) economics and that can be meaningfully used within the discipline.

The application of an economics lens to analysis means that researchers will derive and explain their findings in terms that are meaningful to economists. Coast's work on understanding societal decision making, for example, was couched in terms of agency relationships and disutility (Coast 2001a, 2001b). Bertone and Lagarde's research on health worker incomes highlights issues such as fragmentation of incomes, income stability and financial incentives (Bertone and Lagarde 2016). Cruz and McPake's research on management of poor performance in aid effectiveness in the Ugandan health sector was framed in terms of agency theory and focused on aid performance appraisal systems, donor incentives and contracting issues (Cruz and McPake 2010). It does not mean that economists should be limited to existing economic theory, much of which is deductively derived from axioms and assumptions that may have questionable validity, but that they should apply an economic lens drawing on the underlying concerns of economics: scarcity, resources, allocation, distribution, value, utility, demand, supply, equity, choice and efficiency. A good example of analysing data through an economic lens is provided by a recent paper by Walker et al., who focused on understanding the economic issues affecting patients and their carers when undergoing dialysis for kidney disease, and the extent to which economic issues dictate the choice of dialysis modality (Walker, Howard, et al. 2016). They found three main themes arising from their data: '(i) productivity losses associated with changes in employment; (ii) the need for personal subsidization of home dialysis expenses; and (iii) the role of socio-economic disadvantage as a barrier to home dialysis' (Walker, Howard, et al. 2016, p. 634).

The generation of outputs that take the form of models is advantageous both because most of economic theory is conceptualized in terms of models and because this is how economists tend to think. Here the term 'model' is not used in the sense of the decision analytic models that health economists might be particularly familiar with but in the more general economic sense, of a set of relationships that can explain an economic phenomenon. Models might be large in scope, focusing on whole aspects of the health economy, such as in Coast's exploration of health care rationing (Coast 2001a), or they may be smaller in scope, for example, relating to aspects influencing demand for a particular service, as in the work of Coast and colleagues to generate attributes to explain demand for different types of dermatology services (Coast and Horrocks 2007). Further, the overall model may depend purely on the qualitative findings, as in the rationing example earlier, or on the combination of qualitative and quantitative findings, as in the dermatology example (Coast, Salisbury, et al. 2006). Importantly, such models typically go beyond the generation of rich description; for some other disciplines this may be a valuable endpoint from qualitative research, but it is unlikely to be considered fully useful within the economics discipline. The description of context alongside models developed from the data is, however, vital in understanding the applicability of the resultant model. It is particularly important for economics where much theory development takes place in a contextual vacuum and where the resultant causal models can therefore be problematic when applied to practical situations. Nevertheless, the familiarity of economists with such models, and their training in using them, means that they tend to be adept at seeing linking connections when conducting qualitative analysis. Economists may also find it easier to take the sort of reductive approach to qualitative data analysis that such models ultimately require than those researchers in other disciplines more used to descriptive approaches to qualitative data analysis; for economists, perhaps, the trick is to give due attention to the description of context alongside the theoretical development, to ensure that models are rich and grounded in the data: 'It is the context that provides for interpretative meaning. Good . . . accounts point out the multiplicity of meanings and perspectives, and the rationality of these perspectives, by setting forth the context(s)' (Altheide and Johnson 1994, p. 496).

GENERAL APPROACHES TO ANALYSING DATA

Although the first section of this chapter advocates a particular way of thinking about qualitative analysis, it is worth being clear that there are many aspects of qualitative analysis that are common across the different philosophical and methodological approaches (Miles and Huberman 1994; Rapley 2011; Creswell 2013). These may, however, be expressed in different terminologies and may have different emphases in terms of the importance with which they are seen within the different approaches; there are also some aspects of analysis that differ between approaches (Creswell 2013). Creswell's work, on five different approaches to qualitative research, provides a current and very useful introduction to the similarities and differences between the major analytic approaches for the reader who wants more understanding of these issues (Creswell 2013). Specialized forms of analysis focusing on language, conversation and discourse are not considered here but are covered elsewhere (Heritage 2011; Sidnell and Stivers 2013).

As well as the different philosophical and methodological approaches, analytic approaches also differ according to the extent to which they focus on deductive or inductive forms of analysis. Some forms of analysis employ coding or categorization systems developed prior to the conduct of the research (e.g., template analysis/qualitative content analysis [Crabtree and Miller 1992; Morgan 1992; Miles and Huberman 1994; Sandelowski 2000]), and others are entirely or almost entirely dependent on the data obtained (Glaser and Strauss 1968; Hammersley and Atkinson 1983; Strauss and Corbin 1990; Addison 1992); yet other approaches explicitly allow for both deductive and inductive coding to be used, as in framework analysis (Ritchie and Lewis 2003; Gale, Heath, et al. 2013). Essentially, the difference between these approaches relates to the extent to which research is guided from the beginning by existing evidence and the extent to which theory emerges during the analysis (Barbour 1998). All of these approaches have been used within health economics. For example, Russo and McPake in a study of medicine prices in Mozambique used deductive coding based on the neoclassical structure-conduct-performance framework (Russo and McPake 2010), McKie and colleagues began their coding of principles for resource allocation from codes derived from the literature but added to this on the basis of the research data (McKie, Shrimpton, et al. 2011) and in a study of priority setting in Jordan, codes were generated inductively from the data (Lafi, Robinson, et al. 2012).

There are, however, as identified by Miles and Huberman, common elements to the process followed by much qualitative data analysis, which involve the following:

- *Affixing codes to a set of field notes drawn from observations or interviews.*
- *Noting reflections or other remarks in the margins.*
- *Sorting and sifting through these materials to identify similar phrases, relationships between variables, patterns, themes, distinct differences between subgroups, and common sequences.*
- *Isolating these patterns and processes, commonalities and differences, and taking them out to the field in the next wave of data collection*
- *Gradually elaborating a small set of generalisations that cover the consistencies discerned in the database*
- *Confronting these generalisations with a formalised body of knowledge in the form of constructs or theories.* (Miles and Huberman 1994, p. 9)

In a similar vein, Rapley identifies central methods that cut across the majority of qualitative data analysis:

- *Always start by engaging in some kind of close, detailed, reading of a sample/section/bit of your archive of data . . .*
- *Always read and systematically label your archive of data . . .*
- *Always reflect on why you've done what you've done . . .*
- *Always review and refine your labels and labelling practices . . .*
- *Always focus on what you feel are the key labels and the relationship between them . . .*
- *Always make notes of your thinking behind why you've done what you've done . . .*
- *Always return to the field with the knowledge you have already gained in mind and let this knowledge modify, guide or shape the data you want to collect next.* (Rapley 2011, pp. 278–9)

Rapley feels that the last two of these are aspects that are central but are not included in some approaches (Rapley 2011).

The ideal is that data from one piece of fieldwork should be coded before the next fieldwork is undertaken (Hammersley and Atkinson 1983; Miles and Huberman 1994) and that the ongoing analysis influences the sampling of further data (Glaser and Strauss 1968; Rapley 2011). Analysis thus goes on throughout the research process, with the researcher continually forming and re-forming explanations and testing hypotheses while generating data, hence acquiring deeper understanding (Glaser and Strauss 1968; Hammersley and Atkinson 1983; Strauss and Corbin 1990; Addison 1992; Gold 1997; Rapley 2011). Glaser and Strauss advocate the constant comparative method, in which new data are compared, initially to previous data and, as the analysis progresses, to the properties of emerging categories (Glaser and Strauss 1968). Such comparisons facilitate the development of a tightly integrated theory, with so-called negative cases accounted for in departures from the main findings (Gold 1997).

In conducting analysis it is important to be close to the data in the sense of having full knowledge of and familiarity with these data (Hammersley and Atkinson 1983; Richards 1998). Coding/categorizing/labelling the data is a key aspect of analysis and is ongoing throughout the analytic process (Rapley 2011). Sensitivity to the data is important (Hammersley and Atkinson 1983); theoretical sensitivity can be enhanced using a number of techniques related to questioning the data (Strauss and Corbin 1990). Writing is of key importance and can encompass both brief memos and much longer analytic accounts (Rapley 2011); memos can be used to note down theoretical insights during the analysis (Strauss and Corbin 1990). Various forms of software can be used to facilitate coding and retrieval of data, from basic word processing packages to more sophisticated software (Reid 1992; Ziebland 1996; Gale, Heath, et al. 2013).

An essential part of analysis is synthesis and interpretation of data, including the ability to abstract (Rapley 2011) and thus provide understanding that may escape informants who are closely involved with a particular situation (Richards 1998). This synthesis of data may be achieved through a number of techniques, including the writing of detailed analytic accounts, the use of charts or matrices that facilitate the identification of contrasting and similar data and the use of various visualization techniques. All of these methods have been used by qualitative studies in health economics. For example, Coast developed detailed descriptive accounts and generated comparative matrices for her work on citizen–agent relationships in health care decision making (Coast 2001a, 2001b), Geneau et al. used data matrices including supporting quotes and sequentially generated visual representations of their conceptual framework in understanding willingness to pay for cataract surgery (Geneau, Massae, et al. 2008) and Stevens generated matrices of sub-themes for areas of health-related quality of life that kept the language used by the children participating in the study and then mapped relationships between themes and sub-themes on a large chart (Stevens 2010).

DATA ANALYSIS IN PRACTICE: DETAILED EXPLORATION OF ANALYTIC TECHNIQUES FOR HEALTH ECONOMICS

Making analytic choices

Within the case studies presented in this book, there are broadly two analytic strategies. It is notable that both draw heavily on approaches that are not bound to particular qualitative theoretical perspectives: one approach draws on aspects of grounded theory, in particular a constant comparative approach to analysis (Glaser and Strauss 1968; Glaser 2005; Charmaz and Bryant 2011), and the other focuses on thematic content analysis aligned with framework analysis with its systematic approach to charting (Ritchie and Lewis 2003; Gale, Heath, et al. 2013). The first of these approaches is used in chapters led by Vosper (Chapter 10), Canaway (Chapter 12), Bailey (Chapter 14) and Kinghorn (Chapter 16). The second is used in chapters led by Stevens (Chapter 11), Husbands (Chapter 13); Martínez-Álvarez (Chapter 18) and Eckhard (Chapter 19); the chapter by Martínez-Álvarez is particularly useful in setting out the use of the framework approach in an economic context. Two other chapters make slightly different analytic choices, but those are also similarly not bound with any specific qualitative theoretical perspective: Baker and colleagues use thematic categorization to generate statements for a Q-sort (Chapter 9), and Robinson (Chapter 15) uses modified induction drawing on the work of Miles and Huberman (1994). Smith (Chapter 20) discusses the value of using multiple analytic approaches, and De Allegri (Chapter 17) is focused specifically on design and sampling issues in her work.

These choices are also reflected in published research. Much work has drawn on grounded theory and constant comparative approaches to data analysis (Coast 2001a, 2001b; De Allegri, Sanon, et al. 2006b; Coast and Horrocks 2007; Geneau, Massae, et al. 2008; Al-Janabi, Flynn, et al. 2012; Sutton and Coast 2012, 2014; Canaway, Al-Janabi, et al. 2017). For example, one study focusing on better understanding how households arrive at their decisions about their willingness to pay for cataract surgery in Tanzania used a grounded theory approach given the complex and multidimensional nature of the phenomena being studied (Geneau, Massae, et al. 2008). The authors started by generating open coding and initial lists of categories, which were then combined as they explored how the different categories were interconnected. Much work has also drawn on thematic (Robinson and Bryan 2013) and framework approaches (Grewal, Lewis, et al. 2006; Stevens 2009, 2010; Kinghorn, Robinson, et al. 2014; Bertone and Lagarde 2016; Miners, Llewellyn, et al. 2016).

These analytic choices are important because, on the whole, they allow researchers to operate explicitly within an economics framework: using an economic lens for analysis and focusing on models as the outputs from the analysis. They emphasize slightly different aspects of the analytic process, with the constant comparative approach explicitly drawing out aspects of theoretical development and providing useful techniques for enhancing theoretical sensitivity (Strauss and Corbin 1990), and the structure of the framework approach enabling, sometimes larger, research teams to handle high quantities of data with relative ease (Gale, Heath, et al. 2013).

Researchers have to make their own analytic choices. These will depend in part on their philosophy, in part on what they want to achieve and the depth with which they want to achieve it, and in part on their own strengths and weaknesses. It should also be noted that these analytic choices range from the very theoretical to the quite mundane! As an indication of what is meant by this, we outline briefly some of the choices that Coast has made in her own data analysis:

- Taking a subtle realist approach to the analysis, meaning that she sees a single reality that she is trying to access through her analysis of qualitative data but that she believes that reality has to be accessed through layers of context and perception (Hammersley 1992)
- Using a constant comparative approach (Glaser and Strauss 1968; Strauss and Corbin 1990) to generate models and allow her work to relate to economic theory, although she has used framework in the past and has recommended it to others for analysis in particular contexts, including the work by Husbands in this book (Chapter 13)
- Comparing newly generated data initially to previously generated data and then, as the analysis progresses and categories have been established, comparing new data to these emerging categories, enabling her to generate explanations and to continually re-form these in the light of new data arriving. Essentially, Coast is working within a circular, iterative process where she is generating new hypotheses from the data and testing them on new data, to generate a deeper understanding of a particular area (Glaser and Strauss 1968; Strauss and Corbin 1990; Gold 1997)
- Categorizing data (coding) through the process of cutting and pasting data within a word processing software package, which she finds provides greater convenience than the use of physical transcripts and greater flexibility than the use of dedicated qualitative computer packages
- Using the process of writing extensively, generating analytic accounts that describe the data, develop and clarify ideas, and that create and test theoretical models

And while many qualitative texts retain an air of mystique around the analytic process, there are increasingly descriptions available of what researchers actually do with their data, which can be particularly helpful for the novice in this area (Rapley 2011; Creswell 2013). That is also the focus for the rest of this section, which first outlines step-by-step details of an approach to analysis that can form the basis for the application of an economic lens and the generation of economic models and then provides a case study of data analysis within health economics. The case study thus illustrates the various steps of data analysis within an analytic approach that draws on the method of constant comparison (Glaser and Strauss 1968; Strauss and Corbin 1990) and also on the writing of analytic accounts.

The analytic process

This section focuses on describing a number of steps associated with the analytic process.

Initial analytic design issues

Before starting the analysis, there are some issues associated with the design of the analysis that researchers have to consider. An initial question that analysts may have to decide on if they have more than one data source is how to deal with these: should they be all joined together from the start? Or should they be dealt with separately? Data may be derived just from one type of data collection or through different data collection methods; they may also be derived from one or more sources. How the analyst should deal with this issue is likely to be related to both the research question posed and the depth of data achieved through different sources. For example, if different data sources and types of informants are all providing different interpretations on the same question, it makes sense to analyse the data together. If they are providing interpretations on slightly different questions, it may make sense to conduct the analysis separately, at least initially.

A second issue for some research occurs where the qualitative data are collected in a language that is not the final language that the analysis will be reported in. See, for example, recent economic studies by Geneau and colleagues conducted in Tanzania and collecting data in Kiswahili but transcribing the data into English and conducting the analysis in English (Geneau, Massae, et al. 2008) and by Abiiro and colleagues conducted in Malawi with data translated into English before analysis (Abiiro, Leppert, et al. 2014). Here the researcher has to decide whether to analyse the data in the language of origin or to translate prior to analysis. This may be a pragmatic decision; if the researcher cannot speak the original language, then translation may be required. There are issues in working with translated data, however, in terms of the choices that are made in translation and the extent to which these choices influence the data analysis, that researchers should be aware of in conducting their analysis (Temple, Edwards, et al. 2006).

Managing the data

A key aspect of analysis is the choice about how to manage the available data. Interview and focus group data will generally be audio-recorded, but to make it manageable for analysis, it will need to be transcribed. Then there is the question of how analysts will physically conduct the process of coding and organizing their work. This physical process of data analysis can be conducted in a number of ways. Coast has worked with researchers using techniques that varied from the least technical of highlighting printed transcripts, cutting these up and moving them around on the floor through similar cutting and pasting of data within word processing packages to the more technical application of codes within a dedicated qualitative software package. Her own preference is to cut and paste data within word processing packages, as she tends to find the dedicated software packages too restrictive as the analysis progresses; her interpretation of data is enhanced once she starts the process of writing, and having everything pre-coded is then unhelpful. The flexibility of being able to move excerpts of data around a word processing package enables new insights to be readily accommodated in the ongoing analysis, without having to recode data within the dedicated package. Others, however, prefer the comprehensiveness and structure of dedicated software packages. This choice about data management can thus hinge on the degree of flexibility required in using the data as well as preferred working practices and the methodological approach being taken. Decisions about data management may also rest on the size of the research team and the data set, and dedicated software packages may be particularly valuable for larger research teams with large quantities of data and multiple coders.

Immersion in the data

Knowing the data is a vital aspect of analysis, and there is much value in spending sufficient time on this process. Immersing oneself in the data will enable insights to be generated and connections to be made (Hammersley and Atkinson 1983; Hansen 2006). There are many ways of achieving this immersion: listening to tape recordings, transcribing the data, listening to tape recordings while checking transcripts and reading and re-reading the transcripts.

Initial categorization

Once analysts are familiar with their data, the process of categorization or coding can begin. Saldaña defines a code as 'a word or short phase that symbolically assigns a summative, salient, essence-capturing, and/or evocative attribute to a portion of language-based or visual data' (Saldaña 2015, p. 4). It is helpful to start this process with hard copies of the transcripts, with sufficiently large margins to enable writing to be clearly visible. The idea is to make notes on a line-by-line basis of what is being said in the transcripts. It is helpful if these categories are generated in a hierarchical manner to avoid having very many unconnected codes (Miles and Huberman 1994).

At the start of this process of writing down coding notes on the transcript, these 'categories' will usually be a single word. For example, in early text stating 'I think priority should be given to children, yes, rather than the elderly', initial code notes written on the transcript might be 'priority' and 'children'. As the analysis progresses, other connected types of phrases might be noted, such as 'Well as regards self-induced illnesses like sclerosis of the liver or obesity, unless it's a glandular problem some people can't help it they're overweight, I wouldn't prioritize those'. The code note for this second phrase might be something like 'personal fault'. As more of these justifications for prioritization arise, the code note on the transcript might change from just 'personal fault' to something that more explicitly places the code note into a potential hierarchy, for example, 'priority-justification-personal fault'. Essentially, but still with nothing fixed, the analyst is starting to see and draw the data into potential families of categories.

This early open (Strauss and Corbin 1990) or expansive (Merriam and Tisdell 2016) coding in the initial stages of the early analysis should be carried out on a small number of these transcripts. It is important to note that the codes can be applied to single words, phrases, sentences or slightly longer pieces of text. It is also important to note that more than one code can be applied to any piece of text.

Seeing what is in the data is an important part of this coding (Hammersley and Atkinson 1983; Strauss and Corbin 1990), and there are techniques that can help with this. Strauss and Corbin outline a number of effective approaches that are 'especially useful in analyzing the first few interviews, field observations and document, because they help to "see" what is in the data' (Strauss and Corbin 1990, p. 94). These include the use of 'questioning' – asking 'who', 'what', 'why', 'when', 'where', 'how' and 'how much' of the data and the issues arising from the data – and using this to enable the analyst to see both what is in the data and what might need to be pursued in further interviews. For example, in the two excerpts used earlier, the analyst might ask questions such as 'why' children should be prioritized or self-induced illnesses should be de-prioritized, but also how this should happen, at what point, who should do it, the extent of the prioritization and so on.

Strauss and Corbin also include techniques focusing on specific words, phrases or sentences to open up meaning, making comparisons at the extremes of dimensions (referred to as the 'flip-flop' technique), systematically comparing two or more phenomena (Strauss and Corbin 1990). These techniques are not intended to impose the views of the researcher onto the data but rather 'they function to sensitize a researcher to know what to look for. They are designed to free up thinking, and awaken sensitivity' (Strauss and Corbin 1990, p. 94).

It is at this point that the economic lens starts to be applied to the data. The aim is not to blindly impose existing economic theory – which, after all, may have been generated in a very deductive manner and may have limited validity – but rather to be sensitive to economic concepts arising in the data; applying the economic lens to what is there in the data. For example, in the two excerpts earlier, the economic lens in conjunction with the questioning outlined earlier may start to suggest that these excerpts perhaps express a concern with fair innings (in the first case) or culpability (in the second), and further data within the transcript may be used to explore these issues and to broaden out these concepts as the analysis progresses.

In generating a coding schedule to use to start to formally code the data, it can then be helpful to use visualization techniques such as spider diagrams or mind maps to start to put the potential categories onto a single page, to clarify what the categories and subcategories might be and also to start to see where categories might overlap. This process is aided if there has already been an element of hierarchical thinking included in this initial coding.

Ideally, this process of the initial coding should be carried out by more than one person, for example, different members of the research team, or the doctoral student and all of the supervisory team. The terms used and potential coding schemes generated can then be compared and discussed so that the coding scheme eventually applied draws on different expertise and experience and thus has greater validity.

Reviewing and refining through writing analytic accounts

Once this initial categorization or open coding has been applied to the first set of data, the data can be organized according to these codes and the process of bringing these data back together can begin. Essentially, through the process of comparison, the analyst is looking for connections within the data and between categories (Strauss and Corbin 1990; Maxwell 2012). In relation to grounded theory, for example, Strauss and Corbin talk about this process in very structured ways, in terms of what they refer to as 'axial coding', which concerns relating subcategories to categories, following a particular structure that ultimately links causal conditions to consequences, through thinking about the phenomenon, the context in which it occurs, intervening conditions and what they refer to as action/interactional strategies which relate to a particular approach used by these authors in generating their theory (Strauss and Corbin 1990). In the formal grounded theory approach, the process of conducting this axial coding happens through writing detailed memos that relate to these theoretical links (Strauss and Corbin 1990).

Bringing the data back together can also be achieved through the process of writing analytic accounts that both describe the data in context and make the connections between categories and subcategories. The notion of extensive writing is particularly associated with ethnographic approaches to data analysis (Hammersley and Atkinson 1983; Rapley 2011). As Rapley suggests:

> The focus that writing enables is so incredibly helpful in both establishing what you know (and don't know) and assisting you in making conceptual leaps. Transforming your thoughts onto paper or onto the screen, throughout the life of the project, inscribes them with form and solidity. The act of writing is a rich

> and analytic process as you find yourself not only attempting to explain and justify your ideas, but also developing them. (Rapley 2011, p. 286)

Researchers from many methodological approaches, however, concur with these views: Dey (pragmatic approach, social policy) suggests that 'producing an account is not just a question of reporting results, it is also another method of producing these results' (Dey 2003, p. 245); Charmaz (constructivist grounded theory) indicates that 'you will gain further insights and create more ideas about your data while you are writing. You will see clearer connections between categories and draw implications from them. Thus writing and rewriting become crucial phases of the analytic process' (Charmaz 2014, p. 290); Hansen (writing within health) states that 'writing in fact plays a crucial role in analysing qualitative data' (Hansen 2006, p. 162); and Ritchie and colleagues (framework) suggest that 'the process of actually writing a summarised or synthesised account begins to trigger the vital insights into, or questions about, the data that will lead to the later interpretative stages of analysis' (Ritchie, Spencer, et al. 2003, p. 237).

Writing accounts forces analysts to confront the extent of their understanding and the extent to which their data support or do not support the emerging theoretical framework. The coded data form the basis for these analytic accounts and allow analysts to explore these data within informants' contexts. They include quotes to illustrate points and aim to show where views of informants coincide or contrast. They comprise 'quotes from interviews and interpretative narrative' (Al-Janabi, Flynn, et al. 2012, p. 169). Early accounts tend to be more descriptive (descriptive accounts), and later accounts involve more interpretation (explanatory accounts) as the emerging theory is developed and clarified (Ritchie, Spencer, et al. 2003); this might also be reflected in a changing coding framework. A good example from within health economics is the work of Al-Janabi and colleagues in generating attributes for the ICECAP-A, where early accounts focused on describing the factors that informants spoke about in terms of a good life, and later accounts began to develop the theoretical focus.

> Each transcript was coded in the ATLAS.ti qualitative data analysis package with codes initially reflecting the set of issues covered in the interviews (see 'prompts' in the Appendix) and the emerging understanding about how each of these issues affected capability wellbeing. For subsequent batches of interviews in phase one, the codes used reflected less the specific influences on wellbeing (e.g., work) and more the concepts that could be influenced by multiple factors (e.g., stress). This changing coding framework was used to ensure interview data were organised into themes that represented what was ultimately important in individuals' lives rather than the external prompts introduced during the discussion. (Al-Janabi, Flynn, et al. 2012, p. 169)

It is helpful to formulate these accounts in batches as data collection and analysis progress simultaneously. Coast in her analysis of citizen–agent relationships (see later) used approximately four interview transcripts per batch; Al-Janabi used five to eight per batch in developing the ICECAP-A (Al-Janabi, Flynn, et al. 2012); and Canaway used three to six in developing the ICECAP-CPM (Canaway, Al-Janabi, et al. 2017). Ideally, the quantity of data should be manageable and should relate to the inductive nature of the research and the possibility of returning to the field.

The construction of these analytic accounts may also be supported by the use of theoretical memos (separate notes outlining ideas and insights that occur to the analyst, making connections between categories and so on). These may be particularly useful in starting to generate economic interpretations of the data contained within the analytic accounts, drawing links between the accounts from informants and the existing economic theory.

Determining key relationships through data visualization techniques, external exposure of thinking and more writing

Various data visualization techniques can be helpful in identifying patterns across data. Matrices are one useful technique for facilitating comparison and contrast between informants and providing a concise display of data (Miles and Huberman 1994), and, indeed, in expanded form, provide the main approach to analysis within the framework approach (Ritchie and Lewis 2003; Gale, Heath, et al. 2013). Matrices can be very helpful in avoiding the tendency, pointed out by Miles and Huberman, to find simplifying patterns which may not exist when concentrating only on extended text (Miles and Huberman 1994). These matrices contain textual information and might be generated using pen and paper, or using spreadsheets. Another potentially helpful option is to use hierarchical tree diagrams showing various levels of abstraction within the data (Creswell 2013).

Use of these sorts of techniques might expose areas for further, more detailed investigation. For example, the work discussed by Canaway and colleagues in Chapter 12 identified deviant cases (those that did not conform to the generally emerging pattern) and explored these in greater depth to try to explain differences and improve the explanatory power of the analysis. This work also identified contrasting networks in terms of size and conducted detailed comparisons across these to identify important causal characteristics related to network size.

Testing thinking by exposing the emerging findings to critique is also important at this stage and can help clarify and strengthen thinking. This exposure of thinking can be with informants, with non-informants with similar experience and with academics. It is particularly helpful for health economists to expose their work and ideas within the economics community at this point, to generate feedback and to draw on areas of economic theory that the researcher may not have fully considered.

Further writing, drawing on these visualization techniques and exposure of ideas to others, is then helpful in continuing to draw out relationships and improve the understanding of the data. Using these visualization techniques as an aid, it is helpful to bring all the data together into a single full written account. This full written account may still draw mainly on the data, synthesizing it into a manageable length and fully drawing out the relationships within each of the categories and subcategories.

Reflecting and generating the final model

The final stage of the analysis involves further reflection and generation of the final model, reducing the data to the essential categories required for explanation and using the linking connections between them that have been generated in the earlier analysis. At this stage, the analyst draws on the analytic accounts and theoretical memos generated during the analysis, but also draws on evidence from outside the research in the general literature as a basis for thinking about the typicality of what has been found and linking to any existing relevant theory. There is a very explicit shift at this point to the economic lens and, where relevant, the use of economic terminology.

Again, the model is generated through writing and still needs to be linked to the evidence from the research in the form of quotes, but there may also be a diagrammatic representation of the theoretical understanding that has been generated. There also needs to be consideration of typicality and the extent to which the model might be useful outside the setting in which it was generated.

Case study example: citizen–agent decision making

This case study example is provided by one of the earliest attempts within health economics to use qualitative research to generate better theoretical understanding around an aspect of existing economic theory. The work explored citizen–agent relationships in health care (Coast 2001a, 2001b; Coast, Donovan, et al. 2002), drawing on principal-agent theory (Ross 1973; Smith, Stepan, et al. 1997; Scott and Vick 1999) and developing the application of this theory to health care decision making following the more deductive work of Gavin Mooney and Mandy Ryan (1993) and Lise Rochaix (1998). The research focused on whether a citizen–agent relationship, in which (some) health professionals act on behalf of the general public in making rationing decisions, existed in the UK health care setting. Other issues of interest were who might act as agents for citizens and whether citizens saw the need for such an agency relationship.

Data collection was largely through semi-structured interviews, with members of the public (citizens) and health service workers of various types (potential agents) selected from previous participation in focus groups held to discuss issues around the rationing of health care (Litva, Coast, et al. 2002). The data collected in the focus groups were also included in the final analysis because, although originally collected for a slightly different research question, these data contained valuable insights in relation to values in health care and the agency relationship. The research findings suggested that there was variation in how much citizens wanted to be involved in making decisions about health care rationing, while the health service informants saw a clear need for agents to make decisions on behalf of citizens and identified the grouping who should take on this role. It was also apparent from the findings, however, that any citizen–agent relationship was complex and imperfect and that final decisions did not neatly result from the perfect application of that relationship but instead from interactions between the utility functions of the different actors. It was concluded that 'in practice a system of equivocation can be envisaged in which different groups collude as they attempt to avoid the disutility associated with denying care, with the consequence that the impact of decisions taken on an explicitly societal or citizen basis may be relatively small' (Coast 2001a, p. 159).

Initial analytic design issues

In this case study, there were two data collection sources (individual interviews and focus groups), and there were also two sources of data (citizens and agents). In relation to the question of data sources, for this particular research it made sense to concentrate on the analysis of the interview data as a primary source, as this was where the specific research question was addressed, and to then weave in the focus group data where it addressed aspects of the citizen–agent research question. This was because data from the focus groups were collected with a somewhat different research purpose, with the concern there being primarily around public participation in the rationing process (Litva, Coast, et al. 2002) rather than values in health care or the agency relationship.

In relation to the two data sources, a decision was made to analyse transcripts of interviews held with individuals who had initially attended a focus group as a citizen/member of the public (and the associated focus group transcripts) separately from transcripts of interviews held with individuals who had attended as agents/health professionals (and their associated focus group transcripts). The main purpose of this split in the analysis was to compare and contrast the different perspectives of these two potentially very different sources of data on the specific research question. Analysis of data from the health professional 'agent' informants was carried out once the description across all citizens had been completed (which was also the order in which the interviews were conducted).

Managing the data

For this case study, all interviews were fully transcribed using a consistent standard originally based on work by Poland (1995), ensuring rigour in the transcription process. Analysis was conducted by cutting and pasting the data within a word processing package.

Immersion in the data

Some early transcription was carried out by the researcher and the remainder by an administrative member of staff. All transcripts were checked by listening to the original audio recording while reading the transcript and adjusting for any errors. This ensured that transcripts were accurate and extended the familiarity of the researcher with the data, before formal analysis began.

As interviews were conducted and tape recordings were transcribed, the transcripts were read and re-read looking for broad patterns and themes. Notes were made on the transcripts of phrases considered to have 'meaning' with respect to the central research questions as part of this immersion process.

Initial categorization

Initial categorization took place first with the citizen interview data. Notes were made on the initial transcripts, and the technique of 'questioning' (Strauss and Corbin 1990) was used to enhance theoretical sensitivity. Broad preliminary categories were generated, which seemed to relate to the developing patterns and the interpretation of the phrases noted on transcripts. These were the initially emerging themes. The active way in which themes 'emerge' should be noted here; they do not arrive passively from the data but are the product of the active role played by the researcher (Braun and Clarke 2006).

Details of the rationale for the development of these categories were kept in the form of memos (Strauss and Corbin 1990). In practice, these memos were separate computer files described as 'coding notes' and contained thoughts about the rationale and evidence for the categories and subcategories, explicitly drawing on the questioning technique. Seven categories were developed initially: 'depending', 'constraints', 'choosing', 'communicating', 'knowing', 'telling' and 'preferences and processing' (first-level codes), and subcategories of these codes were also generated (second-level codes). An initial coding schedule, comprising these seven categories, was developed and applied to the first four transcripts. Data were first categorized according to the first- and second-level codes developed. During this first set of analysis, the categories 'communicating' and 'choosing' were very quickly combined as 'choosing', while the 'telling' category was incorporated into the category 'knowing'. Definitions for these first- and second-level codes were generated so that it was clear which data were related to what category (see Table 5.1).

Table 5.1. Example definitions associated with first- and second-level analytic categories for citizen–agent example (Coast 2000b)

Depending	Relying on the health service
Care for all	Who should receive care
Care when needed	When care should be received
Quality care	What types of care should be received
Care without financial ruin	Costs of care
Constraints	Limits on what the health service is able to provide
Nature	Nature of limits on the health service
Changes over time	Changes in the nature of limits on the health service
Awareness	Awareness of the limits on the health service
Reality	Reality of limits on the health service
Morality	Ethical dimensions of limits on the health service
Solutions	Ways of dealing with limits on the health service
Choosing	Deciding what should be provided and to whom
Taking responsibility	Who currently takes responsibility; who should take responsibility; whether the informant wants to have any involvement/take any responsibility for choices; reasons for and against involvement
Principles	Difficulty or conflict in determining principles; definitions of principles
Knowing	Being aware that treatment has been refused – either implicitly or explicitly
Wanting to know	Reasons for wanting to know about restrictions on own care
Not wanting to know	Reasons for not wanting to know about restrictions on own care
Response to knowing	Response (hypothetical or otherwise) to knowing about restrictions on own care
Acting (agents only)	Whom agents perceive themselves, and others, to be acting on behalf of in relation to health care decision making
Politicians	Whom politicians act on behalf of
Health authority	Whom health authorities act on behalf of
General practitioners	Whom general practitioners act on behalf of
Trust	Whom hospital trusts act on behalf of
Hospital doctors	Whom hospital doctors (and other senior health professionals working in hospitals) act on behalf of
CHC	Whom the Community Health Council acts on behalf of

A second categorization of data was then conducted to develop lower-level codes (essentially subcategories) and to relate these codes in a hierarchical manner (Miles and Huberman 1994). Again, the aim was that all meaningful phrases could be accommodated and the 'questioning' technique was again used (Strauss and Corbin 1990).

The categories developed for use with citizens provided a starting point for the initial categorization of agent data. While some of the lower-level subcategories became obsolete, the five broad categories were applicable to the data from agents. It was also necessary to add an additional broad category: 'acting', which was used to code agents' views about whom those holding particular roles within the health care system (including themselves) act on behalf of.

In a similar manner, initial categorization of the focus group data was conducted following the analysis of interview data and using the main categories developed from the interview data.

Reviewing and refining through writing analytic accounts

An analytic account was completed for each of the five major categories generated during the initial categorization, using the data from the first four transcripts. This analytic account provided a detailed description of the data from the included interviews and was about 17,000 words (about forty-five pages) in length, including quotes. This written analytic account was given to an experienced qualitative researcher who provided comments on the categorization as well as further insights into the analysis. An excerpt from this first account is given in Box 5.1.

Subsequent citizen interview transcripts were also analysed in groups of four. Categories and subcategories were modified and extended as the remaining transcripts were analysed, until a comprehensive system of codes was achieved. Looking in detail at only four transcripts at any one time also made the task more manageable than it would otherwise have been. At this point in the analysis, separate analytic accounts were then developed for each individual citizen to ensure that each view was individually captured within its own context.

The transcripts for the agent informants were generally longer than those for citizen informants. Instead of initially forming analytic accounts for groups of four informants, therefore, the analysis was conducted by initially forming individual analytic accounts for each informant (based on the modified coding outlined earlier).

The sequential nature of the analysis meant that, following analysis of each group of transcripts, the analysis was able to inform subsequent interviews (although not to an ideal extent due to time constraints on transcription) and to aid in identifying the point at which saturation of the data was reached in

BOX 5.1. EXCERPT FROM FIRST ANALYTIC ACCOUNT FOR CITIZEN INFORMANT, BASED ON FIRST FOUR INTERVIEWS TRANSCRIBED

Care for all

All four informants talked about the importance of care being available to all.

IB4: I think the – the idea of treatment being available, regardless of your personal circumstances, that you can go and hope to get a reasonable level of medical care. I mean the last thing on earth I would want is to follow, as we do in so many things, follow the American, the United States way of doing things
IA4: . . . I think generally it should be available to all.
IC3: I think there should be care for everyone

A system whereby health care was not available to all was, in contrast, felt to be morally wrong.

IB4: . . . I have (.) on many occasions (.) heard of other people having experiences over there [USA] and feeling that it was just totally wrong.

Various reasons were given for this view. One reason was that the provision of health care was felt to be of great importance, and a system of care which was not available to all automatically could leave some people without health care or with very poor care.

IC3: Umm (. . . . . .) yes, I remember (.) as a child (.) living (.) in very (.) poor and what the medical service was like to those at the bottom end of the (.) scale so I think we have such a lot to be thankful for (.) umm [J: what was the medical service like?] non-existent unless you had (..) money or the barest (.) medical provision umm (.) yes yes (.) I remember my mother being terribly ill (.) umm (..) actually (.) yes she did have an operation but she was in the poor quarters . . . of the hospital you know, it was definitely the rich and the (.) and the poor
IC3: well because its so essential, so many of us a- of us are dependent on it aren't we? . . . for health care (..) I mean (.) what's my option (.) I don't have any umm private (..)

IG3: Yeah. I know that err (.) you know there's the wealthy element of society, and there's a poor element and so (.) um, (.) I think er not everybody can afford all these er insurance policies and err so forth and so uh (.) that's why I think it's important then you have a system there to help everybody, you know, I think it's a an important thing because it's to do with your health and you know and your well being.

Linked with this was the notion that those who would be unable to afford care privately might have greater need than others.

IA4: . . . people like income support? yes, I think they should [receive free health care] they probably need it more than people who have paid . . . so I think, yea

A further reason given was that, in practice, everybody eventually requires health care.

IB4: . . . everyone at some time or another needs to use the NHS or the vast majority of people do

terms of the generation of theory. Throughout the analysis, memos referred to as 'theoretical notes' were used to note down theoretical insights, particularly in terms of links with economic concepts (Strauss and Corbin 1990).

Determining key relationships through data visualization techniques, external exposure of thinking and more writing

Large matrices were developed to aid the visualization of data (Miles and Huberman 1994). For citizens, one large matrix was developed for each of the five main categories generated for the citizen informants. This was also the case for the agent informants, but with the additional 'acting' category also producing a further, sixth, matrix. For this study, these matrices were essentially comparative tables developed on large sheets of paper. They contained informants down the side of the table and categories across the top. Some of these categories were very basic, relating to socio-demographic information; others were more complex and related to the emerging theory, for example, around issues such as whether informants wanted to know about their own care. The purpose of the matrices was to aid in spotting factors that coincided across informants with the main data being contained in the analytic accounts. Unlike in framework analysis (Ritchie and Lewis 2003), therefore, these matrices did not attempt to provide evidence or detailed information but rather to reduce the data into whether a factor was relevant for a particular informant or not. At this point, data from the analytic accounts were also presented to groups of health economists, social scientists and study participants for comment, and again this provided further insights and clarifications.

The individual analytic accounts and the matrices were then used to generate two comprehensive comparative accounts of the major themes across all citizens and across all agents who were interviewed. This included checking

BOX 5.2. EXCERPT FROM FINAL ANALYTIC ACCOUNT FOR CITIZEN INFORMANT, BASED ON ALL INTERVIEWS

Making choices in health care: citizens or their agents?

Perhaps the most important question to be tackled using the data from the interviews with citizens concerns whether or not these citizens want to be directly involved in making choices in health care or whether they would rather someone else made those choices on their (i.e., society's) behalf. Do citizens want agents to make choices on their behalf? There was wide variation in the views of the informants interviewed here. This section attempts to make sense of this variation, and to explain why some individuals perceive the need for an agent, while others wish to be involved in making choices directly.

The data are described separately for three groups of individuals. These groups can be broadly categorized as follows:

- *Group 1*: those informants who were unequivocal in their view that they personally did not want any involvement in health care decision making.
- *Group 2*: those informants who were more equivocal in their views about whether they did or did not want to be personally involved in health care decision making, but still seemed to show considerable reluctance to make decisions that would result in individuals being denied care.
- *Group 3*: those informants who were unequivocal in their willingness to be involved in health care decision making even if this would mean denying care to particular individuals.

The description of each group type considers the level of personal involvement desired, the perceived difficulty of the decisions which informants viewed themselves as having to take, the characteristics that they would desire decision makers to have and the specified reasons for the desired level of involvement.

Group 1

Five individuals fell into Group 1, the group who were extremely reluctant to take part in rationing decisions about health care. The five individuals were IB4, IB7, IB8, IC3 and IG3. These individuals were extremely reluctant to take part in rationing decisions which would involve the denial of care. IC3 likened the situation to both Russian roulette, and to sending someone to the gallows, while IB8 (and to some extent IB7) became extremely agitated at the thought of having to be involved in such decisions. IB4 stated that she was extremely glad that she did not have to make decisions, and IG3 said that he would hate to be in the position to turn anyone down for treatment.

IC3: well, that's how I would see it, as like sending someone to the gallows isn't it, in a way, well not quite the same, no it isn't the same really, but it is, in a sense you're being partly responsible for not continuing that person's life.

IB8: No, I just wouldn't, no I I don't know why, I just, I umm, how would you decide? I I I wouldn't know how to decide, I mean you ask somebody dying with cancer, and somebody with heart problems and another person I don't know with another leukaemia or something like that, I wouldn't be able to decide which umm err things should get the money I w- I, no, and I wouldn't want to, you know I wouldn't

for negative circumstances and attempting to describe fully the nature of the evolving concepts. These accounts were checked by two experienced qualitative researchers who provided further insights and thoughts for the analysis. As an indication of the length of the analytic accounts at this stage, the final citizen account was around 26,000 words long.

It was at this point that information from the focus groups was also integrated into the accounts. As one of the main advantages of focus group data is the opportunity to observe interaction between participants (Kitzinger 1994, 1995; Wilkinson 2011), analysis that focused on this interaction was conducted so that comments were related to the context in which they were made. Detailed notes on the content of each focus group were made, including quotes where applicable. These notes were related to the relevant categories derived during the main analysis and were a valuable source of additional information for the main categories 'constraints', 'choosing' and 'acting'. An analytic account was formed for each focus group. Information from the focus groups was then integrated into each of the overall citizen and agent accounts.

To show how the analytic accounts progress from the early accounts, which are much more descriptive, to these later final accounts, which are more explanatory and contain more of the theoretical development, Box 5.2 contains an excerpt from the full citizen analytic account.

Reflecting and generating the final model

The final model arose from the extensive full analytic accounts with their detailed exploration of relationships based on the earlier individual and group accounts, the matrices exploring relationships and the theoretical memos generated during the analysis. The final model was described as a 'system of equivocation' – a model focusing on the players in the system, the roles that they take, their preferences for engaging in rationing decisions and how these preferences influence the way that the system works: via collusion to avoid explicit involvement in decision making through two mechanisms. The first is the use of obstacles to objective decision making and the second dilution of decisions as they flowed through the system. The model explicitly started from the sort of individualistic viewpoint associated with a neoclassical mode of thinking, and the economic notion of disutility was key to the underlying structure of the model (Coast 2001a).

Consideration was given to both the typicality of the informants and the likely generalizability of the model to other contexts. Citizen informants could have been atypical in that they were willing to get involved in the research and thus may have been more 'community minded' than those choosing not to participate; given the reluctance of these informants to be responsible for decision making, this was not seen as problematic in the final model. Generalizability was seen as being potentially affected by the location of the data collection and the ways of work in that location, the extent to which all 'agent' roles had been included in the research and the temporal generalizability given the constant state of flux within the UK National Health Service.

CONCLUSION

This chapter has outlined approaches to data analysis. It has explored the prospect of conducting analysis that is particularly relevant to health economics, by considering the possibility of analysing data through an economic lens and generating output in terms of models. This is, of course, not the only approach that health economists can use; there are a myriad of analytic choices available within qualitative research (Creswell 2013; Grbich 2013), some of which are aligned to particular qualitative approaches (Creswell 2013; Grbich 2013) and others of which are more atheoretical (Ritchie and Lewis 2003; Rapley 2011; Grbich 2013). The possibilities available are also constantly changing and adapting as new choices become available (Grbich 2013).

Despite these many choices, there are aspects of qualitative data analysis that are common across approaches, and these are also outlined in the chapter. Perhaps most important to note is that all approaches require rigour and time in their application but that the increase in insight afforded by such detailed analysis of rich data makes this endeavour worthwhile. Passing on this insight to others is then the final part of the qualitative research process, and this is discussed in Chapter 7. First, however, the different challenges of conducting secondary analysis with existing qualitative data are explored.

Chapter 6

Understanding secondary data analysis

Hareth Al-Janabi and Amanda Owen-Smith

Secondary data analysis involves the re-analysis of existing qualitative data and studies for a different purpose. Given the wealth of qualitative data that are now collected in health research and the potential value of qualitative research in health economics, there is a strong rationale for undertaking secondary analysis of qualitative data to inform health economics research questions. Secondary data analysis can proceed in various ways (Heaton 2008), and a distinction can be drawn between the re-analysis of 'raw' qualitative data sets and the synthesis of published qualitative research studies (Heaton 2008). This chapter considers both of these approaches and provides worked examples of each.

An important advantage of secondary analysis that ought to appeal to economists is that data collection may be more cost-effective. Data can potentially be accessed more quickly, avoiding the need for further primary research. Furthermore, a broader range of material may be available, meaning that comparisons can often be drawn between different population groups. This can be facilitated by the use of data archives for qualitative research and the ability to search and access qualitative studies easily online. Secondary analysis can also be especially useful when researching sensitive issues in a hard-to-reach population (Long-Sutehall, Sque, et al. 2010) and thus particularly useful for economists who may not have had the opportunity to develop skills to collect data directly in such situations.

Careful consideration, however, needs to be given to questions of ethics and appropriateness. Ethical concerns include, for example, the degree to which informed consent can be achieved for secondary data analysis and participant confidentiality can be maintained through the secondary analysis process. Concerns also surround the potential for secondary data analysis to decontextualize the primary work. In addition, there will clearly be situations where secondary analysis is not an appropriate research strategy. For example, there may simply be insufficient primary data available to address the research question of interest, or existing studies may be so methodologically flawed that their findings cannot be relied upon. In these cases, the research design needs to be reconsidered in the light of the (in)adequacy of the data at hand, encompassing further primary data collection where appropriate.

This chapter focuses on describing the two main approaches to re-analysing qualitative data. The process of re-analysing the raw data from existing primary studies for a new purpose is outlined first. The use of meta-ethnography to synthesize insights from published qualitative studies on a new topic of interest is then discussed. The third section of the chapter highlights some possibilities for how secondary analysis of qualitative data could be applied in health economics and makes recommendations for improving the feasibility of research in this area. The chapter ends with a brief conclusion.

RE-ANALYSIS OF A PRIMARY DATA SET

A popular form of secondary analysis of qualitative data is re-analysis of a primary data set. The advantages to doing so are clear. Qualitative data are time-consuming and expensive to collect, and it is commonplace for only a fraction of data collected to be used (Fielding and Fielding 2000). Re-analysis thus offers a potentially cost-effective solution where resources are tight and may allow access to a larger and more diverse data set than would otherwise have been available (Seale 2011). In addition, there is an ethical argument for making the best use of available data and not unnecessarily overburdening research participants by collecting additional primary data (Seale 2011).

Formal secondary analysis of qualitative data has a relatively short history. The first qualitative data archive (QUALIDATA, now part of UK Data Service [https://www.ukdataservice.ac.uk/]) was established in the United Kingdom in 1994, and published examples of qualitative research based on secondary analysis date to the same year (Thorne 1994). Since that time, several other qualitative data archives have been established, and an increasing number of peer-reviewed journals are now prepared to accept work based on secondary qualitative analysis (Heaton 2008). However, this growth has not been without controversy, and concerns range from the practical issues around getting consent from participants for possible reuse of research data to epistemological concerns about the validity of comparing different data sets and introducing a false separation between data collection and analysis (Boddy 2000).

There are two main approaches to re-analysing a primary qualitative data set (Heaton 2008). First, researchers could re-analyse their own data set for a different purpose or join with colleagues to address a more targeted research question across several comparable data sets (see, e.g., Biddle, Cooper, et al. 2013; Owen-Smith, Coast, et al. 2014). Second, researchers could obtain formally archived qualitative data, which are normally re-analysed without any defined role for the original primary researcher, save for being informed of the purpose for reuse (see, e.g., Savage 2005; Seale and Charteris-Black 2008). Both of these approaches share the advantages outlined earlier, importantly allowing access to a broader range of data that can (arguably) be used for both verification purposes and addressing novel research questions. Both of these approaches are explained in depth; good sources of secondary qualitative data are outlined, and the methodological, ethical and practical challenges posed by each approach are highlighted.

Approach 1: informal data sharing

The most common approach to secondary data analysis is informal data sharing through reuse of in-house data. There are a number of ways to go about this, such as by constructing a new research question that arises across a number of data sets or by simply re-analysing an existing data set with a different purpose in mind (Heaton 2008). The overriding characteristic of this type of data sharing, however, is that the original researcher is normally involved in some way in the new analysis. This circumvents some of the criticism levelled at secondary qualitative data analysis that it is problematic to 'decontextualize' qualitative data through the separation of the data collection and analysis and has obvious advantages for data access.

Based on a comprehensive analysis of the published literature, Heaton has outlined a number of analytic approaches to analysing in-house secondary data. These are as follows:

- Supplementary analysis (most common) – an in-depth analysis of one aspect of the data not fully addressed in the original study
- Supra analysis – aims of the secondary study transcend those of the original research
- Re-analysis – undertaken for confirmation/validation purposes
- Amplified analysis – two or more data sets combined for secondary analysis
- Assorted analysis – re-analysis of existing data supplemented by further primary research or use of naturally occurring data (through observations, documentary analysis, etc.) (Heaton 2004, 2008)

A recent example of a supplementary approach is shown in a publication by Dennis et al., who re-analysed data from in-depth interviews and focus groups with former prisoners with HIV, which had the original purpose of informing a scale measuring motivation to engage with medical treatment (Dennis, Barrington, et al. 2015). However, these interviews also yielded a large amount of rich data relating to participants' experiences of HIV treatment following incarceration, and the authors were able to make a number of in-depth insights into the lived experience of HIV in jail and make recommendations for improvements to current treatment regimens. The re-analysis used original transcripts, re-coding the data and drawing out themes and links as explained earlier in this volume (see Chapter 5), aiming for a more in-depth analysis than that suited to the original purpose of the research. A contrary approach can be seen in a study by Biddle et al., where the authors combined selected data from three in-depth studies on the experience of suicide and self-harm to make broader statements about the experience of qualitative interviewing in vulnerable populations (Biddle, Cooper, et al. 2013).

An example of amplified analysis undertaken by one of the authors (Owen-Smith) will now be discussed in depth so that the process of undertaking a secondary data analysis based on informal data sharing can be understood (Owen-Smith, Coast, et al. 2014). This study reused data from two qualitative studies relating to the experiences of accessing appropriate health care for people with morbid obesity. In the first study, experiences of health care rationing were sought through one-off interviews with morbidly obese (n = 13) and breast cancer patients (n = 18) who were accessing care in shortage areas, with the aim of generating theory through comparison. In the second, a longitudinal approach was taken to research, which integrated both observational and interview techniques to analyse morbidly obese patients' (n = 22) experiences of accessing health care over time. Although the sample size for each study was relatively small, both data sets yielded rich emergent data on the background to attempts to access health care, including issues around self-confidence and interpersonal relationships, as well as previous attempts to lose weight, which affected their interactions with clinicians. Further investigation of these primary accounts became the explicit purpose of secondary data analysis.

Since all data had been coded thoroughly and methodically as part of the initial data analysis exercise in both studies, full re-coding of the data for secondary analysis was not necessary. Instead, coded transcripts were re-read with the objectives of the secondary analysis in mind, with updates being made where necessary. At this point, updates were made *within the coding structures of the original study*. Next, a 'reciprocal translation' process was used, whereby all relevant codes for each study were identified and reciprocally applied across both data sets with the aim of distilling a distinct set of themes explaining the whole data set (Noblit and Hare 1988). To do this, a spreadsheet was set up where all the relevant codes identified across both studies (e.g., 'narrative of weight gain', 'history of depression') were listed in the left-hand column and summaries of the relevant data pertaining to each study were entered into subsequent columns under the headings 'study 1' and 'study 2'. Where it was clear that differently named codes across the two studies encompassed similar data, these were merged until there was one coding structure explaining the entire data set. At this point coding became more analytical, with explanatory links sought between codes and higher-order concepts (and later overarching themes) being identified, in line with standard qualitative analysis techniques (see Chapter 5).

Table 6.1 shows a worked example of the identification of three reciprocal themes across both data sets, showing how original data extracts were coded in individual studies and how these fitted within the higher-order themes identified for the data synthesis.

Table 6.1. Reciprocal translation of selected themes across two qualitative studies

Overarching theme (and definition) applied	*Data extract from Study 1*	*Data extract from Study 2*
Personal responsibility and the morality of health *Participants alternated between accepting and rejecting culpability for their obesity, which often related to feelings of moral failure relating to their current health state*	I was always fit, always healthy, never stopped. . . . We never had sweets, we never had anything fattening . . . always up the gym (Female, Study 1, early in interview) I know that the last few years, because of everything, crap going on, it [weight gain] is self-inflicted (Female, Study 1, later in same interview) *Original codes (study 1): Narrative of weight gain // Self-blame*	You think, 'Is it my head? Can it be fixed with just my head, [or] is there a real problem that could be treated?' . . . And you hope that it is something, to keep you sane, because otherwise you just think, 'Why me? Why can't I just lose weight like a normal person?' (Female, Study 2) *Original codes (study 2): Personal culpability // Aetiology of obesity*
Family structure and the importance of gender *Participants were particularly concerned about the impact of socialization on the development of poor eating habits and often had conflicting feelings with relation to their own parenting styles*	My mum [mother] was one of twenty-three. You ate what was on your plate. . . . With my two, as soon as they say they're full up, that's fine. . . . I've had to change . . . because I don't want my kids fat (Female, Study 1) *Original codes (study 1): Socialisation patterns // Generational cycles*	He's [son, age 26] twenty-four stone. . . . I know it's going to end up [in] diabetes and strokes. . . . I am afraid my son saw how I acted when I was younger, and he sort of copied that – same as me with my father (Male, Study 2) *Original codes (study 2): Socialisation patterns // Fear for own children*

(*Continued*)

Table 6.1. (Continued)

Overarching theme (and definition) applied	*Data extract from Study 1*	*Data extract from Study 2*
The role of emotional distress and the impact on the body *Nearly all participants discussed the role of emotional distress, and this was often seen as key to ongoing cycles of weight loss and regain*	I put on an awful lot of weight through stress. . . . I was just getting bigger and bigger and bigger – and then becoming – less and less active, because I was struggling then, where I'd put on so much weight. . . . And then I was feeling bad because I couldn't go out anywhere and I couldn't do anything, so I'd eat more. And it got worse and worse and worse (Female, Study 1) *Original codes (study 1): Narrative of weight gain // Stress // Vicious cycles*	If he [ex-husband] was drinking I would eat. And if he came home drunk I would go and make a pile of sandwiches and say. 'Look what you have made me do'. . . . It was almost as though I was using it as a weapon, but it was harming me, not him (Female, Study 2) *Original codes (study 2): Narrative of weight gain // Mental health issues // Relationship with spouse*

Source: Quotes contained in Owen-Smith, Coast, et al. (2014).

The particular benefit of secondary analysis in this study was to conduct a further investigation into an important issue that had not been the focus of the research conducted using the individual data sets. However, the secondary data analysis benefited from the involvement of the primary researcher in data collection and analysis for both studies, and more caution needs to be applied where multiple researchers are involved, each potentially working within distinct conceptual frameworks (Seale 2011). It is a hallmark of qualitative data that individual researchers bring something of themselves to the research field, an influence that is generally dealt with adequately through individual researcher reflexivity (Bryman 2004). For example, in the obesity studies described earlier, it was necessary for the researcher to stand back and consider what influence she, as a relatively young female not experiencing difficulties with overweight, had on the level of disclosure from informants and as such the research data collected. Indeed, on one occasion she experienced having a front door shut in her face as the potential informant declared she could 'know nothing' of what it meant to be obese. In the case of secondary analysis, where two or more researchers may have contributed to data collection and analysis, these issues become even more complicated, with individual epistemological standpoints needing further explication to assess their impact on resulting data collection and analysis (Heaton 2008). For example, if the analysis of one data set was undertaken using an inductive grounded theory approach and the other analysed using a highly focused deductive approach, then simply merging the two sets of codes (as earlier) would not be a comparable basis for higher-order analysis, suggesting a complete re-coding exercise should be considered.

In addition, there are a number of practical and ethical issues that need to be addressed with respect to informal data sharing. Of particular importance is attention to informed consent, and it is the responsibility of both the primary researcher and the secondary analyst to ensure that reuse of the data is in line with the initial consent processes undertaken by participants (Seale 2011). Unless a specific request was made for reuse of the data as part of the original consent process, consideration needs to be given to how far the secondary analysis concords with the original contract between researcher and participant, particularly in terms of the research purpose and expected audience (Long-Sutehall, Sque, et al. 2010). In addition, when reusing data it is important to pay attention to confidentiality, and there is a fine balance between ensuring that data are adequately anonymized before sharing and retaining sufficient contextual information so that the new analysis can be undertaken meaningfully. There are also legal issues to consider around data protection, and any original agreements with respect to the storage and carriage of data need to be respected in any secondary analysis undertaken. A useful source for advice on legal and ethical issues in data sharing is provided at https://www.ukdataservice.ac.uk/manage-data/legal-ethical.

Approach 2: formal data sharing

The other major approach to the secondary analysis of qualitative data is to use formally archived data stored in a dedicated data repository. The first national repository for qualitative data was set up in the United Kingdom in 1994 and now hosts over 900 qualitative data sets available for reuse (https://www.ukdataservice.ac.uk). The popularity of the databank is at least in part due to the Economic and Social Research Council (ESRC) making data deposit a condition of funding. However, with advances in information technology making qualitative data deposit more feasible, the profile of formal data sharing can be expected to continue to increase across the social sciences (Seale 2011). There are also three U.S. databases that specialize in the storage of qualitative and mixed-methods data, and the Australian Data Archive launched a dedicated repository for qualitative data in 2010 (Table 6.2). In addition, the U.S. database TalkBank provides a repository for naturally occurring data such as clinic consultations, and the UK initiative Health Talk online has collated in excess of 1,000 qualitative interviews relating to people's experiences of living with different illnesses. There are also a number

Table 6.2. Qualitative data repositories currently available

UK Data Service (United Kingdom) (formerly known as QUALIDATA)	A mixed-methods repository for social science data managed by ESRC. There is a defined and well-supported qualitative arm which offers access to data from over 900 original studies	https://www.ukdataservice.ac.uk/
Inter-university Consortium for Political and Social Research (United States)	Originally a database of survey data, a qualitative repository was added in 2011	http://www.icpsr.umich.edu/icpsrweb/landing.jsp
The Henry A. Murray Research Archive (United States)	A rich source of data from key U.S. longitudinal and mixed-methods studies	http://murray.harvard.edu
The Qualitative Data Repository at Syracuse (United States)	Digital archive of social science data collected using qualitative and multi-method research	https://qdr.syr.edu/
Australian Data Archive (Australia)	A national service for depositing data for secondary analysis. A dedicated qualitative store was added in 2011	http://www.ada.edu.au/ada/home
TalkBank (United States)	A U.S. database of naturally occurring data (e.g., consultation recordings) relating primarily to health services research	http://talkbank.org/
Health Talk Online (United Kingdom)	A rich repository of interview transcripts and audio recordings from people talking about living with illness and accessing treatment. The information is particularly aimed at patients and carers making treatment decisions, but is also available for research and teaching purposes	http://www.healthtalk.org/
Finnish Social Science data archive	A nationally managed archive of social science data for research and teaching	http://www.fsd.uta.fi/en/
Irish Qualitative Data Archive	A relatively new archive of (mainly historical) social science data	https://www.maynoothuniversity.ie/iqda

Source: UK Data Service (https://www.ukdataservice.ac.uk/).

of European qualitative data archives, but, with the exception of the Finnish Social Science data archive and the Irish Qualitative Data Archive, these are generally underdeveloped or still at the feasibility stage (Consortium of European Social Science Data Archives [CESSDA] 2016). A brief description of available databases and Internet links to their content is included in Table 6.2.

In general, the databases are fairly easy to navigate and, with the exception of the U.S. 'Talkbank', include easy-to-use search functions. Data are normally accessible free of charge, but most organizations require researchers to fulfil a brief application process before access is granted. In addition, there is the emergence of specialist archives of qualitative data where the sole purpose of data collection is to create a catalogue of data available for general use (e.g., the publicly funded One in a Million study, developed at the University of Bristol, United Kingdom, which is a dedicated repository of primary care consultations for general research use [Jepson, Salisbury, et al. 2017]).

Despite the availability of a growing number of qualitative data sets online, it is widely accepted that secondary analysis through formal data sharing is a relatively underdeveloped research area (Heaton 2008; Seale 2011). Most of the research studies using qualitative data from UK Data Service, for instance, currently depend on the re-analysis of historical seminal studies. For example, Savage used the original data from Goldthorpe's affluent worker study to re-conceptualize informants' accounts of social class and notions of individuality, and used the findings from more contemporary literature to cast a critical lens over the previous analyses (Goldthorpe, Lockwood, et al. 1969; Savage 2005). An alternative approach to secondary analysis based on formal data sharing was taken by Seale and Charteris-Black, who used Health Talk Online data to address a novel research question relating to the interaction of age and gender in illness narratives around cancer (Seale and Charteris-Black 2008). Given the size and range of the available data set, these researchers used a purposive sampling technique to select 102 interview transcripts from participants meeting their characteristics of interest with respect to age, gender and cancer diagnosis. The researchers then employed a mixed-methods approach to analysis through word frequency counts and a targeted qualitative analysis to understand contextual differences between groups.

The advantages of using a formal data sharing approach to secondary qualitative analysis are clear. A readily available bank of data transcribed and ready for analysis awaits the eager researcher, which in some situations will enable a longitudinal approach to be taken to analysis (see, e.g., Fielding and Fielding 2000; Savage 2005). In addition, ethical and legal issues around informed consent and data protection will have largely been addressed at deposit, so the researcher faces fewer practical barriers to proceeding. The main stumbling blocks with this type of secondary data analysis relate to whether the data the researcher wants to analyse actually exist in sufficient depth and breadth, and contextual issues around whether high-quality analysis can be conducted by a researcher divorced from the original research context. Although there is no way past this hurdle for those who argue that the co-construction of social reality is immediate and irreplaceable, for more pragmatic researchers there are a number of ways to ameliorate its impact.

First, and most important, the depositors themselves must ensure that as much contextual information as possible is made available alongside the data set to assist secondary analysts in their interpretation. Second, secondary analysts must take a reflexive approach to their analysis to assess what preconceptions they bring to the research field, just as if they were conducting primary data collection. Finally, consideration could be given to contacting the original researchers and asking for their comments on any re-conceptualization of the data undertaken (see, e.g., research by Fielding and Fielding, which included the comments of the original authors of the research as part of the published article [Fielding and Fielding 2000]).

The chapter moves now to the discussion of meta-ethnography, which, rather than using raw data sets as described earlier, focuses on the re-analysis of published research studies and conducting evidence synthesis across a wider range of material.

CONDUCTING META-ETHNOGRAPHY

Meta-ethnography is a technique for combining the results of multiple qualitative studies within a particular topic area (Dixon-Woods, Agarwal, et al. 2005). Like a secondary analysis of primary data sets, it offers a means of exploiting existing research findings without the need to conduct primary research. Unlike a secondary analysis, meta-ethnography synthesizes authors' interpretations of the primary data, enriched and illustrated by quotes and extracts from the primary studies. This section aims to highlight the objectives and process of meta-ethnography, with the aim of guiding health economists who might want to apply meta-ethnography to their research.

Meta-ethnography as a form of qualitative synthesis

The secondary analysis of *quantitative* research studies (i.e., meta-analysis) is well established in health economics. Meta-analysis (and the associated meta-regression) has been variously used to determine parameters for economic decision models (Briggs, Sculpher, et al. 2006), examine rates of time preference (Asenso-Boadi, Peters, et al. 2007) and estimate demand elasticities (Gallet and List 2003). However, syntheses of *qualitative* studies may also be useful to health economists, given the contribution that qualitative research can make to theory development and understanding social and economic phenomena.

Meta-ethnography is similar in some ways to a conventional literature review. In both cases, the objective is to develop some overarching explanation of the data, which adds to, and in some sense summarizes, the original studies. However, there are important differences. In a meta-ethnography, studies are typically purposefully (as opposed to exhaustively) sampled, with interpretations (as opposed to summaries) created from the data (Doyle 2003). The critical feature of a meta-ethnography that differentiates it from a simple literature review is the attempt to reinterpret or re-conceptualize research findings rather than simply to link or aggregate them (Campbell, Pound, et al. 2012). Meta-ethnography is based on inductive reasoning, seeking to develop concepts and theories that go beyond the 'sum of the parts' of the individual studies being synthesized (Campbell, Pound, et al. 2003). The aim is an overarching interpretation of the phenomena of interest that is consistent with the studies, but genuinely adds to the body of research (Campbell, Pound, et al. 2003).

Meta-ethnography is not the only method for synthesizing qualitative studies, but it is the most widely cited (Campbell, Pound, et al. 2012). In a strict sense, meta-ethnography is a technique for synthesizing ethnographic studies (Campbell, Pound, et al. 2003). However, the method is flexible enough to be used to synthesize different types of qualitative studies (and sometimes the term 'meta-synthesis' is used to describe these syntheses). This chapter adopts this more flexible interpretation of a meta-ethnography. The origins of meta-ethnography can be traced back to Noblit and Hare's work to develop a framework for synthesizing qualitative research (Noblit and Hare 1988). In broad terms, a meta-ethnography can be summarized in three phases:

- *Identifying studies*: Specifying the research question, the audience and which research studies might address the audiences' interests
- *Recording and comparing studies*: Repeated reading of studies; noting of concepts and metaphors; and the juxtaposition of key metaphors, phrases, ideas and concepts
- *Translation and synthesis*: The interpretation ('translation') of concepts generated in the second phase into individual papers, the development of lines of argument to explain the meaning of the concepts in general and the expression of the synthesis in an appropriate form, with appropriate language and concepts for the audience

The following sections outline key considerations in each of these steps.

Identifying research studies for synthesis

The initial task in a meta-ethnography is to specify the research question. As with any synthesis, careful thought needs to be given to this to ensure the question is important, novel, specific, not so narrow that it is of little interest and not so broad so that it will result in overgeneralization. It may be that the research question is a question in its own right or that it relates to a broader question that will be tackled quantitatively. For example, an economist wishing to quantitatively model preferences for a health care intervention may conduct a meta-ethnography to understand the factors that would encourage take-up of the intervention and then use this information to design a quantitative study, such as a discrete choice experiment, to collect data on patients' preferences. Some iteration is likely to be worthwhile (Walsh and Downe 2005) to determine how broad the synthesis should be in terms of the different contexts and populations that are considered. On the one hand, synthesizing studies that span a number of health care systems or disease areas might be important in order to develop a comprehensive understanding of the phenomena of interest. On the other hand, overgeneralizing might result in an unwieldy mix of studies that are difficult to synthesize. The importance of a good research question cannot be overemphasized; the research question will determine the studies that are included, the process of the synthesis and the way the synthesis is expressed. As with any review, the researcher must set clear inclusion and exclusion criteria, conduct the search and sift identified papers to select the final set of studies for synthesis.

Searching systematically for qualitative research poses problems in addition to those encountered in conducting a quantitative literature search (Patton 2002; Pound, Britten, et al. 2005). First, there is a tendency for the titles and abstracts of qualitative research to be less precisely written than for quantitative research. As a result online keyword searches may miss large numbers of useful studies. Second, qualitative research is often published in book form, which is less likely to be indexed in online databases (although this is starting to change with the increase in e-books). These issues can be dealt with by adopting multiple search strategies (Campbell, Pound, et al. 2012). For example, it may be sensible to manually search recent articles in key journals, take advice from key researchers in the field and use key articles as the basis for forward and backward citation searches. These should complement the standard online keyword searches.

Unlike quantitative meta-analysis, where the aim is to include all relevant studies (Walsh and Downe 2005), in meta-ethnography it may be advisable to limit the total number of studies. Including a large number of studies will increase the range of experiences that the synthesis can draw on, but potentially at the cost of feasibility and overgeneralizing over disparate areas of research. There are not clear rules for researchers on when and how they should reduce a larger set of papers for synthesis as part of a meta-ethnography. For qualitative synthesis, it has been suggested that no more than ten studies should be included (Sandelowski, Docherty, et al. 1997). However, much larger qualitative syntheses have been conducted successfully, and it has been suggested that forty studies might be a more sensible limit for a meta-ethnography (Campbell, Pound, et al. 2012).

One option to limit the number of included studies is to return to the research question and define this more tightly. Another option is to conduct a preliminary set of mini-syntheses on groups of studies that are most similar to one another. This may produce interesting findings on subtopics but could be very time-consuming. A third option is therefore to purposefully sample from the identified set. This requires careful thought and the application of some sort of sifting criteria, but it does have the advantage that it generates a synthesis that focuses on the studies that add most value. Purposeful sampling could be completed prior to the analysis of the individual studies (as would be done with a narrative review or meta-analysis), but equally it could be conducted iteratively, as is often done in primary (qualitative) data collection.

Recording and comparing studies

When a set of studies have been identified for a meta-ethnography, these should be re-read a number of times. Immersion in the qualitative studies is key to a successful synthesis. For each of the studies, the researcher should note characteristics, quotes and concepts relevant to the research question. Concepts are likely to arise inductively, in much the same way as attempts to develop codes for multiple interviews (see Chapter 5). Quotes can be used to illustrate the relevance of the concepts in the study participants' own words. This sort of recording of study characteristics, concepts and codes can be done using simple tables, which have the advantage of enabling multiple studies to be easily compared. At this stage the concern should be to understand the individual studies rather than compare the studies with one another.

The next step is to begin to develop an idea of how the concepts from individual studies relate to one another. Studies can be grouped for comparison in pairs (Al-Janabi, Coast, et al. 2008) or compared with each other chronologically (Pound, Britten, et al. 2005). Concepts and quotes identified during the previous stage can be compared across studies, with attempts made to generate higher-order concepts that encompass the findings of multiple studies. These higher- or 'third-order' concepts can then be used to re-code the material in the individual studies to determine the generalizability of concepts and whether there are contradictions between studies.

Analytic accounts (see Chapter 5) can be used to bring together extracts from multiple studies under these newly constructed third-order concepts. An analytic account can be used to juxtapose related quotes from the individual studies, to better understand how the studies relate to one another and which concepts are common across studies and which are study-specific concepts. Narratives can be added around the quotes, to indicate how the quotes relate to one another and the research question. At this stage the overlap and relationships between the concepts and studies should become more apparent.

Translation and synthesis

It is the translation of studies into one another that truly differentiates the process of a meta-ethnography from a literature review. Essentially, the step of translating the papers requires a comparison of the concepts in one study with those in others (Noblit and Hare 1988). Three possible techniques can be used to draw the data from primary studies together (Noblit and Hare 1988; Dixon-Woods, Agarwal, et al. 2005): *reciprocal translational analysis*, which focuses on translating metaphors, themes and concepts into one another; *refutation synthesis*, where contradictions are identified and an attempt is made to explain them; and *lines of argument synthesis*, which is a general interpretation based on findings of each of the individual studies. The approach taken is supposed to be flexible and able to be adapted to best meet the needs of the researcher (Paterson, Thorne, et al. 2001).

Table 6.3 shows the process of translating a concept relating to 'control' (in the context of a meta-ethnography of the experience of informal care

Table 6.3. Translation of the concept of 'control' into individual studies in a meta-ethnography of six studies of the experience of informal care (Al-Janabi 2009)

Study	*Interpretation of control*
Adamson and Donovan (2005)	Carers feel their duty is controlled by cultural and religious identity. Carers organize work commitments around caring commitments
Baker, Sudit, et al. (1998)	Carers control the situation by managing the stigma and understanding the disease (talking to recipients' children, creating an alternative explanation)
Cheung and Hocking (2004)	Carers don't feel they have long-term control of their lives. Some feel they can adapt to day-to-day living; others are very worried about the lack of control
Harris (1993)	Carers are protective of the caring and are reluctant to relinquish control to people whose caring will be inferior
Lewis, Curtis, et al. (1995)	Control could be linked to respite care. Carers valued being able to find the right type of respite care to relieve the burden of caring
McGarry and Arthur (2001)	Maintaining control was essential when dealing with tasks such as assisting with medication

[Al-Janabi, Coast, et al. 2008; Al-Janabi 2009]) back into each of the individual papers. In this case, the concept 'control' could be related to each individual study. This will not always be the case, and there may be concepts that do not appear in some of the constituent studies. It is important for the translations not to stray too far from the original papers, and maintaining the terminology of the original studies is seen as a way of remaining faithful to the original research (Finfgeld 2003).

For each concept, a 'line of argument' can be developed as a way of bringing together the individual translations. Dixon-Woods, Agarwal, et al. (2005) highlight that the process of line-of-argument synthesis bears similarities with the technique of constant comparison (see Chapter 5). In some cases, the interpretation of a concept in one study may contradict the interpretation of the concept in another; where this happens, this needs to be noted. In the meta-ethnography of the experience of informal care (Al-Janabi 2009), the line of argument for control spanned all the synthesized studies: 'The uncertain nature of the recipients' condition leads many carers to feel a lack of control over their life. Those that had developed ways of controlling their lives generally seemed more satisfied' (Al-Janabi 2009, p. 177).

Following translation, the 'synthesis' must be expressed in some way. Ultimately, the importance of a meta-ethnography lies in the impact it has on the intended audience (Doyle 2003). The synthesis from a meta-ethnography may be in the form of a set of concepts and or lines of argument. For health economics it may additionally be desirable to develop the synthesis into a model, theory or outcome measure. In this case, further testing or validation of the result may be useful.

Reflecting on the use of meta-ethnography to develop attributes for the Carer Experience Scale

The meta-ethnography of studies describing the experience of family caregiving was conducted by one of the authors (Al-Janabi) with the broader aim of developing an outcome measure for carers for economic evaluation, which focused on *care-related* quality of life as opposed to *health-related* quality of life (Al-Janabi, Coast, et al. 2008). A key step in generating an outcome measure is the defining of the domains of life that a measure will focus on. In health economics there is a desire to keep these domains to a minimum, to ensure the resultant measure is both simple to complete and can be valued using preference-based techniques.

This study identified articles about the caring experience through online keyword searches, contents of recent issues of key journals, citation-tracking and expert recommendation. These were purposefully sampled to generate a set of six studies that reflected the experiences of carers, of different ethnicities, of both sexes, of different relationships to the care recipient, and caring for people with different illnesses. Six studies was not a predefined number; rather, it was the minimum number of studies that ensured diversity with respect to the sampling characteristics. These studies were repeatedly read, and concepts and quotes relating to the experience of caring were noted. Ultimately, fifteen cross-cutting concepts were identified and used to structure a descriptive account covering the concepts arising from the papers. Translations and lines of argument for these fifteen concepts were developed (see previous section for an example). These lines of argument were then refined into six attributes of the caring experience.

The final stage was the one that presented most difficulties. The aim was to go from fifteen concepts that were relevant to experience of caring to a shorter set of conceptual attributes that could form the basis of an outcome measure. To reduce these topics down, the overlaps and links between concepts were mapped out. Where possible, concepts were combined. Whether concepts were a description of caring (e.g., 'challenging') or a potentially modifiable aspect of the process of caring (control) was also noted. Ultimately, six attributes of the caring experience were established: social activity, relationship quality, institutional support, informal support, control and duty. These conceptual attributes from the meta-ethnography were further refined through a set of sixteen interviews with carers to determine coverage, language and format for an outcome measure. This supplementation of secondary material through the collection of further primary data has been termed 'assorted analysis' (Heaton 2008).

Challenges with meta-ethnography

The twin challenges with meta-ethnography concern the philosophy of the technique and the way it is practically applied. Among some qualitative researchers, there is some resistance to the very idea of synthesizing qualitative research. Resistance is illustrated with the analogy: 'Can you sum up a poem?' (Sandelowski, Docherty, et al. 1997, p. 336). It is argued that qualitative synthesis decontextualizes research in a way that is anathema to the ideology of much qualitative research (Finfgeld 2003; Zimmer 2006). Even if qualitative synthesis is accepted in principle, there is the question of whether research utilizing different modes of qualitative enquiry, such as phenomenology and ethnography, can be synthesized (Sandelowski, Docherty, et al. 1997; Finfgeld 2003). Different modes of qualitative enquiry are accompanied by different epistemological perspectives, viewpoints on what a good-quality study is and conventions for presentation; these may create difficulties in both identifying a set of studies for synthesis and comparing concepts across studies.

In practical terms, recent papers on a topic may simply confirm earlier papers, as was found in one meta-ethnography (Campbell, Pound, et al. 2012), limiting the insights into theory building that can be generated from synthesizing across the range of research studies. Furthermore, meta-ethnography is likely to be more time consuming than a simple literature review and requires more skills in understanding and doing qualitative research (Walsh and Downe 2005). However, it is unlikely to require the same level of skill or training as conducting primary qualitative research, so it may be useful as a halfway house for students or researchers keen to develop their qualitative research skills.

The challenges associated with meta-ethnography must also be weighed against the potential of meta-ethnography to be more cost-effective than primary data collection and capable of generating new interpretations of existing qualitative research that encompass all of the relevant data. It might be of interest to health economists to know that meta-ethnography has been used to better understand adherence to medication (Pound, Britten, et al. 2005) and select outcomes for economic evaluation (Al-Janabi, Coast, et al. 2008; Jackson and Roberts 2015). It has been proposed as a technique for identifying attributes for discrete choice experiments (Coast, Al-Janabi, et al. 2012). Meta-ethnography avoids researchers constantly reinventing the wheel and has been proposed as a route to making qualitative research more relevant for policy making (Sandelowski, Docherty, et al. 1997; Finfgeld 2003). Despite inevitable challenges associated with a new(ish) research methodology, meta-ethnography has clear potential for research within health economics.

RECOMMENDATIONS FOR USING SECONDARY DATA WITHIN HEALTH ECONOMICS

Health economists who are developing research proposals could find it very helpful to take a look at archived qualitative data, for example, QUALIDATA. For example, one of the raw data sets available on QUALIDATA is the original set of transcripts from Townsend's classic study of poverty in the United Kingdom (Townsend 1979). This could be used to take a longitudinal perspective on the experience of economic poverty and address interesting questions about the interaction between economic circumstances and health. In addition, on a more informal level, simply maintaining good contacts with colleagues and discussing the availability of data sets within individual university departments might yield new and interesting research questions, and opportunities to reuse existing data may emerge. In terms of meta-ethnography, existing published qualitative research may facilitate theory building, particularly as economists working in health move beyond simple rational choice models of behaviour to employ insights from psychology (Perry, Chhatralia, et al. 2015; Trujillo, Glassman, et al. 2015).

Secondary data analysis may also be applied in the economic evaluation of new health care interventions. When conducting economic evaluation, the initial step is to identify the costs and benefits of the interventions (Drummond, Sculpher, et al. 2015). The identification of costs and outcomes for economic evaluation is seldom studied in the same detail as their measurement and valuation, but the identification step is critical for the resulting economic evaluation. Identifying costs and benefits entails thinking logically about the impact the illness (and treatment) has on patients, families and the health care system. Meta-ethnography may offer an ideal vehicle to draw on existing qualitative literature of the experiences of a wide range of stakeholders in relation to an illness or health care. It offers the potential to re-conceptualize participants' experiences as potential costs or benefits of an intervention of interest. The value of drawing on qualitative research seems most pertinent in the context of complex interventions and where a societal perspective to evaluation is taken. In these cases, the range of costs and benefits is likely to be numerous and not straightforward to identify. Without re-analysing the qualitative literature in a systematic way, there is an increased risk that impacts of interventions will remain hidden, or anecdotal, and consequently the range of costs and benefits considered will be partial and skewed.

In terms of developing the scope of secondary qualitative data analysis for health economists, the most obvious first step is to improve the amount of data deposited in formal research repositories. Although QUALIDATA is growing daily in its size and scope, much of this has been driven by the ESRC mandate that makes repository a condition of study funding. With closer consideration of the issues around secondary analysis at the research planning stage (e.g., inclusion of explicit agreement for re-analysis on study consent forms), this databank could be made even more diverse and useful to social scientists of all disciplines. Of particular importance is to ensure that as much contextual detail as possible is provided at data repository so that the information is as useful as possible to future researchers attempting to grapple with the epistemological issues surrounding the reuse of qualitative research.

Qualitative data may be either non-naturalistic (i.e., data produced in a specific research context, such as semi-structured interviews) or naturally occurring, as in the case of routine doctor–patient consultations that are recorded for research purposes. In this chapter, the focus has been largely on the re-analysis of non-naturalistic sources of qualitative data. However, an increasing amount of naturalistic data is placed in the public domain, most notably through social media. The re-analysis of such qualitative data might offer exciting opportunities for health economists and others to study behaviours and attitudes in the health system. For example, messages and blogs on social media might reveal insights about social values in relation to health care rationing or barriers and facilitators to accessing health care.

In terms of enabling more inclusive and wide-ranging meta-ethnographies, attention needs to consistently be paid to best-practice reporting standards for qualitative research so that assessments around relevance and methodological quality can be made more readily by secondary analysts. The most commonly used set of standards is the consolidated criteria for reporting qualitative research (COREQ), which consists of a comprehensive thirty-two-item checklist (see Chapter 7 for further details), and top peer-reviewed journals could lead the way here by insisting on compliance with reporting standards prior to the publication (Tong, Sainsbury, et al. 2007). Finally, and perhaps most obviously, increased attention needs to be paid to the indexing of qualitative research studies in online bibliographic databases so that the methodology used, participants and research purpose are all made explicit in the abstract.

CONCLUSION

This chapter has summarized two key approaches to the secondary analysis of qualitative data and discussed their advantages as well as some difficulties that researchers using these techniques might encounter. Of particular importance across both techniques is the potential for the researcher to access a broader range of data and make use of vibrant research material that may otherwise lie dormant. In addition, using pre-existing data may have benefits in terms of both cost and researcher time, and is an ideal training opportunity to educate new researchers in qualitative analysis techniques where funds are not available for a full primary research study (Long-Sutehall, Sque, et al. 2010).

Nevertheless, there are a number of difficulties inherent in the re-analysis of qualitative data. These relate to practical barriers (e.g., whether the required data are available and how they can best be accessed), ethical issues (particularly informed consent in the case of the re-analysis of primary data) and epistemological concerns (whether the reuse of qualitative data collected in a different context can be considered scientifically valid). With careful consideration of these issues in research planning and the maintenance of reflexivity throughout, however, these barriers are largely surmountable, and the secondary analysis of qualitative data is a promising field of enquiry for health economists and there are a number of potential areas for its use.

In conclusion, secondary analysis of qualitative data is both feasible and potentially desirable for health economists. Primary data from one or more qualitative studies can be re-analysed with a different research question. Multiple published qualitative studies can be synthesized to generate new insights and theories. Secondary data analysis needs to be conducted in a rigorous way to ensure reliable and acceptable results, but it is still very much 'up for grabs' as to the precise way each individual study proceeds. If done well, secondary analysis represents an important addition to health economics toolkit, capable of assisting a wide range of inquiries in normative and positive health economics.

Chapter 7

Presenting and publishing qualitative research in health economics

Joanna Coast

Presenting qualitative data in a manner that both is accessible to health economists and meets the requirements of qualitative research presentation can be challenging. This chapter begins by focusing on these challenges and outlining currently accepted standards for presentation of qualitative research within the health literature. It then examines a number of specific presentational issues that are likely to be of particular concern for health economists, including how best to present findings for an economics audience and how to deal with issues of reflexivity. Finally, the chapter considers some of the issues around publications of qualitative research in high-impact health and economics journals, suggesting that there is still a way to go in this area. It ends with some concluding comments.

PRESENTATION

Challenges in presenting for health economics

Presenting qualitative research to health economists is challenging because of the need to depend on written text (Hansen 2006). Some of these challenges were noted in 2004 by three researchers who had experienced difficulties in presenting and publishing work for health economics audiences:

> Even where health economists accept the methods used in qualitative research, they may dislike presentational norms for qualitative research papers and thus find the research unconvincing. Indeed, health economists conducting qualitative work have in some cases stuck to more familiar presentations of data, reducing data to the customary set of numbers (Cookson and Dolan 1999). Alternatively, they have used empirical qualitative data to provide the basis for

> theory development whilst providing little evidence for the findings obtained (Goddard, Mannion, et al. 2000) or little contextual detail from which to assess transferability.
>
> One accepted norm for the presentation of qualitative papers is to provide a number of quotes. This allows readers to judge the veracity of the interpretation, provides evidence for the range of findings obtained and allows the richness of people's views to be understood. It is, however, an unfamiliar form of presentation for economists and contributes to difficulties with publication (for example, the perception that the use of quotes is 'uninspiring' and 'hard-going'), with referees even expressing the desire to have models presented as purely conceptual, ignoring the contribution of the empirical data. (Coast, McDonald, et al. 2004, p. 173)

It is important that health economists using qualitative research methods find ways of presenting their research that both meet accepted conventions of reporting quality for qualitative research and are engaging for the health/health economics/economics audience towards whom it is targeted. In general, health economists presenting qualitative research will be largely focused on audiences in two areas: economics and health, where the latter encompasses medicine, nursing, allied health, health services research and health policy. It is helpful for economists to draw advice and guidance from both areas in terms of presenting their research in a way that will achieve publication within these target areas. Less often will health economists be focusing on the qualitative health journals, although some studies (particularly when collaborating with sociologists or anthropologists) may also target these journals (e.g., work on living with morbid obesity that arose from a project where the main focus was on rationing [Owen-Smith, Coast, et al. 2014]).

There is much advice within the qualitative research literature on writing qualitative research. This comprises both generic advice (Dey 2003; Marvasti 2011; Grbich 2013) and advice specific to particular approaches such as grounded theory (Strauss and Corbin 1990; Charmaz 2014) and ethnography (Hammersley and Atkinson 1983). There is also advice on writing for those working within health (Hansen 2006).

In general, there is a focus on the importance of the audience, and ensuring that the way the research is written is sensitive to this audience (Strauss and Corbin 1990; Dey 2003; Hansen 2006; Marvasti 2011; Creswell 2013; Grbich 2013; Patton 2015). While a number of authors point out the needs of different audiences in terms of policy versus academic audiences, Hansen also stresses the importance of considering different expectations within diverse disciplines, noting that 'health researchers working within multidisciplinary and applied fields . . . often find it difficult to make decisions about whose work needs to be cited and how to present their data and analysis because they are not working within clear disciplinary parameters' (Hansen 2006, p. 164).

This is undoubtedly also true for health economists where there is little in the way of a disciplinary tradition in relation to qualitative research. Health economists are also likely to have to write differently according to whether they are targeting 'health' or 'economic' journals.

This means that conventions for presentation need to be sought more within the health and, such as it is, economics qualitative research literature. Current conventions within health largely focus around a very useful publication for ensuring that all relevant information is provided transparently within a paper. This is the thirty-two-item COREQ checklist (Tong, Sainsbury, et al. 2007). This consolidated checklist focuses on criteria for studies collecting data through interviews or focus groups, rather than through observation, and was generated from a review of existing published checklists and guidelines for reporting qualitative research (Tong, Sainsbury, et al. 2007). All criteria for assessing or reporting qualitative research were extracted from this literature, resulting initially in seventy-six items, which were reduced by 'removing duplicates and those that were ambiguous, too broadly defined, not specific to qualitative research, or impractical to assess' (Tong, Sainsbury, et al. 2007, p. 351).

The final checklist has thirty-two areas that should be covered and is presented within three domains. The first of these is **research team and reflexivity**. This has two subdomains, *personal characteristics* and *relationship with participants*, and contains specific items focusing on the characteristics of the person(s) conducting the research in terms of their qualifications, experience, gender and occupation; and what the informants knew about them prior to the research. The second domain is **study design**. This has four subdomains: *theoretical framework*, *participant selection*, *setting* and *data collection*. These subdomains include items on the underpinning theory and methodology; the number and selection of participants, how they were approached and how many chose not to take part; where the data were collected, who was present and the characteristics of the sample; the use of an interview guide, repeat interviews, audio/visual recording, field notes and respondent checking of transcripts; and the length of interviews and the achievement of saturation. The final domain is **analysis and findings**. This has two subdomains, *data analysis* and *reporting*, and contains items on number of coders, the use of a coding tree, software and participant feedback and whether themes were inductively or deductively derived; presentation of quotes and their consistency with themes; and the clarity of major and minor themes (Tong, Sainsbury, et al. 2007). A number of medical journals require the use of the COREQ reporting checklist for publication in their journals: examples include all BioMed Central journals, *Plos One*, *Canadian Medical Association Journal*, *Palliative Medicine*, *BMJ Open* and *Journal of Advanced Nursing*.

A small number of health economics journals or journals where health economists publish also require authors to follow the COREQ guidelines either explicitly (e.g., *The Patient – Patient Centred Outcomes Research*) or implicitly through requesting authors to follow guidelines on the EQUATOR network (https://www.equator-network.org/), which is where the COREQ guidelines are located (e.g., *Applied Health Economics and Health Policy*, *PharmacoEconomics*) or have their own reporting guidelines for qualitative research (e.g., *Social Science & Medicine*). Others do not appear to specify any particular guidance for qualitative research papers (e.g., *Health Economics, Journal of Health Services Research and Policy, Health Economics Policy and Law, Health Policy and Planning, Value in Health, European Journal of Health Economics, Health Policy*), and some appear to publish few, if any, qualitative research papers (e.g., *Journal of Health Economics*).

Presenting for health economics

While following the COREQ guidelines is undoubtedly good advice in putting together publications, there are also some aspects of presentation for health economics that it is worth delving into a little more deeply.

Focusing the publication

Much of the advice on publication of qualitative research in the more general, and sometimes older, texts focuses on the production of monographs (Hammersley and Atkinson 1983; Strauss and Corbin 1990). In contrast to many of the traditional qualitative disciplines, health economists are unlikely to publish any of their research in single monographs. Instead, they are most likely to be writing for journals. Strauss and Corbin give some specific advice on writing journal publications and suggest that authors should not try to incorporate all of their work into a single journal publication but rather give a clear message around one or two categories from within their research (Strauss and Corbin 1990). Carving up the work in this way might feel daunting, particularly for those conducting research aimed at improving understanding of general theoretical concepts, but an example of how this might be achieved can be seen in how Coast published her work on citizen–agent relationships for which the analysis was described in Chapter 5. This was published as three papers: the first on the overall model resulting from the work, drawing largely on the categories of ‘choosing’ and ‘acting’ (see Chapter 5) (Coast 2001a); the second concerned with whether individuals want to know about rationing of their own care, drawing on the category of ‘knowing’ (Coast 2001b); and the third focusing on perceptions of rationing, taking largely from the ‘constraints’ category (Coast, Donovan, et al. 2002). Indeed, a well-conducted analysis of a set of interviews is likely to produce many hundreds of pages of data on the general topic of interest, and just as a quantitative data set can be put to multiple uses, pursuing different research questions within the qualitative data set is often legitimate and desirable.

Working in this way, it is also possible to target different aspect of the research towards different audiences. For example, of Coast's publications mentioned earlier, only the first was written primarily for an economics audience (published in *Health Economics*), using explicitly economics language, although a book chapter was also written using economics terminology and drawing on both of the categories of 'knowing' and 'choosing' (Coast 2000a,b). The other two publications were written for a more general health/social science audience and did not use specialist terminology (published in *Social Science & Medicine* and *Health Expectations*).

Locating the work within the relevant economic theory

An important part of applying an economic lens to the research is locating the work within the relevant area of economic theory within the journal publications. There are many examples of how this is done within the literature. Where the aim of the work is to improve quantitative measurement within economics, much of the available empirical work has tended to be located in the area of either preference/utility/health maximization (Geneau, Massae, et al. 2008, Stevens 2010; Stevens and Palfreyman 2012) or capability well-being (Grewal, Lewis, et al. 2006; Coast, Flynn, et al. 2008; Al-Janabi, Flynn, et al. 2012; Sutton and Coast 2014; Canaway, Al-Janabi, et al. 2017). Here, the economic theory also has to be related to the particular topic under investigation; for example, in the work by Sutton and Coast, the focus was on capability well-being for those at the end of life (Sutton and Coast 2014), while for Stevens it was health maximization in children (Stevens 2009). Such research does not tend to challenge theory but rather adds to the body of knowledge about how the theory might be applied within a particular context.

Where research aims to aid understanding of quantitative work, it generally locates itself early within the paper in the particular theory of interest. Much of the existing body of work in this area is located in topics related to health state valuation and tends to focus on a particular methodological issue within the economic theory. Authors here quickly locate their work in the particular technique of interest and discuss the methodological issue that will be investigated in the paper. Examples include work exploring time trade-off techniques (Robinson, Dolan, et al. 1997; Spencer 2003; Robinson and Spencer 2006), visual analogue scales (Robinson, Dolan, et al. 1997), standard gambles (Baker and Robinson 2004; van Osch and Stiggelbout 2008), person trade-off (Robinson and Bryan 2013) and willingness to pay (Smith 2007).

Research in this area tends to contribute to methodological understanding within a particular theoretical area and is presented as such.

Perhaps more difficult is the presentation of research intended to aid understanding, particularly where this comes from a more inductive standpoint. Nevertheless, even in these cases, where researchers have brought their economic perspective and knowledge to the analysis and will have started their research with a particular interest and often with a particular issue that has inspired them to conduct the research, it is important to then locate the publication in this economic theory. Through the paper, researchers should show that they have not been blinkered by the economic lens, but they should acknowledge it and the influence it has on the research, ideally showing how applying this economic lens has enabled them to see the important economic aspects of the data that they collect. Again, there are a number of examples within the literature of the application of different economic lenses to research aiming to aid economic understanding of particular phenomena. These include research by Cruz and McPake, who explicitly located their work on aid effectiveness within principal-agent theory (Cruz and McPake 2010, 2011); Coast also located her work on rationing in this theoretical area (Coast 2001a). Research has also been located in theories around economic rationality (Baker 2006), financial incentives (Bertone and Lagarde 2016) and the demand for health insurance (De Allegri, Sanon, et al. 2006a, 2006b).

Dealing with reflexivity

Dealing with reflexivity in health economics papers is a difficult issue. Creswell, for example, states that 'qualitative writers need to "position" themselves in their writings. This is the concept of reflexivity in which the writer is conscious of the biases, values and experiences that he or she brings to a qualitative research study' (Creswell 2013, p. 216) as well as how these might have influenced the findings (Creswell 2013; Patton 2015). A number of key qualitative researchers are clear that researchers should make their position explicit (Hammersley and Atkinson 1983; Creswell 2013; Patton 2015) although others are more concerned with the taking of a reflexive stance than explicit disclosure of a person's life experience (Charmaz 2014). Where researchers are explicit, there are different views about how this should best be done. Patton, for example, suggests that the methods section of a qualitative paper should acknowledge the role of the researcher in the research (Patton 2015), while Creswell suggests a number of options, from the opening passage through a 'threaded through the study' option to the end of the study (Creswell 2013).

It goes without saying that researchers should be reflexive in their approach to the conduct of the research and particularly the analysis, and they should also be reflective in writing their research for external dissemination, thinking particularly about issues such as their own theoretical perspective and personal experience, and how this might have influenced the research. Certainly, an awareness of the role of the researcher is important, and information should be provided about who conducted the research. Indeed, the COREQ guidance requires some reflexive information of this type (Tong, Sainsbury, et al. 2007). Nevertheless, for an economics publication, with an economics audience, where the vast majority of publications are quantitative, it is probably also the case that going too far in this direction is likely to reduce the chance of publication. Certainly, the use of a first-person active voice giving extensive reflexive information and weaving this through the work (Creswell 2013) is largely unseen in the published examples of health economics qualitative research. Elements of reflexivity are apparent in health economics research in providing both information about the research team (De Allegri, Sanon, et al. 2006b; Canaway, Al-Janabi, et al. 2017) and some discussion about the impact of the researcher on the research (Coast 2001a), but extensive discussion of this type is more likely to be seen in longer documents such as doctoral theses (Coast 2000b; Owen-Smith 2008) than in journal articles.

Presenting the findings for an economics audience

The very start of this chapter highlighted the lack of familiarity of economics audiences with qualitative research, although this may be less true for health economists, particularly those working in health rather than economics academic departments. The excerpt at the beginning of the chapter highlights the concerns that some editors and reviewers might have with the use of quotes in the reporting of findings (Coast, McDonald, et al. 2004). The presentation of quotes as evidence for the findings is important, however, in showing the veracity of the work; in many ways this is akin to the presentation of tables or graphs of data in quantitative studies. As Patton states, ‘Rich, detailed description and direct quotations constitute the foundation of qualitative inquiry. Sufficient description and direct quotations should be included to allow the reader to enter into the situation observed and the thoughts of the people represented in the report’ (Patton 2015, p. 605).

Indeed, in practice, a constant of presentation, seen in almost all health economics qualitative research studies, is the use of quotes both to provide description and to underline the emerging analysis and interpretation. Although some health economists do additionally use other techniques to clarify their interpretation, as discussed later, it is extremely unusual for them not to provide quotes in the text under discussion of the themes or the emerging theoretical model. There are a number of aspects of good practice in the use of quotes. Of greatest importance is that researchers should be careful in providing quotes, such that they do not in any way compromise the confidentiality of informants. Thought should also go into the purpose of the quotes presented. Geneau and colleagues, for example, use quotes to illustrate their findings in two ways (Geneau, Massae, et al. 2008). The first is to illustrate views that were expressed by a number of their informants; the second is to illustrate particular views that diverged from the majority. It is not necessary to provide large numbers of quotes to illustrate each point; one or two should suffice. In choosing quotes, it is helpful to choose those that most clearly illustrate the point being made, but it is also important to include a range of informants overall and avoid using the same one or two informants to provide all the quotes in the paper, as this may undermine the credibility of the analysis. Quotes should be properly and informatively labelled so that the reader can see something of the characteristics of the informant.

It can also be helpful to edit the verbatim quotes somewhat, being explicit in the methods about how this has been done and, obviously, avoiding changing the meaning. This might include omitting substantive text with use of ellipses (. . .) and omitting text without use of ellipses when ‘umms’ and ‘errs’ are omitted because they do not add to the specific point being made and when omitting use of terms such as ‘you know’, ‘sort of’ or ‘I mean’ which do not relate directly to the specific point being made, or when informants repeat a word immediately and this repetition adds nothing to meaning. Such editing of quotes is helpful in two ways. First, it reduces unnecessary length, which is always a key consideration when publishing in journals with restricted word limits. Second, it enables the reader to understand the meaning that is being illustrated rather than having to work this out for themselves. To illustrate this, a full quote is given from the analytic account generated for Coast’s citizen–agent analysis and then the quote that appears in the final paper is given (Coast 2001a).

QUOTE FROM ANALYTIC ACCOUNT: that are trained, and I think really, with the, as the doctors, yes, because the public will take a personal view, will take a personal view, but with the qualified err, fully qualified surgeon or professor, that’s their job so it wouldn’t be a personal view, I mean, if it was err, if it was for the public to decide, nothing would get done, nothing would get done.

QUOTE FROM PAPER: I think really . . . the public will take a personal view, but with the . . . fully qualified surgeon or professor, that’s their job so it wouldn’t be a personal view.

In general, economics papers would also be expected to start their findings with details of the characteristics of those included in the study, often presented in the form of a table. This might summarize the age and sex of informants, as well as other characteristics that are potentially relevant to the interpretation such as health state, living circumstances and professional roles. These should be at a sufficient level of generality to avoid individuals being recognizable. In reporting findings under themes, economists (who come from a primarily quantitative discipline) should avoid the temptation to report frequencies (e.g., seven out of twenty-five informants suggested that . . .). The main reason for avoiding presentation of such frequencies is the purposeful nature of sampling, particularly those forms of sampling that are driven by the ongoing analysis, which means that these frequencies may well be related to the sampling choices. While it can be valuable to indicate where a particular theme or issue was common across most of the sample, or was related just to a particular single case, any sense of precision should be avoided.

Economists may also choose to use other forms of data display (Grbich 2013), depending on their topic. Although it is important to present quotes to show the veracity of the research, other forms of data display may help to illustrate the models that might arise from economic analysis of qualitative data. These might include social networks, matrices, decision trees to show how sequential decisions lead to outcomes, flow charts, ladders, taxonomies and Venn diagrams (Grbich 2013). Existing examples within the health economics literature include the use of a flow diagram by Geneau and colleagues to show the interrelated dimensions of willingness to pay for cataract surgery in Tanzania (Geneau, Massae, et al. 2008), the use of a diagrammatic taxonomy by Goebbels and colleagues in exploring non-health outcomes for a lifestyle behaviour change intervention (Goebbels, Lakerveld, et al. 2012) and the use of a bar graph by van Osch and Stiggelbout to show the focus of attention in completion of standard gambles (van Osch and Stiggelbout 2008). A particular type of taxonomy frequently presented in attribute development studies is the full list of attributes and their levels (Ke, Mackichan, et al. 2013; Abiiro, Leppert, et al. 2014). Economists also quite commonly present themes in tables (Kaltenthaler, Essat, et al. 2014; Kinghorn, Robinson, et al. 2014; Jackson and Roberts 2015) and quotes in boxes (Holmes, Bate, et al. 2009). An example of presenting social networks figures generated during data collection is shown in the work by Canaway and colleagues (Chapter 12).

Presenting qualitative alongside quantitative data

In the case of mixed-methods research, the presentation of the qualitative and quantitative data needs to be organized in a way that makes sense for the particular piece of research. It may be sequentially presented as in papers where the qualitative work forms the basis for attributes for a discrete choice experiment, for example, in work on preferences for types of dermatology appointment (Coast, Salisbury, et al. 2006). Or the two types of data may be integrated throughout the paper, as in Bertone and Lagarde's work on health worker revenues in Sierra Leone (Bertone and Lagarde 2016).

A particular challenge for economists is the brief presentation of qualitative research that has been conducted purely for the purposes of conducting the quantitative research. This may be particularly the case where the qualitative work does not justify its own publication, at least insofar as its purpose in informing the quantitative research; although, often, when this work is conducted by qualitative researchers working with economists, they will also publish the work separately focusing on themes generated around the health issues (Horrocks and Coast 2007; Sutton and Coast 2012). Where work has to be briefly presented within a primarily quantitative publication, it may be that the full COREQ guidance cannot be adhered to. Nevertheless, in relation to attribute development, guidance has been given that the minimum information given should include a rationale for the method, information about the nature of the sample and the sampling mechanism, brief details of the interview schedule and interview conduct, information about transcription and type of analysis and a brief description of the findings including the manipulation of attributes (Coast, Al-Janabi, et al. 2012). Even in a very brief description, it is important to show in the presentation that the research, even as underpinning research, has been conducted rigorously.

PUBLICATION

Publication within economics could target general economics journals but is most likely to be aimed at the discipline-specific health economics journals. Publication within the health literature covers a multitude of disciplines, ranging through health policy, medicine, nursing and allied health. Recent reviews have suggested that publication of qualitative research can be challenging, particularly when targeting the higher-impact journals (McKibbon and Gadd 2004; Gagliardi and Dobrow 2011; Weiner, Amick, et al. 2011).

There is some evidence that it can be difficult to publish qualitative research in the highest-impact medical journals. Evidence from 2011 looked at publication of qualitative papers in the ten top general medical journals (based on four different sets of rankings) (Gagliardi and Dobrow 2011). The proportion of research papers published that used qualitative methods varied by journal from 0 percent (*Journal of Internal Medicine*, *New England Journal of Medicine*) to 0.6 percent (*BMJ*); other journals examined were *American Journal of Medicine* (0.2 percent), *Annals of Internal Medicine*

(0.3 percent), *Archives of Internal Medicine* (0.3 percent), *Canadian Medical Association Journal* (0.3 percent), *JAMA – Journal of the American Medical Association* (0.1 percent), *Lancet* (0.1 percent) and *PLOS Medicine* (0.2 percent) (Gagliardi and Dobrow 2011); in general it appears that more qualitative research is published in nursing journals (McKibbon and Gadd 2004), although this may also reflect the extent of use of different research methodologies in the different disciplines.

There has recently been a lively debate within the medical literature about the value of qualitative research, with extensive discussion over the publication of qualitative research in high-impact medical journals (Clark and Thompson 2016; Greenhalgh 2016; Loder, Groves, et al. 2016) following indications from the *BMJ* that it would treat qualitative research as a lower priority (Greenhalgh 2016; Loder, Groves, et al. 2016). There is much in this discussion that is useful to health economists aiming to present qualitative research both in medical and in economics journals. Clark and Thompson, in particular, present some useful suggestions for engaging with research communities for whom qualitative research is not the usual form of research. These include 'try, try, try again' in relation to choosing to submit papers to the relevant journals rather than settling for a journal with lower impact, making the key messages both clear and matched to the journal being targeted (and being aware of the journal's scope) and being mindful of the advantages of publishing in mainstream journals in terms of connecting with the relevant communities (Clark and Thompson 2016). It is also important to note that while achieving publication may be challenging on occasion, qualitative papers for well-conducted research can be extremely highly cited and influential (Greenhalgh 2016), for example, highly cited work on health care decision making and knowledge management in primary care (Gabbay and le May 2004), on patient non-compliance (Donovan and Blake 1992) and on unvoiced agendas in patient consultations (Barry, Bradley, et al. 2000).

The publication situation does not seem to be that different for the top health services and policy research journals, which includes a number of notable health economics journals. Here, the proportion of qualitative papers in ten top health services research and policy research journals (again based on four sets of rankings) over the same period (1999–2008) ranged from 0 percent (*Journal of Health Economics*) to 6.4 percent (*Quality and Safety in Health Care*) (Gagliardi and Dobrow 2011). Other journals researched were *American Journal of Managed Care* (1.1 percent), *Health Affairs* (1.1 percent), *Health Economics* (0.8 percent), *Health Services Research* (1.8 percent), *Medical Care* (0.8 percent), *Medical Decision Making* (2.1 percent), *Milbank Quarterly* (2.3 percent) and *Value in Health* (0.8 percent) (Gagliardi and Dobrow 2011). Nevertheless, just as highly cited papers can be seen in the medical literature, there are highly cited papers using qualitative methods from health economists on a range of topics including understanding aspects of the health economy in lower- and middle-income countries (McPake, Asiimwe, et al. 1999; De Allegri, Sanon, et al. 2006a), generation of capability attributes (Grewal, Lewis, et al. 2006; Al-Janabi, Coast, et al. 2008; Coast, Flynn, et al. 2008) and priority setting (Litva, Coast, et al. 2002; Bryan, Williams, et al. 2007).

Weiner and colleagues identify several factors that might influence publication rates: the extent to which researchers in the field are actually conducting qualitative research (influenced by both funding for qualitative research and levels of training in qualitative research), choice of publication outlet and the views of journal editors and the reviewers they select (Weiner, Amick, et al. 2011). The concern that funding for qualitative research may be limited has also been expressed elsewhere: 'There is a perception among research funding agencies, clinicians and policy makers, that qualitative research is "second class" research' (Tong, Sainsbury, et al. 2007, p. 356).

The lack of qualitative research published in health economics journals is therefore likely to be the result of all of these factors, a number of which are beyond the scope of this chapter. Rather, it is important to note here that, although 'a natural solution for health economists facing difficulties with publication is to submit to general, rather than economics, journals' (Coast, McDonald, et al. 2004, p. 173), it is important to keep targeting (health) economics journals. This is because the main audience for this work is and should be economists. Despite the fact that qualitative research may challenge the discipline both methodologically and theoretically, it is economists who will most benefit from reading the research and perhaps then taking it forward either quantitatively or qualitatively. Applying the advice from Clark and Thompson from the health arena (Clark and Thompson 2016), by continuing to target the mainstream (health) economics journals, is important not just in getting the research to the right audience but also in changing the cultural acceptability of qualitative research within health economics, something that is already happening during recent years.

CONCLUSION

Qualitative research within health economics can offer important advances in the field, through avenues from improving the quantitative data with which economists work through to improving the theoretical understanding within the discipline. This will be achieved, however, only if economists publish the qualitative research that they conduct and publish it both with rigour and in a way that engages with the health economics community. It is not enough, for example, to do as many of those conducting discrete choice experiments have done in the past, reducing the qualitative element of their research to little more than a couple of sentences along the lines of having conducted focus groups and a number of attributes having emerged (Coast, Al-Janabi, et al. 2012). Not only is such reporting poor, but it is impossible to know whether the research itself has been conducted with any rigour; if not, it casts doubt on the value of the whole of the subsequent quantitative work within the paper (Coast, Al-Janabi, et al. 2012).

Those reading this book with a view to conducting qualitative research within health economics will have already made sound and rigorous choices with regard to their research. The final stage of their work is to do the same with regard to publication!

ACKNOWLEDGEMENTS

I would like to thank Hareth Al-Janabi for comments on an earlier draft of this chapter.

Part II

CASE STUDIES

Chapter 8

Introduction to the case studies

Joanna Coast

The first part of this book has aimed to provide health economists coming to the area of qualitative research with the background and tools that will enable them to design, conduct and interpret qualitative studies of their own. Although practical examples and advice were given within these chapters, researchers coming to this area also need to see, in more depth, how economists have tackled different types of research problems. That is the purpose of this second part of the book.

The chapters are divided into three groups broadly aligned with the purposes for qualitative research in health economics described in Chapter 2. The first comprises chapters whose main purpose is to develop and enhance quantitative research (Chapters 9 to 13); the second comprises chapters whose main purpose is to interpret quantitative findings (Chapters 14 to 16) and the third comprises those chapters where the research aim is to enhance and generate economic understanding and theory (Chapters 17 to 20). Having made this pragmatic divide, which should help economists to identify the chapters most likely to be of relevance to their own work, it is important to note that the chapters are very varied and each also offers particular information beyond these specific issues of purpose.

In being asked to provide a case study chapter for this book, authors were asked to focus on a particular area in which they had expertise or a specific piece of work that they had completed. Beyond this, however, authors were given considerable freedom about the particular nature of their contribution. This was in the interests of having a spread of different types of chapters and a variety of approaches to qualitative research within the case studies. Authors were able to bring their own approach to both the content and the style of presentation.

Some chapters, therefore, provide quite general overviews of a specific area, within which the case study example is situated (e.g., see Chapter 9 by Baker et al. on Q methodology, Chapter 11 by Stevens on the use of qualitative methods in generating preference-based measures, Chapter 12 by Canaway et al. on the use of pictorial data collection methods and Chapter 20 by Smith on the choice of theoretical approach in priority setting research). Other chapters, in contrast, provide detailed exploration of the methods used throughout a particular case study (Chapters 10, 11, 13, 15, 16, 18, 19). Still others drill down more deeply into specific issues within a case study, with Bailey et al. focusing explicitly on three issues in Chapter 14, including conducting research in sensitive contexts, and De Allegri focusing specifically on design issues in the context of a study collecting both qualitative and quantitative data. Chapters also vary in terms of their presentation and the way they are written, with some providing quite personal accounts written in the first person, others providing a more neutral descriptive approach and yet others writing with a more instructive voice, focusing on those readers who want to follow similar methods; these choices are themselves likely to be of interest to economists who are not used to working in a more interpretivist paradigm.

In the first section of the book, links are made to chapters that are of particular relevance to a specific point, and the reader may therefore identify case study chapters that are of particular relevance to their work through reading these initial chapters. Given the variety of the case studies, however, and because each may offer researchers particular information that is not immediately apparent from the title, the remainder of this short chapter is used to briefly describe the key contributions of each case study to the potential reader. This is done in the order in which chapters are presented in the book.

Chapters 9 to 13 focus on research where the aim is to develop and enhance quantitative research. Chapter 9, from Baker, McHugh and Mason, provides an introduction to Q methodology, highlighting the mixture of qualitative and quantitative techniques that forms the basis for the approach. The chapter focuses on one of the main qualitative aspects of the approach, the generation of the 'Q set' that forms the basis for the collection of data that are then used in further quantitative and qualitative analyses. The analytic approach to the qualitative data collected for generating the 'Q set' is quite specific to the approach and involves identifying strong and opposing views from a variety of sources, using a purposeful sampling approach that aims to generate maximum variation, and then selecting a set of statements that represent the totality of those statements. Baker and colleagues set their work in the context of a Q study focusing on views about life extension for people with terminal illness.

Chapters 10 and 11 both focus on using qualitative methods to generate attributes/dimensions/domains for valuation using quantitative techniques.

Chapter 10, from Vosper, Coast and Flynn, describes two case studies of the generation of attributes for discrete choice experiments. Both were conducted on the topic of depression, an area which can be sensitive and challenging to research. The chapter describes the use of two different data collection techniques: semi-structured interviews and focus groups. Of particular interest in this chapter is how the authors conducted the analysis to make decisions about the generation of attributes from their qualitative data, including at times by combining the qualitative findings with other sources of information, particularly the existing academic literature. Detailed examples are presented for a small number of attributes so that the reader can fully understand the process undertaken. The chapter also provides a discussion of the philosophical approach to the research and notes on issues around the reliability of the research.

Chapter 11, by Stevens, describes general approaches to the development of dimensions for preference-based measures, contrasting approaches that have smaller or larger roles for qualitative research methods. She then focuses specifically on the development of the CHU9D, a preference-based measure for children, generated through interviews with children. Stevens takes the reader through the whole research process, including sampling, data collection and data analysis. As well as being of interest to those readers concerned with attribute or dimension development, the chapter will also be of interest to those whose research focus is on childhood.

Chapters 12 and 13 are both situated in the context of research that is intended to develop and enhance quantitative research by thinking more broadly about economic methods, rather than by generating qualitative data to inform a specific piece of quantitative research. Both chapters also provide exploration of methods that are largely novel in the context of health economics qualitative research. Chapter 12, from Canaway, Al-Janabi, Kinghorn, Bailey and Coast, was conducted in the context of generating information about the appropriate scope (in terms of who should be included) for economic evaluations of care at the end of life. Canaway and colleagues focused on obtaining information about the social networks of those at the end of life using innovative (for health economics) pictorial methods. The chapter provides detailed information about a number of the pictorial tools that might be available for such research. It then explores the use of hierarchical mapping in one case study. The chapter also explores the value of such task-based activities in generating rapport between the interviewer and the informant.

Chapter 13, by Husbands, Jowett, Barton and Coast, was conducted in the context of research to explore, and generate better processes for, decision analytic modelling. The chapter focuses on the observational elements of the research, in terms of both non-participant observation of meetings and the innovative use of think-aloud techniques to observe solitary modelling activity; this chapter thus provides the most detailed case study of the use of an observational approach in the book. Husbands and colleagues provide a detailed description of these methods as well as present some illustrative findings and provide a detailed reflection on the methods used.

Chapters 14 to 16 move on to consider research where the main aim is to interpret quantitative findings. Chapter 14, from Bailey, Kinghorn, Orlando and Coast, focuses on the methods used in applying a think-aloud approach to explore measure completion by those at the end of life and their potential proxies. It focuses on three specific issues that were pertinent to the case study. First, it details the methods used for a think-aloud study of this type. The second issue, explored in depth, arises from the end-of-life context in which the work was conducted, and comprises discussion of the challenges associated with conducting qualitative research in sensitive environments. The third issue is the use of different analytic techniques for achieving different purposes within the same dataset.

Chapter 15, by Robinson, uses qualitative methods to explore the validity of techniques for health state valuation, providing hints and tips for others working in this area. The work was undertaken alongside a larger programme of work, and Robinson details some of the design challenges that arose as a result; this is likely to be a common problem in much work conducted by economists. The chapter also provides a detailed description of the sampling, data collection and analytic strategies. Of further interest in this chapter is that Robinson explicitly considers the reporting of her findings, and some of the challenges of publishing health economics research that has used qualitative methods.

Chapter 16, by Kinghorn, Canaway, Bailey and Coast, provides a slightly different focus in terms of the interpretation of quantitative findings. It applies a deliberative approach to valuation of outcomes for family and friends in the context of end-of-life care, first setting the work in the context of a broader overview of deliberative research. The chapter is of interest in three areas: its use of a deliberative approach; its use of focus groups and exploration of associated practical issues around recruiting to, and conducting, such groups; and its discussion of purposeful random sampling.

Chapters 17 to 20 provide case studies where the aim was to enhance and generate economic understanding and theory. Broadly these case studies related to two areas where the use of qualitative methods within health economics has been highest: in generating understanding around different aspects of health systems in lower- and middle-income countries, and in understanding processes around setting priorities for health care. Chapters 17 and 18 concentrate on the first area, and Chapters 19 and 20 on the second.

Chapter 17, by De Allegri, examines the use of qualitative methods in impact evaluation, focusing specifically on a case study of the use of results-based financing in Malawi. The chapter is of particular interest because of its detailed examination of methodological design choices, in the context of a study using a mix of quantitative and qualitative approaches. The chapter details the use of a number of approaches to sampling and data collection in this context and the operational challenges that were faced.

Chapter 18, by Martínez-Álvarez, assesses aid effectiveness using a case study of Tanzania. The chapter provides a detailed account of the use of a variety of methods, including document review, in-depth interviews and non-participant observation. It also provides a useful, step-by-step application of the framework approach to the data, as well as consideration of issues of validity, reliability and reflexivity.

Chapter 19, from Eckard and Nedlund, moves to the area of health care priority setting. This chapter focuses on priority setting processes around setting guidelines in Sweden and uses both observational and interview techniques. It applies a thematic content analysis approach to the analysis of data, using a combination of deduction and induction to generate themes.

Chapter 20 from Smith, provides an overview of the use of qualitative methods in priority setting research, focusing particularly on design issues. The chapter considers the different theoretical and methodological approaches explored in Chapter 2, in terms of their application to priority setting research, and Smith advocates clearly for the importance of taking a theoretical stance within the research. He then explores four specific examples of priority setting research conducted in Canada, focusing on the use of different approaches in terms of both data collection and analysis.

CONCLUSION

Each of the brief aforementioned descriptions should help to orient readers as to which of the chapters might be most helpful to them in their own research. Chapters 1 to 7 also highlight where specific issues are touched upon in the case study chapters, and readers may also want to combine the information given in those chapters with the short descriptions of the specific contributions of each case study highlighted here, in choosing which chapters to focus upon.

Together, these chapters provide readers with a varied set of experiences of the generation, analysis and interpretation of qualitative data in a number of different health economics contexts. They give greater depth on some topics than was possible in the first part of this book, particularly around the use of qualitative approaches in specific contexts such as the generation of Q sets, and in the use of more specialized methods such as think-aloud, pictorial methods and deliberation. The case studies also provide both detailed accounts of the activities undertaken and candid reflections on the research conducted. Importantly, each of these case studies is conducted in a particular context, and these contexts form an important element of each case study, influencing design, sampling, data collection and data analytic choices. Overall, these case studies complement the detailed descriptions of methods in the first part of the book, and will generate greater understanding for readers, of the application of qualitative research methods to health economics.

Part II A

USING QUALITATIVE METHODS TO DEVELOP AND ENHANCE QUANTITATIVE RESEARCH

Chapter 9

Constructing statement sets for use in Q methodology studies

Rachel Baker, Neil McHugh and Helen Mason

Q methodology was conceived by William Stephenson as a means to study 'subjectivity', a term that is used to refer to subjective beliefs, opinions and values (Stainton Rogers 1995). First described in 1935 in a letter to *Nature*, Stephenson's seminal work 'The study of behavior' was published in 1953 (Stephenson 1935, 1953). Q is now a well-established approach to researching subjectivity, and there are numerous publications reporting Q studies in psychology, political science and in various social, environmental and health sciences (Brown 1980; Stenner and Rogers 1998; van Exel, de Graaf et al. 2006; Cuppen, Breukers et al. 2010; Jeffares and Skelcher 2011; McHugh, Baker et al. 2015).

Q is a not a particularly common approach in health economics research and, like qualitative methods, crosses disciplinary boundaries in a way that can cause tensions as well as bear fruit (Coast 1999). We have used Q methods to address questions framed through a health economics lens such as exploring economic models of rationality (Baker 2006) and public priorities for health care provision (Baker, Bateman et al. 2010; Mason, Baker et al. 2011; Baker, Wildman et al. 2014; van Exel, Baker et al. 2015). Like qualitative methods, Q has also been proposed as a means of selecting attributes for, or better understanding findings from, preference elicitation studies (Baker, Thompson et al. 2006). Although it has not been commonly used in this way it has been applied in a small number of stated preference studies in health and environmental economics (Lancsar, Wildman et al. 2011; Armatas, Venn et al. 2014).

Q comprises a set of qualitative and quantitative techniques, and in this chapter we focus on one particular aspect of a Q study – the construction of the 'Q set', which is a sample of items, usually statements, that forms the basis of data collection in Q methodology. We describe the principles that guide Q set design and discuss structured and unstructured Q sets and different approaches to accessing the 'concourse' (a term used to describe the flowing together of statements and arguments) on any given subject.

Before turning to the focus of the chapter and by way of situating our account of Q set design, we give a brief introduction to Q methodology. In doing so, we connect the Q set to the other aspects of Q study design and conduct. The philosophy underlying Q methodology and the techniques associated with Q are detailed in key texts, which we would recommend to those interested in Q methodology (Brown 1980; Watts and Stenner 2012; McKeown and Thomas 2013). We do not attempt to do justice to those here. Instead we characterize Q methodology, in brief, via two key features of Q studies: the means of generating data and the approach to analysis, each of which is summarized and followed by some observations about Q and mixed method research.

GENERATING Q DATA

Participants in Q studies express their viewpoints on a given topic through a card-sort exercise known as a Q sort. The epistemological foundations of Q are based on the assertion that individuals' subjectivity can be made 'operant' for the purposes of study, through the rank ordering of a set of stimuli. Typically, cards are printed with statements of opinion (although images and objects have also been used in Q sorts) sampled carefully to represent the range and breadth of opinion on the subject matter in question. The statement cards are placed into a grid according to a condition of instruction – typically to 'rank order the cards from most agree to most disagree' or 'from most like me to most unlike me'. The Q grid is quasi-normal or pyramid-shaped, permitting ties (all statements placed in the same column are ranked equally); respondents indicate their agreement with, or the importance of, statements by placing them on the grid. Fewer spaces in the columns at the outsides of the grid reflect an expectation that there will be a few issues about which people feel very strongly and more statements that do not resonate with respondents' views. Respondents are usually guided through the Q sort by an interviewer, beginning at the poles, so that respondents place those statements they most (dis)agree with first and work towards the centre of the grid.

Figure 9.1 shows a picture of a sorting grid and a condition of instruction. In this example there are forty-nine statement cards; the number of statements will vary from study to study, and the grid is designed each time to fit.

Q factor analysis

Factor analysis is used to identify a small number of shared views, based on the correlations between the Q sorts. Usually factor analysis is used to identify

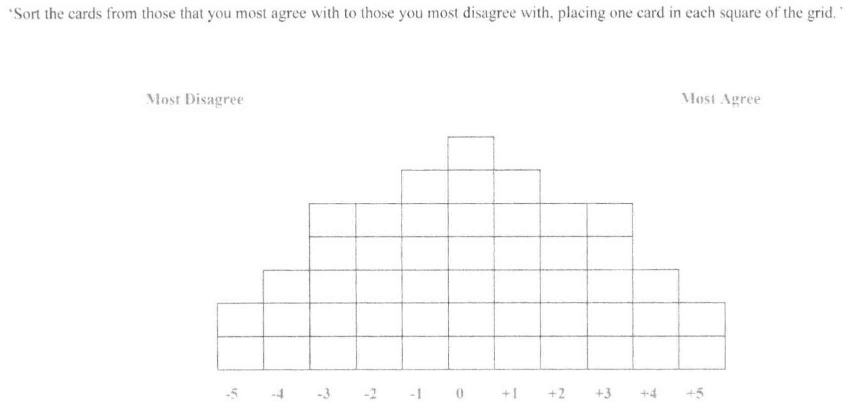

Figure 9.1. Q grid and sorting instruction. Courtesy of the author.

underlying dimensions connecting tests or other measures; for example, several questionnaire items attempting to measure different aspects of quality of life might be connected by a smaller number of underlying dimensions, and those dimensions are drawn out as factors based on correlations between scores. In Q methodology each Q sort is correlated (positively or negatively) with every other Q sort, and those correlations are used to identify patterns of similarity across a sample of Q sorts. Factors in Q methodology are shared perspectives – clusters of similar Q sorts that are distinct from other clusters of Q sorts forming different factors.

Figure 9.2 illustrates factor analysis in Q methodology. The similarity between Q sorts is illustrated using patterns and shading. In this example three factors result and each factor is represented by an 'average Q sort' or 'factor array'.

Importantly, Q depends on an expectation of 'finite diversity' (Rogers, Stenner et al. 1995). Although there are many ways to rank order even a small set of cards, and it follows that it is unlikely that two Q sorters will arrange the cards in exactly the same way, Q methods are based on the assumption that there are a limited number of different ways of seeing an issue. Hence from a large number of Q sorts a small set of perspectives are identified, usually between one and seven factors. Each of the resulting factors is represented by a distinct ordering of statements, calculated as a weighted average of Q sorts that are highly and purely associated with the factor in question, and resulting in a composite or average Q sort for each factor known as an array. It is this factor array that forms the basis of interpretation and description of each factor.

Wherever possible, Q sorts should be conducted face to face (although a growing number are administered online), and each Q sort is followed by a brief interview recording the respondent's summary of their views and an

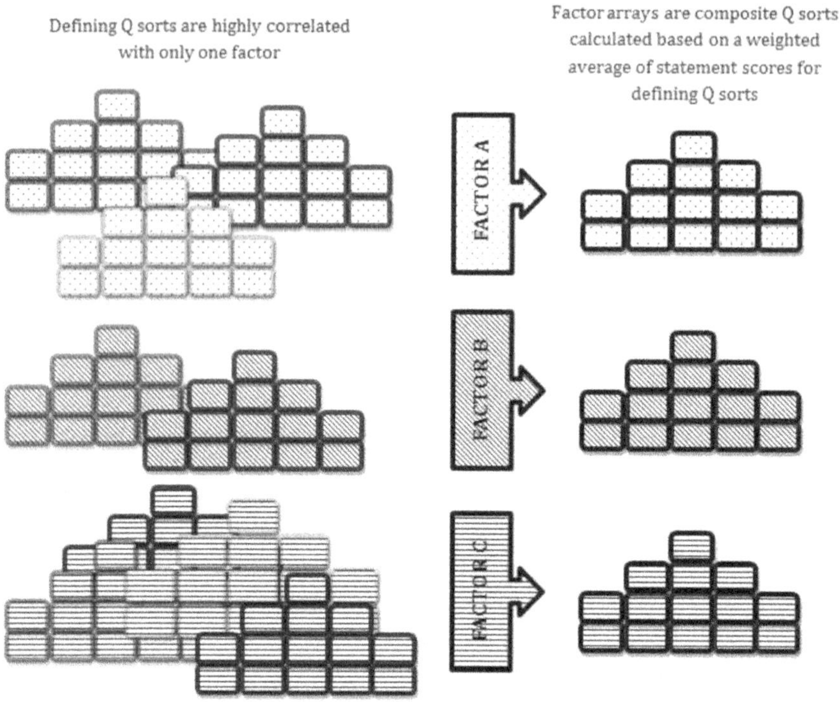

Figure 9.2. An illustration of Q factor analysis. Courtesy of the author.

explanation of the ordering of the Q cards. These qualitative data are then useful in selecting and interpreting a factor solution and in constructing a rich description of the views identified.

Q AND MIXED METHODS

Q methodology has qualitative foundations; Q studies are designed to answer 'what' and 'how' questions of subjectivity rather than measuring 'to what extent'. But Q methods also combine qualitative and quantitative techniques, a feature that perhaps makes Q particularly attractive to researchers who are interested in quantitative as well as qualitative information and who are drawn to interdisciplinary research and cross-disciplinary questions (Coast 1999; Coast, McDonald et al. 2004; Baker, Thompson et al. 2006).

The results of Q studies are, first and foremost, rich descriptions of the different shared perspectives that exist on the topic of interest. Alongside these rich, detailed data to be examined and interpreted, quantitative information is generated. Each respondent's Q sort is correlated with every other respondent's Q sort, resulting in a matrix that expresses similarity between participants' viewpoints, where a value of 1 indicates an identical ranking of the statements and –1 an exactly reversed rank order. Once factors are extracted, correlation coefficients known as 'factor loadings' are calculated indicating the extent to which each respondents' Q sort is similar to each of the factors (i.e., the similarity between individuals' views and the shared perspectives that have been identified). And, when interpreting factors (through, as shown in Figure 9.2, composite Q sorts that represent an average ordering of the statements for people associated with each factor) the *whole* array is of interest (and not simply the differences in the positioning of individual statements between factors). Q factor analysis produces a '*z* score' for each statement which is an indication of the 'contribution', or importance, of the statement to the factor, as well as the ranked position of each statement within each factor array.

THE Q SET

The first step in a Q study, once the subject of the study has been located and specified, is a qualitative matter of accessing and drawing from the 'concourse' in order to design the statement set.

Concourse in Q methodology

The term 'concourse', taken from the Latin meaning 'a running together', is conceptualized as a flow of communication, a coming together of views, of competing and complementary arguments and beliefs. Stephenson described it as:

> A universe of 'statements' so conceived for any situation or context . . . to remind us that the concern is with conversational possibilities, not merely informational. There is a concourse for every concept, every declarative statement, every wish, every object in nature when viewed subjectively. (Stephenson 1986, p. 44)

The starting point of every Q study is to locate access points and find means to 'hear' the flow of communication that is the concourse. We can find entry points to existing conversations or generate new discussion around any topic of concern, from simple subjects, as in Stephenson's example, all subjective possibilities around the subject 'it is raining' (Stephenson 1986), to commonly discussed moral or political issues, such as views on assisted dying or perspectives on the referendum for Scottish independence in 2014.

Different subjects are likely to entail different points of access, but it is usually better to attempt to 'find' rather than construct – by locating the relevant discourse(s) and finding a window into those conversations.

Perhaps the most common way to access the concourse is to make space for points of view to be expressed through interviews or focus groups. By introducing a topic and asking open-ended questions of people who are likely to have different views, the researcher 'collects' statements expressing different thoughts and opinions. Depending on the topic of concern, the questions posed may be more open or more directed in nature. For some topics, respondents may have a strong viewpoint, already articulated; for others their views might not be pre-articulated. Additional statements may be required around a particular theme which would indicate a higher level of direction and questioning (e.g., to add what appear to be missing components to Q sets in development).

To generate the statements from interview data, the aim is not to conduct a full qualitative analysis. Instead, the researcher examines transcripts quite quickly and highlights any and all statements of opinion in relation to the research question under consideration. At this stage it is important not to manipulate or 'clean up' respondents' statements too much – but simply to find and list them. Q statements retain the language of the original expression, wherever possible, and even an element of looseness so that they might be interpreted by different respondents in different ways. This is sometimes alien to researchers accustomed to survey design where the aim is to ensure that there is only one way of interpreting questionnaire items. That said, it is important that Q statements are not overly long and complex, or express multiple points of view (this is sometimes tricky – but the aim is that a respondent will agree or disagree with the statement and not agree with one part and disagree with another).

Researchers should identify interviewees or other source material that gives access to strong views expressed by people with different ideas and experiences. Different research questions will lead researchers to different sources. For example, a societal question such as, 'what is the nature of societal views in relation to the referendum for an independent Scotland?' is relevant to anyone (who is politically engaged) in that country – and perhaps even outside of it. One might consider the political allegiance of respondents and seek views from people of different age groups, ethnic origins and so on. To get a sense of strong and opposing views, political leaders or academic experts might be interviewed, or else published materials from different political parties or lobby groups might be consulted. If we were designing a Q set as part of a study of views about resuscitation in hospital intensive care units, different sources would be identified which would be likely to include clinicians, ethicists, families and patients who have experience of intensive care.

As a growing list of potential Q statements is collected, other sources will be suggested or become obvious and a good technique when conducting interviews is to ask respondents to suggest someone, or another category of respondent, who would give a very different view to their own.

The media is a rich source of views, and statements can be collected by searching newspapers for relevant articles, readers' responses to those articles, television documentaries, political debates and interviews, web-based discussions, social media and anywhere that debate and discussion play out. Policy documents and the public consultations that often accompany policy documents can also be rich sources of statements.

In a recent study of the relative value of life extension for people with terminal illnesses we accessed the concourse in different ways (McHugh et al. 2015). Table 9.1 details the sources we identified to access different aspects

Table 9.1. Sources of statements for study of values and life extension and terminal illness

Source	*Details*
Newspaper Review	Forty-five newspaper articles reporting decisions of NICE committees regarding the approval or rejection of new 'end of life' drugs, including readers' responses following the articles on the newspaper websites. For example: • *Condemned to an early death: Rationing body tells liver cancer victims that life-prolonging drug is 'too costly'* (Hope 2009) • *Cancer drug 'too expensive for NHS'* (Boseley 2012)
NICE Public Consultation	NICE conducted a public consultation on their draft proposal – 'Appraising life-extending, end of life treatments' (National Institute for Health and Clinical Excellence 2008): • End of life treatments: views on the proposition (National Institute for Health and Clinical Excellence 2009b) • End of life treatments: general comments (National Institute for Health and Clinical Excellence 2009a)
Qualitative Interviews	Sixteen in-depth interviews with: • Friends/family with experience of bereavement, n = 6 • Health/medical professionals (doctor, cancer nurse, medical director, palliative care worker), n = 4 • Academic health economist, n = 1 • Cancer charity/patient groups, n = 2 • Pharmaceutical industry, n = 2 • Religious leader, n = 1
Focus Groups	Three general population focus groups (n = 21) recruited via a survey company: • 11 female • Age range 22 to 70+

of the concourse. Ethical approval for this study was obtained from the School of Health and Life Sciences Ethics Committee, Glasgow Caledonian University (reference B11/04).

GENERATING A Q SET

The next stage is to reduce a long list of statements into a manageable Q set. Statements should not be empirical claims or matters of fact but rather sentences that would naturally be preceded with 'in my opinion . . .' or 'it is my belief that. . .'. The aim is to generate a set of statements that will allow Q sorters of all persuasions to express their views. The statement set is the basis for data collection in a Q study, and the design of the Q set is an important part of the research process; it is often the stage of the Q study that takes the most time. Some writers have noted that Q set design is more art than science.

> Mention of arts and crafts should not, however, be taken as a metaphor indicating a lack of system or rigour. Artistic work ordinarily requires great persistence and very high levels of skill. Both of these attributes will be required if you want to produce the best possible Q set. (Watts and Stenner 2012, p. 58)

Methods for sampling a Q set from a concourse are in some ways akin to sampling participants or respondents from a large population – as in survey sampling from the general population or sampling from a population of patients for medical research. The aim is to draw a small number of statements that will represent the population of statements. Rather than sampling randomly, as is often the case in medical trials or population surveys, efforts are made to sample statements from a wide range of different sources and to cover categories of viewpoint. Two researchers embarking on identical Q studies using similar methods would not come up with exactly the same Q set, but assuming they have sampled from the 'whole' concourse, and covered all the issues, they should both arrive at a Q set that is composed of the same broad themes, through which respondents could express their views on the topic in question. Factor analysis and interpretation of factors do not depend on the exact wording of a single statement but the relative positioning of a large number of statements.

Most Q sets are designed around concepts of coverage and balance, and Q methodologists use particular techniques in order to be confident that their Q sets are 'broadly representative of the opinion domain, population or concourse at issue' (Watts and Stenner 2012, p. 58). 'Coverage' refers to the range and extent of the Q set, and 'balance' pertains to issues of bias and a concern that the Q set is not weighed too heavily towards one particular view of the world. Q sets are often piloted before being finalized and pilot participants are asked to complete the Q sort and note any issues they thought were missing or that prevented them from expressing their views.

Inclusion, exclusion and the boundaries of the Q set

Setting out the research question clearly and establishing the condition of instruction that will be used for the Q sort are prerequisites for Q set design. Usually this entails setting some limits around what statements will, and will not, be considered relevant. In the study of views about life-extending treatments presented in Table 9.1, the research question and condition of instruction were as follows:

Research Question:

What are societal perspectives with respect to the relative value of life-extensions for people with terminal illness?

(in the context of a fixed budget in a publicly funded health system, where value is relative to all other potential health gains arising from NHS spending).

Condition of Instruction:

Please read each statement and place on the grid according to your level of agreement or disagreement.

We generated more than 200 statements and set about a process of reducing them – initially by categorizing them loosely into themes and determining whether those themes fell within the remit of the research questions.

During interviews we generated a number of statements around two issues that we then excluded from the Q set on the basis that, although relevant to the broad subject matter, these were outside the boundaries of our research question. These related to:

i) the pricing of pharmaceuticals, for example:

'Don't blame the NHS, which is operating on limited funds. The blame should be laid firmly at the door of the drug companies which are profiteering from people's misery'.

'Drug manufacturers have to make the case for value for money and if every drug is bankrolled by the NHS then there is no incentive to reduce prices'.

ii) arguments in relation to reallocation of government spending to allow growth of the health budget, for example:

'There is so much appalling use of money in this country – of course the drug should be made available. . . . Stop foreign aid to countries who buy luxury government cars, cut benefits to those who visit pubs and clubs or have more than Free View TV, stop funding sports and arts – they will be self-financing if they are worthwhile – saving life must be more important'.

'You just have to find the money for it, and it seems to me – without talking too politically – but it does seem to me that we can always find the money for wars and things like that'.

After extensive discussions among members of the research team, statements in these categories were excluded as not directly relevant to the research question. The process of inclusion and exclusion of statements on the basis of relevance can be difficult and debatable!

Structured and unstructured Q sets

The sample of statements for the Q set can be either unstructured or structured. In the former, items are chosen which are presumed to be of relevance to the study with emphasis on representation and completeness. In the latter, sample items are chosen to represent points in a theoretical matrix.

Stephenson based Q set design around Fisher's experimental design principles (Fisher 1960). An example of a structured Q set design based on 'Jung's type psychology' is presented in *The study of behaviour* (Stephenson 1953, p. 69). This theory involved three main issues: attitudes (introversion/extraversion), mechanisms (conscious/unconscious) and functions (thinking, feeling, sensation and intuition). Stephenson shows how a matrix can be used to structure a Q set by populating each cell with statements that relate to each of the constructs listed in Table 9.2.

Table 9.2. Example of Q set design matrix

Attitudes	*Mechanisms*	*Functions*
(a) Introversion	(c) Conscious	(e) Thinking
(b) Extraversion	(d) Unconscious	(f) Feeling
		(g) Sensation
		(h) Intuition

Adapted from Stephenson, 1953, p. 69, with permission of the International Society for the Scientific Study of Subjectivity.

A Q set structured using the matrix in Table 9.2 would seek to cover combinations of attitudes, mechanisms and functions in sixteen possible combinations (2 × 2 × 4), for example, *ace, acf, acg, ach, ade, adf, adg, adh, bce,* and *bcf.*

Less systematic, theoretically informed designs are also possible. In a study of the health and lifestyle choices of people with type 2 diabetes, Baker categorized statements according to three types of economic rationality: instrumental rationality, procedural rationality and expressive rationality (Baker 2006). Roughly even numbers of statements were collected for each type of rationality in an effort not only to achieve balance and coverage in the Q set but also to examine the usefulness or relevance of the theoretical constructs in this context. Structured Q sets can be used to test the appropriateness of theory in conceptualizing subjective views; emergent factors are not constrained by the theoretical framework used to structure the Q set and the structure that emerges from factor analysis can be very different.

Design of unstructured Q sets should still satisfy concerns of coverage and balance and are suitable for subjects where categories are not clear or theory is underdeveloped (McKeown and Thomas 2013). Unstructured designs can be based on a systematic search for statements and post hoc categorization based on emergent constructs. All statements relevant to the subject would be collected until no different opinions could be identified, and then grouped according to the topic.

For both structured and unstructured designs, there follows a process of deleting duplicate statements and merging similar statements to eliminate overlap and repetition, and the final set of statements should be spread across the categories identified. Following any final piloting of the statements, the complete Q set is printed onto cards ready for the card-sort exercise (or programmed for use in an online Q sorting exercise). And the Q study can begin!

CONCLUSION

Q methodology is used to study qualitative questions about the nature of subjective opinion, and qualitative techniques are used in each step of a Q study from Q set design through to factor interpretation. Such techniques include purposive sampling of respondents, collection of narrative data from existing or new sources, interviewing respondents after their Q sort and interpretation of factors as rich accounts of subjectivity. Q methodology harnesses quantitative techniques for analysis, and this combination of qualitative and quantitative components differentiates it from some of the other case studies portrayed in this book, but in common with all qualitative approaches is the need for reflexivity and critical consideration of the role of the researcher in

Q studies. Most obviously, this reflection would relate to the construction of the Q set, which involves searching for and then representing the conversational possibilities that exist on a topic. Less obvious perhaps is the requirement for reflexivity in Q factor analysis, where the selection of a factor solution is in part statistical but also requires judgement about appropriateness and fit with the qualitative accounts of respondents.

ACKNOWLEDGEMENTS

Some of the work detailed in this chapter has been funded by the Medical Research Council Methodology Panel, grant number 91002324.

Chapter 10

Qualitative methods in discrete choice experiments: Two case studies

Jane Vosper, Joanna Coast and Terry Flynn

Discrete choice experiments (DCEs) are a way of investigating people's preferences and choices in a quantitative way and are used increasingly by health economists. They are a form of forced choice questionnaire that allows investigation of how people weigh up different attributes of a product when they are deciding which option they would choose. For example, if one wanted to predict how people would choose a new car, a DCE would present the different options of possible cars with varying attributes (e.g., colour, number of doors, engine size) and would investigate which attributes appear to drive choices.

Choice is a core concept of interest to economists as it implies the need to weigh up options and choose one option while giving up another. As more health care treatments become available for patients, the issue of choice is becoming increasingly important within health economics, to understand how different treatments and services are valued.

Although DCEs offer the potential for studying preferences from large samples of people, they require an appropriate and relevant choice of attributes and wording if they are to provide useful information about preferences. If a DCE is designed using attributes that are not important to the choice-makers, it will not provide useful information. For this reason, the choice of attributes included in the DCE, and how each attribute varies (the levels), is critical to obtaining meaningful results (Coast and Horrocks 2007; Vass, Rigby et al. 2017).

Over recent years, there has been a growing emphasis on the importance of how DCEs are designed, with qualitative methods emerging as a strong complement to the DCE (Coast and Horrocks 2007; Coast, Al-Janabi et al. 2012). This chapter presents two case studies that used qualitative methods to inform and design discrete choice experiments to investigate patient choices in depression treatment. One study explored preferences for a complex behavioural intervention for patients (the TREAD study) (Chalder, Wiles et al. 2012), and the other explored preferences for drug treatment of depression. Each case study is presented in brief and not all attributes are explored in depth; rather, two illustrative attributes are presented for each DCE. These particular illustrations were chosen as they show how themes may or may not be transformed into DCE attributes.

DECISIONS ABOUT DEPRESSION TREATMENT

There are numerous aspects for patients to consider when making decisions about depression treatment. Understanding patients' preferences for depression treatment may enable health professionals to provide the most useful information for shared decision making about treatment (Raue, Schulberg et al. 2009) and, given the wide variety of different behavioural, psychological and medical treatments now available for treating depression, understanding the factors contributing to patient choices is becoming increasingly important (Kupfer, Frank et al. 2012).

There is some evidence that patients find it very difficult to take in all the information they are given when they are first diagnosed with depression (Oppenheim 2000), which may make their decision-making process more difficult. DCEs offer the potential for practitioners and policy makers to see how patients trade between the different attributes of treatments, and how patients value different attributes, possibly enabling more informed treatment decisions.

CHOOSING ATTRIBUTES FOR DCES

There are many methods that can be used to choose DCE attributes, including literature review, meta-ethnography, expert opinion and use of previous questionnaires (Coast, Al-Janabi et al. 2012). Conducting qualitative research can be particularly useful where there is little previous literature available. As well as allowing flexibility and exploration of the area of interest, using qualitative methods can also instigate subtle changes in the overall aim of the questionnaire (Oppenheim 2000). The original research question can be confirmed as a salient question, or it can be altered, making the research as a whole more likely to be helpfully informative in health care decision making. Once attributes are defined, qualitative research is also useful for exploring the wording of the attributes – recommended for all questionnaires (Oppenheim 2000) – to ensure that respondents and researchers have the same understanding of the phrases used.

Qualitative methods were used in two studies described in this chapter, as they allowed particular tailoring to the areas investigated by the DCEs. For the first study, the 'TREAD study', there were no pre-existing studies of similar interventions, thus qualitative exploration was the main method available. For the second study, the 'drug study', while there were a number of pre-existing studies that served as a guide, qualitative exploration allowed confirmation of the themes identified in the literature. The studies are described and a small amount of illustrative analysis is presented for each, specifically documenting the way that themes from the analysis were converted into 'attributes' for the subsequent DCEs. The illustrative analysis was chosen to represent themes that were either directly transferable to attributes or where the constraints of the research question for the DCE meant the theme could not be used. This description aims to give examples of the additional consideration needed for qualitative analysis used in conjunction with designing DCEs.

NOTE ON PHILOSOPHY

There are some methodological and philosophical difficulties with the use of qualitative methods in designing DCEs (or other questionnaires). One issue is that qualitative research tends to be explorative and expansive, whereas to design a questionnaire it is necessary to be reductive; reducing qualitative accounts can be seen by some as devaluing the research findings (Coast, Al-Janabi et al. 2012). Additionally, the ontological and epistemological stances may be seen as different and incompatible between qualitative and quantitative methods; realist, idealist or relativist stances posit very different understandings of reality (Finch and Lewis 2003; Snape and Spencer 2003). Where studies take different stances the findings can be difficult to reconcile. The stance taken in this research was neither completely realist, idealist nor relativist. Instead, subtle realism was adopted (Hammersley 1992). Subtle realism requires the researcher to be wary of the possibility of error; it is accepted that cultural assumptions must be relied on and have the potential to influence the researcher away from reality (Hammersley 1992). The understanding used was that, although it isn't possible to know reality, reality does exist and through rigorous research it is possible to gain insight and make informed conjectures about phenomena (Hammersley 1992).

In terms of epistemology, quantitative methods are often seen as coming from a positive perspective and qualitative methods are often associated with an interpretivist perspective (Finch and Lewis 2003). Mixed methods research, where a combination of quantitative and qualitative methods and concepts are used (Johnson and Onwuegbuzie 2004), can draw from the strengths of different schools of research. There are numerous advantages of this 'third wave' of research paradigm. For example, words and narratives can be used to expand and give meaning to numerical scores, while numbers can give precision and relativity to words and narrative (Johnson and Onwuegbuzie 2004). The strengths of one method can overcome weakness in another. Research questions are less confined and have the potential to address problems in a broader and more complete way (Johnson and Onwuegbuzie 2004). Using qualitative research for the design of DCEs allows the richness and exploratory nature of the method to gain an insight into patients' decision making about depression treatment, followed by further precision and quantitative weighting of themes/attributes by conducting the subsequent DCEs with a wider population. Additionally, from the quantitative findings, it may then be possible for qualitative researchers to identify and further interview 'archetypal respondents' (with viewpoints at the extremes) to generate a richer understanding of these extremes (Flynn 2016).

Thus, although some philosophical quandaries about mixing methods have been raised (Guba 1990), the potential advantages of mixed methods for investigating a context-dependent subject, such as preferences, could be argued to outweigh the potential philosophical disadvantages. Indeed, in the context of discrete choice experiments, it has recently been suggested that by using a mixed methods approach both qualitative and quantitative findings can enhance the interpretations made bidirectionally (Flynn 2016).

STUDY 1: TREAD STUDY

The first DCE was designed alongside the TREAD trial (TREAtment of Depression with physical activity alongside normal care). This randomized controlled trial was investigating a complex physical activity intervention for depression, with multiple active components, the main component being receiving regular sessions with a physical activity facilitator (PAF) to help people engage with increased activity in an individually tailored way (Chalder, Wiles et al. 2012). The DCE was intended to investigate patients' preferences for components of the intervention, with the research question asking which intervention attributes were most valued by patients. The DCE focus was on attributes of the physical activity intervention that distinguished it from other physical activity schemes and that could potentially be changed by health care professionals. The qualitative work used to develop the DCE was included in ethical approval for feasibility work for the TREAD trial.

Interviews

To generate attributes for the TREAD DCE there were a number of phases of interview. Interviews were used rather than other methods of qualitative data collection as there was no available documentation or previous literature about the novel TREAD intervention. Focus groups were impractical as patients lived in disparate areas of the country. Additionally, they may not have been appropriate due to confidentiality issues associated with taking part in the trial.

Semi-structured interviews were conducted to identify attributes of the activity intervention that were salient to patients as well as distinguishing factors of the intervention. There were few preconceived ideas about what these attributes were. Semi-structured interviews allowed the researcher to focus the conversation on elements of the activity intervention, and explore possible attributes, while also leaving space for new attributes to emerge. Large numbers of informants are not necessarily required for qualitative research; as long as key informants take part it is possible to achieve saturation (Oppenheim 2000). The key informants for this study were PAFs working for the trial, GPs recruiting to the trial and patients who had experienced the TREAD intervention or who had been involved in the trial (and so had thought about trying a physical activity intervention for depression). These informants were included to maximize the number of different perspectives on which attributes were important to the intervention and were important in choices. Although patients had direct experience of the intervention, professionals could give a perspective from working with a wider sample of patients.

Analysis

Thematic analysis was used and was conducted iteratively. The first phase of analysis was carried out with existing interview data generated through the trial. This phase of exploration, in which themes began to emerge, guided the interview schedule for the second phase of interviews, conducted by JV specifically for the purpose of designing the DCE.

Interviews were audio-recorded and transcribed verbatim by an administrator, and double-checked by the author. Transcripts were read a number of times by the author before analysis began. The technique of constant comparison was used (Glaser and Strauss 1968); transcripts were analysed iteratively and codes were allowed to emerge during the process to give the best chance for the attributes to develop from the data, rather than from pre-existing ideas.

To begin defining the themes, 'codes' (labels) were added to chunks of text. As there was no strongly established theory to guide the coding, the analysis was more 'inductive' than 'deductive', allowing flexibility to adapt to the data (Joffe and Yardley 2004). However, given the research question and purpose of the analysis (to design a DCE), the analysis was not purely inductive. The coding started off as low-level and non-exclusive (e.g., a word that categorized something being said). Some codes were spliced or linked (e.g., the codes were either split into separate codes, or some were joined to create one code from a number of others) (Dey 2003). Other codes remained as they were initially coded. Ultimately, the aim was to consolidate low-level themes into higher-order themes. Themes were described in coding frames/descriptive accounts, where they were labelled and defined with examples given from the texts (Joffe and Yardley 2004). To aid rigour within the study, a third of transcripts were coded by both JV and JC and differences between coding were discussed.

TREAD study findings

Recurring themes in the interview data relating to the research question (e.g., which attributes were valued by patients) began to emerge as the research was conducted, such as having a choice about physical activity and receiving financial assistance. These two themes are described as they provide an example of two themes that were initially separate themes, but were then linked into one DCE attribute. This was because, at a practical, service delivery level, they were mutually exclusive and thus formed two levels of one attribute. The two themes are presented with the supporting quotations from different informants, followed by a description of how they were linked to create one attribute in the DCE.

Physical activity choice: theme development

One of the strategic characteristics of the TREAD intervention was that patients were encouraged to do any physical activity of their choice. The choice aspect was a key element of the theory behind the intervention, and was seen as a positive by the majority of patients, PAFs and GPs. All phase one patients (in interviews already conducted by the wider TREAD team), and all phase two patients but one (in specific DCE-related interviews), contributed to this theme, along with all PAFs and two GPs.

Most patients had a fairly clear idea of activities they liked, and often a very clear idea of activities they did not enjoy. Physical activities such as running and going to the gym were often disliked.

> *But I don't think I got a lot out of running and things that like . . . I have done running and I've been to the gym, but I can't say it was the most enjoyable thing. (Mark, 53)*
>
> *I don't like going to gyms . . . that doesn't do anything for me at all. Don't do jogging. . . . (Stephanie, 22)*

However, activities such as swimming, cycling and walking (including dog walking) were more popular.

> *Cycling perhaps, that sort of thing, I do, [like]. . . . Swimming, I quite enjoy (Mark, 53)*

Probably going out for walks and in the countryside . . . we've got friends with dogs and we take those out a couple of weekends a month for a long walk, so yeah, it's kind of good. (Stephanie, 22)

And physical activities involved with tasks such as DIY or gardening could be satisfying and also produce a sense of achievement.

When I go back to my parents'. . . I might help them with some DIY or gardening or fixing a roof. . . and you get exercise doing that . . . and I suppose sometimes I feel better afterwards cos you get the exercise . . . but you also feel like you've done something as well. (Peter, 31)

Choice was also seen as important for individually tailoring the activity to the patient's needs. One GP discussed the need to tailor physical activity for physical and health reasons, suggesting aquaerobics as an example of an activity that is suitable and enjoyable for older people.

No, I think as long as the exercise is geared towards older people, that's not a problem. I don't suppose you'd get the average seventy year old woman to go and do a gym, pumping iron, but there is exercise, aquaerobics, at the gym I go, and many women in their seventies and eighties even are quite happy in the water which supports their weight, and they're being very physically active. (Richard, GP)

In contrast to the general feeling that providing choice was advantageous, one PAF suggested that one of her patients would have preferred a more structured activity plan, and was not comfortable with having to choose what to do by himself.

He didn't seem comfortable with the fact that I couldn't say 'oh this is what I suggest for you particularly'. (Kim, PAF)

Physical activity choice: DCE attribute

The choice of physical activity was a key component of the TREAD intervention and a factor that distinguishes it from other schemes, such as exercise on prescription. Thus there were good theoretical reasons for including it as an attribute in the DCE. The interviews suggested that for many patients, PAFs and GPs (although not all) it was valued. Combining theoretical relevance with the theme from the interviews confirmed the decision to include choice of activity as an attribute.

Financial assistance: theme development

Patients, GPs and PAFs all discussed the possibility of assistance with financial costs as part of an exercise treatment scheme. One phase one patient and one GP described issues associated with this theme, and around three-quarters of the phase two patients and two PAFs subsequently contributed to this theme. The cost of physical activities, such as gym membership, was identified as a possible barrier.

> *People in a lower income bracket might find that, if they're on a really tight budget, the gym can be quite expensive. (Joy, 45)*

It was not only the direct cost of the activity that was considered; cost of travel and equipment purchase were also mentioned as important potential barriers to participation.

> *What would almost be more useful would be being able to access those things, so saying 'right, well, help me out with the bus fare' so you can get to north [city] and go to that class you want to go to. (Nicole, 29)*

> *I'm quite lucky I could take money out of my savings to buy a pair of trainers, it's about fifty quid, and I appreciate that some people can't do that and that was still quite a big financial thing for me, to spend an extra fifty quid. (Nicole, 29)*

One PAF noted that financial help would be extremely beneficial for one of her patients who didn't feel that he could spend money on himself.

> *His was the money barrier with doing stuff . . . and he had a son who he spent most of his money on . . . so he felt that he couldn't spend it on his own activities. (Mary, PAF)*

Additionally, one GP felt that the people most in need of help had fewest resources.

> *It's usually the ones who are most needy who have the least resources to be able to do anything about it. (Richard, GP)*

However, for one patient who could afford to do the physical activity of his or her choice, financial help was not seen as a strong motivator to do more exercise.

> *It is expensive if you go to gyms I suppose or it can be . . . buying equipment and stuff but if I had the motivation to do it I can afford it anyway . . . it's always nice to have people to pay for things for you but if I'd have wanted to do it myself anyway I'd have probably done it. (Peter, 31)*

DCE attribute: combining the themes to create an attribute

GPs, PAFs and some patients felt that financial assistance as part of the intervention could reduce barriers to physical activity. There was an initial possibility of providing financial aid to patients in the TREAD trial, but the practicalities of implementing this were too complicated. Exercise on prescription schemes often offer financial aid with gym membership, so the lack of assistance offered in the TREAD intervention was an important contrast. As there appears to be a trade-off between providing financial assistance and giving patients a choice of physical activity, the contrast between financial assistance and choice of activity was incorporated into the DCE by making them different levels of a single attribute.

Further themes from the TREAD study interviews

The interviews revealed several further important characteristics of the intervention. Choice of physical activity, social aspects of physical activity, financial assistance, goals, time, talking and support, physical benefits of activity, alternative treatments to antidepressants and information provided all emerged as salient aspects of the TREAD intervention. However, only the choice of physical activity, financial assistance, goals, time and talking/ support were included as attributes. The other themes were not included for a number of reasons. Issues such as physical benefits and social contact were seen as outcomes of the intervention rather than direct attributes that could be modified by service providers. (It was for this reason that effectiveness of the intervention was also not included.) Although many patients like the idea of an alternative to antidepressants, this was also not a direct attribute of the intervention as exercise interventions are offered alongside usual care, which may or may not include taking antidepressants.

Interviews were also used to help the process of designing the DCE questionnaire in terms of wording and feasibility. Table 10.1 shows the final attributes and levels included in the DCE questionnaire for the subsequent quantitative study:

Table 10.1. Attributes and levels included in the TREAD discrete choice experiment

- You will not receive support to help you do physical activity
- Receive telephone support to help you do physical activity
- Receive face-to-face support to help you do physical activity
- Receive face-to-face support to help you do physical activity and to talk more generally about your depression

- You will be asked to do the government recommended levels of activity from the start of the programme (30 minutes of activity 5 times per week)

- You will build up your activity levels gradually, starting with small goals
- You will be able to fit your activity into your daily routine

- You will need to use your leisure time to do physical activity
- You will receive financial help to do physical activity, but this will be for only a few months' membership to your local gym
- You will not receive financial help to do physical activities; however, you can do any physical activity of your choice, for example, things like walking, cycling, gardening, salsa dancing, martial arts or yoga.

STUDY 2: DRUG TREATMENT OF DEPRESSION

The initial aim of the second DCE study was to investigate preferences for attributes of drug treatment of depression, including allopathic antidepressant drugs as well as preferences for herbal antidepressant drugs such as St John's wort. The focus group study, which included patients, received NHS ethical approval from the St Thomas Hospital Research Ethics Committee.

Focus groups

Five focus groups were conducted to explore factors that were important to people when making a decision about taking drug treatment for depression: both allopathic and alternative medicines. Focus groups were chosen as the method of data collection for a number of reasons. There was no existing literature that was directly relevant that could be used for attribute development. Focus groups have previously been used to develop DCE attributes (Dwight-Johnson, Lagomasino et al. 2004; Mahadevia, Shah et al. 2006) and were found to give a good picture of the important issues. The group nature of focus groups can have some advantages compared to interviews. Discussion can spark memories in participants, and ideas and thoughts about issues can develop as they are discussed. Participants can ask each other questions that would not necessarily have occurred to the researcher. Additionally, if some members of a group admit to feelings or thoughts that could be considered embarrassing or socially unacceptable, other members may find the confidence to share similar ideas or thoughts (Finch and Lewis 2003). For this reason, focus groups can be a particularly useful way to explore thoughts about treatment for depression: a sense that others in the group understand or even share their thoughts and experiences may allow participants to feel more comfortable talking about their own thoughts, feelings and experiences with depression treatment. However, there can also be challenges with focus groups, particularly when discussing sensitive topics such as mental health. Participants may not feel comfortable sharing personal information or may distort their responses due to social pressure. To maximize the possibility of the group feeling supportive and open, it is important that it is appropriately facilitated and all members choose to attend understanding the nature of the environment.

Considerable thought was therefore given to recruitment, setting and context of the focus groups. Informants were recruited through depression self-help groups and organisations, as well as through a GP surgery. Where focus groups were conducted with people already attending support groups, there was the advantage that participants were already likely to be comfortable talking in that group setting. These focus groups were held concurrently with, but in different rooms from, the self-help groups. Self-help group leaders were present in the focus groups, which provided some extra support for the participants but may also have affected the dynamic of the groups. These group leaders were also able to offer advice before the focus group about any group dynamics that might be present (e.g., members of the group who might typically dominate a discussion).

Although recruiting for focus groups can be challenging, particularly for sensitive topics, conducting groups with the support of relevant charities who can advocate for the need for research as well as represent informants in terms of their well-being can help to facilitate the process. Recruiting solely through other means such as GP surgeries may have presented considerably more challenges.

Three staff members were present for each focus group: one to facilitate, one to aid with transcription of the themes and the third to manage any situations that arose, for example, if a group member became distressed with the conversation and needed to leave. These roles were agreed in advance. When participants arrived for the focus group, introductions were made and the study explained. Confidentiality was assured, and participants were asked to respect each other's confidentiality by not discussing people's views outside of the focus group.

Although literature on perceptions of depression treatment did not specifically suggest attributes to include in the DCE, it highlighted some salient factors. To link these findings with the qualitative research undertaken, the topic schedule for the focus groups was designed with reference to published literature on views of antidepressants (Cooper-Patrick, Powe et al. 1997; Wagner, Jester et al. 1999; Löwe, Schulz et al. 2006; Pellegrini and Ruggeri 2007; Malpass, Shaw et al. 2009). Salient factors, such as side effects, safety, medicine status (herbal versus allopathic) and the need for prescription, were explored. Two topic schedules were designed. One was for the first three groups, aimed at generating attributes. It asked questions about the drug treatments participants were familiar with, and their advantages and disadvantages. Reasons for taking antidepressants and/or complementary medicines were addressed, as well as what things would be off-putting about medication. Views about whether prescription was important, safety and natural status were also prompted if not spontaneously mentioned. The second topic schedule was for the final two groups, used to consolidate attributes and explore wording. It began by asking about participants' experiences with and views on antidepressant medication, both conventional and alternative. After this possible attributes were proposed – participants were asked what came to mind when they heard the wording of the attributes. Alternative ways of describing attributes were offered, and participants were asked if they could think of better words to use.

Analysis

The focus groups were analysed as data collection progressed, so that themes emerging could be explored further in subsequent groups. Participants' memories of decision making about drug treatment were intertwined with their experiences of care from GPs and other health professionals, and thus were discussed within this context. However, the purpose of the focus groups was to generate attributes related directly to drug treatment, so the analysis focused on themes around medicines, rather than general care or other treatments such as psychotherapy.

Thematic analysis involving constant comparison and an iterative approach was used. Transcripts were read twice before analysis began. To begin defining attributes, coding started off as low-level and non-exclusive. As for the TREAD study, some codes were spliced and linked (Dey 2003) to consolidate the low-level themes into higher-order (more generalized) themes. Other codes remained as initially coded. In some cases initial codes were split to form more specific codes. Themes were described in coding frames/descriptive accounts, where they were labelled and defined with examples given from the texts (Oppenheim 2000; Joffe and Yardley 2004).

To enhance rigour, emerging themes were discussed by the author and the researchers who assisted with conducting the focus groups. A summary of the findings was also sent to self-help group leaders (and participants who requested this), and comments were invited.

Drug treatment study findings

Participants in the focus groups generally seemed to be very knowledgeable about depression and the treatments available. Many had extensively researched depression and its treatments, whether through self-help group activities or independently. Most had either long-term or recurrent depression and had tried numerous treatment options over many years.

Important themes around antidepressants were the need for treatment, adverse effects of medication, the effectiveness of the medicine and the nature of its effectiveness (long-term use and the feeling that they are 'hit and miss'), aversion to medication, stigma and the properties of the medicine (whether it's herbal or synthetic). Participants didn't tend to talk about what they were thinking when they were deciding to take antidepressants. Rather, the discussions seemed to be based around their experiences with medication. This could have been because they didn't remember exactly what they were thinking when they were first deciding whether or not to take medication, other than that they needed to do something to treat their condition. Literature on help-seeking for depression and patients' first experiences seeing their GPs suggests that discussing treatment options can be difficult, and that patients are often unable to process all the information provided (Garfield, Francis et al. 2004).

DCE attributes were developed by combining findings from the focus groups with findings from existing literature. The focus groups highlighted issues associated with antidepressants that affect decision making, and the literature was used to further explore these issues. For example, the focus groups emphasized the importance of adverse effects, but the literature helped to identify which adverse effects were important in a variety of contexts.

Increased anxiety: theme development

An adverse effect that was discussed by many of the participants in all the groups was the feeling of increased anxiety, agitation and, in some cases, panic.

> *Agitation, which I think, was definitely caused by the drug. That was venlafaxine. (Linda, 59)*
>
> *I took it for a few days, and I started breaking out into sweats and panicking a lot. (William, 64)*

One participant explicitly described the trade-off he had to consider between decreasing the depression and increasing the anxiety.

> *If you treat the depression . . . with antidepressants, it makes the anxiety worse. Although cures the depression. (James, 54)*

Some participants had experienced extreme anxiety as an adverse effect of their medication and felt they could no longer continue their treatment because the adverse effect was so intolerable.

> *But I became very agitated. I wanted to come off it and the psychiatrist said she wanted me to keep on trying it because it would work if I carried on – so I kept carrying on and I've carried on for six months, and then in the end I just refused to take it. (Linda, 59)*

One participant eventually found the feelings of racing thoughts, inability to 'switch off' and 'buzzing' too detrimental to continue with antidepressants, even though she felt this cessation of medication caused her depression to return.

> *And I couldn't sleep, and I had racing thoughts and eventually, what happened – all the times I couldn't get the dosage right, too much of it and I was just buzzing, it was horrible, you know when your brain just won't switch off . . .*

so eventually, after several years, I had to stop it and that caused the depression to return. (Karen, 49)

Increased anxiety: DCE attribute

Many participants had experienced varying anxiety levels that they attributed to medication. Anxiety and depression are often comorbid (Hirschfeld 2001), so it is possible that the participants were experiencing anxiety independently of medication. However, increased agitation and anxiety are also reported in the literature as an adverse effect of medication (Trinidade, Menon et al. 1998), and participants perceived that stopping medication reduced their anxiety, although their depression worsened. Participants explicitly described trade-offs between their depression and the anxiety caused by their medication. For this reason it seemed important to include an attribute for anxiety and agitation in the DCE.

Greater severity of depression: theme development

One of the adverse effects that participants described as particularly unpleasant was the feeling that depression symptoms worsened for the first few weeks of taking medication.

I think the absolute number one bad side effect has got to be the drugs actually making depression worse. (Michael, 27)

Because there are a small number of people who get very much worse on antidepressants. (David, 59)

The disturbing experience of antidepressants causing the depression to worsen to the point of causing suicidal thoughts was described.

Going back to what I'm saying about suicidal feelings, one SSRI I was put on, I really felt extremely low, and I am pretty well convinced it was because of that drug. (Barbara, 60)

The possibility of depression worsening was seen as an unacceptable side effect of homeopathy; feeling even worse than the current state of depression was intolerable.

I tried homeopathy once for anxiety depression. I can't remember what they said, but when I went back they said 'you're gunna get worse before you get better'. And I couldn't afford – not financially – to get worse so I gave up. Simple . . . that's no good if you're feeling shit and you get worse, I just couldn't handle getting worse. (Richard, 66)

Greater severity of depression: DCE attribute

Although the experience of worsening depression was a particularly unpleasant adverse effect of medication, and one participant explicitly said it was the reason he declined a treatment option, it was not developed into an attribute for the DCE. This decision was made as the literature suggests that the reason people sometimes feel that their depression is worsening is due to a combination of adverse effects such as anxiety and sleep problems (Garfield, Francis et al. 2004). Depression itself worsening due to medication is not reported as an adverse effect in the literature and so including it in the DCE would not be helpful in terms of providing people with accurate information about medication. However, the issue of reporting of adverse effects and which symptoms are seen as being caused by medication and which are associated with depression itself is considered in the discussion. Table 10.2 shows final attributes that were derived from the themes and the literature.

Table 10.2. Attributes and levels included in the drug treatment discrete choice experiment

- There is a 3 in 10 chance you will gain weight
- There is no chance you will gain weight

- There is a 3 in 10 chance you will experience nausea/dizziness/headaches
- There is no chance you will experience nausea/dizziness/headaches

- There is a 5 in 10 chance you will experience drowsiness or sleep problems
- There is no chance you will experience drowsiness or sleep problems

- There is a 2 in 10 chance this medicine will NOT improve your depression
- There is a 3 in 10 chance this medicine will NOT improve your depression
- There is a 5 in 10 chance this medicine will NOT improve your depression
- There is a 7 in 10 chance this medicine will NOT improve your depression

- There is no chance you will experience sexual dysfunction (reduced sex drive or inability to orgasm)
- There is a 3 in 10 chance you will experience sexual dysfunction (reduced sex drive or inability to orgasm)
- There is a 5 in 10 chance you will experience sexual dysfunction (reduced sex drive or inability to orgasm)
- There is a 7 in 10 chance you will experience sexual dysfunction (reduced sex drive or inability to orgasm)

- This is a chemical-based medicine prescribed by a GP
- This is a plant-based medicine that can be bought from a health food shop

- There is a 2 in 10 chance you will experience increased anxiety or agitation
- There is no chance you will experience increased anxiety or agitation

REFLECTIONS ON THE RESEARCH

The qualitative work carried out was key in generating attributes for the DCEs and meant the DCEs had the best possible chance of including the attributes that were important to patients. If the attributes had been defined solely by the author and researchers involved in the studies (as in many conjoint analysis and DCE studies), they would have been different from those that emerged from the qualitative work, and are likely to have had less relevance to the people making the treatment choices. The qualitative work also allowed the direction of the research to change slightly in the drug study. Emphasis moved away from an initial focus on St John's wort and other complementary medicines onto side effects of different allopathic treatments during the focus groups, as this appeared to be a more salient and relevant issue to the participants.

One limitation of the TREAD qualitative work was the small number of interviews conducted in the final phase. It was feasible to interview only two patients in this final phase due to constraints of the TREAD trial. However, wording was also explored in earlier interviews, meaning that the final phase was mostly concerned with refinements of the questionnaire.

For the drug study there was a concern that certain adverse effects might be less likely to be discussed or reported, as they may cause embarrassment or shame. For example, people may feel uncomfortable discussing sexual dysfunction in a group situation. Of course, reluctance to discuss certain adverse effects could also have been an issue had interviews, rather than focus groups, been conducted. This was one of the reasons that additional published literature on antidepressant adverse effects was also used to develop attributes, as filling out anonymous questionnaire studies could make it easier for a patient to report a symptom such as sexual dysfunction as being important.

The terms 'trustworthiness' and 'consistency' have been used to describe 'reliability' for qualitative findings (Hammersley 1992). Seale suggests that practices such as reflexivity (presenting a clear picture of the procedures leading to any conclusions made) can enable qualitative findings to be considered reliable (Seale 1999). Ritchie, Lewis and Elam suggest additional methods that can be used to ensure rigour in qualitative work, for example, attempting to identify all perspectives of a target population, and ensuring selection of participants includes these perspectives (Ritchie, Lewis et al. 2003). Ensuring respondents have the chance to cover all relevant ground can add to the rigour of the study. In the two studies carried out, attempts were made to ensure that a clear and reflexive picture of the research was presented, including clarity about how themes were derived from accounts, and using quotations with sufficient context for meaning to be derived. Additionally, clarity was aimed for in the presentation of choice of attributes from themes, and from present arguments for including or not including themes. Although, in terms of generating attributes for DCEs, random utility theory (RUT) requires inconsistency, the overall themes/attributes should be consistent in the sense expressed by Hammersley (1992), albeit with variability within the levels or importance of the theme to respondents.

In relation to the validity of qualitative studies, Hammersley argues that an account can be seen as true or valid if the features that it intends to describe or explain are accurately represented (Hammersley 1992). This can be achieved, to some extent, by taking research findings back to respondents to confirm if interpretation is validated by those who contributed (Yardley and Marks 2004). Additionally 'trustworthiness' of qualitative research can be increased by triangulation (using other sources such as literature and additional observers). The two studies used previous research, where possible, to guide the attribute development from themes, and used a second coder to check the transcripts and associated codes and themes, thus increasing the trustworthiness of the findings.

CONCLUSION

This research highlights the potential for qualitative work to inform and shape quantitative methods in health economics. The processes of conducting the qualitative research and analysis, and considering the transition of themes to attributes, were described. In the examples given, the transfer of qualitative themes to attributes was not necessarily direct; rather, it was a process of considering which themes were:

- Relevant to the research question,
- Relevant to the patient group and
- Changeable attributes of the treatments.

Following the initial stages of defining the attributes and designing the questionnaires, further qualitative research focusing on details of the attributes and levels generated was conducted (in particular the wording and how understandable the attributes were). There was also rigorous piloting to ensure that the DCEs would provide meaningful results.

Carrying out qualitative research alongside DCEs allows researchers to include attributes that have been developed using views of those decision makers who are actually making the decision of interest. This means the DCE is more likely to elicit patterns of preferences and choices that genuinely reflect the interests of the decision makers (in this case patients/service users), rather than being limited to researchers' own perspectives about important attributes. As well as refining attributes and language of the DCEs, qualitative research also allows the research question itself to be explored and, if necessary, altered to reflect the decisions being made by service users. Failing to define attributes using a rigorous method has the potential to lead to DCEs providing biased or potentially meaningless interpretations of choices and preferences. This chapter has presented some examples of exploring attributes and ways of trying to ensure reliability and validity of choosing attributes for a DCE.

ACKNOWLEDGEMENTS

This research was supported by the MRC Health Services Research Collaboration.

Chapter 11

Using qualitative methods to develop a preference-based health-related quality of life measure for use in economic evaluation: The development of the Child Health Utility 9D

Katherine Stevens

Health-related quality of life (HRQoL) measures typically define the health status of a person in terms of a number of different dimensions of HRQoL, for example, 'sleep' or 'mobility'. Each dimension usually has a number of levels associated with it, indicating different degrees of severity within that dimension. For example, a dimension concerning mobility may have levels ranging from full mobility to no mobility.

HRQoL measures can be preference-based or non-preference-based. The majority of existing HRQoL measures are non-preference-based; that is, they are typically scored by weighting all items equally and their scores are not based on preferences (Brazier, Ratcliffe et al. 2007). Preference-based measures (PBMs) are an attempt to take into account the relative importance of the items (levels of each dimension). Each health state that is defined by a measure's descriptive system has a preference weight associated with it, usually based on a scale where 1 is equivalent to full health and 0 is equivalent to being dead (with negative values for health states judged to be worse than dead) (Brazier, Ratcliffe et al. 2007). PBMs allow the calculation of a common outcome measure (typically the quality-adjusted life-year [QALY]), by combining the value on this scale with length of life. The advantage of QALYs is that they allow for interventions to be compared both within and between clinical areas as they are a common unit of outcome measurement (Brazier, Ratcliffe et al. 2007). When combined with information on relative costs in an economic evaluation, this can help inform decisions about how to use limited health care resources more efficiently.

In this chapter, the use of qualitative methods for the development of preference-based HRQoL outcome measures is demonstrated through the example of the Child Health Utility 9D (CHU9D). First, options for the development of HRQoL measures in general are briefly outlined, of which the use of qualitative methods is one. The application of qualitative methods is then demonstrated through the example of the CHU9D.

DEVELOPING HRQOL MEASURES

The first stage of developing a HRQoL measure is to develop a descriptive system. A descriptive system typically consists of a number of dimensions, each with a set of items/levels. For PBMs a structure that has a limited number of dimensions, usually 9 or fewer (Miller 1956), with a number of ordinal levels for each dimension, is preferred. This makes the descriptive system amenable to health state valuation (by using methods such as time trade-off, standard gamble or discrete choice experiments), a requirement for generating the preference weights for the calculation of QALYs (Brazier, Ratcliffe et al. 2007). If health states have too many dimensions, it is unlikely that respondents will be able to handle all this information when undertaking a valuation task. Non-preference-based measures, such as those frequently used in clinical trials, are not bound by these constraints and therefore can have much larger descriptive systems.

When developing a descriptive system, there are different approaches that can be taken. One is a top-down approach, whereby existing literature, health surveys and instruments are reviewed and items are taken from them to generate an initial pool of candidate items. Further analysis can then be done to reduce and sort these items into a descriptive system, for example, through the use of factor analysis to develop dimensions (Fayers and Hays 1998).

An alternative method is to generate items or dimensions through the use of focus groups or individual interviews. These are termed bottom-up methods (McColl 2005) and are based on using qualitative methods to generate items and/or dimensions for a descriptive system. The use of qualitative methods is common in the development of non-preference-based measures; however, in the field of PBM, until very recently their use was rare. The focus groups or individual interviews take the views of patients or other relevant populations and seek their input on how HRQoL is affected by a particular health problem or condition. Qualitative methods can be used to either generate dimensions directly for a descriptive system (as, for example, with the CHU9D [Stevens 2010]) and the ICECAP measures [Grewal, Lewis et al. 2006; Al-Janabi, Flynn et al. 2012; Sutton and Coast 2014]), or to develop a long list of items that then requires further work to classify these items into dimensions (e.g., in the development of a HRQoL questionnaire for use in asthma [Juniper,

Guyatt et al. 1992] and the development of the Endometriosis Health Profile [Jones, Kennedy et al. 2001]). The item generation approach has a more frequent use of, and reliance on, psychometric, factor analysis or Rasch techniques (Young, Yang et al. 2009) to develop the dimensions. Alternatively, if the dimensions are developed directly from the qualitative data, there isn't necessarily a need for these quantitative techniques.

Top-down and bottom-up methods can be used independently (as in the aforementioned examples of the CHU9D and ICECAP measures, where generation of dimensions is solely through qualitative methods) or in combination (as, for example, with the recent development of the Recovering Quality of life (ReQoL) measure for users of mental health services (http://www.reqol.org.uk/p/overview.html) and the Assessment of Quality of Life (AQoL) instruments (Hawthorne, Richardson et al. 1997). In these instruments, possible items for inclusion were developed using a mixture of bottom-up and top-down approaches. Often the decision over which method to use is based on the purpose of the measure, whether previous research has been done in the area (e.g., a long list of relevant items may already exist) and time and resource constraints.

The most common generic PBMs all used a top-down approach in the development of their descriptive systems (Stevens 2015). For example, The Measurement and Valuation of Health Survey, which was used to develop the EQ-5D questionnaire, took the views of 196 members of the general population to validate five existing descriptive systems by surveying lay concepts (Van Agt and Bonsel 2005). The Health Utilities Index 2 (HUI2) was developed from a review of epidemiological surveys and a review of the literature, which generated a large pool of potential attributes. A sample of child and parent pairs then rated these items to select attributes for inclusion (Cadman, Goldsmith et al. 1986).

Two more recently developed PBMs for children and adolescents – the AQoL-6D (Moodie, Richardson et al. 2009) and the EQ-5DY (Wille, Badia et al. 2010) – were also developed using top-down methods, as they were adapted from existing adult versions (the AQoL [Hawthorne, Richardson et al. 1997] and the EQ-5D [Dolan 1997] respectively).

The first application of qualitative methods to develop a measure intended for use in economic evaluation (although not as a QALY measure) was undertaken by Grewal et al. who developed a measure of capability well-being for older people (Grewal, Lewis et al. 2006). In developing their measure, they interviewed forty people aged over sixty-five years to determine what attributes should be included for a new index focusing on health and social care for older people. In the interviews they explored the respondents' views about what was important to them in their lives. From these interview data they directly developed five conceptual attributes.

The use of a bottom-up methodology using qualitative methods has a number of advantages over more traditional top-down approaches. First, the final measure developed is likely to have more appropriate language and terminology for the population, which should increase the content validity (McColl 2005). Second, there could be an improved responsiveness to change, because the measure would include outcomes directly from the population (e.g., patients) that they feel are relevant (Guyatt and Cook 1994). Third, taking a bottom-up methodology ensures that the measure is developed according to its purpose, rather than relying on information from previous research that may have had different aims and objectives (Stevens and Palfreyman 2012). Finally, measures developed using bottom-up methodology are likely to be more amenable to self-completion by the patient. It is considered desirable in clinical trials and health services research that descriptions of the experience of a health state be elicited from patients, to reflect the actual experience of the disease and its treatment (Fitzpatrick, Davey et al. 1998). The use of qualitative methods is starting to become more common in PBM development, and the Food and Drug Administration (FDA) requirement for the development of patient-reported outcome (PRO) measures, that measures show evidence that their items have been generated through taking account of the experience and perspective of the patient group, is encouraging the use of qualitative methods.

THE DEVELOPMENT OF THE CHILD HEALTH UTILITY 9D (CHU9D)

The Child Health Utility 9D (CHU9D) is a paediatric generic preference–based measure of HRQoL. It was developed in 2008 primarily in response to a lack of child-focused PBMs. In contrast to the development of preceding paediatric PBMs, the CHU9D was developed exclusively with children through the use of qualitative methods (Stevens 2010). Qualitative methods were used for two purposes: first, to generate candidate dimensions; and second, to develop scales (levels) for the dimensions.

Development of the dimensions

There are a number of stages in qualitative research design (Ritchie and Lewis 2003). Each stage involves a series of choices which are often driven by the purpose of the measure being developed. In the case of the CHU9D, the purpose of the measure was to inform health care resource allocation decisions, and so this purpose drove the decisions made at each stage.

Form of data

The first stage of qualitative research is to review your research question and decide what type of qualitative data you require. Qualitative data can take different forms, for example, naturally occurring data (data observed in a natural setting) or generated data (data generated by respondents who give their own interpretation and explanation from interviews). In developing the CHU9D, generated data were obtained as respondents were asked about how their health affected their lives. It is likely that for any development of a PBM, it would also be the case that generated data would be required, as to find out how health affects people's lives you would need to ask them, as these data do not typically occur naturally.

Data unit

Second, you need to consider your data unit and time span (e.g., cross-sectional data at a point in time or over a series of time points). When developing a PBM you are more likely to need cross-sectional data as you are not looking at how individuals' views change over time; instead, you are trying to obtain information about the breadth of the ways in which health impacts on people's lives. This was the case for the CHU9D, and so a series of cases of individuals at a point in time (cross-sectional data) were required.

Data collection

Third, you need to consider how you will collect your data. This may be, for example, through the use of focus groups (two or more participants) or individual interviews. It is also possible to use a combination of the two. Theoretically, an advantage of individual interviews is that they can offer more depth as you can generate increased quantities of data through discussion with a single individual, probing them about how health impacts on their life within an individual interview. It is notable, however, that a study with adult patients' satisfaction with nursing care found that there was no difference in terms of the depth of data generated between individual interviews and focus groups (Thomas, McMillan et al. 1995). Interviews also have the advantage of offering complete privacy and so participants can feel more comfortable in sharing their experiences and ideas; this is particularly important when sensitive issues are touched upon. Focus groups, on the other hand, can often stimulate more discussion as participants can feed off each other's ideas (Ritchie and Lewis 2003).

Ultimately, the decision about whether to use interviews or focus groups is based on factors such as the sensitivity of the topic, the nature of the population being studied and practical issues associated with using each method (McColl 2005). For the CHU9D a decision was made to develop the measure exclusively with children. It was also being developed as a generic measure; therefore, children with a range of health conditions were included in the development. For a generic measure, it may be the case that a focus group is less suitable, as individuals are likely to have different health conditions which they are discussing and so they may prefer to discuss these on an individual basis. The potentially sensitive nature of what children may want to say meant that individual interviews were likely to be more appropriate for the development of the CHU9D. Individual interviews allow for confidentiality and, if focus groups are used, some children may not feel able to freely talk about their health and how it affects them. In addition, when undertaking research with children, it is important to take into account any pre-existing dynamics within groups as this can have an influence on how children may participate in a focus group. The choice of interviews or focus groups for the CHU9D was strongly influenced by the fact that it was a child population being interviewed. Several pilot interviews and focus groups were carried out, and it became clear that on a practical level, individual interviews were easier to manage than focus groups. For these reasons, individual interviews were chosen over focus groups. Further discussion of these issues can be found in Stevens and Palfreyman (Stevens and Palfreyman 2012).

Sampling

Once you have decided what type of data you are collecting and how you are collecting them, you need to devise your sampling strategy (i.e., how are you going to select participants for your research). Potentially relevant groups from whom data could have been gathered included parents/guardians, paediatric health care professionals, the general population, health care decision makers and children (Stevens 2010). As the measure was intended to be child-focused, children were chosen as the population to interview. It was then important to determine the characteristics of children to be interviewed. For development of a condition-specific measure, it is likely you will sample from a population who have the condition of interest. Development of a generic measure is more complex as, to be truly generic, you need to ensure you have breadth of coverage across a wide range of health conditions, both acute and chronic, as well as a range of severity within these conditions. Given this, children with a wide range of health conditions were needed. One approach could have been to sample children via hospitals; however, this would have meant sampling from very poorly children. Many health problems are seen within the general community population, and so children were sampled from the general population via schools to ensure as wide a range as possible of health problems were included, while acknowledging that this would miss children who were very severely or terminally ill (Stevens 2010).

Sampling criteria are used to select respondents with the characteristics you are interested in. This is termed purposive sampling (Ritchie and Lewis 2003). In the development of the CHU9D purposive sampling was used to achieve maximum variation within the sample, with the main criteria being to sample across a range of age (from seven to eleven years) and levels of health (as rated by the parent on a five-point scale from excellent to poor) (Stevens 2010). Secondary sampling criteria of gender and ethnicity were also used to make sure there was representativeness in the sample. The schools that participated in the research were chosen in collaboration with the Children and Young People's Directorate at Sheffield City Council and were chosen specifically to represent the diversity of the child population in Sheffield in terms of social class and ethnicity. Head teachers of the schools were approached in the first instance to see if the school was interested in participating. If they agreed to the research, class teachers in the school were then contacted and sent information sheets. If they were happy for their class to participate, letters, information sheets and consent forms were sent home with the children which also asked the parents to rate their child's health on a scale from excellent to poor in order to allow for the sampling.

Analysis

Finally, you need to decide on what analytical approach you will take for the analysis of your qualitative data. There are different approaches to analysis which can be undertaken in qualitative research (Ritchie and Lewis 2003). In the case of instrument development, you are interested in exploring the themes/issues that are generated through your interviews and/or focus groups. Typically in instrument development in the non-PBM literature, items are identified from the qualitative data and dimensions are developed from these using approaches such as factor or Rasch analysis (Young, Yang et al. 2009). Alternatively, dimensions can be identified directly from the qualitative data, an approach taken by Grewal, Lewis et al. (2006). This approach of identifying dimensions directly was also taken in the development of the CHU9D. As it was being developed specifically to be a PBM and therefore a structure amenable to valuation was desired, the approach to the analysis was to identify dimensions directly from the qualitative data and then develop levels for each of these. The analysis was guided by the research question 'how does health affects children's lives?' and the aim was to identify dimensions of HRQoL (Stevens 2010).

Many of the choices at each of these stages of design are commonly iterative. That is, they are influenced by the previous choice(s). For example in the CHU9D, the choice of interviewing children influenced the choice to use individual interviews rather than focus groups.

Ethical issues

Ethical approval for the CHU9D study was gained from the University of Sheffield Research Ethics Committee. In addition, the study was reviewed by the Children and Young People's Directorate at Sheffield City Council to satisfy their ethical requirements.

Working with children raises several ethical issues that need to be considered prior to undertaking any research with them. In order to work within a school setting in the United Kingdom, a researcher must typically undergo a full police check in line with the practice of the school. There must also be a disclosure policy in place in case anything is disclosed in an interview or focus group which the researcher feels should be disclosed, for example, the child saying something that indicated that he or she, or someone else, were at risk from harm. A school will have a safeguarding officer, and an appropriate policy can usually be worked out in collaboration with them. It is also important that a full consent and assent process is undertaken so that parents/guardians are fully informed and have given consent for the researcher to invite their child to take part and that the child is fully informed, has an opportunity to ask questions and gives his or her assent (where appropriate for age). The researcher also needs to work with the school to ensure there is space for the interviews/focus groups to be undertaken where the researcher will not be alone with the children and another adult is present/nearby, in line with the safeguarding procedures of the school.

UNDERTAKING AND ANALYSING THE QUALITATIVE INTERVIEWS FOR THE CHU9D

Seventy-four interviews were carried out with children aged seven to eleven years, who were sampled from schools in Sheffield based on the criteria outlined previously. After an initial warm-up exercise, a semi-structured interview was undertaken with each child to determine how their health affected their life. Children with a wide range of acute and chronic health problems were included. The interview first asked children to describe their health problem(s) and then went on to ask how the problem(s) impacted on their life. A topic guide was used which included probing to make sure that both acute and chronic health problems were recognized as valid and that all areas of children's lives were considered (e.g., at home and at school). The interviews were designed to understand and explore the consequences of health conditions on children's lives rather than just find out about symptoms. For example, a child talking about eczema might first describe the itching (symptom) but then be probed to ask about how this affected his or her life. Children then discussed how it impacted on sleep (the itching would wake them up throughout the night or they couldn't get to sleep), the impact on their everyday routine due to having to apply cream every day, the impact on their ability to concentrate at school (due to the itching distracting them) and feeling embarrassed about the physical appearance of the eczema (Stevens 2010).

All interviews were recorded and transcribed verbatim. Sampling of children continued until past saturation (no new themes were emerging). This was in order to gain confidence that saturation was reached. The decision that saturation was reached was made intuitively by the researcher as she was undertaking all the interviews and so knew the data well. The analysis of these data was driven by the research question: how does health affect children's lives? Thematic content analysis (analysing the content of interviews to generate themes) used a framework approach (Ritchie and Lewis 2003) as this suited the aim of generating dimensions directly from the data.

Data were first reviewed by listening to all the interviews and reading all the transcripts. During this process, recurring themes, subthemes and ideas were noted and a thematic framework generated. Interview data were then all coded according to this framework. Charting was used to organize the data, with care taken to retain the language and terminology of the children. Charting data involves organising it on a spreadsheet whereby each row is a respondent and each column is a subtheme. In the case of the CHU9D, Excel was used and each tab was a theme with the subthemes charted within it. Themes and subthemes were charted, and then each subtheme was reviewed to look for explanations behind the affected areas of quality of life (Stevens 2010).

Relationships between themes and subthemes were mapped, and dimensions were generated by exploring the consequences of health problems on a child's life. This was undertaken by hand using large poster sizes sheets of paper so that the researcher could visually map all the links between dimensions and subdimensions. The aim was to look at the final impact on a child's life; for example, if a child had to take medication through the night, it often disrupted the child's sleep. If a child had symptoms such as coughing or severe eczema, it also impacted on the child's sleep. This final impact ('sleep') became a dimension of HRQoL.

Other dimensions were generated in the same way, producing a list of candidate dimensions for consideration. Eleven dimensions were generated in total, which were too many for valuation and so further work was needed to reduce these to a maximum of nine, in order to ensure the descriptive system was amenable to valuation (Miller 1956). Before any reduction was undertaken, the eleven dimensions were first developed into a descriptive system by developing scales for each dimension (Stevens 2009).

DEVELOPMENT OF SCALES FOR THE DIMENSIONS

Qualitative methods were also applied in the development of scales for the dimensions of the CHU9D (Stevens 2009). Having reviewed existing paediatric measures and their scales, Stevens determined that none were suitable for use in the CHU9D as the language and terminology of the scales had not commonly been used by children in the interviews to develop dimensions. It was also felt that some terms such as 'moderately' and 'extremely' which are common in existing paediatric scales would not be understood by younger children. Therefore instead of applying a standard scale to each of the dimensions, the qualitative data generated from the interviews were analysed to compile a list of adverbial phrases that children used when describing the dimensions, for example, feeling *very* worried, feeling *quite* worried, feeling *a little* worried. This was done for each of the dimensions in the descriptive system.

Once a list was compiled for each dimension, this list was used to inform whether the dimension should be severity (how much) or frequency (how often) based. All lists clearly demonstrated that children were describing the dimensions in terms of severity, and so each dimension was developed as such. This also suits a descriptive system with a short recall period (today/last night), which is desirable for a paediatric measure as children have short recall periods (Stevens 2009). The adverbial phrases were then presented to children on a series of cards and they were asked to rank the phrases in the order they thought they should go, from highest to lowest (duplicates were allowed). Thirty-two children were included in this ranking study, and the results determined the scales that were applied to the dimensions identified, to form a draft descriptive system (Stevens 2009). One advantage of using qualitative data for this purpose is that the language and terminology of the children is retained in the measure and therefore the validity and practicality of the measure should be increased.

This draft descriptive system was then subject to psychometric testing to produce the final CHU9D ready for valuation (Stevens 2011). The draft descriptive system was tested with both a clinical and general community (school) population. The researcher administered the draft descriptive system on a one-to-one basis, allowing for the collection of quantitative data to test the practicality and validity of the questionnaire, and also allowing for some qualitative data collection, whereby children were asked whether they thought anything was missing from the descriptive system, whether they found any of the wording or questions difficult and whether they had any overall comments (Stevens 2011).

To reduce the eleven dimensions down to nine (the maximum number desirable for a descriptive system that will undergo health state valuation [Miller 1956]) or fewer, two (or more) dimensions had to be removed from the draft descriptive system. The original qualitative interviews were revisited, and the two weakest dimensions ('jealous' and 'embarrassed') were removed. They were the weakest in the sense that they were not strongly put forward by the children in comparison to other dimensions such as 'pain' and 'feeling sad' which had emerged clearly for many reasons, in many contexts and different situations. While the aim was to ensure breadth of coverage, a trade-off had to be made due to the constraints of valuation and the final nine dimensions had far more substantive qualitative data behind them (Stevens 2011). The quantitative and qualitative data collected in the testing phase also informed this decision. There were problems for children in reading and understanding both 'jealous' and 'embarrassed', and some children commented that they didn't understand why 'jealous' was included and could not see how this was connected to health. These two dimensions did not show any significant difference between the general community and clinical populations, and 'jealous' was the dimension with fewest problems reported (Stevens 2011).

REFLECTIONS ON THE RESEARCH

Qualitative methods worked well for the development of this measure. The interviews were successful and children proved to be extremely capable of describing their health and the impact it has on their lives.

The consent process was very helpful for explaining the purpose of the research to children and what was required of them. No interviews had to be stopped early and no disclosure issues arose. The warm-up task which was undertaken prior to the main interview proved to be invaluable as it helped the children feel more comfortable and at ease with the researcher. The recording of the interviews did not bother the children at all, and many were used to recording devices. Interviews varied in length from four to twenty-six minutes and children concentrated well. No negative feedback was received, and some children commented that they had enjoyed the interview. The interview technique was the same for all ages (seven to eleven years), and the topic guide remained the same. However, the older children tended to give more depth in their responses and slightly more probing was needed for the younger children. All children received a certificate with the University of Sheffield logo on for participating which they were very pleased with.

It is always important to reflect on your own role as a researcher when undertaking qualitative work, for example, whether you have any pre-existing views, connections or experience with the type of content being investigated. In this case, my own role as a researcher was as neutral as possible. I had no children of my own to draw experiences from, and no experiences of working with sick or ill children, I was not involved in the care of any of the children in the research, and I did not know them prior to the interviews.

There are several advantages that the use of qualitative methods brings to the development of the CHU9D. The language and content are appropriate and relevant for children, children are more likely to be able to self-complete and the measure was developed to be a PBM from the outset, without including any previous items that may have been developed for different purposes.

CONCLUSION

This chapter has demonstrated how qualitative methods can be applied in the development of PBMs of HRQoL for use in economic evaluation. The example given of the CHU9D demonstrated how qualitative methods can be used in a number of ways: first, to develop the dimensions for a PBM; second, to inform whether these should be severity- or frequency-based; and third, to develop the wording for the levels for each of the dimensions.

Since the development of the CHU9D, other PBMs have also made use of qualitative methods, such as the CATQoL (Carlton 2013) measure. Given the advantages of using qualitative methods, the use of these methods is likely to increase in the future of PBM development.

ACKNOWLEDGEMENTS

This research was funded as part of an MRC Special Training Fellowship in Health Services and Health of the Public Research.

Chapter 12

Incorporating novel qualitative methods within health economics: The use of pictorial tools

Alastair Canaway, Hareth Al-Janabi, Philip Kinghorn, Cara Bailey and Joanna Coast

This research took place as part of a broader programme of work to investigate issues around the economics of end-of-life care. End of life is a time in life when people often rely on family and friends, and thus, care for a person at the end of life may have considerable impact on these family and friends, as well as the person him- or herself. As part of the broad programme of research, a measure was developed using qualitative methods to capture the impacts of end-of-life care on those close to people at the end of life (Canaway, Al-Janabi et al. 2017). While the primary purpose of the research was to identify domains of the bereavement experience of those close to someone at the end of life and generate attributes for the new outcome measure, there were four further interrelated issues that were explored in this piece of qualitative research. The first was how many people are close to those at end of life and thus which individuals might be the focus for use of the 'close person' measure. Second, it was important to determine how to identify who these 'close' people are for the purpose of broadening the evaluative scope; for example, should this new measure be used with carers, family members, friends or other groups? Third, it was desirable to understand more about the nature of 'closeness', what makes a person close to another person and thus what the implications of broadening the evaluative scope of economic evaluation might be. A final issue to explore was how end-of-life care and terminal illness can impact the networks around those at end of life. Again, if an illness or disease impacts upon the networks around that person, it may have important implications in attempting to capture spill-over effects within economic evaluation.

This chapter highlights how the use of pictorial methods alongside in-depth interviews can enhance the quality, understanding and interpretation of research. This chapter will first set the context to the case study and explain the problem that this study sought to address. A number of pictorial methods that can be used are highlighted, the method use within this case study (hierarchical mapping) is detailed and the benefits of using such methods are discussed. Reflections are given on the use of pictorial methods within the analysis and the benefits of pictorial methods as a research tool alongside qualitative interviews.

POSSIBLE METHODS FOR EXPLORING NETWORK COMPOSITION

To examine the networks of persons close to those at the end of life, and to understand the complex reasons underlying the changes in relationships, it was decided at an early stage that a qualitative approach was appropriate. In-depth, one-to-one interviews were arranged with individuals who were either bereaved or had somebody close to them receiving end-of-life care. It was felt, however, that discussion alone would not fully capture these networks and that it would be desirable to incorporate a method or instrument into the interviews that would better enable exploration of the supplementary research questions about the networks.

There are a number of existing tools that can be used to examine 'closeness' and strength of relationships, and so choosing the most suitable method for the task was important. Examples of methods for examining closeness include the use of dyadic tools and strength of tie indicators, and the pictorial tools that form the focus of this chapter. The first of these is briefly outlined before the focus of the chapter turns to pictorial tools.

Dyadic tools

Dyadic tools have often been used to examine concepts such as friendship, closeness and intimacy (Aron, Mashek et al. 2004). The nature of relationships is a well-studied area within the social psychology and communication studies literature, where conceptual frameworks have been developed to help understand the nature of close relationships. Dyadic tools such as the *Other in the Self Scale* (Aron, Melinat et al. 1997) and the *Personal Acquaintance Measure* (Starzyk, Holden et al. 2006) were developed to help quantify the closeness of relationship between two individuals. Such dyadic tools were, however, unsuitable to achieve the goals of this research. Both measures, although used to assess closeness of relationships, only do so between dyads, between the self and the other. Within this research, it was desirable to know the extent of the close person network, and the identity of all those within it. As such, dyadic measures which focused only on the other and the self were too narrow in terms of assessing who, and how many individuals, were within the close person network. Administering a dyadic measure to all those within the close person network would have been both time-consuming, and would not have assisted in the choice about whom the measures should be used with.

Another possibility might have been to examine *Strength of tie indicators* (Granovetter 1973). Early research in this area characterized the strength of ties as being related to a combination of factors including time spent together, emotional intensity and reciprocity (Granovetter 1973), and there are now measures available, such as the *Virtual Tie Scale* (Petróczi, Nepusz et al. 2007), to assess the strength of ties. Such measures again, however, are limited in this context by focusing on the dyad.

Pictorial tools

Pictorial tools are any tools that include the use of pictures, and they have been developed and used in a variety of research areas. Pictorial tools can appear in many forms and have often been used alongside qualitative interviews. Existing tools include genograms (Guerin and Pendagast 1976), family diagrams (Bowen 1978), the Pictor method (King, Bravington et al. 2013), ecological maps (ecomaps) (Hartman 1978), hierarchical maps (Antonucci 1986) and sociograms (Moreno 1934).

Family diagrams and genograms are often referred to interchangeably, but they have slightly differing uses. Family diagrams were developed within the family planning literature by Bowen (1978), and such diagrams aim to record the facts and functioning of multigenerational families. Genograms build upon this by allowing for other contextual information within the diagrams (Guerin and Pendagast 1976).

Expanding on these, there has been the development of further pictorial tools that allow the exploration of a host of sociological phenomena. The Pictor method was developed for use within in-depth interviews to explore how staff experience collaborative working in community settings or across community and acute care settings (King, Bravington et al. 2013). This method requires a large piece of paper, and arrow-shaped Post-it notes to develop a visual representation of the roles and relationships of those providing care to a person (King, Bravington et al. 2013). A similar tool developed for use within social work is ecological mapping (Hartman 1978).

The ecological mapping process typically involves the researcher asking the participants to draw a circle to represent themselves in the centre of a large piece of paper (Hartman 1978; McCormick, Stricklin et al. 2008). The researcher then facilitates the ecological mapping process by asking the participant to add relevant people/services/institutions (nodes) onto the ecomap. A range of different lines and arrows can be used to describe the relationships between the different nodes on the ecological map. For example, thicker lines can be used to describe stronger relationships, arrows can be used to show flows of resources or support, and jagged marks across a line can be used to highlight conflict (Hartman 1978).

Ecological maps (ecomaps) have a long history within social care (Parker and Bradley 2014). They have also been used to describe and examine the different avenues of support within a network and to examine social relationships, particularly in relation to carers (Ray and Street 2005; Rempel, Neufeld et al. 2007). Ecomaps have been used within a number of care-related settings. Ray and Street, for example, used them to analyse sources of support for those caring for somebody with motor neurone disease (Ray and Street 2005), while others have used them to provide information on relationships within a family network (McCormick, Stricklin et al. 2008), and to examine the needs of individuals, and their network, at the end of life (Early, Smith et al. 2000). Ecomaps allow the participant to produce a visual representation of the relationships that exist within their particular context (Tracy, Whittaker et al. 1994) which facilitates the understanding of complex and interconnected relationships.

The Pictor method and ecomapping, although both powerful tools, contain much more information than was required to meet the aims of the research described here. Two other potential pictorial methods of interest were the sociogram and the hierarchical map. Although coming from different research areas, sociograms and hierarchical maps have much in common. The sociogram was developed to examine choices within groups and has been used within a variety of settings, including educational settings (González, Regalado et al. 2010), information systems research (Willis and Coakes 2000) and environmental research (Syme, Dzidic et al. 2012).

Similar to sociograms in style, and the focus of this case study, is hierarchical mapping. Hierarchical mapping was designed to assess the strength of 'closeness' of individuals within a network in relation to a focal person (Antonucci 1986). The hierarchical mapping task involves the use of concentric circles to represent different levels of closeness. Individuals then place members of the close person network (written on an arrow-shaped Post-it note) onto the hierarchical map to generate an image containing all the people who are close to that individual and their relative closeness. This method has been found to be simple, efficient and easy to understand by the general public (Nadoh, Podrebersek et al. 2004), and has been used in a range of situations to examine close person networks. For example, it has been used to explore network size and composition (Antonucci and Akiyama 1987; Hlebec, Mrzel et al. 2009), to examine negative impacts of social relations (Antonucci, Akiyama et al. 1998) and to investigate relationships between generations (Santos and Levitt 2007). It is particularly appropriate for examining the evaluative scope for economic evaluation, given that the focus of an intervention is almost always the individual patient, and it is the relationship to that individual patient and thus the resultant spill-over effects that is important to capture.

WHY INCLUDE PICTORIAL TOOLS WITHIN QUALITATIVE INTERVIEWS?

Despite the increasing use of qualitative methods within health economics, pictorial methods have not previously been employed alongside in-depth interviews. To justify the inclusion of such methods, it is important to understand why a pictorial method can be a useful tool for data generation, not just in its own right, but also as a facilitator within the interview process. There have been a variety of benefits reported within the literature from using pictorial tools as part of the interviewing process. It is often said that 'a picture paints a thousand words', and one of the key benefits underlying pictorial methods is their ability to elicit, and present, complex information in an uncomplicated manner in an interview context (McCormick, Stricklin et al. 2008). This information, when combined with text from interview transcripts, can be combined to generate greater insight and understanding (Hartman 1978). Not only are these methods useful for data generation purposes, they can also help facilitate the interview; they have been reported to generate rapport between the researcher and interviewee (Rempel, Neufeld et al. 2007), while providing the interviewee with the opportunity to reflect and deliberate. Furthermore, the use of a pictorial tool can act as a visual trigger for the interviewee, prompting them to recall information that may otherwise have been omitted from the interview. From the researcher's perspective it has the additional benefit of providing a visual foundation, from which to probe and question (Ray and Street 2005).

CHOOSING A PICTORIAL METHOD

While there are clear advantages to using pictorial tools, there are also some limitations. The most significant drawback is that they can be time-consuming for the interviewee and may distract from the primary goals of the interview. Within this piece of research, exploration of the close person networks was just one goal among others. Consequently, there was a limit to the amount of time that could be devoted to this element of the research, and this influenced the choice of tool. Pictorial methods such as the ecomap and Pictor method were rejected as being typically more time-consuming and involving higher levels of detail and complexity than was required to meet the aims of the research. Hierarchical mapping was chosen for its speed, simplicity and intuitive appeal. It was anticipated that the hierarchical mapping method would facilitate all the objectives of this research, by capturing the scope and scale of the close person network around those at the end of life, while augmenting the interview process. The choice of method is, of course, dependent upon the context, and the goal of the research, and time should be put into deciding what information is required, and which tool best achieves that.

CONDUCTING THE RESEARCH

Twenty-four in-depth interviews were conducted which included the hierarchical mapping task. This gave the opportunity to explore with the participants what the notion 'close' meant to them, and then to probe about the characteristics of a 'close person'. The hierarchical mapping task was conducted to obtain information about the scale and scope of the close person network, as well as to act as a visual tool for further probing and questioning. Ethical approval for this research was obtained through the University of Birmingham's Life and Health Sciences Ethical Review Committee (ERN_12–1338) and North Wales NHS Research Ethics Committee – West (13/WA/0333).

The hierarchical mapping process is relatively straightforward and can be broken down into seven steps.

Step 1

To begin, introduce the topic of interest: here, it was explained that the research was interested in the concepts of 'closeness' and 'close person' networks surrounding the person at the end of life.

Step 2

Introduce to the participant a sizeable sheet of paper, ideally no smaller than A3. The paper should contain large concentric circles moving out from the centre (Antonucci 1986). Explain that the rings represent different levels of closeness, with the inner ring representing the closest relationships, the next ring representing relationships which are very close and the outer ring being less close relationships (Antonucci 1986). That is, the closest relationships are closest to the centre, and those less close are further from the centre.

Step 3

Present the interviewees with a stack of arrow-shaped Post-it notes. Ask them to write the names and, importantly, the relationship of all those who are close on separate arrows. As the task continues, the interviewees can add additional people as and when they desire.

Step 4

Ask the interviewees to place each 'close person arrow' onto the hierarchical map, with the tip of the arrow representing the relative closeness. The distance of the arrow tip to the centre of the hierarchical map represents the relative closeness of the relationship between the close persons and the focal individual.

Step 5

Once all close persons have been added to the hierarchical map, give the interviewees the opportunity to reflect and deliberate on their choices, move arrows around as necessary and add anybody else they feel should be included.

Step 6

Use the map as a basis for discussion with the participant; the details of the hierarchical map can at this point be used as a visual tool to examine the relationships in depth across the whole network of individuals; for example, if the interviewee placed somebody particularly close, or distant, consider probing why that was the case, or referring back to the map to discuss people listed as close but not yet discussed.

Step 7

Once completed, scan the hierarchical maps into a computer and anonymize (in accordance with relevant ethical approvals). These hierarchical maps can then be used alongside the interview transcripts within the analysis. An example of a completed hierarchical map can be seen in Figure 12.1.

Analysis of pictorial tools

One of the strengths of pictorial tools is the ability to use a wide range of analytical methods depending upon the philosophical framework from which the research is being undertaken. King and colleagues, for example, highlight how the Pictor method can be used from narrative, phenomenologist and construct theorist perspectives (King, Bravington et al. 2013). A key component of the analysis is to use the generated picture in conjunction with the

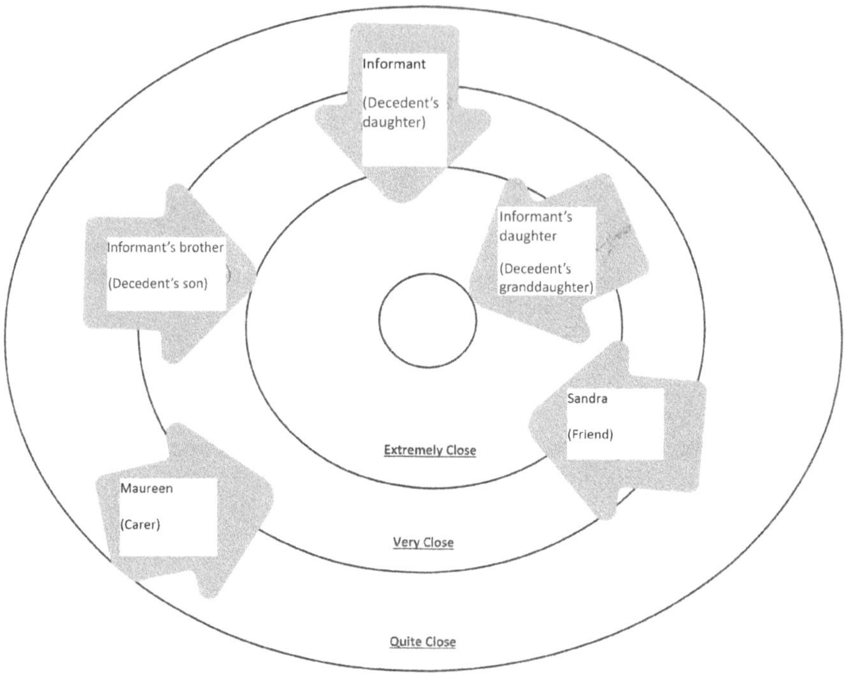

Figure 12.1. Example of completed hierarchical map. Courtesy of the authors.

interview transcript, integration being integral to achieving a richer analysis of the data (King, Bravington et al. 2013).

Within the case study reported here, constant comparative methods (Glaser 1965; Hewitt-Taylor 2001) formed the basis for the analysis of the interview transcripts and hierarchical maps, and were felt to be particularly appropriate in terms of examining the influences of end of life on close person networks. Factors that participants felt impacted upon close person relationships towards the end of life could be probed and further explored within following interviews. Likewise, in examining the attributes that facilitate closeness, the use of constant comparison allowed for attributes of closeness to be elucidated in an iterative process.

The hierarchical maps enabled the use of a host of analytic techniques, both quantitative and qualitative, to address the research goal. Quantitatively, the scope of the network was analysed by examining the number of individuals within each hierarchical map. Simple descriptive statistics were used to examine how many individuals were close to those at the end of life. This simple descriptive analysis also focused on the different levels of closeness, as the closest relationships, within the inner circle, may be the most relevant in exploring spill-overs within economic evaluation. The type of person (e.g., relation/friend) who was close to the person at the end of life was also examined by assessing the hierarchical maps which explicitly state the relationship on each 'close person arrow'.

For the qualitative analysis, the interview transcripts were used alongside the hierarchical maps to explore issues around the nature and size of the network of the person at the end of life. Deviant case analysis (Mays and Pope 2000) was used to explore cases or individuals that appeared to have 'unusual' hierarchical maps and to determine the reasons for these atypical maps. This was particularly relevant in this study where one individual had a vastly contrasting hierarchical map compared to all others; typically at least one family member would be within the inner circle, but in this instance none were present.

To investigate the influences on the size of network at end of life, individuals who reported the largest networks for their end of life 'person' within the mapping task (more than ten) were compared and contrasted with those who reported the smallest networks (fewer than five). This process began with the systematic analysis of the interview transcripts of those with the smallest networks, to identify common patterns and themes which related to network size, and close person relations. This process allowed for the generation of a number of hypotheses relating to the influences on network size. This was then repeated for those with the largest networks, and the hypotheses previously generated were examined in this group. This process helped to identify important potential influences on network size at the end of life. Additionally, a number of sub-analyses of the hierarchical maps were conducted, for example, examining network size and composition by death trajectory, age and ethnicity.

Minimising bias within the process

As with all qualitative research, it is important to consider how the researcher's actions as an interviewer can impact the results. To minimize this, a position of empathic neutrality can be adopted during interviews. Likewise self-reflexivity, which can be defined as a 'confessional account of methodology or as examining one's own personal, possibly unconscious reactions' (Finlay 2002, p. 224), should be conducted following analysis. The idea is to critically appraise research methods to explore how the researcher's pre-existing biases may have impacted upon the results. In this research, the main researcher (AC) had been recently bereaved prior to conducting the interviews. It was therefore particularly important for the researcher to maintain a non-judgemental and open position of empathic neutrality and to ensure that his own issues related to bereavement did not influence the interview. This was achieved by keeping questions open-ended and keeping the interview interviewee-led where possible. Regular meetings with the research or supervisory team were also used to critically examine the data and descriptive accounts to assess whether the interviewer was unknowingly biasing the results.

REFLECTIONS ON THE INCLUSION OF THE HIERARCHICAL MAPPING TASK

The inclusion of the hierarchical mapping task alongside the in-depth interview was valuable in facilitating exploration of all four of the original research aims related to networks at the end of life. It also had other benefits. It gave the interviewees the opportunity to reflect upon their relationships. This allowed more detail to emerge surrounding the networks, with participants often taking the time to make both significant and subtle changes to the composition of the hierarchical maps. For each focal person, the levels of closeness of the different individuals within the network may differ, and these subtleties are captured within the hierarchical map. In contrast, within a standard interview process without such a tool, the differing levels of closeness across a number of people would be near impossible to elicit. For such a question, the hierarchical mapping reduces the response burden of the interviewees, allowing them time to formulate and structure their hierarchical map in a simple and intuitive manner.

Not only did the hierarchical mapping generate data, providing a depth of data that could not be achieved by the use of only the spoken language, it also aided the interview process more generally. By introducing the hierarchical mapping task near the beginning of the interview process it became a useful tool for generating rapport. It was particularly useful in encouraging the interviewee to open up about the relationships involved and their nature, some of which, given the end-of-life context, were difficult for the interviewees to talk about. Asking the participants to articulate their thoughts while conducting the hierarchical mapping task provided a natural method of generating initial conversation between the interviewer and the participants and enabling the participants to feel comfortable with the interview situation.

The task was also helpful in providing a 'springboard' to gain a deeper insight into issues across the remainder of the interview, both in relation to the network and beyond this. In particular, the map provided a valuable reference tool for the remainder of the interview and into the analysis. During the interview itself, and throughout the analysis, it was beneficial for the interviewer, when a name was mentioned, to be able to see at a glance, exactly who that person was, what relation he or she was to the person at the end of life, and how close to the focal person he or she was; this enabled the interviewer to better target follow-up questions and, again, helped with maintaining rapport. Similarly, when analysing the interview transcript, the hierarchical map was extremely valuable in better understanding the data, as, for example, where the participant says something along the lines of 'Dave was very close, and grew closer as John's illness set in'. The hierarchical map allows the researcher to see exactly who 'Dave' is, what his relationship to 'John' is and how close they were, providing important context for analysing the rest of the quote.

CONCLUSION

The use of hierarchical maps alongside interview transcripts provided the opportunity for interviewees to offer detail on the nature of the relationships between the person at the end of life and the members of their network that would otherwise not have been achieved. The maps were used to assess the scope of the networks and to identify the types of individuals who were close to those at the end of life. Influences on network size at the end of life were also explored, and several hypotheses were generated through this process. Using constant comparison methods, 'attributes' of closeness that facilitated close person relationships were also elicited which were useful for interpreting and understanding the various influences on network size.

There are a number of situations where pictorial methods could be utilized. This chapter has focused on those close to the end of life. This examination could, however, be broadened to any population. There has been renewed interest in capturing spill-over impacts within economic evaluation (Al-Janabi, van Exel et al. 2016), and pictorial tools could be used to help identify who could, and should, be included within the evaluative scope. Likewise, the key strength of pictorial methods lies in their ability to collate and convey a lot of information in a quick and intuitive way. Such methods could be particularly useful in succinctly examining complex structures such as service delivery and health care organisation. This could be especially useful in terms of identifying what aspects of services users find valuable, and where services may be failing.

The purpose of this case study has been to highlight how using hierarchical mapping helped to answer a set of research questions of interest to those conducting economic evaluation of interventions at the end of life. As well as addressing the questions, hierarchical mapping had the additional benefit of augmenting the interview more generally. It should be reemphasized that hierarchical mapping is not the only pictorial tool that can be included, and the choice of pictorial tool should be made in the context of the study aims.

ACKNOWLEDGEMENTS

The study described in this chapter was funded by the European Research Council (261098 EconEndLife).

Chapter 13

Using non-participant observation and think-aloud to understand and improve modelling processes

Samantha Husbands, Sue Jowett, Pelham Barton and Joanna Coast

Decision-analytic models are used as a vehicle for economic analysis to compare the costs and health consequences of competing health interventions, and to generate estimates of their relative cost-effectiveness (Buxton, Drummond et al. 1997; Sculpher, Claxton et al. 2006). A decision-analytic model provides a platform for synthesising all relevant data on the health and economic outcomes of comparative health technologies, allowing the long-term costs and benefits of different treatment options to be compared (Kuntz and Weinstein 2001). The use of decision-analytic models in economic evaluation and decision making is advocated by organisations such as the National Institute for Health and Care Excellence in the United Kingdom, the Pharmaceutical Benefits Advisory Committee in Australia and the Canadian Agency for Drugs and Technologies in Health in Canada. Despite the policy importance of these models, it has been suggested that modellers are potentially using inappropriate methods within model development, which could impact on the validity of cost-effectiveness results (Chen, Jobanputra et al. 2006; Roberts, Robinson et al. 2006; Karnon, Goyder et al. 2007). This suggests that research is needed to investigate current model-building processes, to ascertain whether the methods being used by modelling teams require improvement.

This chapter reports on case study research, which used qualitative methods to explore decision-analytic model development, particularly what appeared to be good practice in model building, and where problems were occurring and less robust methods appeared to be being used. The work presented within this chapter concentrates particularly on the use of observational qualitative methods, specifically using think-aloud techniques and non-participant observation; although in-depth interviews were also undertaken, these are not reported here as there are a number of other chapters reporting examples of research using interviews. This chapter offers a detailed overview of how non-participant observation and think-aloud were used to understand the model-building activities carried out by teams of modellers and clinicians, including the results that the methods generated, and some reflections on the qualitative approach taken.

METHODS

Two model-building case studies were undertaken with two separate teams of modellers and clinicians, using non-participant observation and think-aloud methods. The two teams of modellers were sampled purposively, with the aim of capturing potentially diverse model development processes, and thus to strengthen the generalisability of the findings (Polit and Beck 2010). Academic and policy-based case studies were sampled, referred to as Model A and Model B. The modelling teams involved in each of the case studies were also different in terms of the experts who were involved in the development of each model, as Model A had direct input from three modellers and one clinician, and Model B from two modellers and up to twenty clinical experts. These modelling teams were selected because they had good reputations for model building (based on the suggestions of a number of modelling experts interviewed) and were chosen on the assumption that any problems that were encountered within their modelling processes were also likely to be encountered by modellers with less expertise. The objective of this research was to highlight any issues with the modelling methods being used, and potentially suggest ways in which model development processes could be improved.

Non-participant observation was chosen as a method for data collection because of its ability to allow a researcher to directly observe a phenomenon, gain insight into interactions between individuals and record their behaviour (Patton 2002). Non-participant observation was selected with the aim of capturing, as far as possible, the typical processes used by the two modelling teams, with limited disruption to their work. The objective was to observe as many stages of a model's development as possible, which was facilitated by a key informant within each case study, who informed the researcher about when modelling activities were due to take place. Observation entailed 'sitting in' on all meetings that involved any discussion of model building, with the permission of those present. The practicalities of undertaking the observations differed for each case study and the preferences of the key informant. For example, in Model A, the researcher was asked to sit at the table with informants during modelling meetings (although she had no involvement in discussions), whereas in Model B, the researcher was seated at the side of the room. Email communication between the parties involved in model development was also obtained, as the researcher requested to be copied in to all email exchanges. Data collection focused on exploring how each stage of model development was conducted, specifically the methods used and the contribution that the modellers and the clinicians made. Written consent for the case studies was taken prior to any modelling meetings to prevent disruption, and the research was introduced to the informants via the key informant to facilitate the consent process.

Audio recordings of meetings were taken within both case studies, alongside detailed field notes, to generate rich sources for analysis. Descriptive field notes taken at the time of the observation focused on capturing detail on the setting, for example, who was present and what was being discussed, including any direct quotations from informants that appeared relevant (Patton 2002). Analytical field notes were taken in a separate notebook to record the researcher's interpretations of the events being observed, particularly the issues that seemed most important to the research, such as how decisions were being made in model development and how communication worked between the modellers and clinicians. These notes were later used in the analytical coding of the audio-recording data, as identifying key themes during both data collection and analysis allowed for a broader and deeper understanding of the main findings emerging from the data (Miles and Huberman 1984).

The think-aloud method was used to capture data on the tasks that modellers carried out individually. Think-aloud generates data on the 'reasoning processes' that individuals use to undertake particular problem-solving tasks (Fonteyn, Kuipers et al. 1993). More specifically the method works to 'identify the information that is concentrated on during problem solving and how that information is used to facilitate problem resolution' (Fonteyn, Kuipers et al. 1993, p. 430). Data are obtained by asking informants to 'talk aloud' while performing cognitive tasks, capturing verbalisations of their thought processes (Ericsson and Simon 1993). Given that a number of stages of model development were focused on programing and testing the model in computer software, the think-aloud method was used with the intention of permitting an in-depth insight and understanding of how these typically solitary activities were completed.

Think-aloud was undertaken within Model A and was focused on exploring the methods that the modeller used to test the model results, specifically the sensitivity checks that were carried out, and how the modeller made sense of, and interpreted, the results of the analyses. The think-aloud took place in one session, designed to capture the modeller undertaking all planned sensitivity analysis on the model. This was not only to fit in with the scheduled activities of the modeller but also to encourage prolonged application to the task, and to generate uninterrupted verbalisations (van Someren, Barnard et al. 1994). In line with the suggestions of Fonteyn and colleagues, think-aloud was undertaken in a quiet location, in the informant's work office, and with as little interaction from the researcher as possible (Fonteyn, Kuipers et al. 1993). This was to avoid interruption to the informant's thoughts. The informant was instructed prior to the think-aloud to 'speak constantly without regard for coherency' while completing the sensitivity analyses, and was communicated with only to be reminded to 'keep talking' after periods of silence (Boren and Ramey 2000). Where the researcher wanted to ask questions or seek clarification from the informant, these were noted and discussed with the informant after the session. The think-aloud session was audio-recorded with the permission of the informant, and the recording was transcribed verbatim to provide a rich source for analysis.

Analysis of all observational and think-aloud data was undertaken using the framework method (Ritchie and Spencer 1994). Framework involved undertaking five key stages of qualitative data analysis: familiarisation, identifying a thematic framework, indexing, charting and mapping, and interpretation (Ritchie and Spencer 2002). After reviewing all collected material, including observational field notes and transcripts of the think-aloud and modelling meetings, a thematic framework was developed based on the 'key issues, concepts and themes' (Ritchie and Spencer 2002, p. 313) that were emerging from the data. Key themes were identified and developed from the data on the basis of their perceived relevance and importance to the research question, for example, representing stages of the modelling process and problems with model development. This thematic framework was used to sort and label all of the observational and think-aloud material, and was revised as it was applied to the case study data, as new codes emerged and were added, allowing new and important issues to be explored.

Materials were coded by line or passage using NVivo software, with consideration of the meaning of each instance of data and how it related to the thematic framework and data coded previously. After all data had been coded, charts were created to organize the data according to the codes in the thematic framework, and were also separated to account for the method of data collection from which the findings were emerging. Separate charts were created for each of the two case studies, and the charted data included quotations from conversations recorded during observations, extracts from field notes and verbalisations from the think-aloud session. These data were then used to inform the findings of the case study research.

Ethics approval was sought and granted for the research from the Science, Technology, Engineering and Mathematics Ethical Review Committee at the University of Birmingham (reference: ERN_12–1533).

FINDINGS OF THE NON-PARTICIPANT OBSERVATION AND THINK-ALOUD METHODS

This presentation of findings aims to illustrate how the use of non-participant observation and think-aloud methods was able to contribute to the overall findings of this research, showing the types of findings and the ways in which the data can be used and presented. First, the non-participant observation and think-aloud provided a novel insight into the model-building process, including study of the communication between modellers and clinicians, and investigation into how modellers performed the individual tasks required in model development. Second, the findings of the non-participant observation permitted a greater understanding of the data generated through other methods, specifically the qualitative interview findings. Third, the combination of these methods allowed for the in-depth exploration of the entire model-building process, enabling rich data to be generated on the methods that modellers were using to develop decision-analytic models. These contributions will be explored in turn here. In the presentation of the results, informants have been anonymized to protect their identity. Each informant is labelled according to whether he or she is a modeller (M) or clinician (C), whether he or she was involved in Model A or B, and according to an individual number (e.g., MA1 is a modeller belonging to Model A with the unique code 1).

Novel insights into model development

Both the non-participant observation and think-aloud permitted important and novel insights into modelling processes, generating data on how modellers were completing the more 'subtle' aspects of model development, specifically how communication was being managed and how individual modelling activities were being undertaken.

The observation of modelling meetings allowed data to be captured on the communication that occurred between modellers and clinicians, demonstrating how their discussions influenced the development of a model. More specifically, the data showed how the modelling teams were approaching structural development with the clinical experts, and the roles that the modellers and clinicians had in model building. After analysis of the communication recorded within each case study, it became clear that the two modelling teams were taking different approaches to involving clinicians in developing model structure. While the modellers in Model A asked the clinician to talk through the disease pathway of an average patient to structure the model, the modellers in Model B aimed specific questions at the clinicians about an existing model structure that they had developed using previous models and the literature. Comparing these different methods later allowed inferences to be made about which of the approaches to communication seemed to be the better practice.

> MA1 [to clinician]: *It's important to find out from you what the patient pathway would be, as in the patient would have this and then this treatment.* (Modelling meeting, Model A)
>
> MB2 [to clinicians]: *(for patients with) missed [Problem A] . . . will [Treatment 2] be required, so would that be different [Treatment 2] for those identified with [Problem A] or would it be reduced outcomes for delayed [Treatment 2]?*
> CB1: *The [Treatment 2] is much more complicated . . . . because you go onto get secondary problems . . . and (there are) major cost implications for treating those, and loss of quality of life.* (Modelling meeting, Model B)

The observation of communication between the modellers and clinicians also gave an indication of where problems were occurring during discussions between the two parties. For example, clinician understanding of the economic and modelling terminology used by the modellers appeared to cause issues with communication, and delay model development, within the case studies.

> MA2: *Are the utilities different, after the surgery.*
> CA1: *Sorry?*
> MA2: *If the person has [Major surgery 1] for example, the utility might be different then, does the surgery. . .*
> CA1: *The,* ***what*** *will be different sorry?*
> MA1: *The quality of life, so do we assume it's full health when they've had surgery?* (Modelling meeting, Model A)

The use of the think-aloud permitted a detailed understanding of the modelling activities that modellers undertook individually, specifically testing the results of the model. In the following example, the modeller approaches the interpretation of the results of each sensitivity analysis by first predicting the impact that a change in a parameter outcome would have on the model outcome, and then ensuring that the model results moved in the direction expected.

> MA2: *By lowering current practice sensitivity . . . in [Outcome 1] . . . I'm still expecting this effectiveness to be higher than [Strategy E] but the cost-utility might come down to .50, .40, it will still be dominating but at a higher cost. . . . Let's see, so current practice test, lower cost, less effective. . . . Makes sense doesn't it? Yep. I mean it was dominating but now it is less dominating.* (Think-aloud, sensitivity analysis, Model A)

Provide an understanding of the data generated through other methods

Alongside the use of the non-participant observation and think-aloud within the case studies, qualitative interviews were also undertaken with informants, to capture their reflections on the methods used during model development. Although the interview data were useful, the observational data were required to add context to the comments that the informants were making on modelling processes. An example of this is shown in the following quotation from the clinician, and the accompanying excerpt from an observation of a conversation between this clinician and the modellers involved in Model A. In her interview, the clinician (CA1) suggested that she was unhappy with the representativeness of the developed model structure, and on closer inspection of the observational data, it seemed that CA1's dissatisfaction may have been related to how communication was managed within model development, specifically the clinician's lack of influence on decisions made around model structure.

> CA1: *In the model we are mostly concentrating on [Symptom 2] and no [Symptom 2] but then there are some patients who have coexisting conditions like [Symptom 1] . . . [that] are not being accounted for.* (Interview, Model A)
> CA1: *No they are more than an exception to the rule . . . in the prevalence studies they are quoting that 12 to 25% of the population have [Problem 3].*
> MA1: *So my suggestion to you is that our main model excludes this specialist patient group but in the sensitivity analysis we allow the 25% because there are data in the literature.* (Modelling meeting, Model A)

In-depth exploration of, and rich data on, the model-building process

The combination of the use of non-participant observation and think-aloud permitted an in-depth exploration of many stages of model development. This was useful in providing the researcher with an understanding of the methods that the modelling teams were using to develop their models, and also highlighting where the approaches taken were causing issues, later allowing suggestions to be made for improvements to practice. However, the methods also provided rich data on the modelling processes undertaken, which as an output to the research could potentially offer a useful resource to other modellers. This is in terms of other modellers using the methods of these modelling teams to reflect on their own approaches, or where good practices have been identified, using these methods to inform their processes. Having such a detailed resource on the 'real-life' methods used within model development may be particularly helpful to those who are new to modelling, and could be used as guidance in some form. Learning about the problems encountered by these modelling teams may also help others to avoid or overcome such issues themselves, improving the quality of models and the efficiency of model development.

As an example, the following quotation from the think-aloud demonstrates how the modeller resolved an issue related to his interpretation of the results of a sensitivity analysis. MA2 used the strategy of reviewing the base case data and thinking about how the change in scenario (that all patients were assumed to receive the same treatment for a particular problem) would impact on the treatment outcomes of particular groups of patients, and the effectiveness of the competing interventions. By doing this he found that the effectiveness of the most cost-effective strategy decreased because patients who had originally been misdiagnosed by the least effective intervention were now receiving the most appropriate treatment for their condition.

> MA2: *Why did current practice become less effective? There was a high likelihood of a wrong diagnosis for [Strategy E], but if you assume now that these patients will be getting [Minor surgery 1] instead of having the option, patients receive the intervention they would get if they were correctly diagnosed. So you would expect the effectiveness [of Strategy E] to increase.* (Think-aloud, sensitivity analysis, Model A)

REFLECTIONS ON THE METHODS USED

The use of non-participant observation and think-aloud in the exploration of the development of decision-analytic models provided a novel and in-depth insight into how modelling teams were conducting their processes, including problems with the methods used. Gaining these insights allowed inferences to be made about the appropriateness of the practices undertaken, and gave way to suggestions around how methods might be improved. For example, where clinicians were struggling to interpret the research and economic terminology being used by the modellers, communication within structural development may have benefited from clinician training and familiarisation with such terms prior to model building.

Using a triangulation of qualitative methods strengthened the ability of the research to provide a more detailed understanding of good practice and issues in model development, particularly through the combination of the use of non-participant observation and the qualitative interviews. The findings of these two methods complemented each other in the sense that the observational data could provide context to the comments made by the informants in their interviews, and the qualitative interviews could be used as a platform to question, and ask the informants to reflect on, aspects of the modelling practices that were undertaken. In terms of the implications of the research, the use of the qualitative interviews and non-participant observation in conjunction again facilitated suggestions for improvements to modelling practices. Where different approaches were taken by the two modelling teams to communicate and develop the structure of each model with the clinicians, the informants' comments were used to infer which of the approaches appeared to be better practice. For example, in Model B, the modeller involved (MB2) reflected that the method of asking the clinicians questions on only aspects of the model prevented the clinical experts from understanding how the structure had been put together, also leading to the clinicians questioning and requesting changes to elements of the structure late in the modelling process. MB2 suggested that the approach of developing the entire model structure in conjunction with the clinical experts, as undertaken in Model A, would have improved clinician understanding and communication between the modellers and clinicians.

> MB2: *You do get some good feedback on specific bits of it but then they don't see the actual thing happening, so maybe if they did actually see it being built as it goes then that might [help].* (Interview, Model A)

In a similar way, the observational data allowed for a deeper understanding of the findings of the qualitative interviews, with an example being in Model A, where the clinician's unhappiness with the model was seemingly due to her lack of involvement in structural decision making. The implication of this finding was that the clinician, and arguably the clinical validity of the model, would have benefited from more negotiation over the inputs to the structure. Although using the qualitative interviews and non-participant observation in conjunction was a clear benefit of this research, it also highlighted the drawbacks of using these methods alone. Much of the observational data relied on the interviews to expand and follow up on its findings, particularly when making inferences around good and poor practice in model development.

The combination of the use of think-aloud and non-participant observation made it possible to capture in-depth data on many stages of model development. Such a thorough representation of the modelling process was important to the research team's understanding of how model development worked but could also potentially provide a resource for other modellers to refer to in their own model development. Although further consideration is needed around the practical implications of sharing the modelling teams' processes with others, the documentation of their methods through the use of non-participant observation and think-aloud permits insight into the more nuanced, but key, aspects of model development, such as communication between parties and the stages that were undertaken individually by the modellers.

However, there were drawbacks to the use of these methods within this research. Aiming to capture data on all stages of model development was time consuming, and also relied on informants notifying the researcher of when they were undertaking any model-building activities. Although the researcher managed to attend all organized modelling meetings between parties within both case studies, it proved more of a challenge to be present to capture the modellers' solitary model-building activities, as these were typically carried out in a more ad hoc manner. This was particularly problematic within Model B, as these modellers were involved in multiple model-based projects and thus were unable to specify in advance when they would be working on a particular project or activity. Given the unpredictable nature of the modellers' work, the researcher was unable to organize any think-aloud sessions within Model B, given that the method relies on an informant focussing and investing time in verbalising his or her thought processes (van Someren, Barnard et al. 1994). The implication of this was that more data were captured for the stages that were pre-planned, particularly the development of the model structures, and inevitably the majority of the findings and suggestions from the research were based on these activities.

Given the volume and richness of the data collected through the combination of the qualitative methods used in the case studies, ethical considerations were particularly important in this research. Much time was spent during the data analysis stages taking steps to ensure that the identity of the modelling organisations and informants was protected. This involved assigning codes to all identifiable information, including informants' names and job titles, and the details of the medical conditions that were the subjects of the models. Although no ethical issues were encountered, additional time and communication were required at the end of the project to allow the modelling teams the opportunity to review any written work for identifiable information prior to any of the findings being released to the public (Hopf 2004).

Reflecting on the approach to research more generally, it is important to consider how the background and perceptions of the research team may have affected the conclusions of this work (Malterud 2001). On undertaking this research, the main researcher had not worked on any modelling projects previously, with her only exposure to decision-analytic modelling being through a modelling module undertaken on a health economics and health policy MSc course. She felt that this lack of experience of model building was both an advantage and a disadvantage. It was advantageous in that she believed that she did not bring any preconceptions to the research, such as what the main issues with current model development processes were. It was difficult, though, at the outset of the project to follow some of the discussions between the modellers, particularly around the more complex and technical aspects of model development. It is possible that this may have affected the interpretation of some of the model-building activities carried out, although there was the opportunity during the qualitative interviews to clarify understanding of what had been observed with the informants involved; others in the research team also had more extensive modelling experience, which aided interpretation. In addition, the researcher's knowledge of modelling increased as the project progressed.

CONCLUSION

The use of non-participant observation and think-aloud when applied to the processes of decision-analytic model development provided a novel and important insight into how models were being built in practice. The use of these qualitative methods provided an in-depth understanding of the modelling stages that were being undertaken, and allowed the methods and any problems that were occurring within the processes to be documented in detail. With the support of the data from the qualitative interviews, this permitted inferences to be made around the reasons for these problems, and how issues might be avoided or addressed. Such findings are potentially important in improving the quality of decision-analytic models and modelling processes, particularly in light of concerns that modellers do not always use the most appropriate methods.

It was also suggested that the exploration and documentation of modelling processes could provide a useful resource for other modellers, although further thought is needed as to how these data could be shared. To strengthen this research further, future work should focus on using non-participant observation, qualitative interviews and think-aloud methods to explore additional modelling processes, and to identify further ways in which decision-analytic model development might be improved. More generally, these methods could be useful in other areas of health economics to understand and potentially improve the quality and efficiency of health- and economics-related processes.

ACKNOWLEDGEMENTS

The study reported in this chapter was funded by the University of Birmingham.

Part II B

USING QUALITATIVE METHODS TO INTERPRET QUANTITATIVE FINDINGS

Chapter 14

Using 'think-aloud' and interview data to explore patient and proxy completion of health and capability measures at the end of life

Cara Bailey, Philip Kinghorn, Rosanna Orlando and Joanna Coast

This chapter focuses on cases where qualitative information can help economists to interpret the quantitative information that they obtain from economic evaluations, where economic outcome measures are used to assess the benefit of a health or care intervention. The chapter concentrates on the methods used to explore four aspects of outcome measure completion, related to the interpretation of one health and two capability measures in the context of end-of-life care. The issues explored within the research were the making of errors in the completion of outcome measures, views about the feasibility and acceptability of economic questionnaires, the reasons for differing proxy responses in questionnaire completion and whether adaptation leads to adaptive preferences at the end of life.

In economic evaluation of end-of-life care, there is little clarity about which outcomes are most appropriate, with different theoretical views around the welfarist or extra welfarist nature of economic evaluation (Brouwer, Culyer et al. 2008; Coast, Smith et al. 2008), leading economists working in end-of-life care in different directions (Normand 2009; Normand 2012; Round 2012; Coast 2014). Theoretical issues are clearly important in determining which measures to use at the end of life, but methodological and practical issues also are important. It is particularly valuable to understand the extent to which it is feasible for participants in research studies to complete these measures. This may be the case whether they are long-established measures, such as the most commonly used health measure in the generation of quality-adjusted life-years (QALYs), the EQ-5D (Brooks and EuroQol Group 1996; The EuroQol Group 1996; Herdman, Gudex et al. 2011; Devlin, Shah et al. 2016), or newer measures focusing on different evaluative spaces, such as the ICECAP-A capability index for adults (Al-Janabi, Flynn et al. 2012; Al-Janabi, Peters et al. 2013; Flynn, Huynh et al. 2015). It is also important for measures that concentrate specifically on economic evaluation at the end of life, such as the ICECAP-Supportive Care Measure (ICECAP-SCM), which is also concerned with measuring capability well-being (Sutton and Coast 2014; Coast, Huynh et al. 2016).

There are also practical issues in measuring outcome at end of life, and particularly at the very end of life. For people at the end of life, it may just not be possible for them to complete measures, or the burden of asking them to do so may be very great (Shelby-James, Hardy et al. 2011). There are often communication challenges with research involving patients who are living with a terminal or progressive disease or those who are very near the end of life. Verbal communication may be impossible due to the disease itself or the stage of dying. Some patients with motor neurone disease or Parkinson's disease, for instance, may be unable to participate in a research project that involves talking aloud their responses. If this is the case, a proxy could be asked to complete the measure on the patient's behalf, although there is some evidence that proxies may find it hard to separate their own views from the views of the person they are acting as proxy for (Cummins 2002). In a comprehensive review of literature comparing proxy and patient views, McPherson and Addington-Hall provided evidence that suggests that proxies can reliably report on the quality of services, and on observable symptoms (McPherson and Addington-Hall 2003), an issue also highlighted by Feeny and colleagues (Feeny, Eckstrom et al. 2013). McPherson and Addington-Hall identified that agreement between patient and proxy response is worst for 'subjective' attributes including pain, anxiety and depression (precisely the sorts of attributes often included in the generic measures used in economic evaluation) and warn that the choice of measures for assessing the quality of palliative care may affect outcomes (McPherson and Addington-Hall 2003). Poor proxy measures may be particularly problematic if that means that the views of those in the worst states, where proxies are often needed, are not accurately represented (Jones and Feeny 2005).

Even where proxies are not needed, there are often concerns about the collection of data from seriously ill individuals given their potential to adapt both to a poor quality of life and, often a concern at end of life, poor care (Coast 2014). This may happen if individuals alter their hopes and desires in a downward direction to accommodate their new state (Qizilbash 2006; Clark 2009). Taking account of adaptation is seen as important within the capability approach, with measurement of capability seen as a way of enabling evaluations to go beyond utility in addressing the evaluation of aspects of life to which the deprived may be unable to aspire (Sen 1982; Sen 1992). Nevertheless, where capabilities are complex and cannot be easily elicited in an objective manner, such as with the capabilities included in the ICECAP-SCM, assessments may have to rely on self-report or the report of others. These reports may be subject to adaptive preferences in which people have adapted to their situation and, without realising it, have adjusted their responses as a result.

All of these issues are ones where qualitative information can help economists to interpret the quantitative information that they obtain from such studies and can assist in guiding the future research design of quantitative studies. The exploration of patient and proxy completion of health and capability measures at the end of life aimed to tackle a number of discrete issues of interest in interpreting outcome measurement for economic evaluation. The first was the extent to which patients and two kinds of proxy – close persons (family members, friends) and health professionals – are able to complete health and capability measures without 'error' at the end of life (Bailey, Kinghorn et al. 2016). The second was to determine the views of these different groups about the feasibility of completing these measures and how acceptable they are for people to complete at this stage in their life course (Bailey, Kinghorn et al. 2016). The third was around the proxy completion of measures, focusing on the extent to which completion by proxies is similar to completion by the patient and on using the qualitative data to generate understanding of the reasons for differences. The fourth concerned whether it was possible to use these data to explore questions of adaptation and adaptive preferences at the end of life (Coast, Bailey et al. 2014). Each of these different aims used different forms of analysis, with the first, third and fourth aims all achieved by using the quantitative data from the questionnaire completion alongside the qualitative data.

This chapter does not attempt to provide findings but rather explores the methods used in this case study in the context of three issues: the collection of qualitative data for cognitive interviews of the 'think-aloud' type which addressed the first aim and which requires data collection of a different form from most of the other chapters in this book; gaining access to informants, and the conduct of interviews, in a sensitive topic area and the challenges that this context poses; and the ways in which analysis of qualitative data was conducted to achieve each of the multiple aims outlined previously.

COLLECTING DATA FOR 'THINK-ALOUD'

Design

There are a number of different options for using qualitative methods to assess questionnaire completion, largely based on theory from cognitive psychology (Tourangeau 1984; Tourangeau, Rips et al. 2000; Collins 2003). Some, such as verbal protocol analysis, involve probing during the interview to understand the ways in which respondents are completing questionnaires (Ericsson and Simon 1980; Ericsson and Simon 1993; Collins 2003); the difficulty with such techniques is that the use of this probing may influence and interfere with the respondents' thought processes (Mallinson 2002). The work was designed as a 'think-aloud' study. Think-aloud is one form of cognitive interviewing technique in which the participant is asked to speak aloud his or her thoughts while completing the outcome measure, without interference from the interviewer (Ericsson and Simon 1980; Ericsson and Simon 1993; Collins 2003; Willis 2005). It has been used previously in assessing both palliative care instruments (Murtagh, Addington-Hall et al. 2007; Ahmed, Bestall et al. 2009) and capability measures (Al-Janabi, Keeley et al. 2013; Horwood, Sutton et al. 2014). The design here included both a 'think-aloud' element, during which time the researcher asked the participant to think-aloud while completing the different questionnaires, and a subsequent semi-structured interview where the thinking of informants was probed with regard to the different questionnaires.

The study focused on three measures. The first was the EQ-5D-5L (Herdman, Gudex et al. 2011; Devlin, Shah et al. 2016), a relatively new version of the EuroQol EQ-5D measure (Brooks and EuroQol Group 1996), which is expected to have greater sensitivity than the original version because of the increased number of levels available in response to each question. This is one of the most commonly used measures for obtaining QALYs and is recommended in the United Kingdom by NICE for use in economic evaluation (National Institute for Health and Care Excellence 2013a). The second was the ICECAP-A, a measure of capability well-being designed for completion by adults in the economic evaluation of health care and interventions (Al-Janabi, Flynn et al. 2012; Flynn, Huynh et al. 2015). The third was the ICECAP-Supportive Care Measure (ICECAP-SCM), a further measure of capability well-being, but in this case designed for adults at the end of life (Sutton and Coast 2014; Coast, Huynh et al. 2016). ICECAP capability measures are recommended for use by NICE in the economic evaluation of social care (National Institute for Health and Care Excellence 2013b), and by ZorgInstituut Nederland in the evaluation of long-term care (ZorgInstituut Nederland 2016).

Sampling

Numbers in published think-aloud studies have been variable in the past and have often been small; for example, in the area of palliative care, Murtagh and colleagues studied ten patients (Murtagh, Addington-Hall et al. 2007), while Ahmed et al. studied just six health and care professionals (Ahmed, Bestall et al. 2009). The two previous think-aloud studies of capability measures have had higher numbers of participants, one with twenty individuals (Horwood, Sutton and Coast 2014) and the other with thirty-four (Al-Janabi, Keeley, Mitchell and Coast 2013). Here, sampling was concerned with generating both sufficient numbers for the think-aloud scoring and enabling saturation to be reached (Strauss and Corbin 1990) in relation to the issues around views of the questionnaires for each of the different groups involved. It was anticipated that up to thirty-five patient, twenty health professional and twenty close person interviews would be required to achieve saturation; because recruitment of health professionals and close persons would take place through patients, these groups would necessarily be smaller and thus the aim was to achieve sufficient numbers in the two proxy groups.

Sampling was conducted through one urban hospice setting in England. Although the aim was to recruit all patients through the hospice, there was also the aim of assessing people at different stages in their end-of-life trajectories (Lunney, Lynn et al. 2002; Lunney, Lynn et al. 2003; Murray, Kendall et al. 2005) and receiving different forms of care provision, and so patients were recruited in different ways, via the community service, the day hospice and the inpatient unit. This meant engaging three, rather than just one, clinical teams with the research. The research team wanted to enable all types of patients to participate and so inclusion criteria were minimal. Essentially, patients just had to be receiving care from the hospice, be willing to take part and be able to communicate in English (because the aim was to evaluate an English-language questionnaire).

Data collection

Interviews took place at the hospice or a place of the informant's choosing (e.g., the patient's or close person's home). The basic format of the interviews is summarized in Box 14.1. At the start of the interviews, informants were reminded about the purpose of the study and the interviewer explained what would happen during the interview. This included telling the informant that he or she would be asked some basic questions about him- or herself, and that there would be seventeen questions to answer using the think-aloud method, which was very briefly explained at this point. Before proceeding, the interviewer then checked again that the informant was happy that the interview was being audio-recorded and gave a reminder that the interview would be reported anonymously and that the informant could withdraw at any time.

Once this preliminary stage was complete, the interviewer collected some basic socio-demographic information and conducted a warm-up exercise to practice the think-aloud technique (Gilhooly and Green 1996). This involved a first task where the informant was asked to think-aloud as they considered how many health professionals they had had contact with that day, and a second task where the informant was asked to think-aloud as they completed a life satisfaction question. The interview then moved on to completion of the three questionnaires included in the study. The order of questionnaires was randomly allocated, except for patients who were very frail, fatigued or unwell, and not expected to complete all three measures (which did happen in a small number of cases). Because the main aim of the funded research was to generate information about ICECAP-SCM, for this patient group, the ICECAP-SCM was completed first.

At the start of the questionnaire completion, the interviewer reminded participants that they needed to speak aloud as they completed the questionnaire. The interviewer would not interrupt them or distract them, but they would prompt them to keep speaking if they were silent for ten seconds or more. They were also asked not to worry about criticising any of the measures as the aim was to find out about any problems with the questionnaires.

After the informant had completed each of the questionnaires, thinking aloud, the interview moved into a short discussion phase, which took the form of a semi-structured interview. This began with the interviewer asking probing questions about any specific areas of the questionnaire that the informant had seemed to find problematic. Issues for the interviewer to be aware of included problems the informant had experienced with the overall questionnaire instructions, wording of questions and response issues such as wanting to tick two boxes. More general discussion probed what the

BOX 14.1. STAGES OF THE THINK-ALOUD INTERVIEW

Stages of the end-of-life think-aloud interviews were:

- Explanation of the think-aloud process
- Reiteration of issues around withdrawal and consent
- Collection of socio-demographic information
- Conduct of warm-up exercises
- Think-aloud questionnaire 1
- Think-aloud questionnaire 2
- Think-aloud questionnaire 3
- Final discussion phase

informant thought about the questions, including whether they found them off-putting or confusing, whether they had understood the instructions, how easy they had found the questions to answer, whether they thought that having answered one questionnaire had altered how they answered another and how well the different questionnaires could give information about health and quality of life. At the end of the interview, participants were thanked for taking part in the research.

GAINING ACCESS AND CONDUCTING INTERVIEWS IN A SENSITIVE AREA

Recruitment

Given the sensitive topic area and the vulnerable nature of those receiving end-of-life care (Florczak 2014), the researchers worked closely with hospice staff to recruit patients and close persons to take part in the research. Potential participants were identified by the hospice research team, and a hospice nurse made the first contact to gauge whether the person had an initial interest in participating. This minimized the level of intrusion for those who did not want to take part. It was only if they expressed an interest in participating that a full explanation of the study was then given by the researcher.

Recruiting research participants through health professionals in a sensitive area such as end of life is inevitably challenging, and obtaining access to research participants can be difficult. Many health professionals may be concerned about emotional distress in patients or even the potential for symptoms to be exacerbated (Campbell, Bailey et al. 2016), and this may be perceived as unethical or contrary to the philosophy behind supportive care (Hanratty, Lowson et al. 2012; Payne, Preston et al. 2013). Nevertheless, there is evidence that taking part in research at end of life is a positive experience for most people (Gysels, Evans et al. 2012). Here, there were most difficulties, perhaps expectedly so, in recruiting from the inpatient unit where patients are most unwell and staff are likely to feel most protective of their patients. The research team used strategies to try to enable greater access to be obtained where recruitment was proving difficult for this reason. One strategy was to make the researcher more accessible, by spending whole days visibly based in the hospice and thus becoming more obvious to staff, as well as patients and families. A second strategy was to share anonymized comments from previous participants through a number of sources including informal feedback and more formally, through the use of posters and formal feedback sessions.

Consent and the use of a personal consultee

There were four issues faced by the research team around gaining consent because of the sensitive and challenging nature of the research area. First, there were potential difficulties in gaining consent from informants who had particular physical disabilities that prevented them from signing consent forms. This issue was discussed with the ethics group for the programme of work (see discussion) and it was decided that verbal consent could be obtained, ideally with audio-recording. Second, because of the sensitive nature of the research, it was not deemed appropriate to contact close persons of the patient or their health professionals without prior consent from the patient. This was therefore the process followed. Third, there were some patients who were willing to consent to the participation of others on their behalf but did not wish to participate themselves, and such patients were included. Finally, there may be cognitive symptoms that mean a person is unable to provide consent to take part in research and in this case it may be possible to have someone else consent to participation on their behalf. In the United Kingdom this role is known as the 'personal consultee' and in this research, the facility was provided for a personal consultee to consent, on behalf of the patient, to completion of the questionnaire by a nominated close person and/or health professional.

Designing data collection with sensitivity to the context

Both the planning of interviews and their conduct required sensitivity to the end-of-life context. In planning the interviews, and how they would proceed, it was important to be aware of questions that might not be appropriate to the context. A good example of this relates to the warm-up exercise used in the think-aloud element of the study. Often a 'window-counting' question is asked as a warm-up exercise for think-aloud exercises, but this was avoided here because some patients recruited from the inpatient unit might not have expected to see their home again, and it was anticipated that such a question could potentially cause distress unnecessarily. An alternative focusing on contacts with health professionals was used instead.

It was important that interviewers had sufficient training and experience to be able to conduct the interviews with sensitivity. Interviewers all had a combination of skills and expertise that included extensive experience as a health professional and/or training in the conduct of sensitive interviews and/or extensive existing experience in conducting research interviews in sensitive areas. Interviews were conducted with sensitivity. Interviewers found, for example, that gaining rapport with informants who had impairments that 'slowed down' their speed of communication could be achieved by the 'mirroring' of this slow response so that the informant did not feel rushed or uncomfortable. Interviewers also constantly assessed the interview context during the interview, paying particular attention to whether the informant was distressed or fatigued and thus whether the interview needed to be halted either temporarily or permanently. Interviews were generally conducted within the hospice setting, and the research nurse and other hospice staff were on hand if the patient became distressed and at the end of the interview.

Sensitivity to the context also involved being aware that some participants would have rapidly deteriorating (Fischer, Burgener et al. 2012) or highly variable conditions, meaning that data collection had to be designed with flexibility to enable researchers to respond rapidly if necessary, or to wait until a potential informant felt sufficiently well to participate.

Welfare of the research team

The sensitivity of the context can impact on researchers as well as participants. This may lead to emotional strain for staff as a result of constantly dealing with challenging and emotional experiences; such strain may not be limited to 'frontline' research staff but may also be experienced, for example, by those undertaking activities such as transcribing (Kavanaugh and Campbell 2014). The emotional well-being of the researcher was important here and, especially at the start of the project, there was a rigorous use of debriefing sessions for the interviewer with an experienced colleague after each interview. Over time, the debriefing sessions became less frequent and were used in a more ad hoc manner as particular issues emerged. More informal opportunities were also generated for staff involved in transcribing to talk about their experiences of working on the transcripts.

For interviews conducted outside the hospice setting, the physical well-being of the researcher was also an issue, and a lone researcher protocol was used to ensure the physical safety of a team member who was doing fieldwork outside the hospice or university setting. This meant the researcher leaving details of locations of interviews in a sealed envelope with a named contact who would be contacted immediately on completion of the interview. If the researcher did not communicate with the contact within a defined period of time, there were a series of escalating steps defined, culminating with alerting the police if the researcher did not communicate with the contact.

Ethical oversight of the work

The overall programme of research was funded through the European Research Council, and a condition of funding was that an ethics group would be set up to advise on the research. This comprised three senior academics, with expertise in research ethics, ethics of end-of-life care and clinical experience of end-of-life care. The group were able to advise on difficult issues including appropriate use of personal consultees and recording verbal consent for those unable to write because of their condition. Ethics approval was gained from North Wales NHS Research Ethics Committee – West (ref: 12/WA/0076).

ANALYSING QUALITATIVE DATA FOR MULTIPLE PURPOSES

One of the key issues in analysing the data from this research was the different foci for the separate analyses, and the diverse ways in which that analysis was conducted for each different purpose. This is described next in relation to each of these aims, to show how altering the focus of analysis can achieve various ends.

Analysing 'think-aloud' data to assess errors

The process for analysing think-aloud data is relatively structured compared to much qualitative data analysis, and involves detailed examination of the relevant segment of the transcript in light of the response, for each informant for each questionnaire item. Processing the data for analysis involved segmenting each transcript by questionnaire and item and linking it to information about the questionnaire response given by the informant. Each transcript (except where the informant had missing data) thus resulted in seventeen segments, one relating to each questionnaire item on ICECAP-SCM ($n = 7$), ICECAP-A ($n = 5$) and EQ-5D-5L ($n = 5$). Raters were then given each transcript segment and questionnaire response and asked to classify it according to the presence or absence of error (Bailey, Kinghorn et al. 2016). This study used five raters, each of whom undertook this task independently (Bailey, Kinghorn et al. 2016), but other studies in health economics have used three (Horwood, Sutton et al. 2014) or four raters (Al-Janabi, Keeley et al. 2013). The classification of errors was based on a cognitive psychology model suggesting that respondents have to conduct four actions to respond to a question (Tourangeau 1984; Tourangeau, Rips et al. 2000; Willis 2005). These four actions relate to:

- comprehension (i.e., understanding the question in the way that the researcher intended, with errors relating to misunderstanding or explicitly not understanding words or phrases);

- retrieval (being able to retrieve the required information from long-term memory, with errors relating to inability to recall this information or errors in the time frame used);
- judgement (being able to assess how the information that has been recalled should be used in responding to the questionnaire item, with errors relating to use of inappropriate information to come to a decision, including responses that do not match the original researchers' interpretation of the meaning of the question) and
- response (providing a valid response to the questionnaire, with errors relating to the choice of a response category that is not consistent with what has been said, or there not being an appropriate response category available) (Tourangeau, Rips et al. 2000).

This schema was slightly adapted as per earlier work in the capability field in which 'struggles', in which respondents found it difficult to respond to the questionnaire but ultimately made an error-free response, were separately classified (Al-Janabi, Keeley et al. 2013).

The ratings from each of the five independent reviewers were brought together and a decision was made as to whether an error had been made by using a set of rules which involved automatic classification of any errors identified by at least three raters, discussion of errors identified by two or three raters, or where there was disagreement about the type of error, and classification of 'no error' where no error had been identified by more than one person (Bailey, Kinghorn et al. 2016). Where errors were identified, the relevant transcripts were then considered in greater depth to determine where issues with the questionnaires might be leading to errors.

Data from this analysis were presented as percentage error rates for each questionnaire and a more detailed analysis was provided of the error type by respondent type and item for the ICECAP-SCM (Bailey, Kinghorn et al. 2016).

Analysing interview data to assess views and perceptions of the questionnaires

Analysis used constant comparative methods (Strauss and Corbin 1990). Analysis was initiated by reading and re-reading the transcripts, and as themes emerged these were developed into categories and sub-categories. Data were organized and managed using NVivo 10, and associations, relationships and models were developed from the original nodes. For the second part of the analysis, these focused on issues around perceptions of the questionnaires and their appropriateness in the hospice setting, as well as providing insights into issues around how the measures are completed and why completion might result in errors. Themes arising from this analysis were analysed and compared both across questionnaires and according to the persons completing the questionnaire, leading to insights related to both these factors. For example, time frame was identified as a particular issue affecting EQ-5D-5L, while difficulty in completing more 'subjective' items was identified as a particular issue facing health professional participants (Bailey, Kinghorn et al. 2016). Themes were ultimately presented by respondent type using quotes to illustrate the findings of the analysis (Bailey, Kinghorn et al. 2016).

Analysing data to assess proxy completion

While the initial qualitative analysis outlined previously compared themes arising across and within groups, it did not go as far as comparing the qualitative and questionnaire responses to individual questionnaire items between those completing the questionnaire on behalf of the same respondent. That was the focus of the third aspect of the analysis, which focused on exploring why those completing the questionnaire on behalf of a particular patient did not necessarily respond in the same way.

Some statistical analysis was conducted on the proxy responses, concentrating on both crude agreement and chance-corrected agreement. This enabled the identification of contrasting questionnaire items for which agreement was, overall, generally higher or lower, and thus those which were of particular interest for analysis of the qualitative data. The health and capability responses from each participant were then entered into an Excel spreadsheet and explored in sets of triads and dyads according to the data available. Triads included the patient and both a close person and a health professional proxy, while dyads included the patient and one other proxy, either a close person or a health care professional. Graphical illustrations were generated to compare the proxy and patient responses to particular questionnaire items within dyads and triads, enabling the identification of particular triads and dyads where there was agreement or disagreement. Detailed scrutiny and comparison were then applied to the relevant parts of the transcripts to generate theoretical understanding around why proxy completion appears to be strong for some aspects of measures used in economic evaluation and much weaker for others, and to explore the characteristics of those individuals who might make stronger proxies. Presentation of findings includes both graphical illustrations of triad and dyad scores, and illustrative quotes.

Analysing data to explore adaptation

For the purpose of the analysis around adaptation and adaptive preferences the interviews as a whole (i.e., comprising both the think-aloud element and the subsequent semi-structured interviews) were analysed using the methods of constant comparison (Glaser and Strauss 1968; Strauss and Corbin 1990). The primary analysis focused on patients' own assessments but was supplemented by analysis of the data from close persons and health professionals. Initial coding was undertaken following a process of generating familiarity with the transcripts, and a coding framework which identified salient themes was agreed. This analysis focused specifically on issues around adaptation and adaptive preferences. Independent analysis of the adaptation theme was conducted by two researchers using slightly different methods, with one using NVivo 10 to develop associations, relationships and models from the original nodes to generate a theoretical model of adaptation and the second using analytic accounts generated using Microsoft Word that drew on the coded adaptation data but also utilized information about the scores and specific verbal responses to particular questionnaire items where either adaptation or adaptive preferences seemed to be indicated. Both analysts agreed the final interpretation. Findings from this aspect of the analysis presented quotes illustrating the various themes related to the model of adaptation generated and tables showing illustrative quotes, alongside relevant patient responses to the three questionnaires, and relevant close person and health professional responses to the three questionnaires.

CONCLUSION

This chapter has focused on a case study that has used qualitative methods to generate greater understanding of quantitative findings in the area of measurement of health and capability for economic evaluation of interventions at the end of life. The case study has focused on three aspects of methods that might be helpful to health economist readers. The first is the collection and analysis of data for use in 'think-aloud', a technique that has not so far been covered in depth within the book. The second is the use of qualitative methods in a sensitive area; it thus complements the chapters from Canaway and colleagues (Chapter 12), and Kinghorn and colleagues (Chapter 16) which are both also focused on issues around end-of-life care, and the issues contrast somewhat with the chapters by Stevens, which focus on data collection at the other end of the life course (Chapter 11), and Vosper et al., where sensitivity arises through depression (Chapter 10). The third aspect of methods on which the chapter has concentrated is the different forms of analysis that were employed for different aspects of the research. The purpose of including this final section was to illustrate the different ways in which qualitative data can be analysed, and qualitative and quantitative data can be used together to generate innovative findings. Reflecting on the work, one aspect of particular value in the research was the different perspectives brought to the analysis by team members with different disciplinary backgrounds, and experiences of different research topics and analytic approaches, all of which contributed to the final interpretations of the data and credibility of the research.

ACKNOWLEDGEMENTS

The study described in this chapter was funded by the European Research Council (261098 EconEndLife).

Chapter 15

Getting beyond the numbers: Using qualitative methods to explore the validity of health state valuation techniques

Suzanne Robinson

There are a number of economic techniques that can be used to elicit individual's health state preferences, with different techniques often yielding different results (Brazier, Deverill et al. 1999). There has been very little research around the cognitive process that respondents undertake to reach their valuations (Brazier, Deverill et al. 1999; Robinson and Bryan 2013). In the case study reported in this chapter, qualitative methods were used to provide a greater understanding of the processes individuals use, and the experiences they face, when participating in health state valuation exercises (Robinson 2007; Robinson and Bryan 2013). Semi-structured interviews were undertaken with respondents who had participated in an earlier health state valuation exercise which involved valuing health states using the visual analogue scale, time trade-off and person trade-off (PTO) techniques (Robinson 2007; Robinson and Bryan 2013). The interviews explored a number of areas that are relevant to assessing the validity of the instrument and process of elicitation. See Box 15.1 for further details of the study.

This chapter focuses on the methods undertaken in the research with some brief reference to the findings. The interest is around the study design, methods and methodological challenges, and some hints and tips are provided for those who may employ similar techniques in their own work. Finally, some consideration is given to the publication challenges associated with health economics research that utilizes qualitative methodologies.

BOX 15.1. DETAILS OF THE MAIN VALUATION STUDY

Study Title: Valuing health states for use in economic evaluation: an investigation of validity and reliability

Study Aims: To explore the validity and reliability of health state valuation techniques used in economic evaluation.
Health state valuation techniques of interest: Person trade-off and time trade-off techniques
Methodological approaches used: This was a mixed methods study that used quantitative methods to focus on aspects relating to convergent validity, reliability and qualitative methods to focus on the aspects relating to content and face validity. The preference elicitation exercise which is reported in this study forms part of the English contribution to the European Disability Weights Project. Details of the methods used during the preference elicitation exercise are outlined here, and further details of the European Disability Weights Project can be found elsewhere (Essink-Bot, Pereira et al. 2002). The subsequent qualitative analysis was an additional investigation undertaken by the authors and did not form part of the European Disability Weights Project.

The qualitative component was interested in the following elements:

- Content validity, i.e., the extent to which the technique measures what it is designed to measure – in the case of techniques used in economic analysis it is individuals' underlying preferences for different health states. Thus, the interest was in the cognitive aspects relating to what respondents are thinking and doing when participating in preference elicitation exercises, paying particular reference to aspects of utility rationalisation and rational action.
- Issues relating to the framing and process of elicitation.
- An interest in relation to process was that of the impact of discussion and deliberation on health state valuation responses, i.e., does discussion and deliberation in a group setting impact on the individual and aggregate health state valuations?

Further results are available elsewhere (Robinson 2007; Robinson and Bryan 2013).

METHODOLOGICAL APPROACH AND DESIGN

Working out the research design is an important part of any research project, and using qualitative methods is no different than using quantitative methods in that respect. Thus, the methods employed should result from a decision around the research design and methodological approach, rather than an appeal to a certain method (Silverman 2005). For example, just because a researcher may feel more comfortable using certain methods, such as interviews, does not mean this is the right approach. For the case study research reported in this chapter it was felt that the appropriate methodological approach to answering the research question was qualitative. The rationale related to the nature of the questions of interest which were around the cognitive approaches individuals use to reach their valuations, the meaning respondents place on their valuations and the impact of discussion and deliberation on preference elicitation. It was felt that all of these aspects would be best explored using qualitative methods which allow respondents and researchers to explore and understand the meanings respondents place on their valuations and the process of elicitation. The research interest was in the why and how of decision making.

Other factors also influenced the design of the study. The qualitative component was restricted by the broader study protocol. This methodological work was an additional study that ran in parallel to an internationally funded project that aimed to elicit preferences and burden of disease estimates across a number of European countries (Essink-Bot, Pereira et al. 2002). Given the difficulty in gaining research funding to support methodological research, it is not unusual for researchers to include ('add on') methodological components to a study that is funding applied research. Here, for example, the purpose of the main study was to elicit preferences for a number of predefined health states in countries across Europe. The additional qualitative research discussed here aimed to explore the validity of the elicitation approaches used. Working alongside the main study placed a number of restrictions on the qualitative component which included the choice of qualitative method and the timing of the interviews.

The choice of qualitative method used to capture respondents' experiences and perceptions was to some extent driven by the requirements of the main European study, which followed a strict protocol used in all participating countries. Health state valuation exercises used group sessions to elicit preferences, meaning that the use of techniques such as 'think-aloud' (see Chapter 14 for more detail of this approach) was not appropriate for practical reasons. Furthermore, the group sessions took around five hours and it was felt that any additional qualitative components during or at the end of the session could either impact on the health state values obtained or be too burdensome for participants.

METHODS

Ahead of the study, ethics advice and approval were sought following the relevant university ethical processes. This was a low-risk study that posed no ethical challenges or issues either prior or during the research.

Sample and respondents

A purposive sampling technique was used to contact those who had taken part in one of the panel sessions conducted in England. Letters were sent to all individuals who had taken part in the panel sessions, inviting them to participate in a semi-structured interview. Non-responders were then contacted by telephone. All interviews were conducted by the same interviewer (SR) and electronically recorded after assurances of confidentiality were provided. Transcription of tapes was undertaken independently by an individual who had no involvement with the European Disability Weights Project or the qualitative research study. A total of twenty participants were interviewed, which was 40 percent of respondents who were asked to participate in the study. This was a good response rate, and the interviewer felt that saturation was reached during the interviews. Saturation is reached when there is 'enough information to replicate the study, when the ability to obtain additional new information has been attained, and when further coding is no longer feasible' (Fusch and Ness 2015, p. 1408). Here, saturation was reached when no further themes emerged from participants and the data was thick in quantity and rich in depth providing multilayered nuanced and detailed data (see Fusch and Ness for further discussion). Of course, there is no 'magic number' at which saturation is achieved, because the complexity of research questions, the nature of study populations and the designs of research all vary. However, failure to reach saturation can have a negative impact on the validity of a study (Fusch and Ness 2015). Here, the aim was to generate an appropriate study design that would enable saturation in relation to the research question to be efficiently achieved, without necessarily requiring large numbers of participants.

While the research team felt that saturation was reached among the population interviewed in this study, there were also some concerns about the potential for sample bias; one of the groups included in the main European study was general practitioners (GPs) (10 percent of the sample), but in practice it was not possible to recruit GPs to this additional aspect of the research. These busy clinicians, who had already taken part in a five-hour panel session, were reluctant or could not afford to give up extra time to be interviewed; indeed, the difficulty of engaging GPs in research is internationally recognized (Hummers-Pradier, Scheidt-Nave et al. 2008; McKinn, Bonner et al. 2015).

Data collection

The method of choice for the research was semi-structured interviews. Semi-structured interviews were chosen because they are a well-established method and are most commonly used for collecting qualitative data (Byrne 2001; DiCicco-Bloom and Crabtree 2006; King and Horrocks 2010). The method is flexible and provides the capacity to generate an in-depth understanding of the research questions. Through semi-structured interviews, researchers can gather detailed rich information on participants' experiences, views and feelings (Buston, Parry-Jones et al. 1998). Furthermore, they can allow respondents the opportunity to really explain and explore their thoughts and perspectives on a range of aspects, sharing their stories and experiences. These aspects were all important in determining the cognitive processes used by individuals and the meanings they place on their valuations. The advantage of semi-structured interviews over unstructured, in-depth interviews was that they allowed for a balance between free-flowing and directed conversation, thus allowing the research questions to be more fully addressed during the time available for the interview.

The study followed the usual practice of using an interview schedule. This was developed in conjunction with the broader research team and piloted with participants who had been involved in an earlier pilot study for the main research. The interview schedule covered themes which had emerged from the literature and discussions that had been observed during the valuation group sessions that took place prior to the conduct of the qualitative research. The interview schedule was used to ensure that all of the themes were covered with each participant; the ordering of questions was changed to follow the natural 'flow' of discussion required for rapport. The interview schedules were helpful for the interviewer in this research, in focusing on relevant topics and checking that all areas of interest had been covered during the interviews. Although in some instances the schedules are sent to the participant in advance of the interview to allow him or her time to reflect and consider responses, this approach was not used here. A number of factors were taken into account in developing the schedule: keeping the information succinct and easy for the interviewer to view; trying not to cover too much given the length of the interview; being clear on the questions/themes of interest and providing prompts to help in exploring areas. This latter aspect was found to be especially useful when respondents provided limited or superficial responses.

The main question in this study was concerned with the process of eliciting valuations and, specifically, how respondents made their choices. The interviews explored four overarching themes that had already been noted in the literature: stimuli presented; context and framing issues; discussion and deliberation, and use of values in decision making (Brazier, Deverill et al. 1999; Robinson 2007). The interview schedule is briefly outlined in Box 15.2. Various stimuli were used to aid the interview process. These included props from the earlier panel sessions and closed questions around the difficulty associated with each technique. The closed-ended questions produced quantitative data that were explored in the interviews. For example, if a respondent said he or she found a technique difficult, the interviewer then went on to explore this further with the participant. Interviewer observations and discussions with respondents at the end of the interview suggested that the props did help interviewees to focus and reflect on the group exercise. Interviewees suggested that the props helped them to visualize the session and remember activities, with comments such as 'It transported me right back to the day, I could visualise what we did and the people in the room'. At the same time, the interviewer also felt that the props helped to build rapport and to focus the research around the questions of interest.

The interview process

There were a number of aspects of the interview process that were particularly important in this study (Silverman 2005; Green and Thorogood 2014). There were issues around the timing of interviews. It was decided that all data should be collected within two weeks of the respondent's participation in the health state valuation exercise, which brought both advantages and disadvantages. There was a practical advantage in that it was not felt feasible to ask participants to undertake interviews immediately following a five-hour preference elicitation exercise. Moreover, the time between participation in the health state valuation exercise and the interview is advantageous insofar as it allows time to reflect on the exercises undertaken. This may enable individuals to shift their cognitive framework from that of engagement in the health state valuation exercise and how to undertake the tasks, to a more reflective and thoughtful consideration as to the 'how' and 'why' of decision making. A limitation, however, is that respondents may struggle to fully recall the exercise and its aftermath; this could impact on their perspective and the interest is in collecting their thoughts and feelings while they are undertaking the exercise. As noted previously, other methods

BOX 15.2. OUTLINE OF THE INTERVIEW SCHEDULE

The interview began with open questions, followed by more focused closed-ended questions.

Stage 1: The interviewer explained the interview process and stressed that the interview was separate from the European Disability Weights Project.

Stage 2: VAS method was reviewed using props from the panel session. These included the stimuli presented for valuation, the VAS instructions and thermometer. Respondents were then asked to explain the process they used to reach their VAS scores. Questions explored included:

- aspects of the stimuli (disease card) focused on by respondents;
- how respondents used the numbers on the VAS;
- could respondents disregard future prognosis, economic aspects and effects on carers, when they valued health states?

Stage 3: PTO method was reviewed using props from the session. Respondents were then asked to review the PTO method and explain the process they used to reach their valuations. Questions explored included:

- aspects of the stimuli focused on by respondent;
- framing of the question and the use of quadriplegia as an anchor state;
- hypothetical scenarios and assumptions used, how did respondents respond to the societal perspective?

Stage 4: Time trade-off method was reviewed using props from the session. Respondents were then asked to review the time trade-off method and explain the process they used to reach their valuations. Questions explored included:

- framing of the question and its effect on the valuation;
- context and perspective of question;
- could respondents disregard future prognosis etc.?
- did respondents trade and why?

Stage 5: Closed-ended questions were used to ask respondents the level of difficulty they associated with each technique; the answers ranged from 'easy' to 'extremely difficult'. Respondents were also asked to explain their answers.

Stage 6: This stage of the interview explored the effects of group discussion and the process of deliberation. Respondents were asked to discuss their feelings on the panel process. The interviewer also tried to explore whether the group session had any influence on the valuation given.

such as 'think-aloud' or interviews immediately following panel sessions may capture maximum participation as well as the exercises being fresh in participants' minds.

There were also issues around the need for interview training. Those not familiar with qualitative research could be forgiven for thinking that the process of interviewing is fairly easy – after all it is basically a conversation, something we tend to do most days. However, interviewing is much more than that and researchers wanting to conduct qualitative research, even in a study that is predominantly quantitative, do need to understand qualitative methodologies and what they offer to the research setting, alongside a good understanding of the methods they will be utilising. The researcher involved in this study undertook research training in qualitative research methods and had advice from experts in the field which proved invaluable to the success of the study. For example, undertaking practice interviews as part of the training allowed the researcher to understand the role of the interviewer and to provide her with techniques to support the interviewee and to facilitate the generation of information.

A further aspect of importance was the role of the interviewer in the research. An interview is more than a conversation. It involves suspending judgement and being inquisitive, actively listening and helping the interviewee to make connections. Here, the interviewer began by trying to build rapport, by putting the interviewee at ease. During the interview, the interviewer aimed to probe effectively, by summarising what had been said every so often and by asking the interviewee to elaborate and provide examples. The interviewer also tried to avoid any concern with silence during the interview as silence can, for some, be important to their thinking process, allowing them time to think and develop their thoughts. The trick for researchers is to allow for silence and not feel the need to fill gaps which can distract a respondent's thinking process. Allowing silence can empower respondents to develop the direction of the conversation and shows the interviewer (researcher) what their perspective and viewpoint is on the subject in question (Mackie 2016).

Finally, and occasionally difficult, the interviewer tried to avoid interjecting too much into the interview. This was especially difficult when the researcher was excited by the discussions or keen to explore a topic! But it was to be avoided as otherwise the result is a reflection of the interviewee in the data. The interviewer tried to work to a rule of thumb that at least 80 percent of the words spoken during the interview should come from the interviewee (Bernard 1995).

A final aspect of importance was around recording and reflecting on each interview. First, it was important to take a voice recording of the interviews, rather than taking notes, so that the interviewer was able to give the interviewee their full attention. This also resulted in much stronger data, with transcripts from the recordings fully capturing all of the interview conversation. Second, following each interview the interviewer took time to write his or her reflections on the interview, including the main themes that had emerged, a reflection on the process and any additional information they would like to explore in future interviews. This was extremely helpful, both in directing the future course of the research and later when analysing the data.

Data analysis

Data analysis consisted of a modified analytic induction, in which thematic categories identified in the previous literature were used as sensitising devices in developing the analysis (Silverman 2005). These draft codes were modified and extended through iterations to ensure that all of the available data could be accounted for. The analysis built on available prior themes, yet it was free to extend beyond them to accommodate new additional aspects. The data then changed the codes as these codes became more data-driven, both as gaps in the existing theory became apparent and as new and emergent themes and categories were generated to accommodate the data. The approach used drew on the work of Miles and Huberman (1994). It enabled a systematic refining of the data and the development of inductive categories in an ongoing iterative process of interpretation, essentially of dialogue between prior categories and new data. Particular attention was paid to 'negative cases' that did not fit the emergent frameworks. Generating interpretations that could accommodate these negative cases moved the analysis forward, providing a more measured, credible analysis and increasing its internal validity.

Data coding followed the convention of Miles and Huberman in which around a third of the available data were taken and common ideas and emergent themes, based on both prior work and from within the data, were written on separate sheets of paper as a provisional coding scheme (Miles and Huberman 1994). This process was continued for the next third of the data and categories were further refined and developed. Following modifications, the final third of data were analysed and the coding frame was further refined. Once finalized, the coding frame was applied to all of the data, and all data relating to each of the codes were brought together for further analysis, in which patterns and paradoxes were explored. This final stage was conducted using a data-handling software package, NVivo.

An important stage in the analysis and coding was to explore and discuss the findings with the wider research team. The resultant discussions allowed for further exploration of emerging findings and enabled the team to challenge potential assumptions and subjectivity related to an individual researcher's views and standpoints.

Data reporting

The analysis reported from the study used exemplar quotations from interviews to illustrate findings as well as some summarising and interpretation. The reporting also combined findings from the study with assumptions and evidence from the literature. Some studies present qualitative results and then have a separate 'discussion' section or chapter to combine the new findings with those from the literature. In this case the researchers felt that the combining of the qualitative results with existing knowledge allowed more in-depth detailed analysis and allowed for richer interpretation. It also reduces repetition and had the advantage of reducing the word count which was advantageous when writing for publication! As the main purpose was to generate and describe themes, no descriptive quantitative analysis was given. However, where appropriate, some simple quantification of findings was presented relating to information collected from the closed-ended questions used in the study, such as responses to the level of difficulty associated with the techniques.

Reflections and methodological challenges

Many of the methodological challenges faced by this research related to the restrictions placed on the research by the broader study. These included restrictions on design. Specifically, the qualitative research team believes there was a missed opportunity to use non-participant observation during the sessions. Such observation as was conducted was concerned with only deviations from the protocol. Future studies could benefit from using observational methods to capture and code behaviours and activity taking place during the group exercises; this could then be triangulated with information collected from interviews to provide a more robust analysis.

Further limitations to the design included the restrictions on the timing of interviews, choices in relation to the type of stimuli presented, the health state valuations used and the nature of the informants as 'informed respondents' (through having already completed the elicitation exercise). However, the strengths of being part of a large study included working with many experts from across the field of health state valuation who provided important insights that fed into the design of the study and the interpretation of its findings, as well as access to funding (Robinson 2007).

In retrospect and on reflection, the research team also felt that it would have been advantageous to provide respondents with some of the themes that would be discussed in the interview so that they had more opportunity to reflect on these issues.

CASE STUDY RESULTS AND THEIR DISSEMINATION

While the chapter has highlighted a number of methodological considerations, the results from the study were encouraging and provided rich insightful data which related well to the questions of interest. In summary the qualitative results challenged some of the underlying theories around the idea that individuals have well-constructed preferences that they can draw upon even when making the most complex decision. The qualitative data suggested that individuals use simplifying heuristics when undertaking health state valuation exercises. The research also highlighted the need to look at the influence of the administrative process on the preferences elicited. For example, if respondents do not have well-constructed preferences, then the process may need to give them time to reflect and 'try on' a value to see how it 'fits'. Giving respondents the opportunity to deliberate and reflect on their valuations may be an important part of any complex decision process. The research concluded that using qualitative methods to explore the effect of incorporating time for reflective thought is important both for future health economics studies and in relation to other decision settings in health care and beyond.

Despite the importance of the findings generated through the research, dissemination of these findings also proved to be challenging. Peer-reviewed journals in health economics may find it difficult to access reviewers with qualitative or mixed methods expertise. The experience here was that reviewers often had a quantitative background, often with a negative perception and lack of understanding about the nature of qualitative research and a focus on issues generally associated with quantitative research such as validity, objectivity and representative sampling. It remains a challenge to raise the profile of qualitative research and achieve its dissemination to the wider academic community of health economists and those involved in health care decision making.

CONCLUSION

The case study reported in this study demonstrated the importance of qualitative methodologies in progressing our understanding of the validity of health state valuation techniques. The study produced rich data that allowed for sense making around the valuation (quantitative) data collected in the group sessions, allowing for the exploration of the 'how' and 'why' in relation to the earlier preference elicitation exercises. The study raises a number of issues that have implications for decision makers in the field of health economics and for other stakeholders involved in resource allocation decisions throughout health care systems. This information generated could not have been gained from just focusing on quantitative analysis. Thus the qualitative approaches undertaken in this study provided complementary analysis that informed our understanding in the complex field of preference elicitation.

ACKNOWLEDGEMENTS

The preference elicitation exercise that formed the early part of this study was supported by a grant from the BIOMED II Programme of the European Union (project number BMH4-98-3253). The author would also like to acknowledge the European Disability Weights Project team members for their support and guidance.

Chapter 16

Use of deliberative methods to facilitate and enhance understanding of the weighting of survey attributes

Philip Kinghorn, Alastair Canaway, Cara Bailey and Joanna Coast

The ICECAP-Close Person Measure (ICECAP-CPM) is a new measure designed to capture broad outcomes from end-of-life care as they are experienced by 'close persons' (family and friends) (Canaway, Al-Janabi et al. 2017). It is an instrument that seeks to assess well-being in terms of capability, the ability of a person to live a life that he or she has reason to value. There has been an increasing interest within the health economics discipline in operationalising Amartya Sen's capability approach (Sen 2010), and much of the progress so far has been in relation to the development, validation and valuation of capability-based instruments (Coast, Kinghorn et al. 2015; Kinghorn 2015). However, Sen's capability approach is often regarded as being underspecified (Nussbaum 2003), and researchers are left to make key decisions based upon principles from Sen's writings.

Sen advocates tackling some of the more practical steps in operationalising the capability approach (e.g., establishing the value of particular capabilities) via reasoned consensus, involving public discussion and democracy (Sen 1999), and it is this vague guidance which has led to recent interest in public deliberation among capability researchers (Burchardt 2014) and health economists working within the capability approach. Indeed, it was Sen's suggestion to address the practical steps involved with operationalising the capability approach via public discussion and democracy that inspired our use of public deliberation in the study which forms the case study for this chapter.

Although deliberative methods can be both expensive and time-consuming (although still involving small samples), there is evidence that the public are willing to take part in decisions, readily adopt a community perspective and are able to address complex policy questions (Coote and Lenaghan 1997).

Much of this evidence stems from a time of enthusiastic experimentation with deliberative methods by the UK National Health Service in the 1990s which coincided with a requirement from the Department of Health for a greater public role in health care priority setting (Abelson, Forest et al. 2003).

The research reported in this chapter commenced in 2014, using a series of focus groups involving participants from the general population. The focus groups formed one task from a wider four-year European Research Council (ERC)-funded project, EconEndLife, investigating the economic evaluation of care at the end of life. The objective of the focus groups was twofold: to elicit deliberative values for the ICECAP-CPM, and to explore views relating to priority setting and resource allocation in the context of supportive end-of-life care. The former of these two objectives, the valuation of attributes from the ICECAP-CPM, forms the focus of this chapter.

AN OVERVIEW OF PUBLIC DELIBERATION

In seeking to use public deliberation, we are following in the footsteps of both colleagues working in health services research and those in environmental economics. In environmental economics, as in health economics, contingent valuation has been needed to quantify, in monetary terms, goods and services not traded freely, because of the existence of market failure (or government responses to market failure). Contingent valuation 'presupposes a connection between preference satisfaction and *individual* welfare' (Sagoff 1998, p. 214 [emphasis added]). But treating individuals as citizens in the context of public goods is problematic (Soderholm 2001), for the reason that in this context they may not prioritize maximising individual well-being or have well-articulated exogenous preferences.

Traditional contingent valuation methods 'seriously constrain' the articulation of public or citizen preferences (Jacobs 1997, p. 216), which incorporate an ethical concern. Environmental economists have therefore adopted deliberative valuation (or 'public valuation') as an alternative mechanism which allows individuals to formulate and express carefully weighted public (or citizen) preferences.

Monetary values were not elicited in the case study that we outline here, but the values are considered as having been expressed from the citizen perspective.

What is deliberation?

Just as it can be challenging to define qualitative approaches (Snape and Spencer 2003), it can be challenging to define public deliberation (Burkhalter,

Gastil et al. 2002). We will adopt here the same definition of public deliberation suggested by Burkhalter et al.: that deliberation takes place face to face within small groups, at a specific time and place (Burkhalter, Gastil et al. 2002). Our focus is therefore on 'deliberation in its external collective aspect' (Goodin 2000, p. 81), as opposed to internal/individual deliberation. A 'small group' here is assumed to involve a minimum of three participants (Burkhalter, Gastil et al. 2002), and deliberation is the careful weighting of alternative options and views. The core principles of deliberative approaches are that participants be informed and representative and that there be free, open and reflective debate (Abelson, Blacksher et al. 2013).

How does it work?

'Deliberation' is best thought of as an umbrella term, incorporating a range of possible approaches.

Focus groups

Listed by some as an option for 'citizen involvement' rather than explicitly as a deliberative approach (Coote and Lenaghan 1997), focus groups have nonetheless been used by health economists (Dolan, Cookson et al. 1999) in the context of health care priority setting, as well as by environmental economists for deliberative valuation (Soderholm 2001). Coote and Lenaghan rather dismissively say of focus groups, 'While some information is provided, this is strictly limited and the purpose is to probe uninformed opinion in more depth than can be achieved in opinion polls' (Coote and Lenaghan 1997, p. 7). The limitation of focus groups in terms of there being a limited amount of time for information to be presented, for participants to form relationships and for in-depth discussion, should therefore be acknowledged.

Citizens' workshops

A citizens' workshop will tend to bring twelve to twenty participants together for one day and be structured in a similar way to a focus group (Timotijevic and Raats 2007). The advantage is that there is time for participants to develop stronger relationships and, of course, for that all important reflection and discussion (Timotijevic and Raats 2007).

Community deliberation

Community deliberation is a technique used by Carman et al. in which participants were brought together for two 2.5-hour deliberative sessions, separated by a one-week gap (Carman, Mallery et al. 2015). In the first week (the first face-to-face deliberative session), twelve participants considered educational materials and then issues stemming from a case study. In the week between the two deliberative groups there was an online interaction (discussion between participants and experts). In the second deliberative session there was a return to the first case study and consideration of a second (Carman, Mallery et al. 2015).

Deliberative polling

Associated with the work of Fishkin, deliberative polling involves four steps: drawing and interviewing a random sample of respondents; sending those who agree to take part a selection of carefully balanced briefing materials; bringing participants together to a single site for deliberation (usually over a weekend); re-polling views following this deliberation (Fishkin and Luskin 2005). The advantages of the approach are mainly relative to more traditional polling methods: it avoids capturing opinions which are 'cognitively threadbare' (Fishkin and Luskin 2005, p. 287). A distinguishing feature of deliberative polling is that even after deliberation, it is individual views that are polled.

Citizens' juries

Citizens' juries are usually commissioned by an organisation which has authority to act on the public's recommendations (Coote and Lenaghan 1997). They typically involve between twelve and sixteen 'jurors', sampled to be broadly representative of their community. Jurors are brought together for between two and five days and are presented with information relating to the question being addressed, scrutinize this information (or 'evidence') and cross-examine witnesses. The juror's conclusions (the 'verdict' need not be unanimous) are summarized in a report.

The various approaches outlined next generally share a series of common steps. The four steps to public deliberation outlined by Carman et al. are: (i) convene ('individuals with a broad range of perspectives'); (ii) learn (an 'objective overview of background, issues and options [are] presented'); (iii) deliberate ('participants exchange reasons, perspectives and values'); (iv) report ('a summary or transcript of deliberation is prepared for the sponsor') (Carman, Mallery et al. 2015, p. 12).

Who is involved?

Lenaghan warns that 'too often, public involvement exercises confuse or misunderstand the different perspectives of the patient and of the citizen'

(Lenaghan 1999, p. 47). The argument made by Lenaghan is that the public often has two roles, as consumers (or, rather in this case, service users) and citizens. In holding both of these roles, participants will face conflicting interests which are potentially, on the one hand, short term and self-interested and, on the other hand, longer term and more community focussed (Lenaghan 1999). The argument here is essentially the one outlined previously in the context of contingent valuation. Whereas it would be relevant to involve service users in a qualitative exercise aimed at understanding service user priorities, anxieties and experience, when deciding upon the allocation of resources for that specific service, in relation to others, it may be deemed more appropriate to adopt Rawls' 'veil of ignorance'. Depending upon the question and the issue under consideration we are all capable of displaying more of a tendency towards the consumer or the citizen. It may be impossible to fully understand in advance the agenda of those recruited to participate in deliberative methods, and those facilitating deliberation can only encourage conditions in which participants are encouraged to think as consumers. The crucial consideration, however, is whether participants are recruited *because* they are service users; that is, they are part of a special interest group.

CASE STUDY: VALUATION OF OUTCOMES IDENTIFIED AS RELEVANT IN THE CONTEXT OF SUPPORTIVE END-OF-LIFE CARE

Study design

Two sets of focus groups (with significant overlap in terms of content) were conducted with two sets of participant: focus groups with the general population and focus groups with policy makers and service managers. Members of the general population were recruited via the edited electoral register, whereas policy makers were recruited via direct contact with targeted individuals and organisations. This chapter concentrates on the focus groups conducted with the public, although some comparisons will be drawn in later sections.

Prior to commencement of recruitment, ethics approval was obtained from the University of Birmingham's Science, Technology, Engineering and Mathematics Ethical Review Committee (ERN_11–1296).

Sample and recruitment

The sampling strategy essentially involved purposeful sampling of geographical areas (in this case electoral wards), based on socio-economic and geographical considerations, and then random sampling within those specific areas – essentially a purposeful random sampling approach (see Chapter 3). Electoral wards within the West Midlands Region of the United Kingdom were rank ordered in Microsoft Excel, according to their 2007 index of multiple deprivation score (published by the Office for National Statistics), and then divided into tertiles. A smaller number of wards within these tertiles were then selected with the intention of achieving diversity in terms of population density, palliative care provision and geographical spread over the region. Participants were recruited from across six electoral wards (two in Birmingham, one in Wolverhampton and three in Warwickshire). Population densities varied between 0.11 and 0.18 in the Birmingham wards, and 0.01 and 0.06 in the Warwickshire wards. Edited electoral registers were purchased from the relevant local authority and contained between 1,300 and 11,600 names and addresses.

Within each spreadsheet (each for a different electoral ward), a random number was generated for each row (i.e., each entry on the register) and the data then rank-ordered according to that random number. A selection of names were copied into a new sheet of Excel and where there were a number of individuals at the same address all but the first name/row were deleted. Names and addresses were sent to an external company, who sent invitation letters, information leaflets, forms to indicate interest in participating and prepaid reply envelopes out to the selected addressees. Once a batch of invitations had been sent a contact log was opened to record correspondence, queries, expressions of interest and, in a minority of cases, complaints.

The only inclusion criterion was that the addressee had received the invitation and was willing to participate, although in order to adhere to the conditions of our ethical approval, potential participants were excluded if they had been bereaved within the last six months; these people were sent a letter thanking them for returning the form but informing them that they had not been selected for the focus group (they were told of the reason). Those eligible were contacted by telephone and if they were available on the date and time of the focus group they were also sent a confirmation letter (as an email attachment where feasible). The recruitment process is summarized in Figure 16.1.

Initially, 200 invitation letters were sent out to the first three electoral wards (the three city wards). Due to an extremely low response rate (of just 0.5 percent, or one positive response), the focus group planned for a low deprivation area of Wolverhampton was cancelled and additional invitation letters were sent out to the other two wards within Birmingham (an additional 50 and 100, respectively, to a mid- and a high-deprivation ward).

From the 250 invitations sent out to the mid-deprivation ward, five positive responses were received (2 percent); all five individuals were sent confirmation of the focus group and three actually attended. From the 300 invitation letters sent out in the high-deprivation ward, six positive responses were

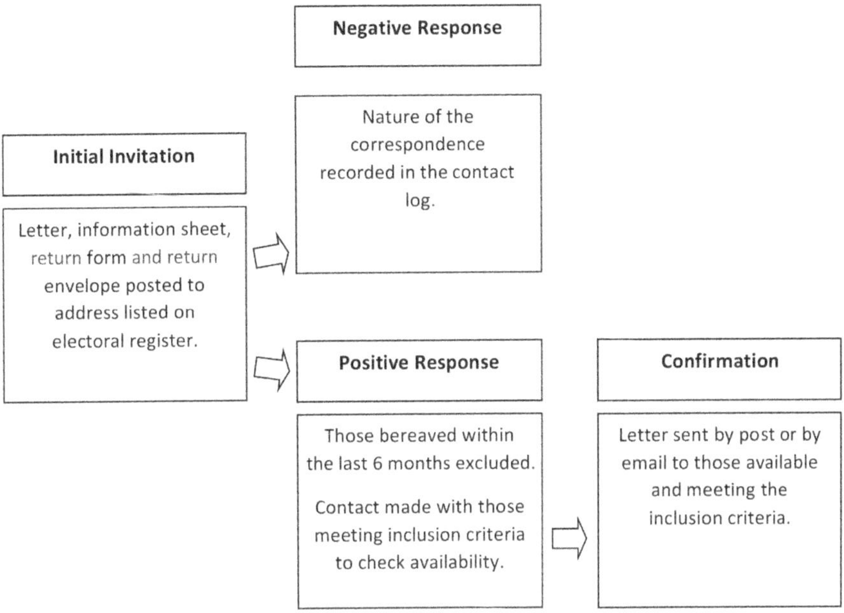

Figure 16.1. Recruitment process for public. Courtesy of the authors.

received (also 2 percent), from which two individuals were excluded due to recent bereavement and four were sent confirmation; one participant actually attended. This 'focus group' coincided with an unusually warm summer evening.

The number of invitation letters sent to the most populated of our county wards (a mid-deprivation ward) was increased to 300. There was a positive response rate of 2.7 percent from the 300 invitations sent to the mid-deprivation ward; six of the eight individuals who were sent confirmation actually participated. For the remaining two, more rural county wards, 500 invitations were sent and response rates were 4.2 percent and 5.4 percent, with the highest response rate overall being achieved in the ward with the lowest population density and the second-lowest index of multiple deprivation score.

The sample was predominantly white British – probably a result of the high proportion of participants recruited from rural, low-deprivation wards – and female (63 percent). Older groups were also over-represented, possibly as a result of the topic under discussion.

In total, thirty-eight individuals participated from the public. The first focus group (as explained previously) was cancelled. Because of the high response rate from the last two rural wards it was decided to split individuals across two focus groups in each ward, meaning that seven groups were held in total. The 'focus group' with the single participant was excluded from the analysis and hence reference will be made in the following section to thirty-seven participants.

Data collection

Venues were booked within the relevant electoral ward and most focus groups took part in the evening. Venues included a Methodist church hall, a Quaker meeting house, a leisure centre and a meeting room in town council offices. Focus groups were facilitated by a minimum of three researchers with varying degrees of qualitative experience. Key roles undertaken at every focus group included a lead facilitator (who introduced the tasks and 'chaired' discussions), a supporter (who welcomed latecomers, helped to respond to questions and sometimes led a specific task) and a note-taker (recording who was speaking throughout the discussion and a few initial words from each new speaker to enable the transcribed text to be linked to specific participants). Focus groups were audio-recorded from the point at which the consent forms had been completed by all participants.

Participants in the public groups completed three related tasks and there were, in total, five topics for group discussion:

- Initial discussion around why participants had chosen to attend the focus group, and their understanding of the purpose and nature of end-of-life care.
- Task one: scaling of attribute levels from the ICECAP-CPM (including group discussion).
- Task two: relative weighting of the attributes from ICECAP-CPM (including group discussion).
- Task three: relative weighting of the importance of outcomes for patients at end of life versus close persons (including group discussion).
- Final discussion relating to priority setting and rules for economic evaluation in the context of end-of-life care.

All of the tasks were introduced in a workbook, as well as verbally by the lead facilitator. Tasks required basic written responses by participants, which were entered into the workbook. The workbooks were linked to participants by a unique identity number prefixed by the electoral ward reference (e.g., A01, A02; B01, B02). An example of one question from task one is presented in Figure 16.2. The top level on each ICECAP-CPM attribute was fixed at 100 on a visual analogue scale, and the worst level (the level indicating the lowest level of ability) was fixed at zero on the same scale. Participants were asked to indicate where on the scale they felt the intermediate three levels would fit. The six questions (one for each ICECAP-CPM attribute) were preceded by

This question is about your view of the importance for family and friends of *being able to have good communication with those providing care services* (e.g., doctors, nurses and carers). This includes things like:

- being able to get information about the person's health and care,
- being able to have a say in the care that the person receives
- being able to ask questions, have them answered and have views respected.
- being able to have rapport with those providing care

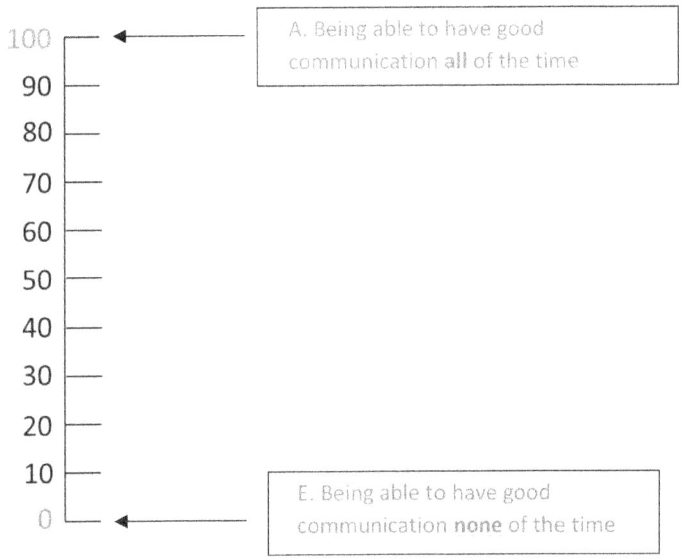

The missing levels are:
B. Being able to have good communication **most** of the time
C. Being able to have good communication **some** of the time
D. Being able to have good communication **a little** of the time

Please show with crosses where you want to put 'B', 'C' and 'D' on the scale.

After the group discussion, would you:

Keep original answer ☐

Change answer ☐

please note your changes: B = ...; C = ...; D = ...

Figure 16.2. Task one example question. Courtesy of the authors.

an example question (relating to happiness) and a practice question (relating to hospital waiting times). Participants completed each task individually, a discussion followed and then participants had an opportunity to change their responses using the box at the bottom of the page.

Task two involved participants splitting 100 tokens between the six ICECAP-CPM attributes, presented within a pie chart, a method referred to by Mullen as budget pie (Mullen 1999). Participants were permitted to give zero tokens to one or more of the attributes if they desired, or to give all 100 tokens to a single attribute. Once again, they completed the task individually, discussed their responses with the rest of the group and then had an opportunity to change their responses if they had been influenced by the group discussion.

Task three was presented as a pie chart (see Figure 16.3) with two segments and participants were asked to split an additional 100 tokens between

Do you think it is important for policy makers to take account of the benefits to family and friends?

Yes ❑ No ❑

If you answered 'Yes': please think about how important it is for policy makers to take account of the impacts to family and friends, and say how much importance you would want to give to family and friends.

Please split your 100 tokens between people at the end of life and family and friends of these people.

If you answered 'No': please write 0 into the box for 'family and friends' and 100 into the box for 'people at the end of life'.

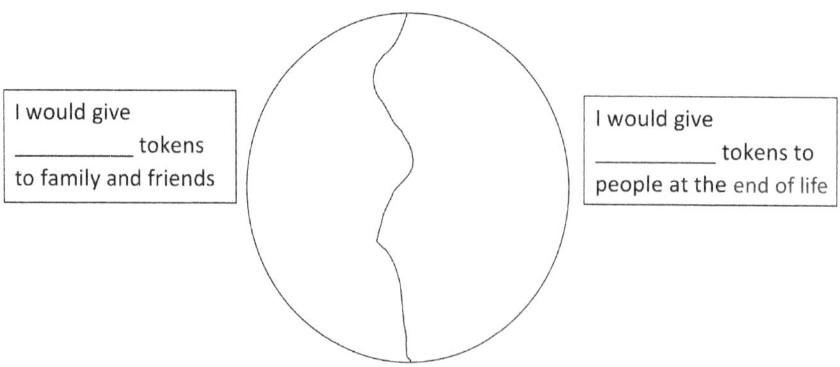

Figure 16.3. Patients versus close persons (task three). Courtesy of the author.

services targeted at/outcomes experienced by the patient and services targeted at/outcomes experienced by close persons (family, informal carers and friends). Participants were asked to consider the value of services and interventions, rather than their cost.

The final discussion which concluded the focus group did not involve deliberative methods and so is not discussed in further detail here.

The focus groups were scheduled to last for up to two hours and this included time for a short break.

Data analysis

All discussion within the groups was audio-recorded, with the recording starting from the point at which written consent was obtained. The whole recording was transcribed verbatim, and to enable the linking of text within the transcript to the identity of a particular participant (or researcher), a member of the project team was solely responsible for recording the first few words spoken (or one or two memorable points made) by each person. To assist with this, each participant wore a name sticker, introduced himself or herself at the start of the group, and a seating plan was recorded. All names were subsequently replaced with the identity number from the front of the workbook (which also linked to the consent form).

The first step, in terms of analysis, was to enter the responses from the workbook into a Microsoft Excel spreadsheet. The values pre- and post-discussion were entered from the visual analogue scale (task one) and the two budget pie tasks (tasks two and three). We then explored: (i) mean values (and range) within each group; (ii) mean values (and range) for the entire sample and (iii) the number of people within each group who changed their responses following the group discussion.

The method adopted in terms of qualitative analysis was a constant comparison. Transcripts of the groups were allocated to one of two batches, one batch within which more changes were recorded (as a response to the discussion), and one batch within which participants were less inclined to change their responses (or did not change at all).

Initially, transcripts were read in full and then coded (an example is found in the first two columns of Table 16.1). Themes emerged from within one batch of transcripts (see the third column of Table 16.1). A specific section of text could relate to more than one theme. Themes from the first batch were compared and contrasted with themes from the second batch. Particular attention was given to the nature of the contributions and interactions in the first batch, versus those in the second. An analytic account for each theme was then developed.

Table 16.1. Coding and the emergence of themes

Text (quote)	*Coding*	*Theme*	*Scope of theme*
'A person should be cared for preferably by the family.'	Family responsibility Care needs	Responsibility for informal care	**Care needs:** 'The family should be encouraged to look after the person unless [there are specific clinical needs that require medical attention].' **Gender:** 'Yes. I think it's important for a married woman to feel that she fulfils her marriage vows – in sickness and in health.' **Culture:** 'And maybe I come from Indian background we do look after our you-know families.' **Geographical distance:** A report from one participant of her mother's death in Scotland and support she received from neighbours

OBSERVED IMPACT AND MECHANISM OF THE DELIBERATION

Deliberation I: what do the statistics tell us?

As a crude indicator of the impact of deliberation, this section presents evidence in response to four questions:

1. How many participants changed their responses following discussion within the group?
2. Are some participants just more amenable to influence and/or less confident of their responses? That is, do we observe that the same participants change their responses across multiple tasks?
3. Can those who changed their responses be characterized by a distinguishing demographic?
4. Where participants changed their responses, did responses move towards the original mean for the group?

Of the thirty-seven participants included for analysis, nineteen (51 percent) recorded one or more changes within their workbook. Only one person changed his or her response on all three tasks (see Figure 16.4), seven people

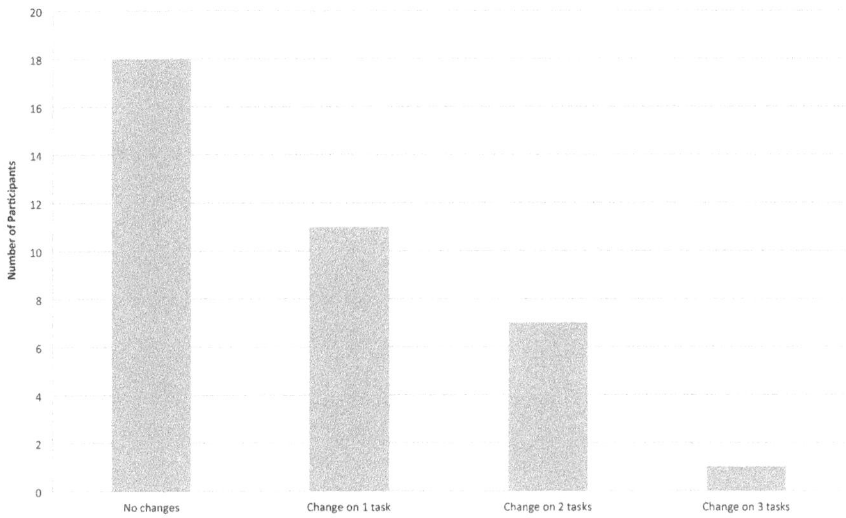

Figure 16.4. Number of participants recording a change on one or more tasks. Courtesy of the authors.

changed their responses on two tasks, eleven people changed their responses on only one task and eighteen people recorded having made no changes.

Thirteen participants changed at least one of their responses to task one. There were 222 chances for a change to be recorded on task one (six questions, each completed by thirty-seven participants); twenty changes were actually recorded. The majority (nine) of participants who changed their response did so to one of the six questions, three participants changed their response to two questions and one participant changed his or her response to five of the six questions.

On task two, five people changed their responses, only three of whom had previously changed their responses on task one, and only two of whom went on to change their response to task three. Ten participants in total changed their response on task three.

Nothing stood out as being distinctive about the characteristics of those who changed their responses on any of the tasks, the age and sex of those participants (mainly older and female) is representative of the overall sample (also mainly older and female). As an indicator of participants holding strong views for task two, participants were identified if they allocated one or more attributes zero tokens; allocated one attribute fifty or more tokens; or both of these were observed. There were eleven (29 percent) participants for whom these types of response were observed, and two of these participants had changed their responses following discussion.

Three participants expressed a 'strong view' for task three (defined as a zero weight for either the patient or friends and family), two of whom changed their response to the task following discussion. Both participants moved from an allocation of zero weight to friends and family to a 20–100 split (with 20 to friends and family). In six out of ten cases participants moved towards the group mean when changing their responses to task three.

To summarize:

1. Nineteen (51 percent) of participants recorded having changed at least one of their responses following the group discussion.
2. Of the nineteen participants who recorded a change to their response, half (eight) changed their response on two or more tasks and only one changed their response on all three tasks. It does not follow therefore that those who make any form of change are somehow more susceptible to influence or indecision across all tasks.
3. It is simply not possible, given the sample size and the fact that the sample was dominated by a certain demographic profile, to say that participants would be any more or less likely to change their responses if they are male or female, older or younger, or from a low-, mid- or high-deprivation electoral ward. What is noticeable is that there were fourteen instances across tasks two and three where a participant expressed a 'strong view' and in only four cases did they change their mind following discussion.
4. Revised responses did not always tend towards the group mean; this was the case for six out of ten participants for task three.

Deliberation II: what does the qualitative analysis tell us?

Given the differing nature of qualitative data, an alternative set of questions are posed and answered here:

1. Can we identify reasons why participants chose to take part?
2. Can we identify participants who appeared to have a strong or weak influence on the group and, if so, how are these participants characterized?

Participants were not asked individually why they had taken part and, had they been pressed on this, some participants may have struggled to explain a simple sense of altruism or curiosity. It is, however, possible to identify *some* reasons why participants were drawn to the topic of end-of-life care and why they felt that they had a view and experience to share. Some participants had relevant professional experience (which ranged from a registrar for births, deaths and marriages, to nursing and a junior doctor); many had personal experience as a patient, relative or carer, and some gave an indication of having an awareness of their own mortality. With respect to awareness of own mortality, this phenomenon is perhaps best summed up from a male participant in the first focus group, who said of his wife and himself in relation to end-of-life care, 'We're at an age where it's at the back of your mind to a certain extent.'

Two groups appeared to have particular influence in terms of deliberation, and these groups were, first, those who offered a new perspective, and secondly those broadly labelled as 'supporter-challengers'. Those who offered a new perspective often did so through personal disclosure; they did not dominate discussion but their experience did resonate with and influence the views of others in the group. Some participants shared the experiences of friends and family, to whom they had offered support (i.e., they had a close insight), and this was termed 'disclosure by proxy'. Supporter-challengers were often seemingly more confident and contributed to the discussion not so much by sharing personal experiences but more by questioning the research team and other participants, vocalising their agreement and challenging other people's viewpoints. Supporter-challengers demonstrated a willingness to change their responses following discussion.

A further group which did not appear to carry strong influence was labelled as being 'agenda driven'. Those showing characteristics associated with being agenda driven were often the first to speak in the initial discussion, set out their personal views early in the discussion and in some cases appeared to have pre-empted that 'their topic' would be a focus of the research. Those who demonstrated characteristics associated with the label 'agenda driven' did not change their responses following the discussion.

Another group identified as being of interest was those labelled as being 'professional experience orientated', a group who referred to and drew upon their professional experience as a reference point without attempting to dominate discussion or claim a uniquely correct or valid viewpoint. In reality, of course, some participants demonstrated characteristics associated with two or more groups and some did not align to one of the four groups outlined here. For example, some of those with professional experience also disclosed personal experiences which resonated with and challenged the perceptions of the rest of the group.

In answer to the questions just posed:

1. It appears that most participants had some personal or professional experience of, or link to, supportive end-of-life care and others attended the group with a clear agenda in terms of what they expected to, or wanted to, discuss.
2. We can identify characteristics of those who were influential in the focus groups and those who appeared to be less influential and hence broadly

label those displaying the characteristics associated with these groups. Those who disclosed personal experience without seeking to dominate the discussion were strongly influential, whereas those with a dominant personal agenda appeared to have little influence. Those with professional experience did not use this to dominate discussion, and those who confidently supported and challenged others within the group helped to bring about greater value from the discussion in terms of the benefits typically associated with focus groups.

REFLECTIONS, LESSONS AND PRACTICAL CONSIDERATIONS

Recruitment and sampling

Although it is likely that those who are motivated to participate in a deliberative exercise will feel some personal or professional connection, by recruiting the general public and by giving as many people the opportunity to take part as possible, then a wide range of perspectives and experiences are likely to be achieved. It is quite different for those with a wide range of experiences loosely connecting them to a topic to select in to the sample than for a narrow range of individuals to be targeted because they are part of a special interest group. Indeed, based on findings from the case study, it is unlikely that those with a strong personal agenda will change their views following deliberation.

Those who were older, female and white were over-represented in the sample from the case study. Carman et al. did achieve a study sample which reflected the key demographic characteristics of each of the local populations they targeted in their U.S. study, although recruitment was via a commercial recruitment firm (Carman, Mallery et al. 2015). Achieving representative sampling is therefore likely to require significant resources and specific expertise, particular in accessing 'hard to reach' groups.

Practical issues and considerations

A number of practical obstacles and challenges were encountered during the study and, briefly, these included:

- Obtaining electoral registers: the study coincided with national elections in England and hence councils were pre-occupied and slow to respond to requests for the registers.
- Time of year: it is likely that the unusually hot weather experienced in early summer when the focus groups were held explained some of the

non-attendance and it actually made taking part in some of the groups uncomfortable (given that local venues did not have air conditioning).
- Reminders/over-recruiting: The case study clearly shows the need to (i) send out a high number of invitations (given that positive response rates varied between 0.5 percent and 5.4 percent); (ii) over-recruit to each group (to account for non-attendance) and (iii) to set up a system of reminders, possibly text message (to mitigate against non-attendance).
- Confidentiality in a small community: our highest participation rate was achieved in the electoral ward with the lowest population density, and this led to concern among the research team at the time about confidentiality.
- Beliefs about recruitment: even though the information leaflet clearly stated that individuals' names and addresses had been obtained from the edited electoral register, some believed that they had been targeted because of their use of a particular GP, hospital, hospice or social care service. It is therefore important for the information sent out in the invitation to be as clear as possible, and it may be useful to re-emphasize how participants were recruited at the start of the deliberation exercise.

Conceptual issues and considerations

There were also some conceptual issues that arose during the research.

- When does deliberation start? Fishkin states that the deliberation process starts (in the case of deliberative polling) from the moment at which participants are selected and sent pre-reading materials. The exchange of information (explicit or inferred) about beliefs, values and experiences began from the first moment of the first discussion in the case study. We may have focused discussion towards particular topics at particular points in the focus group, but it is likely that participants were influenced by discussion at all stages.
- Can deliberation occur within a focus group? Focus groups allow less time for learning and deliberation and so it cannot be regarded as a serious deliberative method, although free and open discussion occurred and participants were influenced by the views and experiences of others in a way that can be evidenced by both the quantitative and qualitative data.

CONCLUSION

This chapter has provided a case study of the use of deliberation within focus groups. The research aimed to provide information for valuation of a new measure for use in the end-of-life care setting. As well as discussion of the deliberative process, and explanation of the various deliberative tasks included in the research, the chapter also outlined some of the challenges associated with recruitment to, and conduct of, this research.

There are many different types of deliberation, as indicated at the start of this chapter. The case study focused on one of the less intensive methods, the use of focus groups, and, although it can be argued that there is less time for deliberation with this method, it still provoked valuable discussion. Scope for the use of more intense deliberative methods within health economics remains.

FUNDING STATEMENT

The study described in this chapter was funded by the European Research Council (261098 EconEndLife).

Part II C

USING QUALITATIVE METHODS TO ENHANCE AND GENERATE ECONOMIC UNDERSTANDING

Chapter 17

Using qualitative methods in impact evaluation: The case of the results-based financing for maternal and neonatal care impact evaluation in Malawi

Manuela De Allegri

Over the past few decades, the concept of evidence-informed policy making has gained prominent attention. Evidence-based policy making has emerged in response to increasing public calls for accountability and is defined in relation to policy formulation and implementation that is informed by evidence on the potential effects of a given policy or program (Moat and Lavis 2013; Newman, Capillo et al. 2013). This renewed interest in evidence-based policy making has fed into an increased demand for impact evaluation studies, that is, studies that systematically assess the impact of a given policy or program on a set of pre-defined outcomes (Gertler, Martinez et al. 2010).

Health economists have played, and continue to play, an important role in conducting impact evaluation studies on health care policies and programs. These impact evaluation studies are expected to generate the evidence that is needed to inform health policy formulation and implementation. They rest on the assumption that the application of rigorous scientific methodologies allows the possibility of distilling the impact of a given intervention and distinguishing it clearly from what would have occurred in the absence of such an intervention. In line with this assumption, impact evaluation studies have traditionally relied on quantitative methods of data collection and analysis, largely 'borrowing' from the experimental tradition of medicine. Health economists have acquired substantial experience in conducting experiments with random assignment of participants to a given policy or program, replicating what would normally happen in clinical randomized controlled trials (Gertler, Martinez et al. 2010; Bernard 2013). Building on a specific expertise in econometrics, health economists (and economists more generally) have also made substantial use of quasi-experimental designs, such as designs relying on difference-in-differences models and regression discontinuity analysis, to assess the impact of a given policy or program in the absence of randomisation (Shadish, Cook et al. 2002; Shadish and Cook 2009).

In more recent years, the supremacy of the experimental and quasi-experimental approach in the field of impact evaluation has been challenged by a number of authors who have argued that, while quantitative methods can be useful to measure impact, they fall short of exploring and explaining causal pathways to change, thus providing only partial evidence to inform policy making (Patton 2002; Craig, Dieppe et al. 2008; Creswell and Plano Clark 2011; Richards and Hallberg 2015). Likewise, increasing awareness has emerged that quantitative methods of analysis fall short of capturing the complexity of the social systems within which policies and programs are implemented, leaving many relevant questions on their effectiveness unanswered. This is largely because the very nature of quantitative enquiry relies on the ability to identify discernible and quantifiable outcomes, while in real life, policies and programs often produce change that is not so easily discernible and/or quantifiable. In addition, the change produced by a given policy or program is largely context-dependent, requiring that attention be paid to the circumstances of the intervention to explain the impact on the single-outcome variables. Moreover, by exploring dimensions that reach beyond the hypothesis originally formulated at the beginning of a study, qualitative methods are more suitable to identifying unexpected effects of an intervention, shedding light on potential externalities derived from the implementation of a given policy or program (Padgett 2012; Datta and Petticrew 2013).

These considerations have led to a general recognition that the field of impact evaluation needs to move beyond the exclusive application of quantitative methods to integrate qualitative methods of data collection and analysis (Bamberger, Rugh et al. 2012; Richards and Hallberg 2015). This renewed recognition of the potential value of qualitative methods in impact evaluation has led to the emergence of purely qualitative and, more frequently, mixed methods designs, with the latter integrating quantitative and qualitative methods of data collection and analysis within a single impact evaluation effort. While qualitative methods have long found an application in other domains of evaluation (e.g., formative, summative and process evaluation) (MacPherson and McKie 2010), their integration in impact evaluation designs is more recent as testified by the number of pertinent guidelines published over the past few years (Craig, Dieppe et al. 2008; Garbarino and Holland 2009; Creswell and Plano Clark 2011; Bamberger 2012; Ellis 2015).

In this chapter, I wish to describe the experience of integrating qualitative methods of data collection and analysis within the framework of an impact evaluation of a results-based financing program on the quality of maternal and newborn health care services in rural Malawi. Hereafter, I describe our field experience and focus specifically on the methodological choices we operated and the challenges we faced in applying qualitative methods within the framework of an impact evaluation. It is important to note that a large number of people contributed towards this study and that in my function of principal investigator, I acted mostly as senior advisor and overall coordinator, ensuring coherence and continuity across the single data collection and analysis components. Therefore, the work described is a reflection of a large collaborative effort and all those who contributed towards it are individually acknowledged at the end of this chapter.

WHAT IS RESULTS-BASED FINANCING?

To understand our research, the reader needs first to be acquainted with the type of intervention being evaluated. 'Results-based financing' (RBF) is a generic term used to refer to the provision of financial incentives aimed at modifying either health care workers' or their clients' behaviour in relation to provision or consumption of health care services. RBF ties the delivery or consumption of a given health care good or service to a specific financial incentive. Incentives that target health care workers are generally defined within the framework of performance-based financing (PBF) schemes. These schemes normally combine financial incentives tied to specific pre-agreed performance targets, to a wider set of provisions, including improved supervision and increased autonomy at the level of the single facilities. Incentives that target clients normally take the form of conditional cash transfers (CCTs), that is, financial rewards disbursed to clients upon consumption of a specific health care good or service (Grittner 2013). Given that their diffusion in low- and middle-income countries (LMICs) largely corresponded with the introduction of the Millennium Development Goals (MDGs), RBF schemes have mostly been implemented to incentivize the provision and use of mother and child health care services, with the explicit aim of fostering progress towards MDG4 and MDG5 (Grittner 2013; Health Results Innovation Trust Fund 2015).

PBF schemes are conceptually rooted in the principal-agent model. In brief, the provision of financial incentives is meant to re-align the behaviour of the agent (the health care worker) towards the provision of the health care services that the principal (the purchasing institution, most frequently the government and its development partners) is interested to purchase in a specific setting, given a particular set of social and health circumstances. The introduction of PBF rests on the idea that traditional input-based financing systems are characterized by the absence of well-defined financial incentives, adequate supervision and autonomy. In turn, this leaves health care workers with little motivation to align their behaviour with the agents' interests, resulting in inefficient health care provision (defined both in relation to the quantity and the quality of the care provided).

CCTs are conceptually rooted in the understanding that attaching a financial incentive to consumption of a given good or service will alter clients' behaviour through two parallel, albeit related, mechanisms. In the first place, the financial incentive is used to signal the importance of consuming a given good or service and the mere expectation of gaining a financial reward is expected to motivate potential clients to use that given good or service. In the second place, the same financial incentive yields an income effect, meaning that clients using a given service will increase their overall income compared to those who do not. In turn, this additional income is expected to facilitate service use by compensating clients for the direct and indirect costs associated with seeking care. This income effect is of fundamental importance in countries where no adequate means of social health protection are in place (Ensor 2004).

Albeit the two interventions are in principle complementary, one acting on the supply and one acting on the demand side, in practice PBF schemes have rarely been combined with CCT schemes. Lack of evidence on the combined effect of the two is what motivated our scientific enquiry in Malawi.

THE RESULTS BASED FINANCING FOR MATERNAL AND NEONATAL HEALTH INITIATIVE IN MALAWI

Malawi is a low-income landlocked country in Southern Africa, with extremely high rates of maternal (460/100,000 live births) (World Health Organisation, UNICEF et al. 2012) and neonatal mortality (24/1,000 live births) (UN Inter-Agency Group for Child Mortality Estimation 2013). Prior to our work in Malawi, evidence had already shown that limited access to obstetric care and poor quality of service provision due to lack of adequate resources were largely responsible for delays in care which ultimately resulted in the death of women and their infants (Kongnyuy, Mlava et al. 2009).

The Results Based Financing for Maternal and Neonatal Health (RBF4MNH) Initiative was set to address these system inadequacies by combining CCT (to address challenges pertaining to access to obstetric services) with PBF (to address challenges pertaining to quality of service provision). The RBF4MNH Initiative represents one of the few experiences in sub-Saharan Africa (SSA) of combining PBF with CCT within the framework of a single intervention. The Initiative has been funded by the German Development Bank (KfW) and by the Norwegian Ministry of Foreign Affairs and implemented by the Malawian Ministry of Health with technical support from the U.K.-based consultancy Options. It has been active in four districts in Malawi (Balaka, Dedza, Ntcheu, Mchinji) since 2013.

The intervention has been described in detail elsewhere (Brenner, Muula et al. 2014). In brief, within the framework of the PBF component, financial incentives are paid to facilities against the achievement of a pre-defined set of quantity and quality indicators. The additional remuneration is partially distributed among the staff working at the facility (70 percent) and partially re-invested in quality improvements at the facility (30 percent). Within the framework of the CCT component, women residing in the catchment areas of the intervention facilities are registered during antenatal care and, upon delivering in the concerned facility, they receive a cash transfer. This transfer is meant to help them to recover the costs associated with transport and with staying at the facility for at least forty-eight hours after delivery. Delivery services are provided free of charge within the framework of Malawi Essential Healthcare Package.

After an initial pilot in eighteen Emergency Obstetric Care (EmOC) facilities starting in 2013, the RBF4MNH Initiative was later scaled up to a total of twenty-eight EmOC facilities starting in 2014. The implementation of the PBF and the CCT components was preceded by an infrastructure upgrade, ensuring that the facilities had sufficient material resources to provide EmOC services meeting basic quality standards. Due to operational challenges, the CCT component was delayed compared to the PBF component and was fully effective in all facilities concerned (including the ones added at scale-up) only by mid-2014.

OUR IMPACT EVALUATION DESIGN

The impact evaluation accompanying the implementation of the RBF4MNH Initiative was originally envisioned to adopt a sequential explanatory mixed methods design (Brenner, Muula et al. 2014), combining quantitative and qualitative methods of data collection and analysis into a single evaluation effort. Methodological decisions were theory-driven, meaning that prior to the definition of the design and the specific methods of data collection and analysis, we defined and described a theory of change (Rogers 2014) and aligned all of our subsequent decisions with it.

In brief, the quantitative component was envisioned as a pre- and post-test design with independent controls (EmOC facilities in the same four districts not affected by the RBF4MNH Initiative). Data were collected at three time points (baseline, midterm and endpoint) using a variety of structured closed-ended tools, namely, a population-based survey, client-structured exit interviews, provider-patient direct clinical observations, facility infrastructural assessments, structured health care worker survey. The quantitative component was set to measure the effect of the RBF4MNH Initiative on a number of pre-defined outcome indicators. Primary outcome indicators were proportion of women using obstetric care services; quality of obstetric health care services (measured using composite scores addressing inputs, processes and outcomes of care); women's perceived quality of care (measured using psychometric scales) and health care workers' motivational profile (measured using a psychometric scale).

The qualitative component was initially envisioned as a defined series of interviews to be conducted at midterm and endpoint to explain and complement emerging quantitative findings. As the evaluation progressed, however, the qualitative component expanded to respond to emerging research questions and became a central, rather than a side, element of the research. Hereafter, I describe this process in detail, explaining the adjustments that we made *in itinere* to both the nature and the scope of the qualitative component.

The study received ethical clearance from both the Ethical Committee of the Medical Faculty of the University of Heidelberg and by COMREG at College of Medicine in Malawi.

BASELINE FINDINGS AND THE DECISION TO MODIFY THE IMPACT EVALUATION DESIGN

The original study design had envisioned a defined set of qualitative interviews at midterm and endpoint with both health care providers and clients (women using obstetric services) to explain emerging quantitative findings and to explore the experiential dimension of service provision. The decision to limit the application of qualitative methods to an explanatory function was motivated by our initial understanding that an impact evaluation should primarily be based on the quantitative measurement of the effect of an intervention on a series of well-defined outcome measures. Our original assumption was that qualitative methods should help us explain what could not be explained through the application of statistical methods. Specifically, we expected qualitative methods to explain heterogeneity in outcomes, meaning that we expected to use qualitative methods to explain differences in outcome measures across sample units (facilities and their catchment areas).

The analysis of the baseline data, however, quickly induced us to change our initial methodological approach and to increase the weight of qualitative methods in our impact evaluation. The starting point for the shift came from observing that baseline values for several of the defined outcome measures (those pertaining to service utilisation and perceived quality of care) were already so high that capturing further changes would have been challenging, unless all quantitative samples could be increased to a level that would have made data collection unaffordable, even for the most generous of field budgets. In addition, baseline findings indicated very little heterogeneity across facilities and communities, challenging from the very onset the conceptual explanatory framework serving as the basis for our qualitative design.

Specifically:

a. The analysis of the population-based survey revealed that use of obstetric services (in particular facility-based deliveries) was already much higher than reported in official statistics, with values reaching over 90 percent across intervention and control facilities.
b. The analysis of the structured exit interviews showed that women expressed very high ratings on the quality of obstetric services across intervention and control facilities. Furthermore, these high ratings appeared rather surprising given that our more clinically oriented tools (infrastructural assessment and provider-patient clinical observations) consistently identified a generalized status of poor quality of service delivery.
c. The structured health care worker survey proved not to be an effective tool in discerning health care workers' motivational profile, with the dimensions pertaining to extrinsic and intrinsic motivation not being clearly distinguishable.
d. The analysis of the infrastructural assessment tool and of the provider-patient clinical observations revealed large discrepancies in the quality of care provided, with some procedures being carried out according to the guidelines and others being consistently bypassed. Furthermore, quantitative analysis did not detect a direct association between quality of clinical processes and availability of supplies and material.

In light of these baseline findings, we decided to revise our original impact evaluation design and to move from an explanatory to a triangulation mixed methods design, allowing qualitative methods of data collection and analysis to hold greater weight within the overall impact evaluation than originally envisaged. In an explanatory design, qualitative methods of data collection and analysis generally hold a smaller weight than quantitative methods, while in a triangulation design the two sets of data generally hold equal weight (Creswell and Plano Clark 2011). In a triangulation design, the focus is on a single phenomenon (in our case the implementation and impact of the RBF4MNH Initiative), but quantitative and qualitative methods are used to explore different aspects of that phenomenon. The rationale for such a design is that of combining strengths and weaknesses of the two methodological approaches, allowing one approach to provide and compensate for what the other approach cannot deliver. In our specific case, baseline data clearly indicated a need to look well beyond the quantifiable measurement of impact into aspects pertaining to the overall health system context and specifically to the intervention of the RBF4MNH Initiative. These aspects could not be captured in a standard quantitative impact evaluation approach.

We maintained our initial ambition to measure the change produced by the RBF4MNH Initiative on the originally defined set of outcome measures, but we enlarged the scope of the qualitative component to take a closer look at each of the hints for research that emerged from the baseline data. Doing this entailed that we recognized enhanced value in using qualitative methods also to explore causal pathways and measure impact, moving away from our original assumption that an impact evaluation should be primarily quantitative in nature. We accepted the challenge that measuring impact through the application of qualitative methods could lead us to identify changes that could be described, but not necessarily captured, by a single quantifiable measure.

This shift in scope and focus was possible thanks to the emerging nature of qualitative designs (and mixed methods designs), whereby research questions, data collection tools and samples can be modified *in itinere* to respond to the cues that emerge from the research environment (Given 2008).

FOUR PARALLEL QUALITATIVE STUDIES WITHIN THE FRAMEWORK OF ONE IMPACT EVALUATION: DECISIONS ON RESEARCH QUESTIONS

The quantitative baseline findings described previously pointed to the need for different strains of qualitative research to understand the context within which the RBF4MNH was being implemented and to explore its impact in a comprehensive manner, beyond mere measurement of effect on a number of restricted outcome measures. Specifically, reflecting the same order in which I introduced the quantitative baseline findings previously, we identified four specific research objectives worthy of further qualitative scientific enquiry:

1. To investigate why utilisation rates for obstetric services were so much higher in our sample than indicated in official statistics, exploring what factors could have motivated rapid changes in health-seeking behaviour since the latest round of official statistics from 2010.

2. To ascertain whether the high-quality ratings reported by women truly corresponded to their perceptions and experiences concerning the quality of service delivery, given that the evidence from the infrastructural assessment and direct clinical observations suggested rather poor quality of service delivery.
3. To explore health workers' experiences with service delivery, their perceptions of the work environment and its relationship to motivation, and their understanding and response to the implementation of the RBF4MNH Initiative.
4. To examine the discrepancy in health care service provision to explain why certain clinical procedures were consistently bypassed even when relevant supplies and material would have been available.

The first two objectives were combined in one qualitative study, primarily targeting women in their communities. The third objective was addressed by a qualitative study, targeting health care workers at RBF4MNH facilities. The fourth objective was addressed by a qualitative study, addressing health care workers in all EmOC facilities in the four districts, irrespective of their RBF4MNH status.

The first two studies adopted a longitudinal design, interviewing women and health care workers at different time points during the course of the overall impact evaluation. The third study adopted a cross-sectional design, interviewing health care workers only once. The different approaches were justified by the fact that while the first two studies aimed at exploring and understanding how processes related to the relevant research dimensions changed over time also as a function of the RBF4MNH Initiative, the third study only sought additional understanding of one specific issue related to clinical performance.

These three qualitative studies were complemented by an additional longitudinal qualitative study to explore and analyse the process of policy formulation and implementation related to the RBF4MNH Initiative.

FOUR PARALLEL QUALITATIVE STUDIES WITHIN THE FRAMEWORK OF ONE IMPACT EVALUATION: DECISIONS ON SAMPLING STRATEGIES

All four qualitative studies adopted a theoretically driven approach to sampling, with respondents being identified on the basis of a defined set of purposively selected criteria (Patton 2002; Given 2008). Next, I do not describe findings from our studies (those are reported in single papers) but rather focus on illustrating the link between research questions and sample selection.

Qualitative study on women's health-seeking behaviours and perceived quality of obstetric care

This study targeted both women having used and women not having used obstetric care services. Different sampling and data collection decisions were made during the first round of data collection (2014) compared to the second round (2015). The thematic focus also evolved as we progressed through our impact evaluation. While the first round of data collection focused primarily on understanding health-seeking patterns and difficulties related to rating quality of care in a structured manner, the second round of data collection built on issues emerging from the first round in relation to the implementation of the RBF4MNH Initiative and explored more comprehensively how the implementation of PBF and CCT had changed women's experiences of care.

In 2014, the sample included women from the catchment areas of both intervention and control facilities and data were collected using a combination of in-depth interviews (with women being identified and interviewed on facility premises upon existing services) and focus group discussions (FGD) (with women being identified and interviewed in the community). We selected facilities and relevant catchment areas where to conduct our interviews and FGD based on the quality of care ratings derived from the baseline quantitative exit interviews. Although the ratings were generally very high, we based our sampling decisions on the limited heterogeneity observed across facilities. In addition, we included facilities from all four districts.

In spite of our explicit focus on clients' experiences and perceptions, as we proceeded with the planning of our study and especially once we began our data collection, we noted the importance of also interviewing health care workers at the sampled facilities. This served as a means of triangulating the information received from women. In 2014, we conducted a total of twelve in-depth interviews with health care workers alongside thirty-six in-depth interviews and fourteen FGD (each with eight to twelve participants), both with women with a recent history of pregnancy.

In 2015, given that we had understood the issues at the core of women's quality of care ratings and had a better understanding of what service delivery attributes were important to them (and could not be captured in our quantitative exit interviews), we made the explicit decision to narrow the size and the scope of the sample. This sampling decision was aligned with the thematic decision to focus more explicitly on issues related to the effects of the RBF4MNH Initiative on experiences of care and with the need to follow up themes which had emerged during the prior data collection round (e.g., misunderstanding concerning CCT, social representations of new clinical procedures being introduced by the RBF4MNH Initiative). Thus, in 2015, we interviewed women and providers exclusively at RBF4MNH facilities and in their matching catchment areas. Specifically, we sampled facilities and matching communities based on the preliminary results from the quantitative assessment of the impact of the RBF4MNH Initiative on quality of service delivery and purposely selected facilities that experienced changes of different magnitude. Given that in 2014 the individual in-depth interviews had not proven to be as informative as we would have wished, in 2015, we conducted only FGD and in-depth interviews with health care workers (again as a source of information triangulation). We conducted a total of fifteen FGD (each with eight to twelve participants) with women and twelve in-depth interviews with health care workers. Women for the FGD were sampled based on residence in one of the sampled communities (attached to a specific health facility as described previously) and on having a recent history of pregnancy. A Malawian public health researcher with extensive experience in qualitative research conducted this set of interviews and FGD, using the local language and was assisted in the field by three research assistants and note-takers.

Qualitative study on health care workers' responses to the RBF4MNH initiative and motivational profile

This study targeted exclusively health care workers at RBF4MNH facilities and aimed at exploring their experiences with service delivery, their perceptions and interactions with the work environment, and specifically their understanding and response to the implementation of the RBF4MNH Initiative. Rather than being descriptive in nature, this study aimed at unravelling causal pathways between the dimensions of the work environment that were modified by the RBF4MNH Initiative and the subsequent changes observed in health care workers' motivational profile and performance. Adopting qualitative methods allowed us not only to gauge the extent of change produced by the RBF4MNH on motivation and performance but also to explore the pathways through which this change was produced.

To achieve our objective, we conducted a total of twenty-four interviews in 2014 and twenty in 2015. Given that our ambition was to explore responses to, and effects of, the intervention across the range of facilities and health care workers targeted by the RBF4MNH, we applied maximum variation sampling (Patton 2002) to select health care workers employed at intervention facilities. Respondents were purposively selected to represent different levels of care (primary- versus secondary-level facilities), the four different districts, different sexes, differing levels of seniority, different ages and different levels of service within the public sector. This approach to detailed sampling was made possible by the availability of precise information obtained through the structured quantitative health care worker survey. Given high personnel turnover, however, we could reach out to the same health care workers in 2014 and 2015 only in very few cases.

A specific challenge within interviews was the difficulty in eliciting responses on conceptual and abstract themes. We consistently noticed a great willingness to discuss the RBF4MNH intervention, its implementations and its risks and benefits, but we also noted some difficulties when asking health care workers to reflect and describe their source of motivation to conduct the work they do. We encountered this difficulty irrespective of how we structured the interview and approached the conversation, and it can probably be attributed to a combination of two factors. On the one hand, health workers in rural Malawi may not be accustomed to reflecting in such abstract terms on their work. On the other hand, since we collected all information in one single encounter, it may not have been possible for the interviewer (a German psychologist, who had worked in the Malawian health care system and who received training in qualitative interviewing prior to fieldwork, conducted all interviews [in English] with health care workers) to establish a sufficiently trusting relationship to elicit such complex responses.

Qualitative study on health care workers' views on quality of service provision

This third qualitative study adopted a cross-sectional design, with data being collected only once in 2014 with the specific objective of explaining the weaknesses in quality of service provision detected by the structured provider-patient clinical observations. Given that our focus was on unravelling reasons behind apparent discrepancies, specifically completing some procedures, but not others and/or not completing some procedure in spite of needed material and supplies being available, we applied extreme sampling techniques (Patton 2002). Based on the preliminary findings from the structured provider-patient observations, we identified sixteen facilities with either a very high or a very low quality of care score and with either high levels or low levels of discrepancy and interviewed one health care worker at each of these facilities. The sample of health care workers for this study was more restricted since we interviewed only skilled birth attendants (health personnel with a specific training in managing labour and delivery). Since the interview guide addressed specific clinical procedures and looked into the details of how these procedures were carried out, this set of in-depth interviews was carried out by a trained Malawian obstetrician, who for the occasion received additional training in qualitative interviewing.

As with the study on health care workers' motivation and performance, this study also aimed specifically to unravel causal pathways behind health workers' behaviour. By understanding the causal pathways behind carrying out or not carrying out a given clinical procedure, we wished to generate evidence to inform the selection of the indicators to be rewarded by the RBF4MNH Initiative and to inform any subsequent quality improvement intervention.

Qualitative study on policy formulation and implementation

Finally, we conducted a series of semi-structured interviews with policy and implementation stakeholders to analyse the process of policy formulation and implementation, paying close attention to issues pertaining to the introduction of the concept of RBF in Malawi and to fidelity in the implementation of the RBF4MNH Initiative. Our operational definition of fidelity included exploring adoption and adaptation among stakeholders at all levels of the policy and implementation hierarchy, since these are essential elements in determining the success or failure of complex health system interventions.

In line with our overall methodological approach, this study also adopted an emerging design. We had originally envisioned one single round of data collection in 2014, but decided to repeat interviews in late 2015 because the intervention was unexpectedly expanded to include an additional ten EmOC facilities. Thus, in our second round of interviews, we explored both issues related to keeping up and allowing the intervention to mature and issues related to the challenges derived from this sudden scale up.

We conducted a total of twenty-three interviews during the first data collection round and twenty-one during the second data collection round. Respondents included representatives of the funding agencies supporting the RBF4MNH Initiative (KfW and Norway), the implementing partners (the Malawian Ministry of Health Reproductive health unit and the U.K.-based consulting agency Options) and District Management Team Officers. This set of interviews was conducted in English by a physician with public health training and by a psychologist, both having received specific training in qualitative interviewing prior to fieldwork.

OPERATIONAL CHALLENGES IN CONDUCTING OUR QUALITATIVE WORK

All research efforts require great amounts of coordination and management. Conducting a mixed methods impact evaluation, however, is probably particularly challenging, since it entails integrating multiple strains of data collection and analysis in the form of single studies. In this chapter, I have described only the qualitative component of our impact evaluation, but the reader needs to appreciate that alongside these four qualitative studies, we were also engaged in three additional large-scale quantitative data collection efforts.

Reflecting on the key success factors that made it possible for us to collect and analyse this large amount of data within the framework of a four-year period, I immediately think of the close collaboration between the participating institutions, primarily the Institute of Public Health of the University of Heidelberg in Germany and the College of Medicine (University of Malawi) in Malawi, with support from colleagues from Harvard School of Public Health and from the University of Bergen in Norway. We had a large team of researchers, with different sociocultural backgrounds, different levels of seniority and different scientific expertise. The one common trait was our openness towards the group and an intrinsic capacity to smile when confronted with a new methodological challenge and to review one's academic point of view as we moved along. This is what made it possible for me as overall coordinator to move the team from an explanatory towards a triangulation design, allowing everyone to see that qualitative methods of data collection and analysis could play a greater role in impact evaluation than we had originally envisioned.

It is worth noting that accepting that baseline findings clearly pointed to the need for a shift in design was not something easy to accept and internalize immediately for everyone in our team. This difficulty stemmed from two different sets of considerations. On the one side, a shift in design leading to a wider application of qualitative methods implied acquiring new skills and/or further enlarging the original team to include competencies and expertise not originally envisioned as necessary. On the other side, the nature of emerging designs represents a foreign concept for researchers raised primarily in the quantitative tradition of social science research, where decisions on design and sample are made ex ante and not modified *in itinere* (Given 2008). Accepting that our overall approach could be emerging and modifiable as we moved along our impact evaluation required a substantial leap of faith for some researchers in the team.

As noted earlier, increasing the qualitative weight in our impact evaluation entailed recruiting additional researchers to our team and offering everyone involved additional training and continuous support in qualitative methods of data collection and analysis. This point deserves particular attention within the framework of our impact evaluation, since our contractual arrangements included specific provisions towards capacity building. This means that in practice several of our team members were junior researchers working towards their PhDs. The decisions made on a methodological level obviously yielded important implications for their training, since the junior researchers were basically left with no option, but to acquire extensive skills in both quantitative and qualitative methods of data collection and analysis. Although there was backup for these mixed methods approaches within the team, there was a high level of effort required by the junior scientists.

An additional challenge one needs to consider when conducting such complex evaluations, including multiple qualitative longitudinal data collection tools, is that of ensuring non-overlapping samples. This was a real challenge in our case, especially when it came to health care workers, given the limited number of EmOC facilities (33) from which we could draw respondents in the four districts. From a methodological point of view, interviewing the same health care workers using a diverse set of interview guides would not have been problematic. The issue was rather pragmatic, since given the overall shortage in health personnel typical of these settings, it would have been both unfeasible and unethical to require time for multiple interviews from the same health care worker. Thus, we spent an extensive amount of time mapping our samples, to match scientific rigor with feasibility concerns.

CONCLUSION

By reporting on our experience in Malawi, I have illustrated the role and value of including qualitative methods in impact evaluation in the health care sector. The experience reported, both in terms of its achievements and challenges, is not restricted to the evaluation of RBF interventions and can surely serve as an example of how qualitative methods can be used within the framework of the evaluation of complex health system interventions. In our specific case, the benefit of including qualitative methods clearly outweighed the challenges. Qualitative methods were not only fundamental to make sense of the context within which the intervention took place but were also key to measuring and explaining change and causal pathways to change in a way that quantitative methods alone would have never allowed us to do.

ACKNOWLEDGEMENTS

As indicated in the text of this chapter, the work presented was the product of the efforts of many different people. I do not list here the entire research team involved in the impact evaluation but only those who had a specific role in relation to the qualitative studies I described and discussed. Prof. Adamson Muula from the College of Medicine in Malawi was co-PI of the overall impact evaluation and, together with me, coordinated all research efforts, especially in relation to their fieldwork component. Christabel Kambala is the PhD candidate in charge of the qualitative study on women's perceived quality of care. Julia Lohmann is the PhD candidate in charge of the study on health care workers' motivation and performance. Sister Joyce Chika Ezeugo and Dr Brenner were in charge of the qualitative study on discrepancies in quality of health care service provision. Danielle Wilhelm is the PhD candidate in charge of the qualitative study on policy formulation and implementation.

The study described in this chapter was funded by the United States Agency for International Development under Translating Research into Action, Cooperative Agreement No. GHS-A-00-09-00015-00 and by the Royal Norwegian Embassy in Lilongwe and NORAD.

Chapter 18

An assessment of an international declaration on aid effectiveness through qualitative methods at the country level

Melisa Martínez-Álvarez

International declarations are signed with the goal of galvanising efforts towards improving development, and help to concentrate development efforts towards a set of *priority* common goals. They influence global and national health strategies: the period of 2000–2015 was guided by the Millennium Development Goals, and from 2015 to 2030 development strategies will follow the priorities set out by the Sustainable Development Goals. International declarations on development financing, although not health-specific, also have a substantial impact on how the health sector is funded and managed.

Evaluations of these development financing declarations have mainly used quantitative methods to assess progress towards targets (e.g., improvements in the health status of their population and the use of results-based evaluation frameworks) and compare findings across countries (Wood, Betts et al. 2011; Department of Economic and Social Affairs of the United Nations Secretariat 2015). Further, low- and middle-income country annual health sector evaluation frameworks are often guided by international declarations. These frameworks are also quantitative in nature (e.g., in Tanzania and Uganda [Department of Economic and Social Affairs of the United Nations Secretariat 2015; Ministry of Health of the Republic of Uganda 2015]). Less attention has been paid to how international declarations are adopted and interpreted at the country level. This is important because the political, economic and institutional contexts in which these declarations are implemented, how actors interpret the different principles of declarations and the relationships between implementing actors play a key role in determining the success of international declarations (Eyben 2006; Sundewall and Sahlin-Andersson 2006). Qualitative methods are much better suited than quantitative techniques to explore these contextual influences of international declarations on aid effectiveness in health.

The aim of this chapter is to describe how international declarations can be analysed through qualitative methods at the country level, using the example of the implementation of the Paris Declaration on aid effectiveness in the Tanzanian health sector.

DEVELOPMENT ASSISTANCE FOR HEALTH AND THE PARIS DECLARATION ON AID EFFECTIVENESS

Development assistance for health (DAH) flows from high-income countries and private funders to low- and middle-income countries, with the aim of improving the health status of citizens of recipient countries. The amount of DAH globally has increased from $7.2 billion in 1990 to $36.4 billion in 2015 (Institute for Health Metrics and Evaluation 2016). However, there is increasing recognition that inequitable targeting, fragmentation and over-reliance on project-based financing, volatility and inadequate institutional arrangements all limit the effectiveness of DAH (Quartey 2005; Celasun and Walliser 2008; Frot and Santiso 2010; Institute for Health Metrics and Evaluation 2016). It should be noted that increased recognition of the importance of recipient countries in implementing development strategies post the Busan Partnership (2008) has signified a shift from the use of the terms 'aid' to 'development assistance', and 'donors' to 'development partners'. In this chapter the term 'aid effectiveness' is used only when discussing the Paris Declaration; otherwise, 'development assistance' (or 'DAH') is used.

Through a series of high-level meetings (Monterrey [2002], Paris [2005], Accra [2008], Busan [2011] and Mexico City [2014]), the international community has agreed on novel approaches to deliver development assistance and address these shortcomings. Each meeting resulted in a new declaration on aid effectiveness. To date the most important declaration has been the Paris Declaration, where recipient countries and development partners agreed on an approach to aid-giving based on five principles (Organisation for Economic Co-operation and Development 2005):

1. Country ownership over their national development strategies
2. Development partner alignment to national strategies and financial systems
3. Development partner harmonisation and coordination of actions, working in a transparent and collectively efficient manner
4. Management for results
5. Mutual accountability

Reflecting these global priorities, development partners have adopted new modes of cooperation and aid delivery modalities. One such approach is the sector-wide approach (SWAP), which involves a partnership between all development partners working in a particular sector and the partner government (Hutton and Tanner 2004). Although SWAPs are implemented differently in different settings, they are characterized by being led by the partner country, having a single programme and budget framework, and promoting development partner coordination, harmonisation and the use of country systems (Sundewall and Sahlin-Andersson 2006). Although SWAPs predate the Paris Declaration, they promote the same principles of cooperation and are often seen as vehicles to implementing the Paris Declaration's agenda (McNee 2012).

A QUALITATIVE APPROACH TO ASSESSING THE IMPLEMENTATION OF THE PARIS DECLARATION IN THE TANZANIAN HEALTH SECTOR

The aim of this study was to assess whether and how the Tanzanian health SWAP had achieved the principles of the Paris Declaration, using a theoretical framework based on principal-agent theory (Martens, Mummert et al. 2002). The study had five specific objectives:

1. To describe the history and the current structure of the Tanzanian health SWAP policy landscape
2. To develop a set of indicators to measure whether the implementation of the Tanzanian SWAP is consistent with the principles outlined in the Paris Declaration
3. To apply the indicators developed to assess the extent to which aid effectiveness principles have been achieved
4. To explain the achievement of the Paris Declaration through an analysis of institutional factors and relationships between the actors present in the Tanzanian health SWAP using a political economy framework
5. To develop policy recommendations based on the findings for national policy makers implementing SWAPs, development partners and researchers at the national and global level

To achieve these objectives, a mix of qualitative methods was used. In particular, qualitative methods were used to construct a map of health sector management in Tanzania, including budgeting processes, policy strategies and stakeholders involved; to develop and apply a set of indicators to assess the Paris Declaration in the Tanzanian health SWAP; to understand quantitative financing trends and the use of different financing modalities; and to explore the relationships present in the 'aid system'. Some of the indicators developed required the use of quantitative methods, but these are discussed elsewhere (Martinez Alvarez 2014).

Qualitative methods used included document and literature review, in-depth interviews and non-participant observation. The rest of this section describes the study methods, including the reasons for selecting a case study approach. Ethical approval for this study was obtained from the following Institutional Review Boards: London School of Hygiene and Tropical Medicine (UK) (Ref: 6061), Ifakara Health Institute (Tanzania) (Ref: IHI/IRB/No. 22–2011) and National Institute of Medical Research (Tanzania) (Ref: NIMR/HQ/R.8a/Vol.IX/1468).

Using a case study approach to assess the Paris Declaration

A case study approach has been recommended by the World Bank's series on Evaluating Development Effectiveness (White 2005), and has the advantage of providing political, historical and social context. Although there have been concerns about the lack of generalisability and applicability of findings arising from case study research (Yin 2009), they allow for the development of, or contribution to, theory (Green and Thorogood 2009). I selected a case study approach because it allows for the in-depth study of policy responses to factors hindering aid effectiveness.

I chose Tanzania as a case study country because it is one of the top recipients of DAH globally and is heavily dependent on external health funding (which accounted for 40 percent of total health expenditure in 2009 [Ministry of Health and Social Welfare 2012]). In addition, Tanzania has a long history of democratic institutions, is a signatory to all major international declarations on aid effectiveness and (at least on paper) has kept its promises, and has been hailed as a success story in aid (Tripp 2012). In addition, in the Tanzanian health sector, development partners and the government have been working under a sector-wide approach since 1998.

Time period of study

This study involved a two-week pre-fieldwork visit (June 2011) and one year of fieldwork (October 2011–September 2012). Being based in-country allowed me to build the necessary relationships and gain an in-depth understanding of the local context.

The Tanzanian aid landscape underwent important changes between 1998 and 2012, with the adoption of the Paris Declaration, the design of national aid effectiveness and health sector strategies, and the introduction of the health SWAP. It was therefore important to reflect these political events by considering changes in the delivery and use of DAH over time, rather than at a single point.

DATA GENERATION

Document and literature review

I conducted a document review to understand the national and international political context in relation to the implementation of the SWAP. To look for relevant documents, I undertook a search in Eldis, Google and Scholar Google using the following search terms: *Tanzania*, *SWAP*, *health*, *DP*, *development partner* and *basket fund* on their own and in combinations. This was complemented by a search of development partner, Tanzanian government and Tanzanian civil society websites (e.g., Sikika and Twaweza). To identify further documents, I checked the references of selected documents and study participants were also asked to recommend documents. Documents were included if they described the SWAP, domestic and external health financing mechanisms and health policy strategies in Tanzania, were in English and were published in the time period 1995–2012 (from the conception of the SWAP to the time when the search was conducted). Although most documents were in English, some civil society documents were in Swahili and were therefore excluded. All documents were read in full, and coded and analysed as described here.

I undertook a literature review to inform the development of indicators to assess whether the health SWAP had achieved the principles of the Paris Declaration. I searched the Global Health, EconLit and Web of Science databases. In addition, to avoid publication bias, I consulted key websites for grey literature, including Eldis, the OECD and government and development partner websites. The following search terms were used: *aid*, *aid effectiveness*, *health*, *Paris Declaration*, *ownership*, *basket*, *results*, *results-based management*, *harmonisation*, *coordination*, *accountability*, *sector-wide approach* and *SWAP*. Terms were used alone and in combination. To obtain as wide a selection as possible, no restriction was placed on sector or date of publication. Papers in English, Spanish and French (languages readily spoken) were included. Papers were included only if they had a definition of indicators to measure at least one of the Paris Declaration principles. Snowballing was used to find further relevant material by searching references of relevant articles and reports. In total 221 abstracts were reviewed, and 108 papers and reports were identified and included for full text review. The only information extracted was the definition of one of the five Paris Declaration principles and/or the indicators used to assess them.

A final source of documentary evidence was the field notes taken during the year-long fieldwork period and two-week pre-fieldwork visit. Field notes are a useful way of recording what researchers are seeing and feeling, and provide ideas for modification of the data generation and analysis methods (Ritchie and Lewis 2003). In this study field notes recorded informal conversations and interactions, news articles, as well as personal thoughts and reflections on the experiences during fieldwork. I recorded handwritten notes in a notebook (in total I filled three A4-sized notebooks). I took notes on an ad hoc basis, during and after every interview and observation, but also after every event of interest (e.g., an informal conversation). I also kept an electronic archive of all the news articles of interest during the period of study. Field notes helped understand the context, fed into the design of the study tools and assisted with the interpretation of the results.

In-depth interviews

In-depth interviews were conducted to explore health sector stakeholders' perceptions of how the Paris Declaration had been implemented in the Tanzanian health SWAP, including what the Paris principles meant to them, how they felt they should be measured, whether they felt the principles had been achieved and what incentives faced the individuals interviewed as well as their organisations.

Formative research

To design the interview tool and identify key stakeholders I undertook twelve key informant interviews during the initial visit in June 2011 (Table 18.1). Key informants were initially identified through online searches of health SWAP meetings and by contacting the participants in these meetings by email. Further key informants were identified through contact-tracing (asking respondents to suggest relevant stakeholders). Respondents were asked about the structure and management of the health SWAP, important actors and to identify factors that they thought were working well and those that were not. These interviews were highly informative in terms of context, data sources and identification of relevant stakeholders. Key informant interviews were informal and were not recorded so as to generate a better rapport and encourage greater honesty. During interviews, efforts were made to elicit key

Table 18.1. Key informant and in-depth interview participants

Stakeholder type	*Key Informant Interviews June 2011*	*In-depth interviews April–July 2012*
Central government	2	4
Regional and council health management team		8
Development partner	4	7
Non-government	6	3
Total Interviews	**12**	**22**

health policies and documents, identify important areas to investigate within the health SWAP and aid effectiveness, and identify key actors.

The interviews

Two principles were taken into account when designing the definitive interview tool: structure and flexibility (Ritchie and Lewis 2003). The tool was semi-structured. It started with ice-breaker questions on the role of the participant and of their organisation, which were followed by open questions on the Paris Declaration, the SWAP, DAH priorities and institutional relationships between different actors (e.g., the government and development partners). The tool had a set of probing questions under each of these topics to achieve depth (Ritchie and Lewis 2003). For instance, the question 'Do you think donors work under a harmonised approach?' was followed by the probes: 'which donors are harmonised?', 'are there mechanisms for promoting harmonisation?', 'which ones?', 'which are most important/effective?', 'does the SWAP mean donors are more harmonised?'.

Initially, interviewees were sampled purposefully to represent all the main actors in the health sector who are engaged in the health SWAP dialogue. Further participants were identified through contact-tracing of respondents. Four key informants from the preparatory visit were identified as meeting the inclusion criteria and were re-interviewed using the definitive interview tool. The preparatory visit had also revealed the importance of going beyond national-level stakeholders and so one regional health team (mainland Tanzania has twenty-five regional health areas) and two district health teams (known as council health management teams) within it were chosen as case study sites for accessing local stakeholders. The region was selected purposively, based on geographic access and where there were pre-existing research contacts. Within the region, one remote and one accessible district were selected. At the regional and district levels, the criteria for selecting respondents were those who participated in health planning and reporting exercises. Stakeholder access was greatly facilitated by being based at a local research institute (Ifakara Health Institute).

In total, twenty-two in-depth interviews were conducted with representatives from two central government ministries (the Ministry of Health and Social Welfare and the Prime Minister's Office for Regional Administration and Local Government), regional and council health management teams, civil society and development partners (Table 18.1).

The interviews were conducted between April and July 2012. They were conducted face to face to facilitate interaction between the researcher and interviewee (Ritchie and Lewis 2003), in English and lasted for about an hour. The amount of direction and structure in the interviews depended on the behaviour of the respondent. For some respondents, introductory questions such as 'What changes have you observed since you have worked in your role?' would elicit a response that would cover most of the points in the topic guide, and would require only some further probing questions for further explanations of some statements. Other respondents were noticeably less at ease during interviews. In these cases, the interviewer played a more active role, asking questions more precisely and answering frequent requests for clarification of the aims of the research or of a particular question.

Where the participants agreed, interviews were recorded and transcribed. Where participants did not agree, notes were taken during the interview and typed up immediately. Some national participants (particularly from the government) did not agree to be recorded or quoted (in total only eleven interviews out of twenty-two were recorded). This inevitably had an impact on the accuracy of the account of the results. To increase the representation of national voices, the sample size from the central government was increased from two to four and their views were reported in the narrative without quotes.

Non-participant observation

The aim of non-participant observation was threefold: to observe stakeholder behaviour and interactions; to triangulate findings from other sources and to identify, gain access to and develop relationships with key stakeholders who subsequently participated in the in-depth interviews.

Nine meetings were attended and observed. These included development partner coordination meetings, meetings between development partners and the Ministry of Health and Social Welfare, and SWAP meetings, where all actors active in the health sector were present. To minimize influence on the content of the meetings attended, efforts were made to remain 'inconspicuous' to the other participants. This was easier in some of the bigger meetings but harder in meetings where participants sat around a table, or where there were a very small number of foreign participants. Non-participant observation took place throughout the period of fieldwork. During meetings detailed notes were taken of topics discussed and interactions between participants. Notes were typed up immediately.

DATA ANALYSIS

Qualitative analysis takes place through a process in which analytical categories are developed to describe and explain the data (Pope, Ziebland et al. 2000). This process can be undertaken deductively, by applying a set of pre-determined categories to the data, or inductively, where categories 'emerge' from the data (Glaser and Strauss 1967).

I found the framework approach to be the most appropriate method of analysis because it allows for systematic analysis of data with enough flexibility to accommodate inductive and deductive approaches. It has recently been recommended for multidisciplinary mixed methods research (Gale, Heath et al. 2013). The framework approach involves five steps of data analysis, as described next in relation to the analysis of the aid effectiveness data. I use the aid effectiveness principle of mutual accountability (one of the themes emerging from the study) to illustrate how the analysis was conducted. As is usual with framework, data analysis was undertaken once all the data for the study had been collected.

Step 1: familiarisation with the data

Familiarisation with the data was accomplished by reading all the field notes, notes from non-participant observation and interview transcripts (those that were recorded were read while listening to the interview recording, which also allowed for quality-checking of the transcription). This enabled immersion within the data to get an initial feel for the main themes emerging from the study.

Step 2: development of an analytical framework

An analytical framework is a list of the key issues, concepts and themes that can then be applied to index the whole data set (Pope, Ziebland et al. 2000). The analytical framework used here was developed using a mix of deductive and inductive approaches, through a process known as *coding*. A code is a conceptual label applied to a data excerpt (Gale, Heath et al. 2013). The process of developing an analytical framework involves creating a list of codes, which can subsequently be grouped into a coding tree of themes.

An initial analytical framework was developed from the interview topic guide, which included the five principles of the Paris Declaration. Six transcripts were then chosen at random and coded inductively by reading them line by line and identifying emerging codes from the data. The analytical framework was then modified to incorporate new codes that arose from this exercise. This involved both altering the initial codes and adding additional ones. See Figure 18.1 for the analytical framework developed to assess 'mutual accountability'. An example of a code that emerged from the data rather than the initial analytic framework was 'dialogue', which respondents often referred to when discussing the relationships between the government and development partners.

Paris Declaration

Definition
Donors and partners are accountable for development results

Indicator
Number of partner countries that undertake mutual assessments of progress in implementing agreed commitments on aid effectiveness including those in this Declaration.

Analytical framework

Accountability
- Accountability lines – to whom? (all actors including parliamentary commission)
- Accountability processes
- Accountability for what?
- Corruption
- Consequences/enforcing conditionality
- Transparency
- Aid modalities
- DP responsibilities
- Government responsibilities
- Cost effective / value for money
- Other

Thematic matrix

Case	Accountability lines	Accountability process	Accountability for what?	Etc.
Interview 1	Quote summary	Quote summary	Quote summary	
Document 1	Quote summary	Quote summary	Quote summary	
Etc.				

Figure 18.1. Example of analysis of the theme 'mutual accountability'. Courtesy of the author.

Step 3: applying the analytical framework

The analytical framework was applied to code the data (a process known as indexing), including interview transcripts, notes from meetings and interviews, and documents. Sometimes a single data excerpt was allocated multiple codes. Codes were recorded using NVivo software. During this process, the analytical framework was further refined to incorporate any additional emerging themes. In this way, several iterations of indexing took place, until no further themes arose and all the data had been indexed.

Step 4: charting

The next step was to chart the coded data into a 'framework matrix' using NVivo. One matrix framework was created for every key theme (a 'thematic matrix'). (See Figure 18.1 for an illustration of the thematic matrix developed to assess mutual accountability.) Thematic matrices are essentially tables plotting cases (e.g., interview transcripts, documents, notes, in the rows) against themes (columns). Each cell contains all the data coded under a particular theme. Rather than using the original data, however, the content of each cell was summarized to help manage and 'reduce' the amount of data (Gale, Heath et al. 2013). To avoid over-summarising, there was regular cross-checking between the data and the summarized categories.

Step 5: mapping and interpretation

In this final step of data analysis the thematic matrices were used to define and categorize concepts and identify relationships between different themes to provide explanatory accounts of the findings (Pope, Ziebland et al. 2000). Thematic matrices were extracted to Excel for ease of use, and explored by reading the data in the thematic matrices to identify broader themes. During this process of categorisation the original data were often re-visited to ensure the broader themes were representative of data they were based on.

The final part of the analysis involved mapping and interpretation to explore the relationships between the broader themes generated. To do this, cases were first grouped into sub-groups (e.g., the different respondents were categorized as development partner, government and non-government). Then, associations between the different broader themes were tested and explored. When searching for explanations, original transcripts and synthesized data were reviewed, and potential associations were drawn into mind-maps and spider diagrams. Emerging hypotheses were then contrasted with theory and other empirical studies. For instance, themes mapping the incentives of individuals and the institutional set-up of the SWAP helped explain the apparent inability of development partners to hold the government to account.

This process sometimes resulted in important changes to the study. For instance, it was by moving between the data and theory that I found that institutional and political factors were key in explaining the extent to which the Paris Declaration was achieved. This in turn led to the modification of the initial principal-agent framework to incorporate elements from policy analysis.

VALIDITY AND RELIABILITY

Validity is the precision and correctness of the research (Ritchie and Lewis 2003), or the extent to which an account accurately represents the social phenomena to which it refers (Hammersley 1990). Two approaches were undertaken to maximize validity. First, using a constant comparative method helped ensure the internal validity (Silverman 2010). This approach tests hypotheses from one part of the data on the others (first within a case, then across cases in the same group and finally across different groups). Second, care was taken to represent views across the different stakeholders, particularly when these differed. This was done through a process known as deviant case analysis (Silverman 2013), which involved exploring cases that both fitted and contradicted emerging patterns and explanations. Deviant cases were always reported, and sometimes further explorations of their views led to explanatory accounts in themselves. This was the case for one particular development partner, whose answers consistently disagreed with all the other development partners, and often with the Tanzanian government. However, the answers provided by this deviant case, together with policy documents and non-government respondent views, were pivotal in shedding light on certain issues, such as the different levels of dialogue between development partners and the Tanzanian government. In addition, there were some limitations in the availability of documentary data, as often annual reports were not available for every year, and in the reliability and accuracy of documents, such as minutes from meetings. Wherever possible, validity was cross-checked during interviews and non-participant observation, although it was more difficult to verify older documents as stakeholders were not able to recall beyond a certain period.

Reliability refers to the replicability of research findings (Ritchie and Lewis 2003; Green and Thorogood 2009). There are debates in the literature regarding the possibility of replicating qualitative work, given its dynamic nature and the role of the researcher's interpretations in influencing the results (Hammersley 1992). Nevertheless, several steps were taken during fieldwork and analysis to maximize the reliability of the study. During fieldwork, notes taken during non-participant observation and interviews were immediately typed up (or as soon as was feasibly possible) to ensure accuracy. Each interview transcript was reviewed to ensure the accuracy of the transcription. To check the reliability of the analytical framework, a colleague co-coded one transcript; any disagreements were discussed and incorporated into the coding framework where appropriate. Finally, care was taken to select a representative sample of actors active in the health SWAP dialogue.

REFLEXIVITY

The researcher can influence the outcomes of research both through his/her background and beliefs. I conducted all the interviews myself. I am white, female and younger than all the people who took part in the study. During the time of fieldwork I was affiliated with the London School of Hygiene and Tropical Medicine and the Ifakara Health Institute. This had different effects on different study participants. For those of Tanzanian origin, being foreign raised a level of distrust about what would happen to the data and the purposes of the research. This affected my ability to collect quantitative data as well as to attend meetings and to elicit data through interviews. Being affiliated with a local institution opened doors into the government, but many participants still viewed me as a development partner representative and, as a result, may have felt less comfortable sharing information. My relative youth meant I was perceived by non-Tanzanian stakeholders as inexperienced but also less threatening. Aside from the polite greetings, all communication related to the research took place in English. All research participants spoke fluent English; however, it may have had an influence on how comfortable they were in participating in the research and the level of trust they had on me as the researcher. My background (I have an undergraduate degree in biology and a master's degree in control of infectious diseases) and ideology (my ethical and political beliefs include social justice and human rights, including access to health care and good standard living conditions) may have also had an influence on the interpretation of results and attitude towards study participants. Further, the field notes show an increasingly pessimistic tone as the fieldwork went on, reflecting feelings of disappointment with the 'aid world' and human desire and ability to make a positive contribution to development, which was reflected in early drafts of the results.

CONCLUSION

The results of this study are presented elsewhere (Martinez Alvarez 2014). The study found that using qualitative methods added an immensely valuable dimension to a topic that has been studied from a predominantly quantitative lens. Three key contributions of qualitative methods to the study can be highlighted.

First, qualitative methods allow for a flexible research approach, which is well suited to analysing complex phenomena. This study found that some government stakeholders not directly working for the Ministry of Health were very influential in decisions affecting the size and targeting of the health sector budget. It was possible to identify these stakeholders through conducting a preliminary visit, contact-tracing through interviews, document review and non-participant observation. This led to the modification of fieldwork and analysis plans to include these stakeholders, which had a profound and positive impact on the results, by increasing the depth of understanding of the budgeting process and power structures within the Tanzanian government.

Second, qualitative methods allowed a broader evaluation of international declarations beyond their (quantitative) pre-designed targets. Taking into consideration the views of national-level stakeholders in charge of implementing the strategies agreed upon globally added an important dimension to understanding the socio-political context in which these declarations are implemented. This was particularly important in the evaluation of the Paris Declaration as the definitions of the five principles are rather vague and open to interpretation but will also be relevant for other international declarations.

Third, it was important to assess the extent to which the Paris Declaration principles had been achieved through qualitative indicators. Quantitative methods had previously been found to be restrictive in evaluating the Paris Declaration (Martini, Mongo et al. 2012). This study found the Paris Declaration and the declarations that succeeded it emphasize having certain processes in place. For instance, the evaluation of the Paris Declaration bases its assessment of the principle of managing for results quantitatively according to whether or not the recipient country has a performance assessment framework in place (Organisation for Economic Co-operation and Development

2008). The evaluation of the Paris Declaration does not explore whether the performance assessment framework is used to assess progress, or whether its use results in development partners and governments adopting an approach to development underlined by managing for results

Evaluating the Paris Declaration qualitatively in Tanzania involved extensive efforts to access all the relevant stakeholders and documents. Limitations were encountered in terms of willingness to participate, to be recorded and availability of documents. Nevertheless, these methods provided valuable insights to understanding the implementation of the Paris principles at the country level. In addition, direct observation of processes was immensely valuable to understand the relationships and interactions between the Tanzanian government and development partners. Similarly, the process of analysis was iterative and time-consuming, but the modification of the analytical and theoretical frameworks was key to understanding the inadequacy to the local context of some of the processes established in response to the Paris Declaration.

Two main recommendations arise from this study. More country-based qualitative evaluations of international declarations should be undertaken, and global assessments of international declarations should incorporate open questions to enable national stakeholders to contribute their perceptions.

ACKNOWLEDGEMENTS

This work would not have been possible without the help of all the participants, my supervisors Anna Vassall, Josephine Borghi and Arnab Acharya, my advisor Neil Spicer. Special thanks to Josephine Borghi for kindly reviewing this chapter.

This work was funded by the UK Economic and Social Research Council.

Chapter 19

Using cost-effectiveness evidence in making priority gradings: The case of the Swedish National Guidelines for heart diseases

Nathalie Eckard and Ann-Charlotte Nedlund

Traditionally, health economics, based on quantitative research methods, is used to present and compile information on cost-effectiveness, often provided as decision support. However, this methodological approach does not tell us how cost-effectiveness evidence is considered and actually used when making decisions or generating policies. In this chapter we present a study that aimed to explore *how* health economics, in particular, evidence about cost-effectiveness, was *actually* used in a policy-making process.

The policy-making process concerned the National Guidelines for heart diseases in Sweden. The National Guidelines are key national policy documents issued by the National Board of Health and Welfare (NBHW) following the notion of evidence-based policy aiming to govern and inform health care actors, from political, administrative to clinical levels, in explicit prioritisation. Besides giving clinical guidance in the practitioners' meeting with the patients, the Swedish National Guidelines also give guidance to decision-makers on how to allocate resources within different areas (see http://www.socialstyrelsen.se/nationalguidelines/abouttheguidelines). Thus, the Guidelines have a broader perspective, include economic aspects and consist of recommendations in the form of priority gradings (Grip, Lindahl et al. 2011).

In this study we followed the Prioritising Group (PG) that was involved in the production of the policy document 'National Guidelines for Heart Diseases'. A qualitative methodology was used to explore the use of evidence in the process of producing the policy document for health care policy making. A specific focus was to determine in what situations economic arguments impacted the reasoning behind the priority grading made by the PG.

In this chapter we will first give a brief background to the programme of the National Guidelines in the context of priority setting and resource allocation more broadly. We will then discuss the context and actors involved in making priority gradings, the methods used, research findings and implications for health economics.

THE NATIONAL GUIDELINES AND PRIORITISATION

Before describing the work with the National Guidelines we need to situate the research in its context; this is an important part of qualitative study since it helps the reader to understand the interpretations made by the researchers. The NBHW, a government agency in Sweden under the Ministry of Health and Social Affairs, is responsible for producing the National Guidelines. Their work has been influenced by that of the National Institute for Health and Care Excellence (NICE) in the UK (Hutton and Brown 2002; Nixon, Phipps et al. 2002; Dakin, Devlin et al. 2015). Through the National Guidelines, the NBHW aims to support explicit priority setting in health care, as well as letting ethical considerations influence the recommendations. The goal of the Guidelines is to ensure that patients receive high-quality medical care within the context of the need to allocate scarce resources. According to Swedish law, health care should be offered on equal terms, effective, evidence-based, patient-focused and secure (Ministry of Health and Social Affairs 1982). When allocating resources and making prioritisation decisions in health care three ethical principles, the so-called 'ethical platform', are ruled into law (Ministry of Health and Social Affairs 1982) and have to be followed in a hierarchical order:

Human dignity principle: All individuals have equal value and rights regardless of their personal characteristics and social position.
Needs and solidarity principle: Healthcare resources should be allocated according to need. Those with greater healthcare need should be prioritised.
Cost-effectiveness principle: Resources should be used in the most effective way without neglecting fundamental duties to improve health and quality of life (QoL) aiming at a reasonable relation between cost and effect (Ministry of Health and Welfare 1997).

These three principles represent the basis for how priorities should be set, and their influence permeates the National Guidelines. To date, there are National Guidelines for nine different disease areas, including stroke care, diabetes care and musculoskeletal diseases. The National Guidelines for heart diseases were among the first to be published in 2004. They were substantially revised in 2008 and have been updated since.

One criterion used by the NBHW for choosing disease areas is that they should cover large groups of patients with a serious chronic illness that makes a claim on society's resources.

THE PRODUCTION OF GUIDELINES

Once the NBHW have decided to work on a new guideline, several groups of qualified experts, both medical and health-economic groups, are involved in the process of producing the National Guideline. The process of developing the policy document consists of two steps. The first step involves proposing pairs of medical conditions and interventions, denoted as the prioritisation objects (POs). The POs are chosen by the experts to give guidance in those specific situations in clinical practice where the need for guidance is the greatest; the aim is to focus on typical cases, representing large volumes and/or controversial areas where there are differences in accepted practice and/or new expensive treatments or uncertainty. The medical and health-economic groups are responsible for conducting systematic literature searches, reviewing and compiling the current available scientific knowledge for each PO (Socialstyrelsen 2008a). The second step in the production of the National Guidelines involves the PGs. There are separate PGs for each National Guideline, always multi-professional in composition. The PG is responsible for making a priority grading, that is, a recommendation for each PO. The PG work process involves being informed on the compiled evidence provided by the group of experts. The material includes information about cost-effectiveness for each PO. In the case, here, of National Guidelines for heart diseases, the PG comprised twenty-one experts in the clinical topic including a health economist and an ethicist. Physicians were in the majority; for example, cardiologists, thoracic surgeons and clinical physiologists and other stakeholders such as general practitioners, nurses and physiotherapists were also represented. Among other information, the PG thus had access to compiled information about the cost-effectiveness of interventions, or had information that cost-effectiveness evidence was not available. The evidence was provided in the form of a worksheet, which included a box specifically for cost-effectiveness evidence; a lack of information in this box meant that there was no cost-effectiveness information to be presented (see Figure 19.1).

Once information is available, a consensus process is used to grade each PO on a scale ranging from 1 to 10, with 1 denoting the highest priority intervention and 10 denoting the lowest. Certain medical conditions could be given higher priority grading, that is, allocated more resources than others, depending on the seriousness of the medical condition. In general, a low ranking reflects insufficient scientific evidence about effectiveness, often at perceived high cost (Eckard, Janzon et al. 2014).

In our project, the focus was on how the PG used economic information about cost-effectiveness when prioritising in the case study of Swedish National Guidelines for heart diseases. The National Guidelines represent a policy document that systematically incorporates research evidence, both clinical and economic, into policies. We were interested in exploring and

Medical condition *Intervention*	Severity of the condition	Effect of intervention	Evidence of effect	Cost per LY/ QALY gained	Health economic evidence	Ranking
1	2A			2B		3

1 Medical conditions and interventions are identified and paired, forming prioritisation objects (POs). The POs should be clinically relevant and possibly limited, focusing on typical cases, representing large volumes as well as controversial areas where there are differences in medical praxis.
2A Medical experts review and compile current scientific knowledge of the severity of the condition, effect of intervention and evidence of effect.
2B The health economic experts review and compile current scientific knowledge of cost-effectiveness, integrated in the medical review.
3 The PG produces a recommendation or priority grading for each PO based on available evidence provided by the experts. The priority gradings are ranked on a scale from 1 to 10 for each medical condition and intervention.

Figure 19.1. Schematic description of the work process for the National Guidelines. Courtesy of the authors. Using information from Socialstyrelsen 2008b.

understanding the process of policy, and how policy workers actually handled and made sense of various forms of evidence and values, as well as how they came to agreements in the ambiguous and uncertain situation of making priority grading. In other words, we were interested in the practice of producing evidence-based policies in a national health care context. We regard policy not simply as an outcome but as a process, both collaborative and interactional. Policy work involves all actors involved in the creation of policy, and policy workers thus refer to these actors (Nedlund 2012). The case serves as an example of being able to follow the dynamic and non-linear process of producing, compiling and presenting the underlying (cost-effectiveness) evidence. This evidence would later be used by decision makers, health care actors, from political, administrative to clinical levels, in explicit prioritisation situations.

RESEARCH DESIGN: OBSERVATIONS AND IN-DEPTH INTERVIEWING

The study design consisted of observations and interviews. The design was exploratory since the aim was to provide knowledge about how and why the PG used the underlying evidence to produce recommendations (priority gradings) and how collective agreement arose in producing the policy document. An exploratory study is used in areas where little is known or if the key objective is to understand how participants' conceptions or values emerge through their speech and their narrative (Ritchie and Lewis 2003). The aim of the study was to explore both how economic evaluations matter and are used in actual policy-making and how the PG reached a collective agreement. Consequently, both observations of the PG work process and interviewing were used to fully understand the context of the group's behaviour, as well as their individual views (Esterberg 2002). Observation involves the systematic and detailed observation and recording of what people say and do. Observations are useful in developing a descriptive 'picture' of a process, that is, a course of events during a time period. Interviews alongside the observations are valuable for gaining insight into the perceptions and values of the informants by using their own language as a way of understanding and giving meaning (Gillman 2000; Ritchie and Lewis 2003).

A decision had to be made about which elements of the process to observe. It was decided to follow the work of the PG, rather than the experts who provide decision support to the PG, as decisions about priorities are made by the PG rather than the experts. It is interesting to note, however, that the work described in Chapter 13 by Husbands et al., who followed the process of model development, would be more akin to this earlier stage of exploring the development of the supporting evidence for decision making. The importance of being able to access the PG in conducting this work cannot be over-emphasized, not least since the work of producing this type of guideline is commonly highly sensitive, and this is a key aspect of conducting this type of exploratory research.

The design of the research was to use observation and interview methods iteratively, to supplement each other in explaining how participants in the PG made sense of the prioritisation process, generated reasoned arguments and used these arguments to come to agreement. Documents associated with the PG meetings, including information on the formal task of the PG, the clinical and health-economic evidence used as decision support and the NBHW organisation, were also read as background material, though not analysed in depth.

Data generation

Observations were conducted in the period 2006 to 2008, by one of the authors (NE) during all PG meetings related to the development of the National Guidelines for heart diseases. All members of the PG were informed about the study and gave their consent. Eleven full-day PG meetings were held over the course of the work process, of which three meetings were of two days. Field notes were taken during all the meetings, which were not audio-recorded. Field notes included a description of the course of events, comprising information about where people sat, who said what, who appeared to lead discussion, tensions arising and so on.

The data were not selected or categorized during the observations. The field notes taken from the observations were transcribed the same day or the day after the meeting, ready for further data analysis.

The face-to-face interviews were conducted by NE in 2009 with PG members. The sample for the interviews was strategically selected, with the help of a senior researcher, in an attempt to achieve diversity, to achieve broad representative coverage, including geographic distribution, and to ensure that various clinical specialties were represented. The health economist was not included in the sample, as the primary research question of interest was how the policy-making group (non-economists), in this case the PG, used available economic evidence that was not in their field of expertise.

A consideration, before conducting the interviews, concerned when to conduct the interviews so as not to disturb the course of events in the work process. The research group decided that the interviews should be conducted after the PG had finished the work process within the group and following the period of observation. All informants were thus approached after the PG had completed their work, so as not to disturb or influence the course of events during the work process of producing the National Guidelines.

An email was sent to each member separately with general information on the overall aim of the study, the procedures of the research project and why they were being contacted, and the value of their participation. The information contained contact details and the voluntary nature of participation, with information about the right to withdraw from the study at any time. Information was also provided that quotes would be displayed in a manner that minimized the risk of identification, and that data would be treated confidentially. Each interview began with a verbal description of the study and a recapitulation of the information previously sent by email. Informed consent, assurances of confidentiality and the consequences of how the collected information would be used were obtained from all the participants before conducting the interviews.

An interview guide was designed with key questions against the background of the data generated from the observations. An interview guide that contained open-ended questions was chosen covering specific topics to explore particularly views about the policy-making process and perceptions of the role of cost-effectiveness evidence. The specific topics addressed during the interviews were questions regarding the use of cost-effectiveness evidence, what information and evidence was available and how these were made sense of and assessed during the group's deliberations. Further topics regarding what worked/did not work in coming to collective agreement and what happened if another member in the PG had an opposing opinion were also of interest. The interview guide was tested on one informant to establish whether it would work or not and a few minor modifications made.

Potential follow-up questions were also specified, which made the interview more dynamic (Kvale and Brinkmann 2009). The topic guide thus contained questions regarding issues concerning what happened if the PG members had divergent and conflicting views, the way in which the group handled the practical tensions of coming to agreement and the ambiguity of working within an evidence-based policy framework. Each interview took between one and two hours.

As observations were part of data collection, the key researcher had access to the PG meetings during the course of their deliberation and thus had access to sensitive data material. A few informants disclosed information and specifically asked that it would not be shared, and at the end of the interview assurances were given that the case study was to reflect the decisions and deliberations made and that the aim was to reflect the PG as a whole, being as representative as possible. After the interview, NE also gave each participant a more detailed description of the study aims and plans, explaining how the interview would be analysed and how the information would be reported. The informants were also assured that their statements would be used for research purposes only and treated confidentially in all dissemination.

Data collection was continued until 'data saturation' or point of no new insights was perceived to be obtained from expanding the sample further (Ritchie and Lewis 2003). This was achieved after nine interviews, given the preceding observations.

Data analyses

Traditionally, quantitative research methods are used in the field of health economics, to present and compile information on cost-effectiveness often provided as decision support. However, the aim of this project was to explore the process of producing the guideline documents, that is, not only how evidence is presented but also how it is communicated, interpreted and used by decision makers in general. A mixed methods approach seemed appropriate, as 'Rather than thinking of qualitative and quantitative research as incompatible, they should be seen as complementary' (Malterud 2001, p. 483). Specific topics were addressed during the interviews regarding the use of cost-effectiveness evidence as decision support in the PG work process. Three main categories evolved during the course of the data analysis to address the primary interest of research. The focus was on how the PG handled the evidence, what evidence was available and whether it was actually used and accepted by the members of the group. Understanding of the explicit use of cost-effectiveness evidence and specific situations in which it mattered also evolved during the data analysis. The interest was not in quantifying the level of use of cost-effectiveness evidence; rather, it was to explore the inclusion of cost-effectiveness evidence as a basis for priority gradings.

All interviews were transcribed verbatim for further analysis. Thematic content analyses were carried out, according to the common practice of interpretation of content, using an inductive approach (Graneheim and Lundman 2004). Qualitative research is often viewed as predominately inductive, but both deduction and induction may be involved at different stages of the qualitative research process. Analytic induction involves an iterative process of defining a problem, then formulating and testing a hypothesis, and redefining the problem until all cases fit. Induction looks for patterns and associations derived from observations of the world. In practice, abduction is often used in case-study-based research processes. Abduction is used as a reflexive methodology and has its point of departure in an empirical basis, like induction, though it does not reject theoretical preconceptions (Alvesson and Sköldberg 2009); the empirical data is adjusted and refined.

The interviews were read in their entirety several times to get a sense of the whole, predominantly by the key researcher, though the first interview was analysed together with a senior researcher. A senior researcher was present throughout the whole analytical process reading excerpts from the interviews. Thereafter, sentences which seemed important for the research questions were extracted, not using a specific software package, but condensing the material onto spreadsheets. The purpose of the analysis was to condense the content while preserving the core and still mirror the content of the interviews. Thus, the primary research questions formed an initial structure for the categorising of research evidence. Throughout the process of data collection, analysis patterns and recurrent topics, themes and sub-themes were identified. Early frameworks and concepts were treated as tentative and were repeatedly refined as new and existing data were analysed. As the aim of the study was exploratory, several possible suggestions for papers emerged during the course of the analysis; the challenge was to frame the abundance of data. We chose to present two papers based on the data set. The two data analyses were conducted separately, covering different areas.

The main focus of the first paper was to explore the practice of evidence-based policy and to provide knowledge about how workers handled and made sense of various forms of evidence and values, and how they came to collective agreement in producing the National Guidelines. In this analysis a combination of deduction and induction was used. We had a theoretical framework but were open in our analysis for the empirical findings to 'speak to us' in a dynamic process. The categories focused on the process of arriving at collective agreement and two main categories evolved during the course of the analyses which related to (collective) group-facilitating activities and what the PG actually did to move the process forward and reach the agreement by resolving practical tensions and avoiding deadlock in the deliberations.

The main focus of the second paper was to explore how economic evaluations matter and are used in actual decision making. The categories that evolved focused on how the PG handled evidence, what evidence was available and whether it was actually used.

Finally, similarities and differences between the data, in both the observations and the interviews, were compared with other sections, in order not to use overlapping categories, and checked to confirm whether different perspectives had been ignored. Interpretations were checked and excerpts of text from the interviews were also read by a senior researcher. Data were presented with the support of informants' quotes as it is important to be as close as possible to the expressions by the informants, to make the study more trustworthy and to enhance the quality of the research.

Preconceptions as a researcher, and ethical considerations

The choice of methods will be affected by a researcher's epistemological orientation and his or her views on different methods for investigating the central phenomena under study (Ritchie and Lewis 2003). A researcher's background and position will also affect what he or she chooses to investigate. The preconceptions of a researcher thus affect the angle of the investigation, the choice of appropriate methods, the consideration of findings and communication of the conclusions (Malterud 2001). However, it is important to point out that preconceptions are not the same as bias unless, of course, the researcher fails to mention them (Malterud 2001). As the key researcher had already made the observations prior to interviewing, this influenced the design of the interviews. Being familiar with the PG through the observations also gave the researcher some preconceptions about access to individual members, but there was an awareness of the responsibility to reflect the group as a whole. Other preconceptions also arose from the key researcher's role as a health economist with a particular interest in the use of cost-effectiveness evidence in decision making. This influence was reduced in part by the choice to present the empirical material, not only from an economic perspective but also in relationship to the policy process as a whole.

Ethical issues were considered and reflected upon throughout the course of the study analyses. Established research ethics practice and ethical guidelines concerning informed consent, assurances of confidentiality and the consequences of how the collected information would be used were followed (Vetenskapsrådet 2002; Ritchie and Lewis 2003; Kvale and Brinkmann 2009). Informed consent was obtained from participants, but one reflection from the research was that achieving truly informed consent might pose difficulties as the nature of the study was exploratory and the researcher could have little advance knowledge of how the interviews and observations would proceed (Kvale and Brinkmann 2009). Throughout the course of the data analysis, consideration was given to how the statements and quotes were displayed to minimize the risk of identification. The informants were assured that their statements would be treated confidentially in all dissemination. The informants not only had the right to withdraw from the study at any time but also had the right to confidentiality, implying that possible identification through their comments should be eliminated.

FINDINGS AND DISCUSSION

Several themes were identified investigating how the PG used cost-effectiveness evidence in making priority gradings (Eckard, Janzon et al. 2014). These were (a) accessibility (available cost-effectiveness evidence and level of understanding), (b) acceptability (reliance and faith placed in the evidence) and (c) use of cost-effectiveness evidence to form priority gradings (Table 19.1).

Cost-effectiveness evidence was accessed, in condensed text form and verbally, through the health economist present at the PG meetings. The involvement of a health economist on the PG reinforced the notion that health economics was perceived as important throughout the group's work. The study supported the idea that health care policy makers at the national level have accepted the use of cost-effectiveness in their policy-making process. Examples were also given of situations when cost-effectiveness evidence impacted priority gradings made and was used in the PG deliberations. Cost-effectiveness evidence did not seem, however, to be used to support decisions in the majority of cases. The priority gradings made by the PG were based on the severity of the disease and clinical effectiveness as well as cost-effectiveness evidence.

When asked to reflect on the use of cost-effectiveness evidence when making priority gradings, a majority of informants had difficulty in isolating the cost-effectiveness evidence from rest of the collected evidence base.

Table 19.1. Identified themes for the use of cost-effectiveness evidence in priority gradings

Accessibility	Available cost-effectiveness evidence to inform priority gradings Level of understanding
Acceptability	Reliance on available evidence Balancing available evidence
Use of cost-effectiveness evidence	Dichotomisation Adjusting priority gradings

Most of the gradings were primarily based on clinical, rather than economic, evidence, as the latter was often lacking. An observation made was that economic evidence played a role in cases of ambiguity and uncertainty, that is, when the PG had difficulty in reaching agreement, and became part of the PG deliberations as a way of avoiding blocks in the discussion, forming a structure for further discussions. Many informants pointed out that they had doubts about using the evidence base when it was weak, although they had to take a position to be able to make priority gradings. The findings suggested that the PG tended to award either a high or a low grading. Of the 300 POs only 31 were ranked as 5 or 6 (the middle rankings). Dichotomising the POs in terms of favouring the medical condition and intervention (high rankings, 1 to 4), or not favouring the treatments (low rankings, 7 to 10), appeared to be used as a solution in making priority gradings.

The observations show that economic arguments were most often used after a preliminary ranking decision had been made that favoured or did not favour the treatment, that is, dichotomising the priority gradings. A priority grading of 10 indicated that a PO was used as an exception in medical praxis and only in cases of affordability. The PG's deliberations were adjourned several times in the course of the work, and significant time was spent considering the 'signal value' of the priority grades.

Even if economic arguments are significant, research has shown that the expected benefits and risks of a treatment are the most important factors in making priority gradings (Singer, Martin et al. 2000). Other studies have reported several important bases for drug priority setting, and no single basis dominated in reaching priority gradings (Hasman, McIntosh et al. 2008). The findings of our study verify the notion that cost-effectiveness evidence is not challenged to the same extent as clinical evidence and that greater weight is given to clinical effectiveness. Economic evidence should thus be viewed as part of the evidence-based knowledge 'package'. The use of cost-effectiveness evidence represented one of many factors that play a part in health policy making.

The research findings suggested that affordability was seen as a pressing issue, often at the core of the PG's deliberations, and in that sense was associated with 'something negative' prior to the work process. According to the informants, the term 'health economics' had undergone a change and was now associated with a broader mind-set that involved producing priority gradings by weighing the evidence and considering cost-effectiveness evidence. The linear and simplistic goal of arriving at collective agreement is presented as an ideal for how to work with evidence-based policy. There is, however, a need to recognize the contextual elements in policy making, and highlight institutional factors and incentives for employing use of cost-effectiveness analyses in policy making (Williams 2013). In practice, all steps involve negotiations and collective sense-making (Nedlund and Garpenby 2014): when evidence is produced; when evidence-informed guidelines in the form of policy documents are produced; and when these guidelines are interpreted and used in practice.

CONCLUSION

In this chapter we have presented and discussed the process of using qualitative research methodology to explore and understand the process of policy. The case study explored how policy workers handled and made sense of various forms of evidence and values, and how they came to agreement in the ambiguous and uncertain situation of making priority gradings. This case study addressed the use of cost-effectiveness evidence in the context of setting National Guidelines for heart diseases in Sweden, and it contributes to a growing body of knowledge about how cost-effectiveness evidence is used in actual policy making, much of it based on qualitative data (Williams and Bryan 2007; Eddama and Coast 2008; Eddama and Coast 2009; Eckard, Janzon et al. 2014; Eckard 2016). Having access to the PG and their deliberations helped to understand phenomena around how policy workers reach agreement and use economic evaluation evidence in producing recommendations. This could not have been done without the use of qualitative research methods. The findings showed the various ways in which the use of cost-effectiveness evidence played a vital role in cases of ambiguity and uncertainty. These included cases when the PG had difficulty in reaching agreement, those which involved minimising 'blocks' in the PG's deliberation when the overall evidence base was weak, and those which involved the introduction of new expensive medical technologies. Answers to these 'how' and 'why' questions would not have been revealed without the use of in-depth observational and interview techniques.

ACKNOWLEDGEMENTS

We thank the National Board of Health and Welfare for granting us access to meetings.

Chapter 20

Contributions of qualitative methods to the study of priority setting and resource allocation in health care

Neale Smith

In health care, by no means uniquely, potential demand for spending inevitably exceeds available funds. Consequently, priority setting and resource allocation are key functions which health sector managers and providers must fulfil. Research in this field is burgeoning, including studies aimed directly at improving practice, and projects that aim to better understand the nature of priority setting and the factors which affect such practices. This chapter considers the role of qualitative methods in priority setting research.

The chapter provides an overview of the qualitative research landscape, and examples and practical suggestions as to how qualitative methods might be applied in research on health care priority setting. These comments are explicitly rooted in the methodological literature. This issue has previously been considered from a largely conceptual perspective (Smith, Mitton et al. 2009) – here the goal is to offer some concrete examples of the value, and challenges, of employing qualitative approach(es).

HEALTH CARE PRIORITY SETTING AND RESOURCE ALLOCATION RESEARCH

First, definitions. Kenny and Joffres argue that 'while priority setting and resource allocation are often conflated, they are distinct but related process' (Kenny and Joffres 2008, p. 146). Priorities are areas or issues upon which the organisation feels it most pressing to act. The choice of these areas is priority setting, or prioritisation. Sometimes priorities can be tackled with only minor implications for organisational budgets, but more often what is truly important is revealed when resources are allocated. Recognising that resources are inevitably limited relative to demand, this process is sometimes called rationing, which draws attention to the fact that some potential beneficiaries of services cannot receive them. Changing the mix among formal activities can lead to disinvestment, meaning to various people anything from a reduction in the relative rate of growth of a program, to its complete termination (Williams, Robinson et al. 2012). For convenience, we use the umbrella term 'priority setting and resource allocation', or PSRA, throughout this chapter to refer to all of these concepts.

PSRA is conducted and studied at micro-, meso- and macro-levels (Kapiriri, Norheim et al. 2007). The micro-level refers to what is also known as clinical or bedside rationing, for instance, in distributing the scarce supply of donor organs (Coombes and Trotter 2005) or the scarce supply of funding for morbid obesity surgery (Owen-Smith, Donovan et al. 2015). The boundaries of meso- and macro- are occasionally blurred in the literature; here we employ them as follows. Meso- is about allocation between programs and portfolios within a health ministry, service delivery organisation or sub-component of such (Mitton, Patten et al. 2003; Dionne, Mitton et al. 2009); macro- is about allocation at the system level. This can include allocation between health and other social determinants of health, or even non-health purposes; while rare, Mooney et al. allude to instances where this has been pursued in the context of aboriginal health (Mooney, Jan et al. 2002).

PSRA is largely an applied or practical field interested in what happens in the real world. We study it with the aim of helping it improve in practice. It may be helpful to distinguish between research 'for' priority setting and research 'on' priority setting. That is, some research, often conducted in partnership with decision making, is explicitly aimed at making priority setting better. The full gamut of quality improvement, evaluation and research can be brought to bear here (Lowe and Cook 2012). Then, there is research aimed at learning more abstractly about the nature of priority setting and resource allocation in the health sector. Examples may include learning about the value placed on different services by both members of the public and other stakeholders, as an input to PSRA (Coast 2001b); values held by policy makers, providers and the public can be compared (Lees, Scott et al. 2002; Rosén and Karlberg 2002). Academics have designed and tested approaches to public engagement in priority setting, for example, through deliberative forums (Abelson, Eyles et al. 2003; Menon and Stafinski 2008). They have also investigated issues around how priority setting happens in practice (Coast 2001a; Bryan, Williams et al. 2007; Eddama and Coast 2009). However, even such work ultimately is aimed at supporting real-world improvements. Thus, research for and research on should be read as tendencies rather than sharp dichotomies or reflective of an inherent academic-practice divide.

It seems generally recognized that PSRA is a management practice (Donaldson, Bate et al. 2008) that relies upon a variety of forms of evidence. That is, while economic evidence is an important contributor to informed decision making, other factors are influential too. In studying PSRA, then, researchers draw on contributions from fields like ethics and political science/policy as well as economics; other social science disciplines like sociology, anthropology or organisational psychology also offer relevant insights. Thus it can be characterized as an inter- or multi-disciplinary field with access to a wide array of methods and approaches

So, what kinds of research questions are asked about PSRA in health care? One common approach is to find out about 'what worked, what didn't?' in health organisations' experiences with PSRA (Mitton, Patten et al. 2003; Dionne, Mitton et al. 2009; Goodwin and Frew 2013; Cornelissen, Mitton et al. 2014). Such findings can be shaped into recommendations for future iterations of the priority setting processes under study (Dionne, Mitton et al. 2009). As a result of this focus upon understanding experiences and viewpoints in context, the literature contains many meso-level case studies of PSRA processes implemented by individual organisations or programs. The choice of research methods ought to derive from the nature of the questions to be answered. For much of the published PSRA literature, those questions point us towards qualitative methods and methodologies.

QUALITATIVE METHODS AND METHODOLOGIES

'Methods' can be defined as 'the techniques or procedures used to gather and analyse data related to some research question or hypothesis' (Crotty 1998, p. 3). Qualitative methods are those which, generally speaking, rely upon data in the form of 'text' rather than numbers. What constitutes 'text' should be conceived of quite broadly. For instance, it can include an interview transcript, an annual report, policy manuals, meeting minutes, newsletters, media stories, electronic or paper forms used when clients are enrolled into services, an advertisement, a website, photographs or even the physical layout of a building.

'In general, qualitative research does not seek to quantify data' (Pope, Ziebland et al. 2000, p. 114). It is possible to do so (e.g., through counts of the frequency particular words). Comfort and disciplinary expectations have pushed some qualitative economic work on rationing in this direction (Coast, McDonald et al. 2004). However, qualitative researchers disagree about the appropriateness and usefulness of doing so. What is mentioned by a small number of people, or even one person, is not necessarily a less important insight than is a more commonly expressed view. Sandelowski calls this analytical miscounting, arguing than when qualitative researchers identify a number of themes or patterns in their data, what is needed is to present compelling evidence that such patterns exist and are distinct, rather than how common they might be (which is an aim better suited to more quantitative forms of research) (Sandelowski 2001). In other words, qualitative research does not seek to find generalisable results. In any event, as Lavis et al. argue, decisions about what constitutes an evidence-informed practice should be made not upon the results of single studies but on appropriate systematic review and research synthesis (Lavis, Robertson et al. 2003). Means of doing this with qualitative research have been actively under development (Barnett-Page and Thomas 2009) and are discussed extensively in Chapter 6.

The methods commonly seen to constitute qualitative research fall into three groups (see also Chapter 4):

- Talking to people (i.e., interviews and focus groups). An interview typically collects data from a single respondent; when more than one informant is involved at the same time, this is called a group interview or focus group. There can be very pragmatic reasons for conducting a focus group (Sim 1998), such as taking advantage of venues where very busy health care leaders already gather. It is often used in PSRA research for this purpose. There are also more theoretically informed efforts which are concerned particularly with the unique added value from group interaction (Kitzinger 1994; Sim 1998). Published PSRA studies appear to tend towards the former more than the latter. The inclusion of open-ended questions in a survey also fit into this category, though they typically produce very 'thin' data due to lack of interaction, prompts, clarification and people's unwillingness to spend considerable time in writing out thoughtful and detailed answers.
- Observing what people do. People may not be able to articulate their actual practice, or they may attempt to present themselves in more socially desirable ways when speaking to a researcher. In PSRA, the main observation opportunities tend to be meetings at which resource allocation decisions are made. For example, in observing an executive team discussion, researchers might note which participants are paying attention, who is distracted, who misses portions of the discussion by leaving the room and whether discussion corresponds with prepared material like decision criteria and scoring sheets. This all sheds light upon how decisions are reached, none of which context is apparent in a simple statement of what was decided or a count of yea and nay votes.
- Reading and parsing documents which people have produced. While transcripts and reflective notes are created within the research process itself, this method is usually applied to other documentary materials produced during day-to-day life. In priority setting research, these might include the business cases made for investment or disinvestment proposals, criteria scoring sheets, or email communications which are meant to inform staff

about a PSRA process and its results. Such documents are often polished and deliberately crafted to portray a particular image. But they may also contain gendered assumptions, implicit models of the proper relationship between experts and citizens, or many other social constructs which might be identified and critiqued by researchers.

It has been argued, in relation to the study of evidence-based policy, that researchers need to employ a broader range of methods than has been the case, with researchers calling for greater use of 'observational methods with in-depth descriptions of practices . . . instead of repeating studies of perceptions of barriers and facilitators' (Oliver, Lorenc et al. 2014, p. 7) obtained via interviews. I suggest this holds true for PSRA research as well; the academy has relied overmuch upon the interview method to the exclusion of other tools in the qualitative toolkit, and failed to integrate different types of information to inform analysis and findings.

If we consider the aforementioned, the main qualitative methods, then we can distinguish them from research methodology, defined as 'the strategy, plan of action, process or design lying behind the choice and use of particular methods and linking the choice and use of methods to the desired outcomes' (Crotty 1998, p. 3). Methodologies, as distinct approaches to enquiry, are interwoven with and emerge from particular disciplinary and philosophical perspectives. Examples of methodologies, following Crotty, include those associated with quantitative studies such as experimental research; survey research; those seen as more qualitative in orientation such as ethnography or grounded theory; and those that are amenable to a mix of methods such as action research. A key debate in the qualitative research community is about generic versus theoretically informed research (Caelli, Ray et al. 2003; Kahlke 2014). It has been argued previously (Smith, Mitton et al. 2009) that most of the qualitative research in PSRA is a-theoretical; there seems to be little reason to revise this conclusion based on what has been published since.

Generic qualitative research has been defined as that which blends established methodological approaches, or which does not propose any formal philosophical and methodological framework at all (Caelli, Ray et al. 2003). Such work is criticized for failing to draw upon a well-established body of literature directing data collection and analysis, and so might mishandle the research process (Kahlke 2014). The greatest danger seems to be that, in failing to articulate its stance, such research is blind to the inherent underlying views of the researcher and how these inevitabilities illuminate and obscure research findings.

There is no firm consensus as to what constitutes an established tradition of qualitative inquiry; I will follow Thorne (2000) and Hole (2014) in naming them as phenomenology, narrative, ethnography and grounded theory (see also Chapter 2). Phenomenology, with branches adapted from distinct schools of philosophy, aims to understand lived experience from the subject's point of view, and to represent it in a way that might be understood by others (Thorne 2000). Narrative, which takes many of its cues from literary theory, is primarily concerned with stories and how people use story-telling techniques to order the events and experiences of their lives in a way which makes it meaningful. Narratives are often used in micro-level studies, of individual patient and providers, but they certainly can also be used to inform policy discussions. Robinson et al., for instance, looking at priority setting in UK primary care trusts, describe two 'communities of meaning' – which might be referred to as enthusiasts and sceptics (Robinson, Freeman et al. 2009); Smith et al. describe three narratives of high performance in priority setting in Canadian health care organisations (Smith, Hall et al. 2014). Ethnography has its roots in anthropology and focuses upon the exploration of culture(s), seeking to provide detailed or 'thick' description of these from the insider's point of view. There are some examples of ethnographic approaches applied to micro-level resource allocation decisions (Fraser, Estabrooks et al. 2009). Grounded theory was established initially in sociology; as the name implies, its aim is to work inductively from data to find commonalities or patterns that inform explanatory theory, on the premise that 'fundamental social processes explain something of human behavior' (Thorne 2000, p. 69). While many priority setting studies apply some of the methods of grounded theory, such as constant comparison, and some suggest that they have 'adapted' or 'modified' the approach (Kapiriri, Norheim et al. 2003; Hasman, McIntosh et al. 2008), few report straightforward adherence to its methodological guidance.

If research proposes to use theory in its analysis, then data collection instruments must be built to serve this need. For instance, data collection may employ unstructured, semi-structured or structured approaches. Unstructured interviews, which allow for thick description to emerge, are appropriate for narrative study. Structured instruments, which allow more ready comparison across respondents, are suited to template-based approaches, where one starts with pre-existing codes based on what is expected to be important in the data (Hall, Smith et al. 2016). For discourse analysis, which studies the ways in which language is used and how people interact to communicate ideas, transcriptions need to clearly indicate pauses, hesitates, changes in tone and so on – for thematic analysis, this degree of detail is not required. These choices show, in practical terms, what Crotty's distinctions between method and methodology mean.

Based upon what has been published to date, qualitative researchers in the health economics and priority setting fields have largely failed to articulate why more theoretically informed research could be useful to decision makers as well as have academic value. Use is obviously of paramount interest to decision makers who are asked to invest their scarce time and their organisations' reputation into research efforts.

The additional interpretative effort required to translate the findings of theoretically informed qualitative research into practical guidance makes it more difficult to 'sell' the benefit of such research to stakeholders. One methodology which does clearly serve decision makers interests, and so has been used successfully in PSRA studies, is action research (Patten, Mitton et al. 2006; Airoldi 2013; Cornelissen, Mitton et al. 2014). Compared to other research methodologies, action research has more emphasis on collaboration and action as integral to the research approach. If changes to what an organisation is currently doing, its 'business as usual', historical patterns of activity are an expected result – that is, instrumental use of findings (Weiss 1979) – then action research approaches are helpful in getting buy-in and mobilising people to actually follow through with change (see discussion). Nonetheless, we must remind ourselves that use is not the only acceptable guiding model for studies of priority setting; illuminating social values which are being served and groups which are being disadvantaged by program decisions, for instance, can equally be a rationale for such research (Smith, Mitton et al. 2012).

SPECIFIC EXAMPLES AND FUTURE DIRECTIONS

This section offers some examples of how qualitative methods have been, and might be, used in improving practice and building the knowledge base about PSRA in health care. Four case examples are provided. Since PSRA sits at the intersection of economics and ethics (Gibson, Mitton et al. 2006), particular attention is paid to drawing out the implications of these cases for the latter. The first part of this section focuses upon research for priority setting; these studies have been explicitly conducted in partnership with decision makers to lead to improvement in PSRA processes within these decision makers' own organisations. It draws from past published literature, the author's own work as well as that of close colleagues; the author bears sole responsibility for the interpretations of this work presented here.

Example one: action research

This was a well-documented action research project in a Canadian regional health authority (2001–2003). The project received ethics approval from the University of Calgary Conjoint Health Research Ethics Board, 2001. The objective was for researchers and senior executive decision makers in the Calgary Regional Health Authority (RHA) to co-design and implement a formal, explicit and systematic process for PSRA, which the decision makers had identified as an important organisational need.

Recent and existing priority setting practices were documented (Mitton, Patten et al. 2005); then, decision makers reflected upon and critiqued those practices (Mitton and Patten 2004; Mitton, Patten et al. 2005). The researchers, together with decision makers, designed a context-specific priority setting process for the RHA, based upon the Program Budgeting and Marginal Analysis, or PBMA, model (Mitton, Patten et al. 2003; Mitton, Donaldson et al. 2003). The model was implemented to identify resource release and reinvestment for the coming fiscal year. Afterward, decision makers and researchers reflected upon their use of PBMA and identified possible improvements or refinements (Mitton, Patten et al. 2003; Mitton and Patten 2004; Patten, Mitton et al. 2005; Patten, Mitton et al. 2006). The process was again implemented, incorporating the recommended changes (Patten, Mitton et al. 2006). Finally, researchers again worked with the decision makers to reflect upon their experiences in implementing PBMA and to identify how to move forward with the approach in subsequent years (Mitton, Patten et al. 2004; Patten, Mitton et al. 2006).

This example shows how the different methods of qualitative research, described previously, can be deployed in complementary fashion. Observation was used initially to document processes and group dynamics and to note what sources of evidence were publicly drawn upon in decisions and if decision makers appeared to understand and appeal to economic principles (Mitton, Patten et al. 2003; Mitton, Patten et al. 2005). Observation notes informed the drafting of interview and focus group guides. These were able to go beyond descriptions of decision maker views and behaviours, to jointly explore strategic thinking about how to explain PSRA patterns and change practice (Mitton, Patten et al. 2005). At the time, such qualitative reflection to refine management processes was new to health economics–related research (Patten, Mitton et al. 2005).

Several aspects of action research are particularly notable in this case (Patten, Mitton et al. 2006). To begin, the issue was one that had real salience for decision makers. The researchers established ongoing relationships with the leadership team; their presence helped to catalyse self-reflection, leading to increased understanding for all about the nature of the local context, and the particular complexities involved in inserting formal PSRA methods into this setting.

The conclusion, co-authored by researchers and decision makers, was that the PAR experience was a success. 'The PAR process promoted group belonging, fostered creativity and critical thinking, promoted change and growth, and served as a means of resolving shortcomings' (Mitton, Patten et al. 2005, p. 54). 'It is clear that PAR was a vehicle that enabled organisational change'

(Patten, Mitton et al. 2006, p. 130). There were, however, concerns that the change might lack sustainability following researchers' withdrawal from the scene. The 'perceived need for sustained consultation and assistance indicates that organisational change is a process that may take more time than typically allocated from a research project's perspective' (Patten, Mitton et al. 2006, p. 1130). The researcher's exit from practitioner or community partnerships is inherently an ethically fraught aspect of action research approaches. Implementing changes which flow from the research is the logical culmination of such approaches – their whole purpose, in fact. Yet often this involves advocacy and the invocation of researchers' social capital in ways that sit uncomfortably with the values and skills which prevail in most academic training and socialisation experiences.

Example two: retrospective evaluation

This was a retrospective evaluation of a priority setting process in a children's hospital – the Isaak Walton Killam Health Centre – which serves as the main tertiary care centre for Canada's four Atlantic provinces (2011–2014). As with example 3, this project received ethics approval from the UBC Behavioural Research Ethics Board (Ref. #H13–01455) and the IWK Health Centre Research Ethics Board (Ref. #1014616). Decision makers had identified a need to find a better and more acceptable way to meet budget constraints imposed by the funder, the Nova Scotia provincial government. The evaluation was conducted using interview methods.

The qualitative evaluation of the new process – again, PBMA – employed two distinct templates. One of these was the multiple streams theory of policy change advanced by John Kingdon (Kingdon 1995; Smith, Mitton et al. 2016), and the other consisted of identified elements of high performance in priority setting (Smith, Mitton et al. 2016; Smith, Mitton et al. 2016). The multiple streams analysis looked backward to consider the PBMA implementation as the successful result of the opening of a policy window. In Kingdon's model, this occurs from the convergence of three streams: problems, policies and politics. Interview transcripts were reviewed to identify these three streams. The high-performance framework identifies nineteen elements in four domains (structures, processes, attitudes/behaviours and outcomes) which literature and Canadian case studies found to characterize effective priority setting at the organisation-wide level. For the second template analysis, the same transcripts were reviewed a second time to see whether the elements of high performance identified from previous research were mentioned by respondents and whether the organisation was characterized as strong or weak in them. There was some overlap in findings between the two analyses (e.g., each analysis identified the importance of staff engagement). The high-performance findings were relatively actionable; that is, they pointed to specific parts of the priority setting process that could be improved. Analysis using more abstract models like multiple streams is reputedly more difficult to draw practical lessons from (Lomas and Brown 2009; Oliver, Lorenc et al. 2014), so particular attention was paid to these implications (Smith, Mitton et al. 2016).

This example shows the benefits of providing multiple analytic approaches to the data, a ripe opportunity in qualitative research given the diversity of methodologies, relative to quantitative perspectives where there is generally only a single 'proper' way to analyse data. The same qualitative data can be compared and contrasted using different methodological strategies (Wilkinson 2000; Burck 2005), a concept sometimes called theory or perspective triangulation (Patton 1999). This can overcome researchers' preconceived biases, for instance, a tendency to see only data which 'fit' a pre-determined template. Recall, of course, that data collected with one primary theoretical frame in mind may not be fully suited for analysis from alternative perspectives. The analyses reported here were led by the same authors; it may have been stronger if the work could have been done by different members of the team (though this implies a sufficiently large, diverse and skilled research group with dedicated time for qualitative data analysis). In contrast to the previous example, in this case the researchers applied their own frames to assess and explain decision-maker actions. If not done with great care, this might diminish or dismiss health care leaders' agency and impose on the record interpretations with which those leaders might disagree. Treating research participants as objects rather than subjects of ethical analysis should be challenged whenever it seems to occur.

The remainder of this section focuses on research into priority setting that comes from more established qualitative traditions, and consequently might be seen as falling towards the 'research ON' end of the spectrum. The author re-presents methodology proposals from an ongoing program of research with Canadian colleagues. These are extracted from grants that were not funded or not executed in the end as planned; drawing on such material increases the pool of examples available. While these examples highlight some of the challenges to applying qualitative research methods to priority setting, they nonetheless illustrate innovative approaches that hold promise for future investigations, when conditions are right.

Example three: policy analysis of narratives

The goal here was to consider factors that facilitate or inhibit implementation of new policy, such as an organisation-wide approach to PSRA. Interviews were the method of choice. Administrators and clinicians who were involved in the implementation of a new approach to PSRA would be purposively selected as key informants and asked to 'tell their story', their experience with this new local approach to PSRA. These stories embody what the narrators themselves understand and believe to be true of the world. Interviews would focus on eliciting and representing the reasons behind the adoption of the new approach. In other words, how and by whom was the need for change from usual practice identified and how were others convinced of this need? What options were considered? And why, from among these, was the new approach selected? How was the new process implemented into existing organisational routine? What issues and challenges were encountered? Narrative interviewing is typically more unstructured than structured, with participants allowed to present the chronology and meaning of their experience as they understand it, with limited intervention from the researcher (Greenhalgh, Russell et al. 2005; Shaw 2010). However, individual stories, because of their very uniqueness, may tend to identify participants and potentially threaten confidentiality and anonymity. Researchers working in this tradition will need to cultivate the skill of 'fictionalising' details in a way that does not distort the essence of the underlying data.

We framed this research using a policy analysis of narratives methodology, 'where different methods – both from literary theory and social science – are used to analyse the relations among conflicting policy narratives in order to develop policy advice on how to proceed' (van Eeten 2006, p. 252). A policy narrative has several core elements: 'a setting, a plot, characters (hero, villain, and victim)' (Shanahan, Jones et al. 2011, p. 539). Importantly, it is 'disseminated toward a preferred policy outcome' (Shanahan, Jones et al. 2011, p. 539) – the 'moral' of the story. In other words, key actors involved in any policy context will attempt to frame perceived problems in such a way that the story leads to a compelling conclusion based on the actors' preferred policy solution.

Organisations likely have more than a single narrative; while there may be a dominant story to which most subscribe, some individuals will almost certainly hold competing perspectives based on their interests and the extent of their power or influence (Shaw 2010). Thus we proposed that narrative methodology would be an appropriate way of bringing forward these different stances and assessing how their co-existence affects the ultimate implementation and success (or failure) of policy choices. In the end, as implementation of the project was negotiated with decision-making partners, the final interview questions proved to be poorly suited for narrative analysis and so this approach to qualitative research was put aside in favour of others.

Example four: institutional ethnography

The goal of this proposed study was to transfer knowledge about factors conducive to health performance in health care priority setting – in the form of a framework and evaluative tool (Hall et al. 2016). Two Canadian health care organisations would take up the framework, and their efforts to incorporate it into local decision making would be followed over time, to understand processes both of PSRA and knowledge translation. A combination of interview, observation and document review methods was proposed. The application and integration of these research methods would be guided by principles of institutional ethnography (IE) (Green, Moehr et al. 2004; Smith 2006). 'IE is uniquely capable of investigating work practices . . . everything people do to accomplish the organisation of everyday activities including decision making' (Allen, Griffiths et al. 2004, pp. 3–4). We expect that the full effects from a planned intervention to change priority setting practices, based on knowledge of what constitutes high performance – and evidence of its incorporation into standard working – can only be observed over time. Thus, this research proposed longitudinal data collection over a two-year period. Campbell's IE of a quality improvement initiative applied in a Victoria long-term care facility is a useful model (Campbell 1998). IE seeks to preserve participants' situated understandings of their context as an entry point to explicating social relationships. 'Unlike other qualitative methods, institutional ethnograph[y] actively avoids developing thematic analysis. [It does] not collapse the data into broad categories [or] generic concepts' (Rankin and Campbell 2009, p. 4). In our case this relates to how efforts to achieve high performance in PSRA are negotiated and enacted by managers in these health service delivery organisations. IE investigates the 'relations of power . . . within institutional cultures [that] condition/proscribe people's everyday lives' (Hole 2014, p. 167). Because IE studies activities and relations rather than 'people as such', it can pose a puzzle for academic and organisational ethics review boards; there are not necessarily any 'human subjects of research' as these are ordinarily understood (Campbell and Gregor 2008, p. 57). In the end, this study would have produced a thick description of longitudinal PSRA activity, which could help grapple with some of the largely unaddressed questions about implementation – whether priorities set at the senior management level in fact are translated into intended change through the actions of middle managers and front-line practitioners – and about the sustainability of formal methods over time.

CONCLUSION

Health economics is a key contributor to both the practice and study of priority setting. Evidence about the cost-effectiveness of policy, program and service choices is an important input to resource allocation. But PSRA is not simply the technical application of economic analysis. It is a management practice that can be fully comprehended only when the contributions of other disciplines and other types of evidence are considered. PSRA choices are also ethical choices, and should be understood and assessed through that lens.

Qualitative methods, in consequence, have long played a larger role in PSRA research than in many other areas in which health economists act. As an applied topic, PSRA is concerned with questions such as 'how do health care organisations make resource allocation decisions?' and 'how can they do so better?' Research methods should be appropriate to the questions, and such questions are often best addressed with qualitative techniques.

This chapter has given some examples from the experience of the author and colleagues of how qualitative research has been used to study PSRA. While successes can be reported, researchers and decision-maker partners also need to further stretch their application of these methods. Qualitative research has several well-established and distinct conceptual traditions with a rich theoretical and methodological body of literature; too much PSRA research eschews these in favour of generic – and at worst, ill-defined – study designs. In other words, there is far more to qualitative research than extracting 'themes' from a comparison of individual interviews.

Studies that draw upon these perspectives offer different points of access into the topic; narrative and phenomenological approaches often adopt a micro-level lens, focused on individual patient or provider experience; ethnographic studies consider organisations to be examples of 'cultures' that can be entered into and explored. Knowing how theories might be applied in a research study can and must be used to develop better instruments for data collection. This chapter has given some examples of how proposed PSRA research might proceed along these lines.

Much of the health economics and health care PSRA literature can best be viewed as research for the purposes of improving practice, because of its orientation to applied science – a compelling commitment to improve decision-making practices among health care leaders. These efforts should continue. Other research efforts intend to increase our understanding of PSRA practices and the conditions which influence them; such research also needs to continue and expand. The former has more obvious relevance to decision makers and it is thus easier to enlist them as partners and research sites for such research, but a broad combination of both lines of study promises the best opportunities to use qualitative techniques effectively as one component of the larger study of PSRA. This has become firmly established over the past few decades as a fruitful and significant scientific enterprise.

ACKNOWLEDGEMENTS

The project described as example one received funding from the Canadian Health Services Research Foundation and the Alberta Heritage Foundation for Medical Research. The projects described as examples two and three were funded by the Canadian Institutes of Health Research, Evidence-Informed Health Care Renewal funding stream (Ref. #FAS F12–03532).

Part III

AFTERWORD

Chapter 21

Afterword: Walking the disciplinary tightrope

Joanna Coast, Hareth Al-Janabi, Louise Jackson, Philip Kinghorn and Amanda Owen-Smith

While there is a burgeoning availability of books on qualitative research, both in terms of general methodological contributions and specific disciplinary approaches, this book is the first contribution devoted to the use of qualitative methods in health economics. Although it is still a developing area, there are now a number of health economists with experience and expertise in using qualitative methods, and thus it seemed that the time was ripe for such a contribution. It is particularly advantageous that this book was able to draw on work conducted across a number of research teams, in diverse settings, on a variety of topics and using a range of theoretical and methodological approaches. Indeed, this ability to draw on a broad set of studies shows the increasing strength of qualitative methods within health economics.

Although there is a growing body of health economics research involving qualitative methods, many of the disciplinary challenges outlined by Coast and colleagues more than ten years ago (Coast, McDonald et al. 2004) remain. Many economists still appear to view their discipline as purely quantitative and are suspicious of the notion of using qualitative methods. Basole and Ramnarain note that economists 'resist attempts to introduce [qualitative methods] into the profession on the ground that this is "not economics". . . . Even as economics expands its domain of analysis, it refuses to accept methodological pluralism' (Basole and Ramnarain 2016, 138). These issues contribute to the sort of publication difficulties outlined previously by Coast and colleagues (Coast, McDonald et al. 2004) and in this book by Robinson (Chapter 15). Indeed, it is notable that an analysis of qualitative papers published in the ten top journals in health services research and policy found that it was one of the key health economics journals (*Journal of Health Economics*) that was the only one of these journals that had published no qualitative research papers (Gagliardi and Dobrow 2011) (see Chapter 7 for more details of this work).

It is not clear why there seems to be such reluctance to expand the methodological domain of economics. In part, it appears to arise from the sorts of philosophical and theoretical considerations discussed in Chapter 1, but it may also stem from economists' lack of experience in methods for generating data, as opposed solely to its analysis (Berik 1997; Basole and Ramnarain 2016). More fundamental, perhaps, are differing views on what it means to be an 'economist' (or a 'health economist'). Is being an economist about having a quantitative toolbox? Is it about understanding a particular 'economic' body of theory? Or is it about a focus on, and specific ways of thinking about, economic issues of resource allocation and distribution? Answers to these questions of disciplinary boundary are likely to differ, and might then determine the extent to which economists of different persuasions feel that qualitative research is an appropriate focus for health economists. For instance, if economists feel that it is their quantitative econometric methods that define them as an economist (even if their focus is on issues more commonly associated with epidemiology for example), then they may be less accepting of qualitative methods than those economists who see the core of economics as being the study of issues around resource allocation.

From the perspective of this book, the primary focus of economics is on issues of resource allocation and distribution, drawing, where relevant, on the body of theory that comprises 'economics', but also generating new theory where current explanations are insufficient. With this approach, health economics could be seen as reclaiming its identity as a social science utilising the full range of methodological tools to address these core interests around resource allocation. With such a definition of economics, the use of qualitative methods as part of the health economist's toolkit becomes not only possible but also highly desirable, given the additional insights that these methods can produce. If economists are to truly understand complex health economies, then their understanding will be much enhanced if they do not restrict themselves to quantitative analysis, particularly the quantitative analysis of existing datasets that have been collected routinely or for a different purpose.

A further challenge for health economists conducting research using qualitative methods is that the perception that economics is an entirely quantitative discipline is not held just by economists. Such views are also surprisingly common in the sort of population health research environment where health economists are often based. It may be that the view of economists as analysers, but not producers, of data contributes to the perception (implicit or explicit), often prevalent in these environments, that economists and statisticians are largely interchangeable. Such views can make it challenging for health economists to achieve funding for qualitative research in the population health environment; there may be a lack of understanding on the part of panels (and indeed those putting in proposals) that the most appropriate person to conduct qualitative research around topics of resource allocation and distribution might be a health economist.

Perceptions of training may again be an issue here, given that most health economists tend to gain their experience in qualitative methods at the doctoral level, rather than through undergraduate training. It is understandable that researchers from a sociological or anthropological background might question the economist's understanding of ontological and epistemological concerns, given that these do not form a key part of economists' undergraduate training, at least in some settings. But it is also the case that the economist grappling with these issues in doctoral research or beyond will tend to generate a sophisticated understanding of their nature, precisely because of the need to navigate the various disciplinary waters. Whatever the reason, it is clear that health economists working in the area of qualitative research methods need to become better at addressing these perceptions, and demonstrating the strengths that they can have in conducting qualitative research.

Despite these continuing issues, during the writing of the various book chapters, it has been heartening to realize how much more accepted the use of qualitative methods in health economics has become in some quarters over the last twenty years. In a small number of research areas, these methods are now seen even as normal or required. For example, in the generation of attributes for discrete choice experiments (DCEs), it is now probably more acceptable to include qualitative research methods than to not include them. Indeed, Vass and colleagues reported that only 44 percent of DCE papers published since 2001 did not use qualitative methods, and that, of those that did not, a number went on to discuss the lack of qualitative data as a study limitation (Vass, Rigby et al. 2017). These advances are also seen, albeit to a somewhat lesser extent, in other pockets of health economics research, often those that are most complex or difficult to study using quantitative methods. Research areas where qualitative methods tend to be seen as a strength in the research include researching health systems/economies in lower- and middle-income countries; researching priority setting and decision making at all levels from micro to macro; and researching sensitive areas such as end-of-life care.

There are, of course, many other areas of health economics research that could benefit from increased use of qualitative methods, particularly in relation to generating greater understanding of health systems. By providing, for the first time, a book setting out approaches to qualitative research methods from a health economics perspective, the journey of new researchers coming to this area should be eased. They will find a description of relevant approaches to basic aspects of qualitative research, and also a large number of examples from which they can draw as they develop their own research plans. Perhaps more importantly, they will also find, for the first time, the suggestion of a specific economic analytical approach, drawing on the application of an economic lens and the generation of outputs in the form of models.

It is hoped, therefore, that this book will contribute to both the increasing acceptance of qualitative research methods within health economics and the individual journeys of those researchers just beginning their use of qualitative methods. The more health economists who develop experience themselves in using qualitative methods, the greater the possibilities for training others and the larger the network of health economists with such expertise will be. And, ultimately, that will lead to a more informed theoretical foundation for health economics, a stronger basis for empirical work and improved health systems with better experiences for patients and the public.

References

Abelson, J., E. Blacksher, K. Li, S. Boesued and S. Goold (2013). 'Public deliberation in health policy and bioethics: mapping an emerging, interdisciplinary field'. *Journal of Public Deliberation* **9**(1): 4–30.

Abelson, J., J. Eyles, C. B. McLeod, P. Collins, C. McMullan and P.-G. Forest (2003). 'Does deliberation make a difference? Results from a citizens panel study of health goals priority setting'. *Health Policy* **66**: 95–106.

Abelson, J., P. G. Forest, J. Eyles, P. Smith, E. Martin and F. P. Gauvin (2003). 'Deliberations about deliberative methods: issues in the design and evaluation of public participation processes'. *Social Science & Medicine* **57**: 239–251.

Abiiro, G. A., G. Leppert, G. B. Mbera, P. J. Robyn and M. De Allegri (2014). 'Developing attributes and attribute-levels for a discrete choice experiment on micro health insurance in rural Malawi'. *Health Services Research* **14**: 235.

Adamson, J. and J. L. Donovan (2005). ' "Normal disruption": South Asian and African/Caribbean relative caring for an older family member in the UK'. *Social Science & Medicine* **60**: 37–48.

Addison, R. B. (1992). Grounded hermeneutic research. *Doing qualitative research*. B. F. Crabtree. London, Sage: 110–124.

Adler, P. A. and P. Adler (2001). The reluctant respondent. *Handbook of interview research: context and method*. J. F. Gubrium and J. A. Holstein. Thousand Oaks, CA, Sage.

Ahmed, N., J. C. Bestall, S. A. Payne, B. Noble and S. H. Ahmedzai (2009). 'The use of cognitive interviewing methodology in the design and testing of a screening tool for supportive and palliative care needs'. *Supportive Care in Cancer* **17**(6): 665–673.

Airoldi, M. (2013). 'Disinvestments in practice: overcoming resistance to change through a sociotechnical approach with local stakeholders'. *Journal of Health Politics, Policy and Law* **38**(6): 1149–1171.

Al-Janabi, H. (2009). *Measurement and valuation of the caring experience for economic evaluation*, University of Bristol.

Al-Janabi, H., J. Coast and T. N. Flynn (2008). 'What do people value when they provide unpaid care to an older person? A meta-ethnography with interview follow-up'. *Social Science & Medicine* **67**: 111–121.

Al-Janabi, H., T. N. Flynn and J. Coast (2011). 'Estimation of a preference-based carer experience scale'. *Medical Decision Making* **31**: 458–468.

Al-Janabi, H., T. N. Flynn and J. Coast (2012). 'Development of a self-report measure of capability wellbeing for adults: the ICECAP-A'. *Quality of Life Research* **21**: 167–176.

Al-Janabi, H., T. Keeley, P. Mitchell and J. Coast (2013). 'Can capabilities be self-reported? A think aloud study'. *Social Science & Medicine* **87**: 116–122.

Al-Janabi, H., T. J. Peters, J. Brazier, S. Bryan, T. N. Flynn, S. Clemens, A. Moody and J. Coast (2013). 'An investigation of the construct validity of the ICECAP-A capability measure'. *Quality of Life Research* **22**: 1831–1840.

Al-Janabi, H., J. van Exel, W. Brouwer and J. Coast (2016). 'A framework for including family health spillovers in economic evaluation'. *Medical Decision Making* **36**(2): 176–186.

Allen, D., L. Griffiths and P. Lyne (2004). 'Accommodating health and social care needs: routine resource allocation in stroke rehabilitation'. *Sociology of Health & Illness* **26**(4): 411–432.

Altheide, D. L. and J. M. Johnson (1994). Criteria for assessing interpretive validity in qualitative research. *Handbook of qualitative research*. N. H. Denzin. London, Sage.

Alvesson, M. and K. Sköldberg (2009). *Reflexive methodology: new vistas for qualitative research*. London, Sage.

Angrist, J. D., G. W. Imbens and D. B. Rubin (1996). 'Identification of causal effects using instrumental variables'. *Journal of the American Statistical Association* **91**(434): 444–455.

Antonucci, T. C. (1986). 'Hierarchical mapping technique'. *Generations* **10**(4): 10–12.

Antonucci, T. C. and H. Akiyama (1987). 'Social networks in adult life and a preliminary examination of the convoy model'. *Journal of Gerontology* **42**(5): 519–527.

Antonucci, T. C., H. Akiyama and J. E. Lansford (1998). 'Negative effects of close social relations'. *Family Relations* **47**(4): 379–384.

Armataki, E., E. Karampli, J. Kyriopoulos and E. Pavi (2014). 'Health technology assessment of medicines in Greece: pharmaceutical industry executives' views'. *International Journal of Technology Assessment in Health Care* **30**(2): 226–232.

Armatas, C. A., T. J. Venn and A. E. Watson (2014). 'Applying Q-methodology to select and define attributes for non-market valuation: a case study from Northwest Wyoming, United States'. *Ecological Economics* **107**: 447–456.

Aron, A., E. Melinat, E. N. Aron, R. Darrin Vallone and R. J. Bator (1997). 'The experimental generation of interpersonal closeness: a procedure and some preliminary findings'. *Personality and Social Psychology Bulletin* **23**(4): 363–377.

Aron, A. P., D. J. Mashek and E. N. Aron (2004). Closeness as including other in the self. *Handbook of closeness and intimacy*. D. J. Mashek and A. Aron. Mahwah, NJ., Lawrence Erlbaum Associates, Publishers.

Arvidsson, E., M. Andre, L. Borgquist and P. Carlsson (2010). 'Priority setting in primary care – dilemmas and opportunities: a focus group study'. *BMC Family Practice* **11**(71): 1–9.

Asenso-Boadi, F., T. J. Peters and J. Coast (2007). 'Exploring differences in empirical time preference rates for health: an application of meta-regression'. *Health Economics* **17**: 235–248.

Ashmore, M., M. Mulkay and T. Pinch (1989). *Health and efficiency: a sociology of health economics*. Milton Keynes, Open University Press.

Atkinson, J. M. and J. Heritage (1999). Jefferson's transcript notation. *The discourse reader*. A. Jaworski and N. Coupland. London, Routledge: 158–166.

Atkinson, P. (1995). 'Some perils of paradigm'. *Qualitative Health Research* **5**(1): 117–124.

Austen, S., T. Jefferson and V. Thein (2003). 'Gendered social indicators and grounded theory'. *Feminist Economics* **9**(1): 1–18.

Bailey, C., P. Kinghorn, R. Orlando, K. Armour, R. Perry, L. Jones and J. Coast (2016). '"The ICECAP-SCM tells you more about what I'm going through": a think-aloud study measuring quality of life among patients receiving supportive and palliative care'. *Palliative Medicine* **30**(7): 642–652.

Baker, R., I. Bateman, C. Donaldson, M. Jones-Lee, E. Lancsar, G. Loomes, H. Mason, M. Odejar, J.-L. Pinto-Prades, A. Robinson, M. Ryan, P. Shackley, R. Smith, R. Sugden and J. Wildman (2010). 'Weighting and valuing quality-adjusted life-years using stated preference methods: preliminary results from the Social Value of a QALY Project'. *Health Technology Assessment* **14**(27).

Baker, R. and A. Robinson (2004). 'Responses to standard gambles: are preferences "well constructed"?' *Health Economics* **13**: 37–48.

Baker, R., C. Thompson and R. Mannion (2006). 'Q methodology in health economics'. *Journal of Health Services Research & Policy* **11**(1): 38–45.

Baker, R., J. Wildman, H. Mason and C. Donaldson (2014). 'Q-ing for health – a new approach to eliciting the public's views on health care resource allocation'. *Health Economics* **23**: 283–297.

Baker, R. M. (2006). 'Economic rationality and health and lifestyle choices for people with diabetes'. *Social Science & Medicine* **63**: 2341–2353.

Baker, S., M. Sudit and E. Litwak (1998). 'Carer burden and coping strategies used by informal caregivers of minority women living with HIV/AIDS'. *The ABNF Journal* **9**(3): 56–60.

Bamberger, M. (2012). *Introduction to mixed methods in impact evaluation*. Washington, DC., Interaction.

Bamberger, M., J. Rugh and L. Mabry (2012). *Real world evaluation: working under budget, time, data and political constraints*. Thousand Oaks, CA, Sage.

Bansback, N., J. Brazier, A. Tsuchiya and A. Anis (2012). 'Using a discrete choice experiment to estimate health state utility values'. *Journal of Health Economics* **31**: 306–318.

Barbour, R. S. (1998). 'Mixing qualitative methods: quality assurance or qualitative quagmire?' *Qualitative Health Research* **8(3)**: 352–361.

Barnett-Page, E. and J. Thomas (2009). 'Methods for the synthesis of qualitative research: a critical review'. *BMC Medical Research Methodology* **9**(59).

Barry, C. A., C. P. Bradley, N. Britten, F. A. Stevenson and N. Barber (2000). 'Patients' unvoiced agendas in general practice consultations: qualitative study'. *BMJ* **320**(7244): 1246–1250.

Basole, A. and S. Ramnarain (2016). Qualitative and ethnographic methods in economics. *Handbook of research methods and applications in heterodox economics*. F. S. Lee and B. Cronin. Cheltenham, Edward Elgar: 135–164.

Bennett, M. I. (2007). Principles of designing clinical trials in palliative care. *Research methods in palliative care*. J. M. Addington-Hall, E. Bruera, I. J. Higginson and S. Payne. Oxford, Oxford University Press: 13–26.

Berik, G. (1997). 'The need for crossing the method boundaries in economic research'. *Feminist Economics* **3**(2): 121–125.

Bernard, H. R. (1995). *Research methods in anthropology: qualitative and quantitative approaches*. Plymouth, Rowman Altamira.

Bernard, H. R. (2013). *Social research methods: qualitative and quantitative approaches*. Thousand Oaks, CA, Sage.

Berndt, C. (2015). 'Behavioural economics, experimentalism and the marketization of development'. *Economy and Society* **44**(4): 567–591.

Bertone, M. P. and M. Lagarde (2016). 'Sources, determinants and utilization of health workers' revenues: evidence from Sierra Leone'. *Health Policy and Planning* **31**: 1010–1019.

Bhaskar, R. (1989). *Reclaiming reality*. London, Verso.

Biddle, L., J. Cooper, A. Owen-Smith, E. Klineberg, O. Bennewith, J. Donovan, K. Hawton, N. Kapur and D. Gunnell (2013). 'Qualitative interviewing with vulnerable populations: individuals' experiences of participating in suicide and self-harm based research'. *Journal of Affective Disorders* **14**: 356–362.

Biddle, L., J. Donovan, A. Owen-Smith, J. Potokar, D. Longson, K. Hawton, N. Kapur and D. Gunnell (2010). 'Factors influencing the decision to use hanging as a method of suicide: qualitative study'. *British Journal of Psychiatry* **197**(4): 320–325.

Biddle, L., D. Gunnell, A. Owen-Smith, J. Potokar, D. Longson, K. Hawton, N. Kapur and J. Donovan (2012). 'Information sources used by the suicidal to inform choice of method'. *Journal of Affective Disorders* **136**(3): 702–709.

Black, N. (1994). 'Why we need qualitative research'. *Journal of Epidemiology & Community Health* **48**: 425–426.

Blaug, M. (1992). *The methodology of economics. Or how economists explain*. Cambridge, Cambridge University Press.

Boddy, M. (2000). *Data policy and data archiving. Report on consultation for the ESRC Research Resources Board*. Bristol, University of Bristol.

Boren, T. and J. Ramey (2000). 'Thinking aloud: reconciling theory and practice'. *IEEE Transactions on Professional Communication* **43**(3): 261–278.

Boseley, S. (2012). Cancer drug 'too expensive for NHS'. *The Guardian*, **2 February**.

Boulding, K. E. (1969). 'Economics as a moral science'. *American Economic Review* **59**: 1–12.

Bowen, M. (1978). *Family therapy in clinical practice*. New York, Jason Aronson.
Bowling, A. (1997). *Research methods in health*. Buckingham, Oxford University Press.
Braun, V. and V. Clarke (2006). 'Using thematic analysis in psychology'. *Qualitative Research in Psychology* **3**(2): 77–101.
Brazier, J., M. Deverill, C. Green, R. Harper and A. Booth (1999). 'A review of the use of health status measures in economic evaluation'. *Health Technology Assessment* **3**(9): 1–164.
Brazier, J., J. Ratcliffe, J. A. Salomon and A. Tsuchiya (2007). *Measuring and valuing health benefits for economic evaluation*. Oxford, Oxford University Press.
Brazier, J., J. Roberts and M. Deverill (2002). 'The estimation of a preference-based measure of health from the SF-36'. *Journal of Health Economics* **21**: 271–292.
Brenner, S., A. S. Muula, P. J. Robyn, T. Bärnighausen, M. Sarker, D. P. Mathanga, T. Bossert and M. De Allegri (2014). 'Design of an impact evaluation using a mixed methods model – an explanatory assessment of the effects of results-based financing mechanisms on maternal healthcare services in Malawi'. *BMC Health Services Research* **14**(180).
Briggs, A., M. Sculpher and K. Claxton (2006). *Decision modelling for health economic evaluation*. Oxford, Oxford University Press.
Britten, N. (2000). Qualitative interviews in health care research. *Qualitative research in health care*. C. Pope and N. Mays. London, BMJ.
Brooks, R. and EuroQol Group (1996). 'EuroQol: the current state of play'. *Health Policy* **37**: 53–72.
Brouwer, W. B. F., A. J. Culyer, N. J. A. van Exel and F. F. H. Rutten (2008). 'Welfarism vs. extra-welfarism'. *Journal of Health Economics* **27**: 325–338.
Brown, S. R. (1980). *Political subjectivity: applications of Q methodology in political science*. London, Yale University Press.
Bryan, S., I. Williams and S. McIver (2007). 'Seeing the NICE side of cost-effectiveness analysis: a qualitative investigation of the use of CEA in NICE technology appraisals'. *Health Economics* **16**(2): 179–193.
Bryman, A. (2004). *Social research methods*. Oxford, Oxford University Press.
Burchardt, T. (2014). 'Deliberative research as a tool to make value judgements'. *Qualitative Research* **14**(3): 353–370.
Burck, C. (2005). 'Comparing qualitative research methodologies for systemic research: the use of grounded theory, discourse analysis and narrative analysis'. *Journal of Family Therapy* **27**(3): 237–262.
Burkhalter, S., J. Gastil and T. Kelshaw (2002). 'A conceptual definition and theoretical model of public deliberation in small face-to-face groups'. *Communication Theory* **12**(4): 398–422.
Burman, E. (1994). Interviewing. *Qualitative methods in psychology: a research guide*. P. Bannister. Milton Keynes, Open University Press: 49–71.
Buscatto, M. (2011). Using ethnography to study gender. *Qualitative research*. D. Silverman. London, Sage: 35–52.
Buston, K., W. Parry-Jones, M. Livingston, A. Bogan and S. Wood (1998). 'Qualitative research'. *British Journal of Psychiatry* **172**(3): 197–199.

Buxton, M. and J. Ashby (1988). The time trade-off approach to health state valuation. *Measuring health: a practical approach*. G. Teeling-Smith. London, John Wiley & Sons Ltd: 69–87.

Buxton, M. J., M. F. Drummond, B. A. Van Hout, R. L. Prince, T. A. Sheldon, T. Szucs and M. Vray (1997). 'Modelling in economic evaluation: an unavoidable fact of life'. *Health Economics* **6**(3): 217–227.

Byrne, M. (2001). 'Interviewing as a data collection method'. *Association of Perioperative Registered Nurses Journal* **74**(2): 233–235.

Cadman, D., C. Goldsmith, G. Torrance, M. Boyle and W. Furlong (1986). *Development of a health status index for Ontario children. Final report to the Ontario Ministry of Health*. Hamilton, ON, McMaster University.

Caelli, K., L. Ray and J. S. Mill (2003). '"Clear as mud": toward greater clarity in generic qualitative research'. *International Journal of Qualitative Methods* **2**(2): 1–13.

The Cambridge 27 (2001). 'Opening up economics: a proposal by Cambridge Students'. *Post-Autistic Economics Review* **7**.

Campbell, C. L., C. Bailey, K. Armour, R. Perry, R. Orlando, P. Kinghorn, L. Jones and J. Coast (2016). 'A team approach to recruitment in hospice research: engaging patients, close people and health professionals'. *International Journal of Palliative Nursing* **22**(7): 324–332.

Campbell, M. and F. Gregor (2008). *Mapping social relations: a primer in doing institutional ethnography*. Toronto, University of Toronto Press.

Campbell, M. L. (1998). 'Institutional ethnography and experience as data'. *Qualitative Sociology* **21**(1): 55–73.

Campbell, R., P. Pound, M. Morgan, G. Daker-White, N. Britten, R. Pill, L. Yardley, C. Pope and J. Donovan (2012). Evaluating meta ethnography: systematic analysis and synthesis of qualitative research. *Health Technology Assessment* **15**(43): 1–164.

Campbell, R., P. Pound, C. Pope, N. Britten, R. Pill, M. Morgan and J. Donovan (2003). 'Evaluating meta-ethnography: a synthesis of qualitative research on lay experiences of diabetes and diabetes care'. *Social Science & Medicine* **56**: 671–684.

Canaway, A., H. Al-Janabi, P. Kinghorn, C. Bailey and J. Coast (2017). 'Development of a measure (ICECAP-Close Person Measure) through qualitative methods to capture the benefits of end-of-life care to those close to the dying for economic evaluation'. *Palliative Medicine* **31**(1): 53–62.

Carlton, J. (2013). 'Developing the draft descriptive system for the child amblyopia treatment questionnaire (CAT-QoL): a mixed methods study'. *Health and Quality of Life Outcomes* **11**(174): 1–9.

Carman, K., C. Mallery, M. Maurer, G. Wang, S. Garfinkel, M. Yang, D. Gilmore and A. Windham (2015). 'Effectiveness of public deliberation methods for gathering input on issues in health: results from a randomized trial'. *Social Science & Medicine* **133**: 11–20.

Carmerer, C. and G. Loewenstein (2004). Behavioral economics: past, present, future. *Advances in behavioral economics*. C. Carmerer, G. Loewenstein and M. Rabin. Princeton, NJ., Princeton University Press: 3–51.

Celasun, O. and J. Walliser (2008). 'Predictability of aid: do fickle donors undermine aid effectiveness?' *Economic Policy* **55**: 545–586, 590–594.

Chalder, M., N. J. Wiles, J. Campbell, S. P. Hollinghurst, A. Searle, A. M. Haase, H. J. Taylor, K. R. Fox, H. Baxter, M. Davis, H. Thorp, R. Winder, C. Wright, M. Calnan, D. A. Lawlor, T. J. Peters, D. J. Sharp, K. M. Turner, A. A. Montgomery and G. Lewis (2012). 'A pragmatic randomised-controlled trial to evaluate the cost-effectiveness of a physical activity intervention as a treatment for depression: the treating depression with physical activity (TREAD) trial'. *Health Technology Assessment* **16**(10).

Charmaz, K. (2001). Qualitative interviewing and grounded theory analysis. *Handbook of interview research: context and method*. J. F. Gubrium and J. A. Holstein. Thousand Oaks, CA, Sage.

Charmaz, K. (2005). Grounded theory in the 21st century: a qualitative method for advancing social justice research. *Handbook of qualitative research*. N. Denzin and Y. Lincoln. Thousand Oaks, CA, Sage: 507–535.

Charmaz, K. (2014). *Constructing grounded theory*. London, Sage.

Charmaz, K. and A. Bryant (2011). Grounded theory and credibility. *Qualitative research*. D. Silverman. Thousand Oaks, CA, Sage: 291–309.

Chen, Y.-F., P. Jobanputra, P. Barton, S. M. Jowett, S. Bryan, W. Clark, A. Fry-Smith and A. Burls (2006). 'A systematic review of the effectiveness of adalimumab, etanercept and infliximab for the treatment of rheumatoid arthritis in adults and an economic evaluation of their cost-effectiveness'. *Health Technology Assessment* **10**(42): 1–266.

Cheung, J. and P. Hocking (2004). 'The experience of spousal carers of people with Multiple Sclerosis'. *Qualitative Health Research* **14**(2): 153–166.

Chilcott, J., P. Tappenden, A. Rawdin, M. Johnson, E. Kaltenthaler, S. Paisley, D. Papaioannou and A. Shippam (2010). 'Avoiding and identifying errors in health technology assessment models: qualitative study and methodological review'. *Health Technology Assessment* **14**(25): 1–135.

Clark, A. M. and D. R. Thompson (2016). 'Five tips for writing qualitative research in high-impact journals: moving from #BMJnoQual'. *International Journal of Qualitative Methods*, 1–3.

Clark, D. A. (2009). 'Adaptation, poverty and well-being: some issues and observations with special reference to the capability approach and development studies'. *Journal of Human Development and Capabilities* **10**(1): 21–42.

Coase, R. H. (1995). My evolution as an economist. *Lives of the laureates*. W. Breit. Cambridge, MIT Press: 227–249.

Coase, R. H. (1998). 'The new institutional economics'. *American Economic Review* **88(2)**: 72–74.

Coast, J. (1997). 'Rationing should be made explicit at all levels of NHS decision making: the case against'. *BMJ* **314**: 1118–1122.

Coast, J. (1999). 'The appropriate uses of qualitative methods in health economics'. *Health Economics* **1999**(8): 345–353.

Coast, J. (2000a). Explicit rationing, deprivation disutility and denial disutility: evidence from a qualitative study. *The global challenge of health care rationing*. A. Coulter and C. Ham. Milton Keynes. Columbus, OH, Open University Press.

Coast, J. (2000b). *Priority setting in health care: citizens and their agents*. PhD, University of Bristol.

Coast, J. (2001a). 'Citizens, their agents and health care rationing: an exploratory study using qualitative methods'. *Health Economics* **10**: 159–174.

Coast, J. (2001b). 'Who wants to know if their care is rationed? Views of citizens and service informants'. *Health Expectations* **4**: 243–252.

Coast, J. (2014). 'Strategies for the economic evaluation of end-of-life care: making a case for the capability approach'. *Expert Review of Pharmacoeconomics & Outcomes Research* **14**(4): 473–482.

Coast, J., H. Al-Janabi, E. Sutton, S. Horrocks, J. Vosper, D. Swancutt and T. N. Flynn (2012). 'Using qualitative methods for attribute development for discrete choice experiments'. *Health Economics* **21**(6): 730–741.

Coast, J., C. Bailey, R. Orlando, K. Armour, R. Perry and L. Jones (2014). Using a capability based outcome measure, the ICECAP-SCM, to assess benefit in a hospice setting: exploring issues around completion and adaptation. *Human Development and Capability Association Conference*. Athens.

Coast, J., J. Donovan, A. Litva, J. D. Eyles, K. Morgan, M. Shepherd and J. Tacchi (2002). ' "If there were a war tomorrow, we'd find the money": contrasting perspectives on the rationing of health care'. *Social Science & Medicine* **54**: 1839–1851.

Coast, J., T. N. Flynn, L. Natarajan, K. Sproston, J. Lewis, J. J. Louviere and T. J. Peters (2008). 'Valuing the ICECAP capability index for older people'. *Social Science & Medicine* **67**: 874–882.

Coast, J. and S. Horrocks (2007). 'Developing attributes and levels for discrete choice experiments using qualitative methods'. *Journal of Health Services Research & Policy* **12**: 25–30.

Coast, J., E. Huynh, P. Kinghorn and T. Flynn (2016). 'Complex valuation: applying ideas from the complex intervention framework to valuation of a new measure for end-of-life care'. *PharmacoEconomics* **34**: 499–508.

Coast, J., P. Kinghorn and P. Mitchell (2015). 'The development of capability measures in health economics: opportunities, challenges and progress'. *The Patient* **8**: 119–126.

Coast, J., R. McDonald and R. Baker (2004). 'Issues arising from the use of qualitative methods in health economics'. *Journal of Health Services Research & Policy* **9**: 171–176.

Coast, J., C. Salisbury, D. de Berker, A. Noble, S. Horrocks, T. J. Peters and T. N. Flynn (2006). 'Preferences for aspects of a dermatology consultation'. *British Journal of Dermatology* **155**: 387–392.

Coast, J., R. D. Smith and P. Lorgelly (2008). 'Welfarism, extra-welfarism and capability: the spread of ideas in health economics'. *Social Science & Medicine* **67**: 1190–1198.

Cohen, M. Z. and A. Omery (1994). Schools of phenomenology: implications for research. *Critical issues in qualitative research methods*. J. M. Morse. Thousand Oaks, CA, Sage: 136–156.

Colander, D., M. Goldberg, A. Haas, K. Juselius, A. Kirman, T. Lux and B. Sloth (2009). 'The financial crisis and the systemic failure of the economics profession'. *Critical Review* **21**(2–3): 249–267.

Collins, D. (2003). 'Pretesting survey instruments: an overview of cognitive methods'. *Quality of Life Research* **12**: 229–238.

Consortium of European Social Science Data Archives (CESSDA) (2016). National Data Services. https://cessda.net/National-Data-Services.

Cookson, R. and P. Dolan (1999). 'Public views on health care rationing: a group discussion study'. *Health Policy* **49**: 63–74.

Coombes, J. M. and J. F. Trotter (2005). 'Development of the allocation system for deceased donor liver transplantation'. *Clinical Medicine & Research* **3**(2): 87–92.

Cooper-Patrick, L., N. R. Powe, M. W. Jenckes, J. J. Gonzales, D. M. Levine and D. E. Ford (1997). 'Identification of patient attitudes and preferences regarding treatment of depression'. *Journal of General Internal Medicine* **12**(7): 431–438.

Coote, A. and J. Lenaghan (1997). *Citizens' juries: theory into practice*. London, Institute for Public Policy Research.

Cornelissen, E., C. Mitton, A. Davidson, C. Reid, R. Hole, A.-M. Visockas and N. Smith (2014). 'Determining and broadening the definition of impact from implementing a rational priority setting approach in a healthcare organization'. *Social Science & Medicine* **114**: 1–9.

Cornwell, J. (1984). *Hard earned lives: accounts of health and illness from East London*. London, Tavistock.

Cote-Arsenault, D. and E. Denney-Koelsch (2016). '"Have no regrets:" parents' experiences and developmental tasks in pregnancy with a lethal fatal diagnosis'. *Social Science & Medicine* **154**: 100–109.

Crabtree, B. F. and W. L. Miller (1992). A template approach to text analysis: developing and using codebooks. *Doing qualitative research*. B. F. Crabtree. London, Sage: 93–109.

Craig, P., P. Dieppe, S. Macintyre, S. Mitchie, I. Nazareth and M. Petticrew (2008). 'Developing and evaluating complex interventions: the new Medical Research Council guidance'. *BMJ* **337**: a1655.

Creswell, J. W. (2012). *Research design: qualitative, quantitative, and mixed methods approaches*. Thousand Oaks, CA, Sage.

Creswell, J. W. (2013). *Qualitative inquiry & research design. Choosing among five approaches*. Thousand Oaks, CA, Sage.

Creswell, J. W. and V. L. Plano Clark (2011). *Designing and conducting mixed methods research*. Thousand Oaks, CA, Sage.

Crotty, M. (1998). *The foundations of social research: meaning and perspective in the research process*. Thousand Oaks, CA, Sage.

Cruz, V. O. and B. McPake (2010). 'The "aid contract" and its compensation scheme: a case study of the performance of the Ugandan health sector'. *Social Science & Medicine* **71**: 1357–1365.

Cruz, V. O. and B. McPake (2011). 'Global Health Initiatives and aid effectiveness: insights from a Ugandan case study'. *Globalization and Health* **7**(20): 1–10.

Culyer, A. J. (1971). 'Medical care and the economics of giving'. *Economica* **August**: 295–303.

Culyer, A. J. (1989). 'The normative economics of health care finance and provision'. *Oxford Review of Economics and Policy* **5**(1): 34–56.

Culyer, A. J. and H. Simpson (1980). 'Externality models and health: a Ruckblick over the last 20 years'. *Economic Record* **56**: 222–230.

Cummins, R. (2002). Proxy responding for subjective well-being: a review. *International review of research in mental retardation*. N. Ellis, N. Bray and L. Glidden. San Diego, CA, Academic Press. **25:** 183–207.

Cuppen, E., S. Breukers, M. Hisschemöller and E. W. Bergsma (2010). 'Q methodology to select participants for a stakeholder dialogue on energy options from biomass in the Netherlands'. *Ecological Economics* **69**(3): 579–591.

Dakin, H., N. Devlin, Y. Feng, N. Rice, P. O'Neill and D. Parkin (2015). 'The influence of cost-effectiveness and other factors on NICE decisions'. *Health Economics* **24**: 1256–1271.

Danner, M., V. Vennedey, M. Hiligsmann, S. Fauser and S. Stock (2016). 'Focus groups in elderly ophthalmologic patients: setting the stage for quantitative preference elicitation'. *The Patient* **9**: 47–57.

Datta, J. and M. Petticrew (2013). 'Challenges to evaluating complex interventions: a content analysis of published papers'. *BMC Public Health* **13**(568): 1–18.

Davidson, C. (2009). 'Transcription imperatives for qualitative research'. *International Journal of Qualitative Methods* **8**(2): 35–52.

De Allegri, M., M. Sanon, J. Bridges and R. Sauerborn (2006a). 'Understanding consumers' preferences and decision to enrol in community-based health insurance in rural West Africa'. *Health Policy* **76**: 58–71.

De Allegri, M., M. Sanon and R. Sauerborn (2006b). ' "To enrol or not to enrol?": a qualitative investigation of demand for health insurance in rural West Africa'. *Social Science & Medicine* **62**: 1520–1527.

Delli Carpini, M. X., F. Lomax Cook and L. R. Jacobs (2004). 'Public deliberation, discursive participation, and citizen engagement: a review of the empirical literature'. *Annual Review of Political Science* **7**: 315–344.

Dennis, A. C., C. Barrington, S. Hino, D. Wohl and C. E. Golin (2015). ' "You're in a world of chaos": experiences accessing HIV care and adhering to medications after incarceration'. *Journal of the Association of Nurses in AIDS Care* **26**: 542–555.

Denzin, N. K. and Y. S. Lincoln (1994). *Handbook of qualitative research*. London, Sage.

Department of Economic and Social Affairs of the United Nations Secretariat (2015). The Millennium Development Goals Report, United Nations.

Devlin, N., K. Shah, Y. Feng, B. Mulhern and B. Van Hout (2016). *Valuing health-related quality of life. An EQ-5D-5L value set for England*. London, Office of Health Economics.

Dey, I. (2003). *Qualitative data analysis: a user-friendly guide for social scientists*. London, Routledge.

DiCicco-Bloom, B. and B. F. Crabtree (2006). 'The qualitative research interview'. *Medical Education* **40**(4): 314–321.

Dingwall, R., E. Murphy, P. Watson, D. Greatbatch and S. Parker (1998). 'Catching goldfish: quality in qualitative research'. *Journal of Health Services Research & Policy* **3**(3): 167–172.

Dionne, F., C. Mitton, N. Smith and C. Donaldson (2009). 'Evaluation of the impact of program budgeting and marginal analysis in Vancouver Island Health Authority'. *Journal of Health Services Research & Policy* **14**(4): 234–242.

Dixon-Woods, M., S. Agarwal, D. Jones, B. Young and A. Sutton (2005). 'Synthesising qualitative and quantitative evidence: a review of possible methods'. *Journal of Health Services Research & Policy* **10**(1): 45–53.

Dolan, P. (1997). 'Modelling valuations for EuroQol health states'. *Medical Care* **35**: 1095–1108.

Dolan, P. and R. Cookson (2000). 'A qualitative study of the extent to which health gain matters when choosing between groups of patients'. *Health Policy* **51**: 19–30.

Dolan, P., R. Cookson and B. Ferguson (1999). 'Effect of discussion and deliberation on the public's views of priority setting in health care: focus group study'. *BMJ* **318**: 916–919.

Dolan, P. and C. Green (1998). 'Using the person trade-off approach to examine differences between individual and social values'. *Health Economics* **7**: 307–312.

Donaldson, C. (1993). *Theory and practice of willingness to pay for health care*. Aberdeen, Health Economics Research Unit.

Donaldson, C., A. Bate, C. Mitton, S. Peacock and D. Ruta (2008). Priority setting in the public sector: turning economics into a management process. *Managing to improve public services*. J. Hartley, C. Donaldson, J. Skeltcher and M. Wallace. Cambridge, Cambridge University Press.

Donovan, J. L. and D. R. Blake (1992). 'Patient non-compliance: deviance or reasoned decision-making?' *Social Science & Medicine* **34**(5): 507–513.

Donovan, J. L. and J. Coast (1996). Public participation in priority setting: commitment or illusion? *Priority setting: the health care debate*. J. Coast. Chichester, John Wiley & Sons, Ltd.

Downward, P. and A. Mearman (2007). 'Retroduction as mixed-methods triangulation in economic research: reorienting economics into social science'. *Cambridge Journal of Economics* **31**(1): 77–99.

Doyle, L. (2003). 'Synthesis through meta-ethnography: paradoxes, enhancements and possibilities'. *Qualitative Research* **3**: 321–344.

Dreachslin, J. L. (1998). 'Conducting effective focus groups in the context of diversity: theoretical underpinnings and practical implications'. *Qualitative Health Research* **8**(6): 813–820.

Drummond, M. F., M. J. Sculpher, K. Claxton, G. L. Stoddart and G. W. Torrance (2015). *Methods for the economic evaluation of health care programmes*. Oxford, Oxford University Press.

Dugger, W. (1994). Methodological differences between institutional and neoclassical economics. *The philosophy of economics. An anthology*. D. M. Hausman. Cambridge, Cambridge University Press: 336–345.

Durif-Bruckert, C., P. Roux, M. Morelle, H. Mignotte, C. Faure and N. Moumijd-Ferdjaoui (2015). 'Shared decision-making in medical encounters regarding breast cancer treatment: the contribution of methodological triangulation'. *European Journal of Cancer Care* **24**: 461–472.

Dwight-Johnson, M., I. T. Lagomasino, E. Aisenberg and J. Hay (2004). 'Using conjoint analysis to assess depression treatment preferences among low-income Latinos'. *Psychiatric Services* **55**(8): 934–936.

Early, B. P., E. D. Smith, L. Todd and T. Beem (2000). 'The needs and supportive networks of the dying: an assessment instrument and mapping procedure for hospice patients'. *American Journal of Hospice and Palliative Medicine* **17**(2): 87–96.

Eberle, T. S. and C. Maeder (2011). Organizational ethnography. *Qualitative research*. D. Silverman. London, Sage: 53–73.

Eckard, N. (in press). 'Reaching agreement in uncertain circumstances: the practice of evidence-based policy in the case of the Swedish National Guidelines for heart diseases (in press)'. *Evidence & Policy*.

Eckard, N., M. Janzon and L.-A. Levin (2014). 'Use of cost-effectiveness data in priority setting decisions: experiences from the national guidelines for heart diseases in Sweden'. *International Journal of Health Policy and Management* **3**(6): 323–332.

Economic and Social Research Council (2015). *ESRC framework for research ethics. Updated January 2015*. Swindon, ESRC.

Eddama, O. and J. Coast (2008). 'A systematic review of the use of economic evaluation in local decision-making'. *Health Policy* **86**(2–3): 129–141.

Eddama, O. and J. Coast (2009). 'Use of economic evaluation in local health care decision-making in England: a qualitative investigation'. *Health Policy* **89**: 261–270.

Ellis, J. (2015). *Using qualitative methods to assess impact*. London, NCVO Charities Evaluation Service.

Ensor, T. (2004). 'Consumer-led demand side financing in health and education and its relevance for low and middle income countries'. *International Journal of Health Planning and Management* **19**: 267–285.

Ericsson, K. and H. Simon (1980). 'Verbal reports as data'. *Psychological Review* **87**: 215–251.

Ericsson, K. and H. Simon (1993). *Protocol analysis: verbal reports as data*. Cambridge, MA, MIT Press.

Esim, S. (1997). 'Can feminist methodology reduce power hierarchies in research settings?' *Feminist Economics* **3**(2): 137–139.

Essink-Bot, M.-L., J. Pereira, C. Packer, M. Schwarzinger and K. Burström (2002). 'Cross-national comparability of burden of disease estimates: the European Disability Weights Project'. *Bulletin of the World Health Organization* **80**(8): 644–652.

Esterberg, K. G. (2002). *Qualitative methods in social research*. Boston, MA, McGraw-Hill.

The EuroQol Group (1996). *EQ-5D User Guide*. Rotterdam, The EuroQol Group.

Evans, M. J. and C. E. Hallett (2007). 'Living with dying: a hermeneutic phenomenological study of the work of hospice nurses'. *Journal of Clinical Nursing* **16**: 742–751.

Evans, R. G. (1980). Supplier-induced demand: some empirical evidence and implications. *The economics of health and medical care*. M. Perlman. London, Macmillan: 162–173.

Evans, R. G. (1984). *Strained mercy: the economics of Canadian health care*. Toronto, Butterworths.

Evans, R. G. and A. D. Wolfson (1980). *Faith, hope and charity: health care in the utility function*. Vancouver, University of British Columbia.

Eyben, R. (2006). *Relationships for aid.* London, Earthscan.

Fayers, P. and R. Hays (1998). *Assessing quality of life in clinical trials.* Oxford, Oxford University Press.

Feeny, D. H., E. Eckstrom, E. P. Whitlock and L. A. Perdue (2013). *A primer for systematic reviewers on the measurement of functional status and health-related quality of life in older adults.* Agency for Healthcare Research and Quality (US).

Fielding, N. G. and J. L. Fielding (2000). 'Resistance and adaptation to criminal identity: using secondary analysis to evaluate classic studies of crime and deviance'. *Sociology* **34**: 671–689.

Finch, H. and J. Lewis (2003). Focus groups. *Qualitative research practice: a guide for social science students and researchers.* J. Ritchie and J. Lewis. London, Sage.

Finfgeld, D. (2003). 'Metasynthesis: the state of the art – so far'. *Qualitative Health Research* **13**(7): 893–904.

Finlay, L. (2002). 'Negotiating the swamp: the opportunity and challenge of reflexivity in research practice'. *Qualitative Research* **2**(2): 209–230.

Fischer, D. J., S. C. Burgener, K. Kavanaugh, C. Ryan and G. Keenan (2012). 'Conducting research with end-of-life populations: overcoming recruitment challenges when working with clinical agencies'. *Applied Nursing Research* **25**(4): 258–263.

Fisher, R. A. (1960). *The design of experiments.* New York, Hafner.

Fishkin, J. S. (1991). *Democracy and deliberation. New directions for democratic reform.* London, Yale University Press.

Fishkin, J. S. and R. C. Luskin (2005). 'Experimenting with a democratic ideal: deliberative polling and public opinion'. *Acta Politica* **40**: 284–298.

Fitzpatrick, R., C. Davey, M. Buxton and D. R. Jones (1998). 'Evaluating patient based outcome measures for use in clinical trials'. *Health Technology Assessment* **14**: 1–74.

Florczak, K. L. (2014). 'Research at the end of life: a sacred undertaking'. *Nursing Science Quarterly* **27**(1): 12–13.

Flynn, T. N. (2016). Where next for discrete choice experiments? *SSRN Electronic Library.* doi: 10.2139/ssrn.2810444.

Flynn, T. N., E. Huynh, T. J. Peters, H. Al-Janabi, S. Clemens, A. Moody and J. Coast (2015). 'Scoring the ICECAP-A capability instrument. Estimation of a UK general population tariff'. *Health Economics* **24**(3): 258–269.

Flynn, T. N., J. J. Louviere, T. J. Peters and J. Coast (2007). 'Best-worst scaling. What it can do for health care research and how to do it'. *Journal of Health Economics* **26**: 171–189.

Fonteyn, M. E., B. Kuipers and S. J. Grobe (1993). 'A description of think aloud method and protocol analysis'. *Qualitative Health Research* **3**(4): 430–441.

Fraser, K. D., C. Estabrooks, M. D. Allen and V. Strang (2009). 'Factors that influence case managers' resource allocation decisions in pediatric home care: an ethnographic study'. *International Journal of Nursing Studies* **46**(3): 337–349.

Friedman, M. (1994). The methodology of positive economics. *The philosophy of economics. An anthology.* D. M. Hausman. Cambridge, Cambridge University Press: 180–213.

Frot, E. and J. Santiso (2010). Crushed Aid: fragmentation in sectoral aid. *OECD DEVELOPMENT CENTRE.* Working Paper No. 284.

Fusch, P. I. and L. R. Ness (2015). 'Are we there yet? Data saturation in qualitative research'. *The Qualitative Report* **20**(9): 1408–1416.
Gabbay, J. and A. le May (2004). 'Evidence based guidelines or collectively constructed 'mindlines?" Ethnographic study of knowledge management in primary care'. *BMJ* **329**(1013): 1–5.
Gabhainn, S. N. and J. Sixsmith (2006). 'Children photographing well-being: facilitating participation in research'. *Children & Society* **20**: 249–259.
Gagliardi, A. R. and M. J. Dobrow (2011). 'Paucity of qualitative research in general medical and health services and policy research journals: analysis of publication rates'. *BMC Health Services Research* **11**(268): 1–7.
Gale, N. K., G. Heath, E. Cameron, S. Rashid and S. Redwood (2013). 'Using the framework method for the analysis of qualitative data in multi-disciplinary health research'. *Medical Research Methodology* **13**: 117.
Gallet, C. and J. List (2003). 'Cigarette demand: a meta-analysis of elasticities'. *Health Economics* **12**(10): 821–835.
Garbarino, S. and J. Holland (2009). *Quantitative and qualitative methods in impact evaluation and measuring results*. Birmingham, Governance and Social Development Resource Centre.
Garfield, S., S.-A. Francis and F. J. Smith (2004). 'Building concordant relationships with patients starting antidepressant medication'. *Patient Education and Counseling* **55**(2): 241–246.
Geneau, R., P. Massae, P. Courtright and S. Lewallen (2008). 'Using qualitative methods to understand the determinants of patients' willingness to pay for cataract surgery: a study in Tanzania'. *Social Science & Medicine* **66**: 558–568.
Gertler, P. J., S. Martinez, P. Premand, L. B. Rawlings and C. M. J. Vermeersch (2010). *Impact evaluation in practice*. Washington, DC., World Bank Publications.
Gibbs, A. (1997). 'Focus groups'. *Social Research* **19**: 1–4.
Gibson, J., C. Mitton, D. Martin, C. Donaldson and P. Singer (2006). 'Ethics and economics: does programme budgeting and marginal analysis contribute to fair priority setting?' *Journal of Health Services Research & Policy* **11**(1): 32–37.
Gilhooly, K. and Green, C. (1996). *Protocol analysis: theoretical background*. Handbook of qualitative research methods. J. Richardson. Leicester, BPS Books.
Gillman, B. (2000). *The research interview*. London, Continuum.
Given, L. M. (2008). *The SAGE encyclopedia of qualitative research methods*. Thousand Oaks, CA, Sage.
Glaser, B. (1965). 'The constant comparison method of qualitative analysis'. *Social Problems* **12**(4): 436–445.
Glaser, B. (2005). 'The impact of symbolic interaction on grounded theory. (Chapter 10, (The grounded theory perspective III: theoretical coding, Sociology Press, 2005)'. *Grounded Theory Review* **4**(2).
Glaser, B. G. and A. L. Strauss (1967). *The discovery of grounded theory: strategies for qualitative research*. Chicago, Aldine.
Glaser, B. G. and A. L. Strauss (1968). *The discovery of grounded theory: strategies for qualitative research*. London, Weidenfeld and Nicolson.
Gobo, G. (2011). Ethnography. *Qualitative research*. D. Silverman. London, Sage: 15–34.

Goddard, M., R. Mannion and P. Smith (2000). 'Enhancing performance in health care: a theoretical perspective on agency and the role of information'. *Health Economics* **9**: 95–107.

Goebbels, A. F. G., J. Lakerveld, A. J. H. A. Ament, S. D. M. Bot and J. L. Severens (2012). 'Exploring non-health outcomes of health promotion: the perspective of participants in a lifestyle behaviour change intervention'. *Health Policy* **106**: 177–186.

Gold, R. L. (1997). 'The ethnographic method in sociology'. *Qualitative Inquiry* **3**(4): 388–402.

Goldthorpe, J. H., D. Lockwood, F. Bechhofer and J. Platt (1969). *The affluent worker in the class structure*. Cambridge, Cambridge University Press.

González, M. C., M. M. N. Regalado and J. T. Guerrero (2010). 'Teaching and learning social values: experience of resolution of conflicts in the classroom of physical education across the learning of social skills'. *Journal of Human Sport and Exercise* **5**(3): 497–506.

Goodin, R. E. (2000). 'Democratic deliberation within'. *Philosophy and Public Affairs* **29**: 81–109.

Goodwin, E. and E. J. Frew (2013). 'Using programme budgeting and marginal analysis (PBMA) to set priorities: reflections from a qualitative assessment in an English Primary Care Trust'. *Social Science & Medicine* **98**: 162–168.

Graça Moura, M. da. and N. Martins (2008). 'On some criticisms of critical realism in economics'. *Cambridge Journal of Economics* **32**(2): 203–218.

Graneheim, U. H. and B. Lundman (2004). 'Qualitative content analysis in nursing research: concepts, procedures and measures to achieve trustworthiness'. *Nurse Education Today* **24**(2): 105–112.

Granovetter, M. S. (1973). 'The strength of weak ties'. *American Journal of Sociology* **78**(6): 1360–1380.

Grbich, C. (2013). *Qualitative data analysis. An introduction*. London, Sage.

Green, C., J. Moehr and M. Campbell (2004). *Governing health regions/informing board members*. Proceedings of the 37th Hawaii International Conference on Systems Science, Big Island, Hawaii.

Green, J. and N. Thorogood (2009). *Qualitative methods for health research*. London, Sage.

Green, J. and N. Thorogood (2014). *Qualitative methods for health research*. London, Sage.

Greenhalgh, T. (2016). 'An open letter to The BMJ editors on qualitative research'. *BMJ* **352**(i563): 1–4.

Greenhalgh, T., J. Russell and D. Swinglehurst (2005). 'Narrative methods in quality improvement research'. *Quality and Safety in Health Care* **14**(6): 443–449.

Grewal, I., J. Lewis, T. N. Flynn, J. Brown, J. Bond and J. Coast (2006). 'Developing attributes for a generic quality of life measure for older people: preferences or capabilities?' *Social Science & Medicine* **62**: 1891–1901.

Grip, L., B. Lindahl, L.-Å. Levin, C. Kärvinge, K. Eklund and L. Wallentin (2011). 'From European to National guidelines on heart disease'. *Scandinavian Cardiovascular Journal* **45**(1): 3–13.

Grittner, A. M. (2013). Results-based financing. Evidence from performance-based financing in the health sector. Bonn, German Development Institute.

Guba, E. G. (1990). *The paradigm dialog*. Newbury Park, CA, Sage.

Guerin, P. J. and E. G. Pendagast (1976). Evaluation of family system and genogram. *Family therapy: theory and practice*. New York, Gardner Press: 450–464.

Guyatt, G. H. and D. J. Cook (1994). 'Health status, quality of life, and the individual'. *JAMA* **272**(8): 630–631.

Gysels, M. H., C. Evans and I. J. Higginson (2012). 'Patient, caregiver, health professional and researcher views and experiences of participating in research at the end of life: a critical interpretive synthesis of the literature'. *BMC Medical Research Methodology* **12**: 123.

Hall, W., N. Smith, C. Mitton, J. Gibson and S. Bryan (2016). 'An evaluation tool for assessing performance in priority setting and resource allocation: multi-site application to identify strengths and weaknesses'. *Journal of Health Services Research & Policy* **21**(1): 15–23.

Hammersley, M. (1990). *Reading ethnographic research: a critical guide*. London, Longmans.

Hammersley, M. (1992). *What's wrong with ethnography? Methodological explorations*. London, Routledge.

Hammersley, M. and P. Atkinson (1983). *Ethnography: principles in practice*. London, Tavistock.

Hancock, B. (1998). *Trent focus for research and development in primary health care. An introduction to qualitative research*. Nottingham, Trent Focus.

Hanratty, B., E. Lowson, L. Holmes, J. Addington-Hall, A. Arthur, G. Grande, S. Payne and J. Seymour (2012). 'A comparison of strategies to recruit older patients and carers to end-of-life research in primary care'. *BMC Health Services Research* **12**(1): 1.

Hansen, E. C. (2006). *Successful qualitative health research. A practical introduction*. Maidenhead, Open University Press.

Harris, P. (1993). 'The misunderstood carer? A qualitative study of the male caregiver of Alzheimer's Disease victims'. *The Gerontologist* **33**(4): 551–556.

Harrison, S. and M. Mort (1998). 'Which champions. which people? Public and user involvement in health care as a technology of legitimation'. *Social Policy & Administration* **32(1)**: 60–70.

Hartman, A. (1978). 'Diagrammatic assessment of family relationships'. *Social Casework* **59**: 465–476.

Hasman, A., E. McIntosh and T. Hope (2008). 'What reasons do those with practical experience use in deciding on priorities for healthcare resources? A qualitative study'. *Journal of Medical Ethics* **34**(9): 658–663.

Hausman, D. M. and M. S. McPherson (1994). Economics, rationality and ethics. *The philosophy of economics. An anthology*. D. M. Hausman. Cambridge, Cambridge University Press: 252–277.

Hausmann, D. M. (1994). Introduction. *The philosophy of economics. An anthology*. D. M. Hausmann. Cambridge, Cambridge University Press: 1–50.

Hawthorne, G., J. Richardson, R. Osborne and H. McNeil (1997). *The Assessment of Quality of Life (AQoL) instrument construction, initial validation and utility scaling*. Working paper 76. Melbourne, Australia, Monash University.

Health Research Authority (2014). *Consent and participant information sheet preparation guidance*. UK.
Health Results Innovation Trust Fund (2015). *Achieving results for women's and children's health. Progress report 2015*. Washington, DC, World Bank Group.
Heaton, J. (2004). *Reworking qualitative data*. London, Sage.
Heaton, J. (2008). 'Secondary analysis of qualitative data: an overview'. *Historical Social Research* **33**(3): 33–45.
Herdman, M., C. Gudex, A. Lloyd, M. F. Janssen, P. Kind, D. Parkin, G. Bonsel and X. Badia (2011). 'Development and preliminary testing of the new five-level version of EQ-D (EQ-5D-5L)'. *Quality of Life Research* **20**: 1727–1736.
Heritage, J. (2011). Conversation analysis: practices and methods. *Qualitative Research*. D. Silverman. London, Sage: 208–230.
Heukelom, F. (2014). *Behavioral economics: a history*. New York, Cambridge University Press.
Hewitt-Taylor, J. (2001). 'Use of constant comparative analysis in qualitative research'. *Nursing Standard* **15**(42): 39–42.
Hirschfeld, R. M. A. (2001). 'The comorbidity of major depression and anxiety disorders: recognition and management in primary care'. *Primary Care Companion to the Journal of Clinical Psychiatry* **3**(6): 244–254.
Hlebec, V., M. Mrzel and T. Kogovsek (2009). 'Social support network and received support at stressful events'. *Metodoloski Zvezki* **6**(2): 155.
Hodgson, G. (1986) 'Behind methodological individualism'. *Cambridge Journal of Economics* 10: 211–224.
Hole, R. (2014). Qualitative health research. *Health research methods: a Canadian perspective*. K. Bassil and D. Zabkiewicz. Oxford, Oxford University Press: 165–189.
Hollis, M. (1994). Positive science: the empiricist way. *The philosophy of social science*. M. Hollis. Cambridge, Cambridge University Press: 40–65.
Holmes, R. D., A. Bate, J. G. Steele and C. Donaldson (2009). 'Commissioning NHS dentistry in England: issues for decision-makers managing the new contract with finite resources'. *Health Policy* **91**: 79–88.
Hoover, K. D. (2010). 'Introduction: methodological implications of the financial crisis'. *Journal of Economic Methodology* **17**(4): 397–398.
Hope, J. (2009). Condemned to an early death: rationing body tells liver cancer victims that life-prolonging drug is 'too costly'. *Daily Mail*, **20 November**.
Hopf, C. (2004). Research ethics and qualitative research. *A companion to qualitative research*. U. Flick, E. von Kardorff and I. Steinke. London, Sage.
Horrocks, S. and J. Coast (2007). 'Patient choice: an exploration of primary care dermatology patients' values and expectations of care'. *Quality in Primary Care* **15**: 185–193.
Horstman, M., S. Aldiss, A. Richardson and F. Gibson (2008). 'Methodological issues when using the draw and write technique with children aged 6 to 12 years'. *Qualitative Health Research* **18(7)**: 1001–1011.
Horwood, J., E. Sutton and J. Coast (2014). 'Evaluating the face validity of the ICECAP-O capabilities measure: a 'think aloud' study with hip and knee arthroplasty patients'. *Applied Research in Quality of Life* **9**(3): 667–682.

Hughes, J. (1990). The interpretative alternative. *The philosophy of social research.* J. Hughes. London, Longman: 89–113.

Hummers-Pradier, E., C. Scheidt-Nave, H. Martin, S. Heinemann, M. M. Kochen and W. Himmel (2008). 'Simply no time? Barriers to GPs' participation in primary health care research'. *Family Practice* **25**(2): 105–112.

Hunter, D. (1993). *Rationing dilemmas in healthcare.* Birmingham, NAHAT.

Hutton, G. and M. Tanner (2004). 'The sector-wide approach: a blessing for public health?' *Bulletin of the World Health Organisation* **82**(12): 893.

Hutton, J. and R. E. Brown (2002). 'Use of economic evaluation in decision making: what needs to change?' *Value in Health* **5**(2): 65–66.

Hycner, R. H. (1985). 'Some guidelines for the phenomenological analysis of interview data'. *Human Studies* **8**: 279–303.

Institute for Health Metrics and Evaluation (2016). *Financing Global Health 2015: development assistance steady on the path to new Global Goals*. Seattle, WA, IHME.

Jackson, L. J. and T. E. Roberts (2015). 'Conceptualising quality of life outcomes for women participating in testing for sexually transmitted infections: a systematic review and meta-synthesis of qualitative research'. *Social Science & Medicine* **143**: 162–170.

Jacobs, M. (1997). Environmental valuation, deliberative democracy and public decision making institutions. *Valuing nature? Economics, ethics and environment*. J. Foster. London, Routledge.

Jeffares, S. and C. Skelcher (2011). 'Democratic subjectivities in network governance: a Q methodology study of English and Dutch public managers'. *Public Administration* **89**(4): 1253–1273.

Jefferson, T., S. Austen, R. Sharp, R. Ong, G. Lewin and V. Adams (2014). 'Mixed-methods research: what's in it for economists?' *The Economic and Labour Relations Review* **25**(2): 290–305.

Jepson, M., C. Salisbury, M. J. Ridd, C. Metcalfe, L. Garside and R. K. Barnes (2017). '"The One in a Million Study": creating a database of UK primary care consultations'. *British Journal of General Practice* (in press).

Joffe, H. and L. Yardley (2004). Content and thematic analysis. *Research methods for clinical and health psychology*. D. Marks and L. Yardley. London, Sage: 56–68.

Johnson, J. C. and S. C. Weller (2001). Elicitation techniques for interviewing. *Handbook of interview research: context and method.* J. F. Gubrium and J. A. Holstein. Thousand Oaks, CA, Sage.

Johnson, J. M. (2001). In-depth interviewing. *Handbook of interview research: context and method.* J. F. Gubrium and J. A. Holstein. Thousand Oaks, CA, Sage.

Johnson, R. B. and A. T. Onwuegbuzie (2004). 'Mixed methods research: a research paradigm whose time has come'. *Educational Researcher* **33**(7): 14–26.

Jones, C. A. and D. H. Feeny (2005). 'Agreement between patient and proxy responses of health-related quality of life after hip fracture'. *Journal of the American Geriatrics Society* **53**(7): 1227–1233.

Jones, G., S. Kennedy, A. Barnard, J. Wong and C. Jenkinson (2001). 'Development of an endometriosis quality-of-life instrument: the Endometriosis Health Profile-30'. *Obstetrics & Gynecology* **98**(2): 258–264.

Junghans, A. F., T. T. L. Cheung and D. D. T. De Ridder (2015). 'Under consumers' scrutiny – an investigation into consumers' attitudes and concerns about nudging in the realm of health behaviour'. *BMC Public Health* **15**(336): 1–13.

Juniper, E. F., G. H. Guyatt, R. S. Epstein, P. J. Ferrie, R. Jaeschke and T. K. Hiller (1992). 'Evaluation of impairment of health related quality of life in asthma: development of a questionnaire for use in clinical trials'. *Thorax* **47**(2): 76–83.

Kahlke, R. M. (2014). 'Generic qualitative approaches: pitfalls and benefits of methodological mixology'. *International Journal of Qualitative Methods* **13**(1): 37–52.

Kaltenthaler, E., M. Essat, P. Tappenden and S. Paisley (2014). 'Identification and review of cost-effectiveness model parameters: a qualitative study'. *International Journal of Technology Assessment in Health Care* **30**(3): 333–340.

Kapiriri, L., O. F. Norheim and K. Heggenhougen (2003). 'Public participation in health planning and priority setting at the district level in Uganda'. *Health Policy and Planning* **18**(2): 205–213.

Kapiriri, L., O. F. Norheim and D. K. Martin (2007). 'Priority setting at the micro-, meso- and macro-levels in Canada, Norway and Uganda'. *Health Policy* **82**(1): 78–94.

Karnon, J., E. Goyder, P. Tappenden, S. McPhie, I. Towers, J. Brazier and J. Madan (2007). 'A review and critique of modelling in prioritising and designing screening programmes'. *Health Technology Assessment* **11**(52): iii–iv, ix–xi, 1–145.

Kavanaugh, K. L. and M. L. Campbell (2014). 'Conducing end-of-life research: strategies for success'. *Nursing Science Quarterly* **27**(1): 14–19.

Ke, K. M., F. Mackichan, J. R. Sandy, A. R. Ness and W. Hollingworth (2013). 'Parents' perspectives on centralized cleft services for children: the development of a DCE questionnaire'. *Oral Diseases* **19**: 185–192.

Keeley, T., H. Al-Janabi, P. Lorgelly and J. Coast (2013). 'A qualitative assessment of the content validity of the ICECAP-A and EQ-5D-5L and their appropriateness for use in clinical research'. *PLoS ONE* **8**(12): e85287.

Kelly, M. (2010). 'The role of theory in qualitative health research'. *Family Practice* **27**: 285–290.

Kenny, N. and C. Joffres (2008). 'An ethical analysis of international health priority-setting'. *Health Care Analysis* **16**(2): 145–160.

King, N., A. Bravington, J. Brooks, B. Hardy, J. Melvin and D. Wilde (2013). 'The Pictor Technique: a method for exploring the experience of collaborative working'. *Qualitative Health Research* **23**(8): 1138–1152.

King, N. and C. Horrocks (2010). *Interviews in qualitative research*. London, Sage.

Kingdon, J. (1995). *Agendas, alternatives and public policy*. New York, Addison-Wesley Educational Publishers Inc.

Kinghorn, P. (2015). 'Exploring different interpretations of the capability approach in a health care context: where next?' *Journal of Human Development and Capabilities* **16**(4): 600–616.

Kinghorn, P., A. Robinson and R. D. Smith (2014). 'Developing a capability-based questionnaire for assessing well-being in patients with chronic pain'. *Social Indicators Research* **120**: 897–916.

Kitzinger, J. (1994). 'The methodology of focus groups: the importance of interaction between research participants'. *Sociology of Health and Illness* **16(1)**: 103–121.

Kitzinger, J. (1995). 'Introducing focus groups'. *BMJ* **311**: 299–302.

Kitzinger, J. (2006). Focus groups. *Qualitative research in health care. 3rd edition.* C. Pope and N. Mays. Oxford, Blackwell**:** 21–31.

Klein, R. (1984). The politics of participation. *Public participation in health.* R. Maxwell. London, King Edward's Hospital Fund for London**:** 17–32.

Kongnyuy, E. J., G. Mlava and N. van den Broek (2009). 'Facility-based maternal death review in three districts in the central region of Malawi: an analysis of causes and characteristics of maternal deaths'. *Women's Health Issues* **19**(1): 14–20.

Krugman, P. (2009). 'How did economists get it so wrong?' *New York Times,* **2 September**.

Kuntz, K. M. and M. C. Weinstein (2001). Modelling in economic evaluation. *Economic evaluation in health care: merging theory with practice*. M. Drummond and A. McGuire. New York, Oxford University Press**:** 141–171.

Kupfer, D. J., E. Frank and M. L. Phillips (2012). 'Major depressive disorder: new clinical, neurobiological, and treatment perspectives'. *Lancet* **379**: 1045–1055.

Kvale, S. (1996). *InterViews*. Thousand Oaks, CA, Sage.

Kvale, S. and S. Brinkmann (2009). *Interviews: learning the craft of qualitative research interviewing*. Los Angeles, Sage.

Labelle, R., G. Stoddart and T. Rice (1994). 'A re-examination of the meaning and importance of supplier-induced demand'. *Journal of Health Economics* **13**: 347–368.

Lafi, R., S. Robinson and I. Williams (2012). 'Economic evaluation and the Jordan Rational Drug List: an exploratory study of national-level priority setting'. *Value in Health* **15**: 771–776.

Lancsar, E., J. Wildman, C. Donaldson, M. Ryan and R. Baker (2011). 'Deriving distributional weights for QALYs through discrete choice experiments'. *Journal of Health Economics* **30**: 466–478.

Lavis, J. N., D. Robertson, J. M. Woodside, C. B. McLeod and J. Abelson (2003). 'How can research organizations more effectively transfer research knowledge to decision makers?' *The Milbank Quarterly* **81**(2): 221–248.

Lawson, T. (1995a). 'The "Lucas critique": a generalisation'. *Cambridge Journal of Economics* **19**: 257–276.

Lawson, T. (1995b). 'A realist perspective on contemporary "economic theory"'. *Journal of Economic Issues* **24**(1): 1–32.

Lawson, T. (1996). 'Developments in economics as a realist social theory'. *Review of Social Economy* **54**(4): 405–422.

Lawson, T. (1997). *Economics and reality*. London, Routledge.

Lawson, T. (1999). Critical issues in economics as realist social theory. *Critical realism in economics. Development and debate*. S. Fleetwood. London, Routledge**:** 209–258.

Lawson, T. (2003). *Reorienting economics*. Abingdon, Oxon, Routledge.

Lawson, T. (2006). 'The nature of heterodox economics'. *Cambridge Journal of Economics* **30**: 483–505.

Lawson, T. (2009). 'The current economic crisis: its nature and the course of academic economics'. *Cambridge Journal of Economics* **33**(4): 759–777.

Lechner, M. (2010). 'The estimation of causal effects by difference-in-difference methods'. *Foundations and Trends in Econometrics* **4**(3): 165–224.

Lee, F. S., X. Pham and G. Gu (2013). 'The UK Research Assessment Exercise and the narrowing of UK economics'. *Cambridge Journal of Economics* **37**(4): 693–717.

Lees, A., N. Scott, S. N. Scott, S. MacDonald and C. Campbell (2002). 'Deciding how NHS money is spent: a survey of general public and medical views'. *Health Expectations* **5**(1): 47–54.

Legard, R., J. Keegan and K. Ward (2004). In-depth interviews. *Qualitative research practice: a guide for social science students and researchers*. J. Ritchie and J. Lewis. London, Sage.

Lenaghan, J. (1999). 'Involving the public in rationing decisions. The experience of citizens juries'. *Health Policy* **49**: 45–61.

Leontief, W. (1982). 'Academic economics'. *Science* **217**: 104–107.

Lewis, J. (2004). Design issues. *Qualitative research practice: a guide for social science students and researchers*. J. Ritchie and J. Lewis. London, Sage.

Lewis, M., M. Curtis and K. Lundy (1995). ' "He calls me his Angel of Mercy": the experience of caring for elderly parents in the home'. *Holistic Nursing Practice* **9**(4): 54–65.

Lincoln, Y. S. (1992). 'Sympathetic connections between qualitative methods and health research'. *Qualitative Health Research* **2(4)**: 375–391.

Lincoln, Y. S. (1995). 'Emerging criteria for quality in qualitative and interpretive research'. *Qualitative Inquiry* **1(3)**: 275–289.

Litva, A., J. Coast, J. Donovan, J. Eyles, M. Shepherd, J. Tacchi, J. Abelson and K. Morgan (2002). ' "The public is too subjective": public involvement at different levels of health-care decision making'. *Social Science & Medicine* **54**: 1825–1837.

Loder, E., T. Groves, S. Schroter, J. G. Merino and W. Weber (2016). 'Qualitative research and The BMJ'. *BMJ* **352**(i641): 1–2.

Lomas, J. (1997). 'Reluctant rationers: public input to health care priorities'. *Journal of Health Services Research & Policy* **2(2)**: 103–111.

Lomas, J. and A. D. Brown (2009). 'Research and advice giving: a functional view of evidence-informed policy advice in a Canadian ministry of health'. *Milbank Quarterly* **87**(4): 903–926.

Long-Sutehall, T., M. Sque and J. Addington-Hall (2010). 'Secondary analysis of qualitative data: a valuable method for exploring sensitive issues with an elusive population?' *Journal of Research in Nursing* **16**(4): 335–344.

Louviere, J. (2000). 'Why stated preference discrete choice modelling is NOT conjoint analysis (and what SPDCM is)'. *Memetrics White Paper* **1**: 1–11.

Louviere, J. J., T. N. Flynn and A. A. J. Marley (2015). *Best-worst scaling. Theory, methods and applications*. Cambridge, Cambridge University Press.

Löwe, B., U. Schulz, K. Gräfe and S. Wilke (2006). 'Medical patients' attitudes toward emotional problems and their treatment. What do they really want?' *Journal of General Internal Medicine* **21**(1): 39–45.

Lowe, N. K. and P. F. Cook (2012). 'Differentiating the scientific endeavors of research, program evaluation, and quality improvement studies'. *Journal of Obstetric, Gynecologic, & Neonatal Nursing* **41**(1): 1–3.

Lunney, J., J. Lynn, D. Foley, S. Lipson and J. Guralnik (2003). 'Patterns of functional decline at the end of life'. *JAMA* **289**: 2387–2392.

Lunney, J., J. Lynn and C. Hogan (2002). 'Profiles of older Medicare decedents'. *Journal of the American Geriatric Society* **50**: 1108–1112.

MacDougall, C. and F. Baum (1997). 'The devil's advocate: a strategy to avoid groupthink and stimulate discussion in focus groups'. *Qualitative Health Research* 7(4): 532–541.

Mackie, A. (2016). 'Enjoy the silence – active listening for qualitative interviewing'. *Exploring Youth Issues*. https://oldmanmackie.wordpress.com/.

MacPherson, I. and L. McKie (2010). Qualitative research in programme evaluation. *The SAGE handbook of qualitative methods in health research*. I. L. Bourgeault, R. Dingwall and R. G. De Vries. London, Sage.

Mahadevia, P., S. Shah, S. Mannix, J. Brewster-Jordan, L. Kleinman, C. Liebman and L. O'Dowd (2006). 'Willingness to pay for sensory attributes of intranasal corticosteroids among patients with allergic rhinitis'. *Journal of Managed Care Pharmacy* **12**(2): 143–151.

Mallinson, S. (2002). 'Listening to respondents: a qualitative assessment of the Short-Form 36 Health Status Questionnaire'. *Social Science & Medicine* **54**: 11–21.

Malpass, A., A. Shaw, D. Sharp, F. Walter, G. Feder, M. Ridd and D. Kessler (2009). ' "Medication career" or "moral career"? The two sides of managing antidepressants: a meta-ethnography of patients' experience of antidepressants'. *Social Science & Medicine* **68**(1): 154–168.

Malterud, K. (2001). 'Qualitative research: standards, challenges and guidelines'. *Lancet* **358**: 483–488.

Manning, W. G., J. P. Newhouse, N. Duan, E. B. Keeler, A. Leibowitz and M. S. Marquis (1987). 'Health insurance and the demand for medical care: evidence from a randomised experiment'. *American Economic Review* **77**(3): 251–277.

Mannion, R., N. Small and C. Thompson (2005). 'Alternative futures for health economics: implications for nursing management'. *Journal of Nursing Management* **13**: 377–386.

Mannion, R. and P. Smith (1997). Trust and reputation in community care. *Changes in health care. Reflections on the NHS internal market*. P. Anand. Basingstoke, MacMillan: 141–161.

March, J. G. (1978). 'Bounded rationality, ambiguity, and the engineering of choice'. *Bell Journal of Economics* **9**: 587–608.

Marsh, D. (1999). 'Studying British politics'. *British Journal of Politics and International Relations* **1**: 1–11.

Martens, B., U. Mummert, P. Murrell and P. Seabright (2002). *The institutional economics of foreign aid*. Cambridge, UK, Cambridge University Press.

Martinez Alvarez, M. (2014). *Development assistance for health in Tanzania: has the sector wide approach achieved the principles of aid effectiveness?* PhD, London School of Hygiene and Tropical Medicine.

Martini, J., R. Mongo, H. Kalambay, A. Fromont, N. Ribesse and B. Dujardin (2012). 'Aid effectiveness from Rome to Busan: some progress but lacking bottom-up approaches or behaviour changes'. *Tropical Medicine and International Health* **17**(7): 931–933.

Marvasti, A. (2011). Three aspects of writing qualitative research. *Qualitative research*. D. Silverman. Thousand Oaks, CA, Sage: 383–396.

Mason, H., R. Baker and C. Donaldson (2011). 'Understanding public preferences for prioritizing health care interventions in England: does the type of health gain matter?' *Journal of Health Services Research & Policy* **16**(2): 81–89.

Maxwell, J. A. (2012). *A realist approach for qualitative research*. Thousand Oaks, CA, Sage.

Mays, N. and C. Pope (2000). 'Assessing quality in qualitative research'. *BMJ* **320**: 50–52.

McCabe, C, K. Stevens, J. Roberts and J. Brazier (2005). *Health state values for the HUI 2 descriptive system: results from a UK survey*. Sheffield Health Economics Group, University of Sheffield: 231–244.

McCaffrey, N., L. Gill, B. Kaambwa, I. D. Cameron, J. Patterson, M. Crotty and J. Ratcliffe (2015). 'Important features of home-based support services for older Australians and their informal carers'. *Health and Social Care in the Community* **23**(6): 654–664.

McColl, E. (2005). Developing questionnaires. *Assessing quality of life in clinical trials*. P. Fayers and R. Hays. Oxford, Oxford University Press: 9–23.

McCormick, K. M., S. Stricklin, T. M. Nowak and B. Rous (2008). 'Using eco-mapping to understand family strengths and resources'. *Young Exceptional Children* **11**(2): 17–28.

McDonald, R. (2002). *Using health economics in health services. Rationing rationally?* Buckingham, Open University Press.

McGarry, J. and A. Arthur (2001). 'Informal caring in late life: a qualitative study of experiences of older carers'. *Journal of Advanced Nursing* **33**(2): 182–189.

McHugh, N., R. M. Baker, H. Mason, L. Williamson, J. van Exel, R. Deogaonkar, M. Collins and C. Donaldson (2015). 'Extending life for people with a terminal illness: a moral right or an expensive death? Exploring societal perspectives'. *BMC Medical Ethics* **16**(14): 1–15.

McIntosh, E., P. Clarke, E. Frew and J. Louviere (2010). *Applied methods of cost-benefit analysis in health care*. Oxford, Oxford University Press.

McKeown, B. and D. Thomas (2013). *Q methodology*. Newbury Park, CA, Sage.

McKibbon, K. A. and C. S. Gadd (2004). 'A quantitative analysis of qualitative studies in clinical journals for the 2000 publishing year'. *BMC Medical Informatics and Decision Making* **4**(11): 1–8.

McKie, J., B. Shrimpton, J. Richardson and R. Hurworth (2011). 'The monetary value of a life year: evidence from a qualitative study of treatment costs'. *Health Economics* **20**: 945–957.

McKinn, S., C. Bonner, J. Jansen and K. McCaffery (2015). 'Recruiting general practitioners as participants for qualitative and experimental primary care studies in Australia'. *Australian Journal of Primary Health* **21**(3): 354–359.

McNee, A. (2012). Rethinking Health Sector Wide Approaches through the lens of Aid Effectiveness. *Development Policy Centre Discussion Paper,* Australian National University.

McPake, B., D. Asiimwe, F. Mwesigye, M. Ofumbi, L. Ortenblad, P. Streefland and A. Turinde (1999). 'Informal economic activities of public health workers in Uganda: implications for quality and accessibility of care'. *Social Science & Medicine* **49**(7): 849–865.

McPherson, C. and J. Addington-Hall (2003). 'Judging the quality of care at the end of life: can proxies provide reliable information?' *Social Science & Medicine* **56**(1): 95–109.

Menon, D. and T. Stafinski (2008). 'Engaging the public in priority-setting for health technology assessment: findings from a citizens' jury'. *Health Expectations* **11**(3): 282–293.

Merriam, S. B. and E. J. Tisdell (2016). *Qualitative research: a guide to design and implementation.* San Francisco, CA, John Wiley & Sons.

Miles, M. B. and A. M. Huberman (1984). 'Drawing valid meaning from qualitative data: toward a shared craft'. *Educational Researcher* **13**(5): 20–30.

Miles, M. B. and A. M. Huberman (1994). *Qualitative data analysis: an expanded sourcebook.* London, Sage.

Mill, J. S. (1994). On the definition and method of political economy. *The philosophy of economics. An anthology.* D. M. Hausman. Cambridge, Cambridge University Press: 52–68.

Miller, G. A. (1956). 'The magical number seven plus or minus two: some limits on our capacity to process information'. *Psychological Review* **63**: 81–97.

Miller, J. and B. Glassner (2011). The 'inside' and the 'outside': finding realities in interviews. *Qualitative research.* D. Silverman. London, Sage: 131–148.

Miller, W. L. and B. F. Crabtree (1997). Primary care research: a multimethod typology and qualitative road map. *Doing qualitative research.* B. F. Crabtree. London, Sage: 3–28.

Miners, A. H., C. D. Llewellyn, V. L. Cooper, E. Youssef, A. J. Pollard, M. Lagarde, C. Sabin, E. Nixon, M. Sachikonye, N. Perry and M. Fisher (2016). 'A discrete choice experiment to assess people living with HIV'S (PLWH's) preferences for GP or HIV clinic appointments'. *Sexually Transmitted Infections,* 1–7.

Ministry of Health and Social Affairs (1982). Health and Medical Services Act (SFS 1982:763).

Ministry of Health and Social Welfare (2012). Tanzania Mainland National Health Accounts 2009/10.

Ministry of Health and Welfare (1997). Priority setting in health care (1996/97:60).

Ministry of Health of the Republic of Uganda (2015). Annual health sector performance report. Financial Year 2014/2015.

Mitton, C. and S. Patten (2004). 'Evidence-based priority-setting: what do the decision-makers think?' *Journal of Health Services Research & Policy* **9**: 146–152.

Mitton, C., S. Patten and C. Donaldson (2004). 'Listening to the decision makers. Sustainability of PBMA in Alberta'. *Applied Health Economics and Health Policy* **3**(3): 143–151.

Mitton, C., S. Patten, C. Donaldson and H. Waldner (2005). 'Priority-setting in health authorities: moving beyond the barriers the Calgary Experience'. *Healthcare Quarterly* **8**(3): 49–55.

Mitton, C., S. Patten, H. Waldner and C. Donaldson (2003). 'Priority setting in health authorities: a novel approach to a historical activity'. *Social Science & Medicine* **57**: 1653–1663.

Mitton, C. R., C. Donaldson, H. Waldner and C. Eagle (2003). 'The evolution of PBMA: towards a macro-level priority setting framework for health regions'. *Health Care Management Science* **6**(4): 263–269.

Moat, K. A. and J. N. Lavis (2013). '10 best resources for . . . evidence-informed health policy making'. *Health Policy and Planning* **28**: 215–218.

Moodie, M., J. Richardson, B. Rankin, K. Sinha and A. Iezzi (2009). *Predicting time trade-off health state valuations of adolescents in four Pacific countries using the AQoL-6D instrument. Research paper 43*. Monash University, Centre for Health Economics.

Mooney, G. (1994). *Key issues in health economics*. New York, Harvester Wheatsheaf.

Mooney, G. (1998). '"Communitarian Claims" as an ethical basis for allocating health care resources'. *Social Science & Medicine* **47**: 1171–1180.

Mooney, G., S. Jan and V. Wiseman (2002). 'Staking a claim for claims: a case study of resource allocation in Australian Aboriginal health care'. *Social Science & Medicine* **54**(11): 1657–1667.

Mooney, G. and M. Lange (1993). 'Ante-natal screening: what constitutes benefit?' *Social Science & Medicine* **37**(7): 873–878.

Mooney, G. and M. Ryan (1993). 'Agency in health care: getting beyond first principles'. *Journal of Health Economics* **12**: 125–135.

Moore, G. F., S. Audrey, M. Barker, L. Bond, C. Bonell, W. Hardeman, L. Moore, A. O'Cathain, T. Tinati and D. Wight (2015). 'Process evaluation of complex interventions: Medical Research Council guidance'. *BMJ* **350**: h1258.

Moreno, J. L. (1934). *Who shall survive? A new approach to the problem of human interrelations*. Washington, DC, Nervous and mental disease monograph series.

Morgan, D. L. (1992). Doctor-caregiver relationships: an exploration using focus groups. *Doing qualitative research*. B. F. Crabtree. London, Sage: 205–227.

Morgan, D. L. (1998). 'Practical strategies for combining qualitative and quantitative methods: applications to health research'. *Qualitative Health Research* **8(3)**: 362–376.

Morse, J. M. (1994). Designing funded qualitative research. *Handbook of qualitative research*. N. K. Denzin. Thousand Oaks, CA, Sage: 220–235.

Morse, J. M. (2002). Interviewing the ill. *Handbook of interview research: context and method*. J. F. Gubrium and J. A. Holstein. Thousand Oaks, CA, Sage.

Mulkay, M., M. Ashmore and T. Pinch (1987). 'Measuring the quality of life: a sociological invention concerning the application of economics to health care'. *Sociology* **21**(4): 541–564.

Mullen, P. M. (1999). 'Public involvement in health care priority setting: an overview of methods for eliciting values'. *Health Expectations* **2**: 222–234.

Murphy, E., R. Dingwall, D. Greatbatch, S. Parker and P. Watson (1998). 'Qualitative research methods in health technology assessment: a review of the literature'. *Health Technology Assessment* **2**(16): 1–274.

Murray, S. A., M. Kendall, K. Boyd and A. Sheikh (2005). 'Illness trajectories and palliative care'. *BMJ* **330**: 1007–1011.

Murtagh, F. E. M., J. M. Addington-Hall and I. J. Higginson (2007). 'The value of cognitive interviewing techniques in palliative care research'. *Palliative Medicine* **21**: 87–93.

Nadoh, J., P. Podrebersek and V. Hlebec (2004). 'Cognitive evaluation of the hierarchical approach for measuring ego-centered social networks'. *Metodoloski Zvezki* **1**(2): 379.

National Institute for Health and Clinical Excellence (2009a). *End of life treatments: general comments*. London, National Institute for Health and Clinical Excellence.

National Institute for Health and Clinical Excellence (2009b). *End of life treatments: views on the proposition*. London, National Institute for Health and Clinical Excellence.

National Institute for Health and Care Excellence (2013a). *Guide to the methods of technology appraisal 2013. Process and methods guide*. London, NICE.

National Institute for Health and Care Excellence (2013b). *Process and methods guides. The social care guidance manual*. London, National Institute for Health and Care Excellence.

National Institute for Health and Clinical Excellence (2008). *Appraising end of life medicine. Consultation document*. London, National Institute for Health and Clinical Excellence.

Nedlund, A.-C. (2012). *Designing for legitimacy: policy work and the art of juggling when setting limits in health care*. Linköping, Linköping University Electronic Press.

Nedlund, A.-C. and P. Garpenby (2014). 'Puzzling about problems: the ambiguous search for an evidence-based strategy for handling influx of health technology'. *Policy Sciences* **47**(4): 367–386.

Nelson, J. A. (1995). 'Feminism and economics'. *The Journal of Economic Perspectives* **9**(2): 131–148.

Newman, K., A. Capillo, A. Famurewa, C. Nath and W. Siyanbola (2013). *What is the evidence on evidence-informed policy making? Lessons from the International Conference on Evidence-Informed Policy Making*. Oxford, INASP.

Nixon, J., K. Phipps, J. Glanville, M. Mugford and M. Drummond (2002). 'Using economic evidence to support decision making: a case study of assertive community treatment within the UK National Service Framework for Mental Health'. *Applied Health Economics and Health Policy* **1**(4): 179–190.

Noblit, G. and D. Hare (1988). *Meta-ethnography: synthesizing qualitative studies*. Newbury Park, CA, Sage.

Normand, C. (2009). 'Measuring outcomes in palliative care: limitations of QALYs and the Road to PalYs'. *Journal of Pain and Symptom Management* **38**: 27–31.

Normand, C. (2012). 'Setting priorities in and for end-of-life care: challenges to the application of economic evaluation'. *Health Economics, Policy and Law* **7**(4): 431–439.

Nussbaum, M. C. (2003). 'Capabilities as fundamental entitlements: Sen and social justice'. *Feminist Economics* **9**(2–3): 33–59.
Oakley, A. (1981). Interviewing women: a contradiction in terms? *Doing feminist research*. H. Roberts. London, Routledge & Kegan Paul: 30–61.
Ogwulu, C. B., L. J. Jackson, A. E. P. Heazell and T. E. Roberts (2015). 'Exploring the intangible economic costs of stillbirth'. *BMC Pregnancy and Childbirth* **15**(188): 1–11.
O'Hanlon, M., J. Fox-Rushby and M. J. Buxton (1994). 'A qualitative and quantitative comparison of the EuroQol and time trade-off techniques'. *International Journal of Health Sciences* **5(3)**: 85–97.
Oliver, K., T. Lorenc and S. Innvær (2014). 'New directions in evidence-based policy research: a critical analysis of the literature'. *Health Research Policy and Systems* **12**(1): 34.
Oppenheim, A. N. (2000). *Questionnaire design, interviewing and attitude measurement. New edition*. London, Bloomsbury Publishing.
Organisation for Economic Co-operation and Development (2005). *The Paris Declaration on Aid Effectiveness. Paris Organisation for Economic Co-operation and Development*.
Organisation for Economic Co-operation and Development (2008). 2008 survey on monitoring the Paris Declaration. Effective aid by 2010? What will it take? *Overview Volume 1*. Paris, Organization for Economic Co-operation and Development.
Ormerod, P. (1994). *The death of economics*. London, Faber and Faber.
Owen-Smith, A. (2008). *Knowing about healthcare rationing*. PhD, University of Bristol.
Owen-Smith, A., J. Coast and J. Donovan (2009). '"I can see where they're coming from, but when you're on the end of it . . . you just want to get the money and the drug": explaining reactions to explicit healthcare rationing'. *Social Science & Medicine* **68**: 1935–1942.
Owen-Smith, A., J. Coast and J. Donovan (2010). 'The desirability of being open about health care rationing decisions: findings from a qualitative study with patients and clinical professionals'. *Journal of Health Services Research & Policy* **15**(1): 14–20.
Owen-Smith, A., J. Coast and J. L. Donovan (2014). '"Vicious circles": qualitative accounts of developing and living with morbid obesity'. *Qualitative Health Research* **24**(9): 1212–1220.
Owen-Smith, A., J. Donovan and J. Coast (2015). 'How clinical rationing works in practice: a case study of morbid obesity surgery'. *Social Science & Medicine* **147**: 288–295.
Padgett, D. K. (2012). *Qualitative and mixed methods in public health*. Thousand Oaks, CA, Sage.
Padgett, D. K. (2016). *Qualitative methods in social work research*. Thousand Oaks, CA, Sage.
Paramasivan, S., S. Strong, C. Wilson, B. Campbell, J. M. Blazeby and J. L. Donovan (2015). 'A simple technique to identify key recruitment issues in randomised controlled trials: Q-QAT – quanti-qualitative appointment timing'. *Trials* **16**: 88.

Parker, J. and G. Bradley (2014). *Social work practice: assessment, planning, intervention and review*. London, Sage.
Paterson, B., S. Thorne, C. Canam and C. Jillings (2001). *Meta-study of qualitative health research*. CA, Washington, DC: Sage.
Patten, S., C. Mitton and C. Donaldson (2005). 'From the trenches: views from decision-makers on health services priority setting'. *Health Services Management Research* **18**(2): 100–108.
Patten, S., C. Mitton and C. Donaldson (2006). 'Using participatory action research to build a priority setting process in a Canadian regional health authority'. *Social Science & Medicine* **63**(5): 1121–1134.
Patton, M. Q. (1999). 'Enhancing the quality and credibility of qualitative analysis'. *Health Services Research* **34**(5 Pt 2): 1189.
Patton, M. Q. (2002). *Qualitative research & evaluation methods*. 3rd Edition. Thousand Oaks, CA, Sage.
Patton, M. Q. (2015). *Qualitative research & evaluation methods*. 4th Edition. Thousand Oaks, CA, Sage.
Payne, S. (2007). Qualitative methods of data collection and analysis. *Research methods in palliative care*. J. M. Addington-Hall, E. Bruera, I. J. Higginson and S. Payne. Oxford, Oxford University Press: 139–161.
Payne, S., N. Preston, M. Turner and L. Rolls (2013). *Research in palliative care: can hospices afford not to be involved? A report for the Commission into the Future of Hospice Care*. UK, Help the Hospices.
Pellegrini, N. and M. Ruggeri (2007). 'The diffusion and the reason for the use of complementary and alternative medicine among users of mental health services: a systematic review of literature'. *Epidemiology and Psychiatric Sciences* **16**(1): 35–49.
Perry, C., K. Chhatralia, D. Damesick, S. Hobden and L. Volpe (2015). *Behavioural insights in health care*. London, The Health Foundation.
Petróczi, A., T. Nepusz and F. Bazsó (2007). 'Measuring tie-strength in virtual social networks'. *Connections* **27**(2): 39–52.
Pinto-Prades, J.-L. (1997). 'Is the person trade-off a valid method for allocating health care resources?' *Health Economics* **6**: 71–81.
Poland, B. D. (1995). 'Transcription quality as an aspect of rigor in qualitative research'. *Qualitative Inquiry* **1**(3): 290–310.
Polit, D. F. and C. T. Beck (2010). 'Generalization in quantitative and qualitative research: myths and strategies'. *International Journal of Nursing Studies* **47**(11): 1451–1458.
Popay, J., A. Rogers and G. Williams (1998). 'Rationale and standards for the systematic review of qualitative literature in health services research'. *Qualitative Health Research* **8**(3): 341–351.
Pope, C. and N. Mays (2006). Observational methods. *Qualitative research in health care. 3rd edition*. C. Pope and N. Mays. Oxford, Blackwell: 32–42.
Pope, C. and N. Mays (2006). Qualitative methods in health research. *Qualitative research in health care*. C. Pope and N. Mays. Oxford, Blackwell: 1–11.
Pope, C., S. Ziebland and N. Mays (2000). 'Analysing qualitative data'. *BMJ* **320**: 114–116.

Pound, P., N. Britten, M. Morgan, L. Yardley, C. Pope, G. Daker-White and R. Campbell (2005). 'Resisting medicines: a synthesis of qualitative studies of medicine taking'. *Social Science & Medicine* **61**: 133–155.

Pryce, K. (1979). *Endless pressure: a study of West Indian lifestyles in Britain.* New York, Penguin.

Pujol, M. (1997). 'Explorations-introduction: broadening economic data and methods'. *Feminist Economics* **3**(2): 119–120.

Punch, S. (2002). 'Interviewing strategies with young people: the "secret box", stimulus material and task-based activities'. *Children & Society* **16**: 45–56.

Qizilbash, M. (2006). 'Well-being, adaptation and human limitations'. *Royal Institute of Philosophy Supplement* **59**: 83–110.

Quartey, P. (2005). 'Innovative ways of making aid effective in Ghana: tied aid versus direct budgetary support'. *Journal of International Development* **17**(8): 1077–1092.

Ragupathy, R., J. Tordoff, P. Norris and D. Reith (2012). 'Key informants' perceptions of how Pharmac operates in New Zealand'. *International Journal of Technology Assessment in Health Care* **28**(4): 367–373.

Rankin, J. and M. Campbell (2009). *Institutional ethnography (IE), nursing work and hospital reform: IE's cautionary analysis.* Forum Qualitative Sozialforschung/ Forum: Qualitative Social Research.

Rapley, T. (2011). Some pragmatics of data analysis. *Qualitative research.* D. Silverman. Thousand Oaks, CA, Sage: 273–290.

Ratcliffe, J., E. Huynh, G. Chen, K. Stevens, J. Swait, J. Brazier, M. Sawyer, R. Roberts and T. N. Flynn (2016). 'Valuing the Child Health Utility 9D: using profile case best worst scaling methods to develop a new adolescent specific scoring algorithm'. *Social Science & Medicine* **157**: 48–59.

Raue, P. J., H. C. Schulberg, M. Heo, B. Klimstra and M. L. Bruce (2009). 'Patients' depression treatment preferences and initiation, adherence, and outcome: a randomized primary care study'. *Psychiatric Services* **60**(3): 337–343.

Ray, R. A. and A. F. Street (2005). 'Ecomapping: an innovative research tool for nurses'. *Journal of Advanced Nursing* **50**(5): 545–552.

Reid, A. O. (1992). Computer management strategies for text data. *Doing qualitative research.* B. F. Crabtree. London, Sage: 125–145.

Rempel, G. R., A. Neufeld and K. E. Kushner (2007). 'Interactive use of genograms and ecomaps in family caregiving research'. *Journal of Family Nursing* **13**(4): 403–419.

Richards, D. A. and I. R. Hallberg (2015). *Complex interventions in health: an overview of methods.* Abingdon, Oxon, Routledge.

Richards, I. (1998). 'Closeness to data: the changing goals of qualitative data handling'. *Qualitative Health Research* **8**(3): 319–328.

Riessman, C. K. (2011). What's different about narrative inquiry? Cases, categories and contexts. *Qualitative research.* D. Silverman. Thousand Oaks, CA, Sage: 310–330.

Ritchie, J. (2004). The applications of qualitative methods to social research. *Qualitative research practice: a guide for social science students and researchers.* J. Ritchie and J. Lewis. London, Sage.

Ritchie, J. and J. Lewis (2003). *Qualitative research practice: a guide for social science students and researchers*. London, Sage.

Ritchie, J., J. Lewis and G. Elam (2003). Designing and selecting samples. *Qualitative research practice: a guide for social science students and researchers*. J. Ritchie and J. Lewis. London, Sage: 77–108.

Ritchie, J. and L. Spencer (1994). Qualitative data analysis for applied policy research. *Analyzing qualitative data*. A. Bryman and R. G. Burgess. London, Routledge: 173–194.

Ritchie, J. and L. Spencer (2002). Qualitative data analysis for applied policy research. *The qualitative researcher's companion*. A. M. Huberman and M. B. Miles. London, Sage.

Ritchie, J., L. Spencer and W. O'Connor (2003). Carrying out qualitative analysis. *Qualitative research practice: a guide for social science students and researchers*. J. Ritchie and J. Lewis. London, Sage: 219–262.

Roberts, T. E., S. Robinson, P. Barton, S. Bryan and N. Low (2006). 'Screening for Chlamydia trachomatis: a systematic review of the economic evaluations and modelling'. *Sexually Transmitted Infections* **82**(3): 193–200.

Robeyns, I. (2005). 'The capability approach: a theoretical survey'. *Journal of Human Development* **6**: 93–114.

Robinson, A., P. Dolan and A. Williams (1997). 'Valuing health status using VAS and TTO: what lies behind the numbers?' *Social Science & Medicine* **45**(8): 1289–1297.

Robinson, A. and A. Spencer (2006). 'Exploring challenges to TTO utilities: valuing states worse than dead'. *Health Economics* **15**: 393–402.

Robinson, S. (2007). *Valuing health states for use in economic evaluation: an investigation of validity and reliability*. PhD, University of Birmingham.

Robinson, S. and S. Bryan (2013). 'Does the process of deliberation change individuals' health state valuations? An exploratory study using the person trade-off technique'. *Value in Health* **16**: 806–813.

Robinson, S., T. Freeman, H. Dickinson and I. Williams (2009). What's the story? A narrative analysis of priority setting in the area of World Class Commissioning. *Policy Futures: Social Policy Association Conference*. Edinburgh.

Rochaix, L. (1998). 'The physician as perfect agent: a comment'. *Social Science & Medicine* **47**(3): 355–356.

Rogers, P. (2014). Theory of change. *Methodological briefs: impact evaluation 2*. Florence, UNICEF Office of Research.

Rogers, R. S., P. Stenner, K. Gleeson and W. S. Rogers (1995). Q methodology. *Social psychology – a critical agenda*. Oxford, Blackwell: 248–254.

Rosén, P. and I. Karlberg (2002). 'Opinions of Swedish citizens, health-care politicians, administrators and doctors on rationing and health-care financing'. *Health Expectations* **5**(2): 148–155.

Rosenberg, A. (1992). *Economics – mathematical politics or science of diminishing returns?* Chicago, University of Chicago Press.

Rosenberg, A. (1994). If economics isn't science, what is it? *The philosophy of economics. An anthology*. D. M. Hausman. Cambridge, Cambridge University Press: 376–394.

Ross, S. A. (1973). 'The economic theory of agency: the principal's problem'. *American Economic Review* **63**: 134–139.

Round, J. (2012). 'Is a QALY still a QALY at the end of life?' *Journal of Health Economics* **31**: 521–527.

Russell, J. and T. Greenhalgh (2012). 'Affordability as a discursive accomplishment in a changing National Health Service'. *Social Science & Medicine* **75**(12): 2463–2471.

Russo, G. and B. McPake (2010). 'Medicine prices in urban Mozambique: a public health and economic study of pharmaceutical markets and price determinants in low-income settings'. *Health Policy and Planning* **25**: 70–84.

Russo, G., B. McPake, I. Fronteira and P. Ferrinho (2014). 'Negotiating markets for health: an exploration of physicians' engagement in dual practice in three African capital cities'. *Health Policy and Planning* **29**: 774–783.

Ryan, M. (2004). 'Discrete choice experiments in health care'. *BMJ* **328**: 360–361.

Ryan, M., V. Watson and V. Entwistle (2009). 'Rationalising the "irrational": a think aloud study of discrete choice experiment responses'. *Health Economics* **18**: 321–336.

Ryen, A. (2011). Ethics and qualitative research. *Qualitative research*. D. Silverman. London, Sage: 416–438.

Sagoff, M. (1998). 'Aggregation and deliberation in valuing environmental public goods: A look beyond contingent pricing'. *Ecological Economics* **24**: 213–230.

Saldaña, J. (2015). *The coding manual for qualitative researchers*. Thousand Oaks, CA, Sage.

San Miguel, F., M. Ryan and M. Amaya-Amaya (2005). '"Irrational" stated preferences: a quantitative and qualitative investigation'. *Health Economics* **14**(3): 307–322.

Sandelowski, M. (2000). 'Whatever happened to qualitative description?' *Research in Nursing and Health* **23**: 334–340.

Sandelowski, M. (2001). 'Real qualitative researchers do not count: the use of numbers in qualitative research'. *Research in Nursing & Health* **24**(3): 230–240.

Sandelowski, M., S. Docherty and C. Enden (1997). 'Qualitative metasynthesis: issues and techniques'. *Research in Nursing and Health* **20**: 365–371.

Santos, A. C. (2011). 'Behavioural and experimental economics: are they really transforming economics?' *Cambridge Journal of Economics* **35**(4): 705–728.

Santos, J. D. and M. J. Levitt (2007). 'Intergenerational relations with in-laws in the context of the social convoy: theoretical and practical implications'. *Journal of Social Issues* **63**(4): 827–843.

Savage, M. (2005). 'Working class identities in the 1960s: revisiting the affluent worker study'. *Sociology* **39**: 929–946.

Scott, A. and S. Vick (1999). 'Patients, doctors and contracts: an application of principal-agent theory to the doctor-patient relationship'. *Scottish Journal of Political Economy* **46**(2): 111–134.

Sculpher, M. J., K. Claxton, M. Drummond and C. McCabe (2006). 'Whither trial based economic evaluation for health care decision making?' *Health Economics* **15**: 677–687.

Seale, C. (1999). 'Quality in qualitative research'. *Qualitative Inquiry* **5**(4): 465–478.

Seale, C. (2011). Secondary analysis of qualitative data. *Qualitative research*. D. Silverman. Thousand Oaks, CA, Sage.

Seale, C. and J. Charteris-Black (2008). 'The interaction of age and gender in illness narratives'. *Ageing and Society* **28**: 1025–1045.

Searle, J. R. (2005). 'What is an institution?' *Journal of Institutional Economics* **1**(1): 1–22

Sen, A. (1973). 'Behaviour and the concept of preference'. *Economica* **40**: 241–259.

Sen, A. (1977). 'Rational fools: a critique of the behavioural foundations of economic theory'. *Philosophy and Public Affairs* **6**: 317–344.

Sen, A. (1982). *Choice, welfare and measurement*. Cambridge, MA, Harvard University Press.

Sen, A. (1987). *Commodities and capabilities*. New Delhi, Oxford University Press.

Sen, A. (1992). *Inequality reexamined*. New York, Russell Sage Foundation.

Sen, A. (1993). Capability and well-being. *The quality of life*. M. C. Nussbaum. Oxford, Clarendon Press.

Sen, A. (1999). *Commodities and capabilities*. New Delhi, Oxford University Press.

Sen, A. (2010). *The idea of justice*. London, Penguin.

Shadish, W. R. and T. D. Cook (2009). 'The renaissance of field experimentation in evaluating interventions'. *Annual Review of Psychology* **30**: 607–629.

Shadish, W. R., T. D. Cook and D. T. Campbell (2002). *Experimental and quasi-experimental designs for generalized causal inference*. Boston, Houghton Mifflin.

Shanahan, E. A., M. D. Jones and M. K. McBeth (2011). 'Policy narratives and policy processes'. *Policy Studies Journal* **39**(3): 535–561.

Shaw, S. E. (2010). 'Reaching the parts that other theories and methods can't reach: How and why a policy-as-discourse approach can inform health-related policy'. *Health* **14**(2): 196–212.

Shelby-James, T. M., J. Hardy, M. Agar, P. Yates, G. Mitchell, C. Sanderson, T. Luckett, A. P. Abernathy and D. C. Currow (2011). 'Designing and conducting randomized controlled trials in palliative care: a summary of discussions from the 2010 clinical research forum of the Australian Palliative Care Clinical Studies Collaborative'. *Palliative Medicine* **26**(8): 1042–1047.

Sidnell, J. and T. Stivers, Eds. (2013). *The handbook of conversation analysis*. Chichester, Blackwell.

Silverman, D. (2005). *Doing qualitative research: a practical handbook*. 2nd Edition. London, Sage.

Silverman, D. (2010). *Doing qualitative research: a practical handbook*. 3rd Edition. London, Sage.

Silverman, D. (2013). *Doing qualitative research: a practical handbook*. 4th Edition. London, Sage.

Sim, J. (1998). 'Collecting and analysing qualitative data: issues raised by the focus group'. *Journal of Advanced Nursing* **28**(2): 345–352.

Singer, P. A., D. K. Martin, M. Giacomini and L. Purdy (2000). 'Priority setting for new technologies in medicine: qualitative case study'. *BMJ* **321**: 1316–1318.

Smith, D. E. (2006). *Institutional ethnography as practice*. Toronto, Rowman & Littlefield.

Smith, N., W. Hall, C. Mitton, S. Bryan and B. Urquhart (2014). 'What constitutes high performance in priority setting and resource allocation? Decision maker narratives identified from a survey and qualitative study in Canadian healthcare organizations'. *Health Services Management Research* **27**(3–4): 49–56.

Smith, N., C. Mitton, E. Cornelissen, J. Gibson and S. Peacock (2012). 'Using evaluation theory in priority setting and resource allocation'. *Journal of Health Organization and Management* **26**(5): 655–671.

Smith, N., C. Mitton, L. Dowling, M. A. Hiltz, M. Campbell and S. A. Gujar (2016). 'Introducing new priority setting and resource allocation processes in a Canadian healthcare organisation: a case study analysis informed by multiple streams theory'. *International Journal of Health Policy and Management* **5**(1): 23–31.

Smith, N., C. Mitton, W. Hall, S. Bryan, C. Donaldson, S. Peacock, J. L. Gibson and B. Urquhart (2016). 'High performance in healthcare priority setting and resource allocation: a literature- and case study-based framework in the Canadian context'. *Social Science & Medicine* **162**: 185–192.

Smith, N., C. Mitton, M.-A. Hiltz, M. Campbell, L. Dowling, J. F. Magee and S. A. Gujar (2016). 'A qualitative evaluation of program budgeting and marginal analysis in a Canadian Pediatric Tertiary Care Institution'. *Applied Health Economics and Health Policy* **14**(5): 559–568.

Smith, N., C. Mitton and S. Peacock (2009). 'Qualitative methodologies in health-care priority setting research'. *Health Economics* **18**: 1163–1175.

Smith, P. C., A. Stepan, V. Valdmanis and P. Verheyen (1997). 'Principal-agent problems in health care systems: an international perspective'. *Health Policy* **41**: 37–60.

Smith, R. D. (2007). 'The relationship between reliability and size of willingness-to-pay values: a qualitative insight'. *Health Economics* **16**: 211–216.

Snape, D. and L. Spencer (2003). The foundations of qualitative research. *Qualitative research practice: a guide for social science students and researchers*. J. Ritchie and J. Lewis. London, Sage: 1–23.

Socialstyrelsen (2008a). Nationella riktlinjer för hjärtsjukvård 2008. (National guidelines for cardiac care 2008). Beslutsstöd för prioriteringar. (Decision support for priority-setting).

Socialstyrelsen (2008b). Nationella riktlinjer för hjärtsjukvård 2008. (National guidelines for cardiac care 2008). Bilaga 3 Metod (Annex 3 to decision support documents – Method [modified]).

Soderholm, P. (2001). 'The deliberative approach in environmental valuation'. *Journal of Economic Issues* **35**(2): 487–495.

Spencer, A. (2003). 'The TTO method and procedural invariance'. *Health Economics* **12**: 655–668.

Squires, H., J. Chilcott, R. Akehurst, J. Burr and M. P. Kelly (2016). 'A framework for developing the structure of public health economic models'. *Value in Health* **19**(5): 588–601.

Stainton Rogers, R. (1995). Q methodology. *Rethinking methods in psychology*. J. A. Smith, R. Harre and L. Van Langenhove. London, Sage: 178–192.

Starr, M. A. (2014). 'Qualitative and mixed-methods research in economics: surprising growth, promising future'. *Journal of Economic Surveys* **28**(2): 238–264.

Starzyk, K. B., R. R. Holden, L. R. Fabrigar and T. K. MacDonald (2006). 'The Personal Acquaintance Measure: a tool for appraising one's acquaintance with any person'. *Journal of Personality and Social Psychology* **90**(5): 833–847.

Stenner, P. and R. S. Rogers (1998). 'Jealousy as a manifold of divergent understandings: a Q methodological investigation'. *European Journal of Social Psychology* **28**: 71–94.

Stephenson, W. (1935). 'Technique of factor analysis'. *Nature* (24 August 1935): 297.

Stephenson, W. (1953). *The study of behavior: Q-technique and its methodology*. Chicago, University of Chicago Press.

Stephenson, W. (1986). 'Protoconcursus: the concourse theory of communication (Part 1)'. *Operant Subjectivity* **9**(2): 37–72.

Stevens, K. (2009). 'Developing a descriptive system for a new preference-based measure of health-related quality of life for children'. *Quality of Life Research* **18**: 1105–1113.

Stevens, K. (2010). 'Working with children to develop dimensions for a preference-based, generic, pediatric health-related quality-of-life measure'. *Qualitative Health Research* **20**: 240–351.

Stevens, K. (2015). 'How well do the generic multi-attribute utility instruments incorporate patient and public views into their descriptive systems?' *The Patient* **9**(1): 5–13.

Stevens, K. and S. Palfreyman (2012). 'The use of qualitative methods in developing the descriptive systems of preference-based measures of health-related quality of life for use in economic evaluation'. *Value in Health* **15**(8): 991–998.

Stevens, K. J. (2011). 'Assessing the performance of a new generic measure of health related quality of life for children and refining it for use in health state valuation'. *Applied Health Economics and Health Policy* **9**(3): 157–169.

Strauss, A. and J. Corbin (1990). *Basics of qualitative research. Grounded theory procedures and techniques*. London, Sage.

Sundewall, J. and K. Sahlin-Andersson (2006). 'Translations of health sector SWAps – a comparative study of health sector development cooperation in Uganda, Zambia and Bangladesh'. *Health Policy* **76**(3): 277–287.

Sutton, E. and J. Coast (2012). ' "Choice is a small word with a huge meaning": autonomy and decision making at the end of life'. *Policy & Politics* **40**(2): 211–226.

Sutton, E. and J. Coast (2014). 'Development of a supportive care measure for economic evaluation of end-of-life care, using qualitative methods'. *Palliative Medicine* **28**: 151–157.

Swanson, J. M. and L. Chapman (1994). Inside the black box: theoretical and methodological issues in conducting evaluation research using a qualitative approach. *Critical issues in qualitative research methods*. J. M. Morse. Thousand Oaks, CA, Sage.

Syme, G. J., P. Dzidic and J. M. Dambacher (2012). 'Enhancing science in coastal management through understanding its role in the decision making network'. *Ocean & Coastal Management* **69**: 92–101.

Tafuri, G., P. Stolk, F. Trotta, M. Putzeist, H. G. Leufkens, R. O. Laing and M. De Allegri (2014). 'How do the EMA and FDA decide which anticancer drugs make it to the market? A comparative qualitative study on decision makers' views'. *Annals of Oncology* **25**(265–269).

Teerawattananon, Y. and S. Russell (2008). 'A difficult balancing act: policy actors' perspectives on using economic evaluation to inform health-care coverage decisions under the universal health insurance coverage scheme in Thailand'. *Value in Health* **11**(Suppl. 1): S52–S60.

Temple, B., R. Edwards and C. Alexander (2006). 'Grasping at context: cross language qualitative research as secondary qualitative data analysis'. *Forum: Qualitative Social Research* 7(4[10]): 1–17.

Thomas, L., J. McMillan, E. McColl, C. Hale and S. Bond (1995). 'Comparison of focus group and interview methodology in examining patient satisfaction with nursing care'. *Social Sciences in Health* **1**: 206–220.

Thorne, S. (2000). 'Data analysis in qualitative research'. *Evidence Based Nursing* **3**(3): 68–70.

Thorne, S. E. (1994). Secondary analysis in qualitative research: issues and implications. *Critical issues in qualitative research methods*. J. M. Morse. London, Sage.

Timotijevic, L. and M. M. Raats (2007). 'Evaluation of two methods of public deliberative participation of older people in food-policy development'. *Health Policy* **82**: 302–319.

Toboso, F. (2001). 'Institutional individualism and institutional change: the search for a middle way mode of explanation'. *Cambridge Journal of Economics* 25: 765–783.

Tong, A., P. Sainsbury and J. Craig (2007). 'Consolidated criteria for reporting qualitative research (COREQ): a 32-item checklist for interviews and focus groups'. *International Journal for Quality in Health Care* **19**(6): 349–357.

Tourangeau, R. (1984). Cognitive sciences and survey methods. *Cognitive aspects of survey methodology: building a bridge between disciplines*. T. Jabine, M. Straf, J. Tanur and R. Tourangeau. Washington, DC, National Academy Press: 73–100.

Tourangeau, R., L. Rips and K. Rasinski (2000). *The psychology of survey response*. New York, Cambridge University Press.

Townsend, P. (1979). *Poverty in the United Kingdom*. London, Allen Lane and Penguin Books.

Tracy, E. M., J. K. Whittaker, A. Pugh, S. N. Kapp and E. J. Overstreet (1994). 'Support networks of primary caregivers receiving family preservation services: an exploratory study'. *Families in Society* **75**(8): 481.

Trinidade, E., D. Menon, L. A. Topfer and C. Coloma (1998). 'Adverse effects associated with selective serotonin reuptake inhibitors and tricyclic antidepressants: a meta-analysis'. *Canadian Medical Association Journal* **159**(10): 1245–1252.

Tripp, A. M. (2012). 'Donor assistance and political reform in Tanzania'. *World Institute for Development Economic Research* **37**: 1–26.

Trujillo, A., A. Glassman, L. Fleisher, D. Nair and D. Duran (2015). 'Applying behavioural economics to health systems of low- and middle-income countries: what are policymakers' and practitioners' views?' *Health Policy and Planning* **30**(6): 747–758.

UN Inter-agency Group for Child Mortality Estimation (2013). *Levels and trends in child mortality. Report 2013* New York, UNICEF.

Van Agt, H. M. E. and G. Bonsel (2005). The number of levels in the descriptive system. *EQ-5D concepts and methods: a developmental history*. P. Kind, R. Brooks and R. Rabin. Dordrecht, Springer: 29–34.

van Eeten, M. J. G. (2006). Narrative policy analysis. *Handbook of public policy analysis: theory, politics, and methods*. F. Fischer, G. Miller and M. Sidney. Boca Raton, FL, CRC Press: 251–272.

van Exel, J., R. Baker, H. Mason, C. Donaldson and W. Brouwer (2015). 'Public views on principles for health care priority setting: findings of a European cross-country study using Q methodology'. *Social Science & Medicine* **126**: 128–137.

van Exel, J., G. de Graaf and W. B. F. Brouwer (2006). ' "Everyone dies, so you might as well have fun!" Attitudes of Dutch youths about their health lifestyle'. *Social Science & Medicine* **63**: 2628–2639.

van Mastrigt, G. A. P. G., A. T. G. Paulus, M.-J. Aarts, S. M. A. A. Evers and A. F. G. Alayli-Goebbels (2015). 'A qualitative study on the views of experts regarding the incorporation of non-health outcomes into the economic evaluations of public health interventions'. *BMC Public Health* **15**(954): 1–17.

van Osch, S. M. C. and A. M. Stiggelbout (2008). 'The construction of standard gamble utilities'. *Health Economics* **17**: 31–40.

van Someren, M. W., Y. F. Barnard and J. A. C. Sandberg (1994). *The think aloud method: a practical approach to modelling cognitive processes*. London, Academic Press.

van Wijngaarden, E., C. Leget and A. Goossensen (2015). 'Ready to give up on life: the lived experience of elderly people who feel life is completed and no longer worth living'. *Social Science & Medicine* **138**: 257–264.

Vass, C., D. Rigby and K. Payne (2017). 'The role of qualitative research methods in discrete choice experiments: a systematic review and survey of authors. *Medical Decision Making* **37**(3): 298–313.

Vetenskapsrådet (2002). *Forskningsetiska principer inom humanistisk-samhällsvetenskaplig forskning*. Stockholm, Vetenskapsrådet.

Wagner, P. J., D. Jester, B. LeClair, A. T. Taylor, L. Woodward and J. Lambert (1999). 'Taking the edge off: why patients chose St. John's Wort'. *Journal of Family Practice* **48**(8): 615–619.

Wainwright, S. P. (1997). 'A new paradigm for nursing: the potential of realism'. *Journal of Advanced Nursing* **26**: 1262–1271.

Walker, R. C., K. Howard, A. Tong, S. C. Palmer, M. R. Marshall and R. L. Morton (2016). 'The economic considerations of patients and caregivers in choice of dialysis modality'. *Haemodialysis International* **20**: 634–642.

Walsh, D. and S. Downe (2005). 'Meta-synthesis method for qualitative research: a literature review'. *Journal of Advanced Nursing* **50**(2): 204–211.

Warren, C. A. B. (2001). Qualitative interviewing. *Handbook of interview research: context and methods*. J. F. Gubrium and J. A. Holstein. Thousand Oaks, CA, Sage.

Warren, T., G. Pascall and E. Fox (2010). 'Gender equality in time: low-paid mothers' paid and unpaid work in the UK'. *Feminist Economics* **16**(3): 1993–1219.

Watts, S. and P. Stenner (2012). *Doing Q methodological research – theory method and interpretation*. London, Sage.

Weiner, B. J., H. R. Amick, J. L. Lund, S.-Y. D. Lee and T. J. Hoff (2011). 'Use of qualitative methods in published health services and management research: a 10-year review'. *Medical Care Research and Review* **68**(1): 3–33.

Weiss, C. H. (1979). 'The many meanings of research utilization'. *Public Administration Review* **39**(5): 426–431.

White, H. (2005). Challenges in evaluating development effectiveness. *Evaluating development effectiveness*. G. K. Ingram, O. N. Feinstein and G. K. Pitman. London, Transaction Publishers.

Whyte, W. F. (1955). *Street corner society*. Chicago, Chicago University Press.

Wilkinson, S. (2000). 'Women with breast cancer talking causes: comparing content, biographical and discursive analyses'. *Feminism & Psychology* **10**(4): 431–460.

Wilkinson, S. (2011). Analysing focus group data. *Qualitative research*. D. Silverman. London, Sage: 168–184.

Wille, N., X. Badia, G. Bonsel, K. Burstrom, G. Cavrini, N. Devlin, A.-C. Egmar, W. Greiner, N. Gusi, M. Herdman, J. Jelsma, P. Kind, L. Scalone and U. Ravens-Sieberer (2010). 'Development of the EQ-5D-Y: a child-friendly version of the EQ-5D'. *Quality of Life Research* **19**: 875–886.

Williams, A. (1997). One economist's view of social medicine. *Being reasonable about the economics of health. Selected essays by Alan Williams*. A. J. Culyer and A. Maynard. Cheltenham, Edward Elgar: 38–44.

Williams, I. (2013). 'Institutions, cost-effectiveness analysis and healthcare rationing: the example of healthcare coverage in the English National Health Service'. *Policy & Politics* **41**(2): 223–239.

Williams, I. and S. Bryan (2007a). 'Cost-effectiveness analysis and formulary decision making in England: findings from research'. *Social Science & Medicine* **65**(10): 2116–2129.

Williams, I. and S. Bryan (2007b). 'Understanding the limited impact of economic evaluation in health care resource allocation: a conceptual framework'. *Health Policy* **80**(1): 135–143.

Williams, I., S. Robinson and H. Dickinson (2012). *Rationing in health care: the theory and practice of priority setting*. Bristol, Policy Press.

Willis, D. and E. Coakes (2000). Enabling technology for collaborative working: a socio-technical experience. *Human centred methods in information systems: current research and practice*. S. Clarke and B. Lehaney. London, Idea Group Publishing: 119–130.

Willis, G. B. (2005). *Cognitive interviewing: a tool for improving questionnaire design*. Thousand Oaks, CA, Sage.

Wilmot, A. (2005). Designing sampling strategies for social qualitative research: with particular reference to the Office for National Statistics' Qualitative Respondent Register. *QUEST 2005 meeting*. Heerlens, Netherlands.

Wood, B., J. Betts, F. Etta, J. Gayfer, D. Kabell, N. Ngwira, F. Sagasti and M. Samaranayake (2011). *The Evaluation of the Paris Declaration: Final report*. Copenhagen.

World Health Organisation, UNICEF, UNFPA and World Bank (2012). *Trends in maternal mortality: 1990 to 2010*. WHO, UNICEF, UNFPA and The World Bank estimates. Geneva, World Health Organization.

Yardley, L. and D. Marks (2004). Introduction to research methods in clinical and health psychology. *Research methods in clinical and health psychology*. D. Marks and L. Yardley. London, Sage.

Yin, R. K. (2009). *Case study research. Design and methods*. Thousand Oaks, CA, Sage.

Young, T. A., Y. Yang, J. Brazier, A. Tsuchiya and K. Coyne (2009). 'Making Rasch decisions: the use of Rasch analysis in the construction of preference based health related quality of life instruments'. *Quality of Life Research* **18**(2): 253–265.

Ziebland, S. (1996). 'Software for analysing textual data'. *Journal of Health Services Research & Policy* **1(4)**: 247–249.

Zimmer, L. (2006). 'Qualitative meta-synthesis: a question of dialoguing with texts'. *Journal of Advanced Nursing* **53**(3): 311–318.

Zorginstituut Nederland (2016). *Richtlijn voor het uitvoeren van economische evaluaties in de gezondheidszorg*. Diemen, Zorginstituut Nederland.

Index

Note: *Page references for boxes, figures and tables are italicized.*

abduction, 10, 314
access, to informants, *45*, 49, 52, 56–57, 81, 86, 233, 237, 272, 299–300, 306, 311, 313, 318
accountability, 277, 294, 297, 301–2
action research, 90, 323, 325–27
active listening, 60–61, 67–68, 84, 252
adaptation, 231–33, 242–43, 289
adaptive preferences, 233, 242–43
agency relationship, 32–33, 39, 95, 108, 144, 279, 295, 303
aid. *See* development assistance for health
aid effectiveness, 22, 32–33, 93, 95, 144, 159, 293–306
analytic accounts, 38, 40, 87, 99, 101, 105–7, 112–17, 131, 134, 146, 180, 186, 214, 243, 267
anonymity, 79, 86–88, 125, 211, 221, 235, 329
anthropology, 11, 21, 93, 324
antidepressant drugs, 183–90
attribute development, 4, 8, 14, 16, 20, 28–29, 35–38, 47–49, 53–54, 57, 61, 70–71, 93–94, 96, 106, 133–35, 147–48, 150–51, 156–57, 163, 175–92, 195, 205, 337
audience, for research, 34, 125, 129, 133, 139–40, 143, 145, 150
audio recording, 62, 66, 82–84, 86–87, 102, 110, *126*, 141, 179, 219–20, 235, 238, 264, 267, 311
Australia, 125, *126*, 217

behavioural economics, 4, 10, 17
best-worst scaling, 8, 28
bias, 6–7, 11, 13, 26, 34, 40, 49, 56, 84, 144, 171, 192, 213–14, 248, 297, 315, 328
bracketing, 25
BWS. *See* best-worst scaling

CADTH. *See* Canadian Agency for Drugs and Technology in Health
Canada, 159, 217, 327
Canadian Agency for Drugs and Technology in Health, 217
capability approach, 38, 59, 93, 257
capability measures, 30, 37–38, 49, 56, 70, 93, 106, 143, 150, 195, 231–35, 241, 243, 257. *See also* ICECAP measures
case study research, 21, *45*, 217–27, 293–306

causality, 9, 48, 96, 105, 107, 278, 284, 287–89, 291
chance-corrected agreement, 242
children, 14, 29, 69–70, 94, 99, 103–4, *123*, *132*, 143, 157, 193–204, 279–80, 327
CHU9D, 157, 193–204
citizens, 13–14, 38–39, 49, 55–56, 62, 109–17, 142, 146, 258–61, 294
citizens' juries, 260
citizens' workshops, 259
close persons, 57, 205–16, 233, 235, 237–43, 257, 264, 266–67
coding, 22–23, 34, 53, 97, 99–106, 110, 112, 122–23, 125, 141, 179–80, 186, 219, 243, 248, 253, *268*, 301, 304
cognitive interviews, 30, 233–34
collaboration, 25, 37, 48, 140, 199, 207, 279, 290, 325
community deliberation, 259–60
community perspective, 257
complex interventions, 136
complexity, 27, *45*, 90, 209, 248, 278
concourse, 164, 167–70
conditional cash transfers, 279
confidentiality, 71, 74, 78–79, 86–87, *89*, 90, 119, 125, 179, 185, 198, 248, 312–13, 315–16, 329
conjoint analysis. *See* discrete choice experiments
consent. *See* informed consent
constant comparison, 22–23, 28, 35, 38–39, 93–94, 98, 100–101, 133, 179, 186, 212, 215, 241, 243, 267, 303, 324
constructivism, 4, 12, 15, 17, 23, 39, 106
contact log, 262
content analysis, 97, 100, 159, 201
contingent valuation, 258, 261
conversation analysis, 11
COREQ, 35, 137, 141–42, 145, 148–49
cost-effectiveness, 68–69, 79, 80, 217, 224, 307–18, 330
credibility, 34, 46, 53, 146, 244, 253
critical realism: in economics, 4, 9–10, 15; in qualitative research, 10, 15, 17, 95
crude agreement, 242
Culyer, A. J., 33

DCEs. *See* discrete choice experiments
debriefing, 34, 239
decision analytic modelling, 14, 29, 48, 81, 94, 96, 157, 217–27
deduction, 4, 6, 9, 17, 31, 95, 97, 104, 108, 125, 141, 159, 179, 300, 314
deliberation, observing, 312–13, 315–18
deliberative methods, 14, 31, 38, 78, 158–59, *246*, 247, 250–51, 255, 257–74, 320
deliberative polling, 260, 273
deliberative valuation, 258–59
democracy. *See* deliberative methods
depression, 14, 94, 122, 157, 175–92, 232, 243
descriptive accounts. *See* analytic accounts
design: of discrete choice experiments, 175, 177–79, 183; of impact evaluation, 277–78, 281–85; of Q sets, 163–74; of qualitative research, 15–16, 18, 19–41, 43, 57, 100, 102, 109–10, 120, 130, 141, 156, 158–60, 196–200, 234–35, 238–39, 245–48, 254, 261, 288–90, 310–16, 323, 331
development assistance for health, 294
development partners, 279, 294–96, 299–301, 303, 306
deviant case analysis, 107, 213, 303
deviant case sampling, 47
deviant groups, 80, 83
difference-in-difference, 7, 278
discourse analysis, 85, 324
discrete choice experiments, 4, 8, 20, 28, 48, 53–54, 61, 93–94, 130, 135, 148, 150, 157, 175–92, 194, 337

discussion. *See* deliberation
dissemination, 139–51, 255, 313, 316
distress. *See* distress protocol; sensitive issues
distress protocol, 68, 73, 88–89
documentary analysis, 22, 121, 159, 169, 296–99, 302–6, 311, 322–23
donors. *See* development partners
drawing techniques, 87
dyadic tools, 206–7
dyads, 206–7, 242

ecomaps, 207–9
economic lens, 41, 95–96, 100–101, 104, 108, 118, 143–44, 338
economics as maths, 4, 8
education, 11, 21
efficiency, 15, 34, 96, 224, 227
electoral register, 261–62, 272–73
electoral wards, 261–62, 264, 273
elicitation techniques. *See* preference elicitation
emerging designs, 290
emotional strain, 239
encryption, 83, 87
end of life, 56–57, 143, 157–58, 169, 205–6, 208, 210, 212–15, 231–44, 258, 264
environmental economics, 258–59
epistemology, 3, 5, 7, 11, 23, 95, 177
essence, in phenomenology, 24–25
EQ-5D, 30, 195, 231, 234, 240, 242, 261–62
ethical approval, 36–37, 40, 45, 66, 170, 178, 184, 200, 210–11, 220, 240, 248, 261, 282, 296, 325, 327
ethical issues, in qualitative research, 20, 36–37, 45–46, 53, 59, 86–91, 119–21, 125, 127, 137, 200, 226, 237, 239–40, 258, 291, 315–16, 327–28
ethical principles: in economics, 7; in priority setting, 308, 331
ethnography, 11, 21–22, 26, 93, 134, 140, 323, 329–30
European Disability Weights Project, *246*, 248, *251*, 256
evidence-based policy, 277, 307, 313, 317, 323
evidence-informed policy. *See* evidence-based policy
evidence-informed practice, 322
Excel, 201, 242, 262, 267, 302
extra-welfarism, 4, 7, 28, 231
extreme sampling technique, 288

facilitators. *See* focus groups
fatigue, 64, 236, 239
feminist research, 4, 10–11, 21, 25–26
fieldwork, 34, 81–82, 90, 98, 239, 288–89, 291, 296–98, 300, 304–5
financial incentives, 4, 33, 95, 144, 279–81
Finland, *126*
focus groups: confidentiality, 78–79, 185, 273; facilitators, 76–78, 264; over-recruitment to, 273; reflection and discussion in, 75, 77, 259; reminders, 273; starting/ending, 77–79; time of year, 272–73; venues, 76, 78, 264, 273, 322
formal data sharing, in secondary data analysis, 125–28
formative evaluation, 278
framework analysis, 11, 97, 100, 106–7, 115, 159, 201, 220, 301–3; charting in, 100, 201, 220, 302
framing issues, *246*, 250–51

gatekeepers, 51–52, 55–57, 81, 86
general practitioners, 56, *89*, *111*, 179–82, 184–87, 189, 248–49, 273, 309
grounded theory, 11, 21–23, 26, 28, 38–39, 47, 54, 100, 105–6, 125, 140, 323–24
guidelines: attribute development, minimum reporting, 36; consolidated criteria for reporting qualitative research (COREQ), 35, 141–42;

impact evaluation, 278; information sheets, 86; Swedish National Guidelines, 159, 307–18

halting interviews, *89*, 203, 239
Hammersley, Martyn, 34, 95
'hard-to-reach' groups, 49, 50, 55, 57, 119
harm avoidance, 62, 68, 86, 88–90
health professionals, 73, 108–11, 176, 186, 233, 235–38, 242–43
health state valuation, 30–31, 143, 158, 194, 203, 245–56
heart disease, 307–9, 311, 318
heuristics, simplifying, 255
hierarchical mapping, 69–70, 157, 206–16
hospice, 24–25, 73, 235, 237, 239, 241, 273
human dignity, principle of, 308

ICECAP measures, 30, 37, 194–95; ICECAP-A, 37, 49, 56, 106–7, 232, 234, 240; ICECAP-CPM, 107, 257–58, 264, 266; ICECAP-SCM, 232–34, 236, 240–41
identification. *See* anonymity
identity protection. *See* anonymity
impact evaluation, 158, 277–92; explanatory design, 283; triangulation design, 283
in-depth interviews, 14, 18, 38, 50–53, 60, 67, 73–74, 121, 159, *169*, 205–7, 209–10, 214, 217, 249, 286–88, 296, 298–300, 310–13, 318
Index of Multiple Deprivation, 262–63
individualism, methodological, 6, 10, 17
induction, 17, 31, 38–39, 93, 95, 97, 100, 107, 129, 131, 141, 144, 159, 179, 253, 301, 314, 324
informal care, 132–33, 267, *268*
informal data sharing, in secondary data analysis, 121–25
information leaflets. *See* information sheets
information sheets, 51–53, 67, 81–82, 86–88, 199, 262, *263*
informed consent, 52–53, 74, 81, 86–87, 119, 125, 127, 137, 312, 315; initial consent, 125; verbal consent, 238, 240; written consent, 86, 219, 267
institutional economics, 4, 10, 16
institutional ethnography, 329
institutional review. *See* ethical approval
instrument development. *See* measure development
international aid effectiveness. *See* aid effectiveness
international declarations, 293–95, 297, 299, 301, 303, 305–6
interpretivism, 12, 29, 34, 39, 156, 177
interview guide. *See* topic guide
interviews: silence in, 68, 75, 220, 252; starting/ending, 66–67, 72–73; timing of, 247, 250, 254
interview schedule. *See* topic guide
Ireland, *126*
iterative approaches: analysis, 22, 28, 47, 54–55, 85–85, 91, 101, 179, 186, 212, 306, 314; data collection, 85–85, 91; research design, 12, 43, 311; sampling, 28, 43, 46–48, 54–55, 131

Jordan, 97

key informant sampling, *44*, 46, 48–49, 57, 179, 218–19, 298–99, 329

Lawson, Tony, 9–10, 17, 33
lines of argument, 129, 132–34
LMIC. *See* lower- and middle-income countries
lone fieldworker protocols. *See* safety
lone researcher protocols. *See* safety
longitudinal data collection, 25, 72, 122, *126*, 127, 285, 291, 330
lower- and middle-income countries, 33, 150, 158, 337, 279

mainstream neoclassical economics, 3–11, 14, 16–17, 27, 31–33, 39, 97, 117

Malawi, 102, 159, 277–92
market failure, 258
maternal care, 277–92
maximum variation sampling, 43, 45–49, 56, 156, 199, 287
MDG. *See* Millennium Development Goals
measure development, 193–204: bottom-up, 194–96; meaningful language, 36, 70; top-down, 194–96
memos, 91, 99, 105, 107–8, 110, 114–15
mental health, 184, 195
meta-analysis, 128, 130–31
meta-ethnography, 120, 128–37, 176
meta-regression, 128
Millennium Development Goals, 279, 293
mirroring, 239
mixed methods, 10–11, 166, 177–78, *246*, 255, 278, 281, 283–84, 289, 291, 301, 313
models as output of qualitative research, 28, 38, 40–41, 43, 47, 94–96, 100–101, 108, 117–18, 338
modified analytic induction, 100, 253
Mozambique, 32, 49, 97
multi-level sampling, 49
multiple analytic approaches, 100, 240–43, 328
multiple streams theory of policy change, 327–28

named contact. *See* safety
narrative, 11, 21, 23–24, 33, 93, 106, 122–24, 127, 131–32, 173, 178, 211, 300, 323–24, 328–29, 331
National Board of Health and Welfare, Sweden, 307–9, 311
National Health Service, UK, 33, 40, 47, 52, 55, 63, 72, *114*, 117, *169*, 171, 184, 210, 240, 258
National Institute of Health and Care Research, UK, *169*, 234, 308
NBHW. *See* National Board of Health and Welfare, Sweden
needs and solidarity, principle of, 308
negative cases, 34, 47, 99, 253
neoclassical economics. *See* mainstream neoclassical economics
neonatal care, 277–92
NHS. *See* National Health Service, UK
NICE. *See* National Institute of Health and Care Research, UK
non-maleficence, 86, 88, 90
Norway, 289–90
nursing, 11, 21, 24, 140, 148–49, 197, 270
NVivo, 220, 241, 243, 253, 302

observation, 22, 28–29, 52–54, 80–84, 90, 93, 98, 121–22, 141, 157–59, 217–27, 250, 254, 281, 283, 285, 288, 296, 298, 300–301, 304–6, 310–18, 322–23, 326, 330; covert, 80; non-participant, 80–81, 157, 159, 217–27, 254, 296, 300–301, 304–5; participant, 81–83
ontology, 3, 5, 7–9, 11, 43, 95, 177, 337
organizational ethnography, 22

Paris Declaration on Aid Effectiveness, 294–99, 301, 303, 305–6
patient information sheets. *See* information sheets
PBAC. *See* Pharmaceutical Benefits Advisory Committee
PBF. *See* performance-based financing
PBMA. *See* programme budgeting and marginal analysis
performance-based financing, 33, 279–81, 286
personal consultee, 238, 240
person trade-off, 8, 64, 143, 245, *246*, *251*
pharmaceutical, 32, 49, 171
Pharmaceutical Benefits Advisory Committee, 217
phenomenology, 21, 24–26, 93, 134, 323–24
philosophy: economics, 4, 27; and meta-ethnography, 134; and phenomenology, 24, 93, 324; of

Q methodology, 164; qualitative research, 4, 29, 95, 177–78; of supportive care, 237
photography, 69
physical activity, 178–83
pictorial tools, 156–57, 205–16
Pictor method, 207
piloting, 66, 198, 249; in discrete choice experiments, 191; in Q methodology, 171, 173
plausibility, 10, 34
positivism, 5, 9, 53
preference elicitation, 8, 14, 27–28, 30, 71, 163, *246*, 247, 250, 255–56
presentation of findings, 139–48, 221, 242
principal-agent theory. *See* agency relationship
priority setting, 4, 16, 24, 26, 31–32, 34, 37, 39, 44–47, 50, 55–56, 63, 69, 72, 74–76, 83, 87, 93, 96–97, 108–9, *116*, 117, 122, 137, 140, 142, 144, 150, 156, 159, *169*, 258–59, 264, 307–8, 319–32
Priority Setting and Resource Allocation. *See* priority setting
privacy. *See* confidentiality
probing, 30, 60–61, 68, 79, 197, 201, 203, 209–12, 234, 236, 252, 259, 299–300
programme budgeting and marginal analysis, 326–27
proxies. *See* proxy completion
proxy. *See* proxy completion
proxy completion, 231–44
pseudonymisation. *See* anonymity
PSRA. *See* priority setting
psychology, 21, 24, 93, 163, 172, 206, 234, 240, 321
publication bias, 297
publication, of findings, 36–37, 67, 137, 139–45, 148–51, 245, 254, 335
public deliberation. *See* deliberation
public discussion. *See* deliberation
public valuation. *See* deliberative valuation
purposeful random sampling, 49–50, 56, 158, 262
purposeful sampling, 12, 42, 44–50, 76, 87, 127, 129, 131, 133, 147, 156, 173, 199, 218, 248, 261, 287, 299, 328
purposive sampling. *See* purposeful sampling

QALYs. *See* Quality-Adjusted Life-Years
Q methodology, 29, 156, 163–74
Q set, 15, 29, 156, 159, 163–64, 167–74
Q sort, 29, 95, 164–67, 170–71, 173
Quality-Adjusted Life-Years, 30, 193–95, 231, 234, *310*
Quasi-experimental design, 277
questioning techniques: for data analysis, 22, 39, 99, 104–5, 110, 112; in interviews, 30, 67–68, 210
quota sampling, 46, 48

rapport, 40, 59–62, 66, 69–72, 74–75, 78, 86, 91, 157, 214–15, 238, 249–50, 252, 298
rationality, 6, 8, 16, 29, 95, 97, 144, 163, 173
rationing. *See* priority setting
RBF. *See* results-based financing
recall, 85, 202, 209, 241, 250, 304
reciprocal translation, 122–23, 132
reflections on the research, 14, 25, 31, 190–91, 203–4, 213–15, 224–27, 252–54, 272–73
reflexivity, 12–13, 20, 24, 34–35, 40, 124, 128, 137, 139, 144–45, 159, 173–74, 190, 213, 226, 298, 304–5, 314–16, 326
regression discontinuity analysis, 278
relativism, 12, 15, 17, 23, 43, 177
reliability: of health state valuation, *246*; in qualitative research, 34, 157, 159, 190, 192, 303–4
reporting, of findings. *See* dissemination
researcher preconceptions. *See* reflexivity

researcher skills, in qualitative research, 12, 60–61, 72, 84, 119, 135, 238, 290–91, 327, 329
responsiveness to change, 196
results-based financing, 95, 159, 277–92
rigour, 4, 13–14, 19–20, 34–38, 40, 58, 110, 118, 150–51, 170, 180, 186, 190

safety: emotional safety of researchers, 37, 239; of informants, 88; physical safety of researchers, 37, 239; protocols for lone researchers, 62, 90, 239
sampling: adequacy, 43, 47, 53–55, 58, 120; frame, 42–43, 46, 48, 50–52, 57; saturation, 23, 28, 38, 43, 54, 112, 141, 179, 201, 235, 248, 313; strategy, 43, 47, 49, 51, 198, 261
sealed envelope. *See* safety
secondary data sources, 121, 125–27, 136
sector-wide approach, 295–300, 303–4
self-presentation, 66
self-reflection. *See* reflexivity
semi-structured interviews, 26, 33, 60, 109, 136, 157, 179, 200, 234, 236, 243, 245, 248–49, 289, 299, 324
Sen, Amartya, 38, 257
sensitive issues, 19, 37, 56–57, 62, 68–69, 71, 76, 79, 88, 119, 156–58, 184–85, 197–98, 233, 237–40, 243, 311, 313, 337
Sierra Leone, 32, 148
snowball sampling, 43–46, 48–50, 297
social science(s), 16, 21, 24, 58, 93, 125, 143, 290, 321, 329, 336
sociograms, 207–8
sociology, 21–22, 93, 321, 324
standard gamble, 8, 30, 143, 147, 194
statement set. *See* Q set
Stephenson, William, 163, 167, 172
structured interviews, 60, 324
sub-Saharan Africa, 280
subtle realism, 15, 17, 37, 39, 95, 101, 177
supplier-induced demand, 4, 6, 18
Sustainable Development Goals, 293
SWAP. *See* sector-wide approach
Sweden, 22, 159, 307–18

Tanzania, 18, 22, 102, 147, 159, 293–97, 299, 303–6
template analysis, 97, 324, 327–28
theatre, 21
theoretical sampling, 28, 38, 43, 46–48
theoretical sensitivity, 22, 39, 99, 110
think-aloud, 30, 69, 157–59, 217–27, 231, 233–44, 247, 252
time-consuming: deliberative methods, 257; pictorial tool use, 207, 209; qualitative analysis, 44, 120, 131, 306
time trade-off, 8, 30, 64, 143, 194, 245, *246*, *251*
topic guide, 60, 63–67, 73, 75, 77–78, 141, 148, 179, 185, 200, 203, 249–51, 288, 291, 300, 312–13
topic schedule. *See* topic guide
training: of economists generally, 3, 72, 96, 337; in qualitative methods, 3, 21, 61, 72, 90, 135, 137, 238, 252, 288–90, 337
transcription, 59, 72, 76–77, 83–86, 102–3, 110, 179, 185, 201, 220, 239, 248, 267, 300–301, 304, 312, 314
translation, language, 102, 288, 305
triads, 242
triangulation, 20, 34, 39, 191, 224, 287, 328. *See also* impact evaluation
trustworthiness, 34, 190–91, 315

Uganda, 95, 293
unique identity numbers, 264
United Kingdom, 5, 33, 38, 52, 120, 125, *126*, 127, 135, 200, 217, 234, 238, 262
United States of America, *113*, *126*

validity: of attributes for discrete choice experiments, 192; of axioms in economic theory, 95, 104; content

validity, 30, 196, 202; of cost-effectiveness models, 217, 225; of health state valuation techniques, 158, 245–56; in qualitative research, 34–35, 105, 120, 191, 303–4
veil of ignorance, Rawlsian, 261
veracity, 140, 145, 147
video recording, 84
visual analogue scale, 143, 245, 264, 267
visual representation, 99, 108, 207–8
voluntary participation, 86, 312

welfare of research team. *See* safety
welfarism, 7
willingness to pay, 8, 18, 30, 99, 143
withdrawal, from research, 86, 236
writing, 34, 40, 87, 99, 101, 103, 105–8, 112–17, 140, 142, 144–45, 254

ZorgInstituut Nederlands, 234

Contributors

Hareth Al-Janabi, Senior Lecturer in Health Economics, Health Economics Unit, Institute of Applied Health Research, University of Birmingham, UK.

Cara Bailey, Senior Lecturer in Nursing, Institute of Clinical Sciences, University of Birmingham, UK.

Rachel Baker, Professor of Health Economics and Director, Yunus Centre for Social Business and Health, Glasgow Caledonian University, UK.

Pelham Barton, Reader in Mathematical Modelling, Health Economics Unit, Institute of Applied Health Research, University of Birmingham, UK.

Alastair Canaway, Research Fellow in Health Economics, Warwick Clinical Trials Unit, Warwick Medical School, University of Warwick, UK.

Joanna Coast, Professor in the Economics of Health & Care, Health Economics at Bristol, School of Social and Community Medicine, University of Bristol, UK.

Manuela De Allegri, Associate Professor (Privat Dozent), Health Economics and Health Financing, Institute of Public Health, University of Heidelberg, Germany.

Nathalie Eckard, Health Economist, Department of Medical and Health Sciences, Linköping University, Sweden.

Terry Flynn, Managing Director, TF Choices Ltd., Nottingham, UK.

Samantha Husbands, Research Associate, School of Social and Community Medicine, University of Bristol, UK.

Louise Jackson, Lecturer in Health Economics, Health Economics Unit, Institute of Applied Health Research, University of Birmingham, UK.

Sue Jowett, Reader in Health Economics, Health Economics Unit, Institute of Applied Health Research, University of Birmingham, UK.

Philip Kinghorn, Research Fellow, Health Economics Unit, Institute of Applied Health Research, University of Birmingham, UK.

Melisa Martínez-Álvarez, Assistant Professor, Department of Global Health and Development, London School of Hygiene and Tropical Medicine, UK.

Helen Mason, Reader of Health Economics, Yunus Centre for Social Business and Health, Glasgow Caledonian University, UK.

Neil McHugh, Research Fellow, Yunus Centre for Social Business and Health, Glasgow Caledonian University, UK.

Ann-Charlotte Nedlund, Senior Lecturer, Department of Social and Welfare Studies, Linköping University, Sweden.

Rosanna Orlando, Research Fellow, NIHR CLAHRC, Wessex, University of Southampton, UK.

Amanda Owen-Smith, Lecturer in Medical Sociology/Anthropology, School of Social and Community Medicine, University of Bristol, UK.

Suzanne Robinson, Associate Professor, Health Systems and Health Economics, Faculty of Health Sciences, Curtin University, Australia.

Neale Smith, Research Co-ordinator, Centre for Clinical Epidemiology & Evaluation, Vancouver Coastal Health Research Institute, University of British Columbia, Canada.

Katherine Stevens, Reader in Health Economics, Health Economics and Decision Science, ScHARR, University of Sheffield, UK.

Jane Vosper, Clinical Psychologist, Barts Health NHS Trust, UK; and Clinical Tutor/Lecturer in Clinical Psychology, Department of Clinical Psychology, Royal Holloway University of London, UK.

CPSIA information can be obtained
at www.ICGtesting.com
Printed in the USA
LVHW092142230220
647967LV00004B/22

9 781783 485611